LIGHT BRIGADE

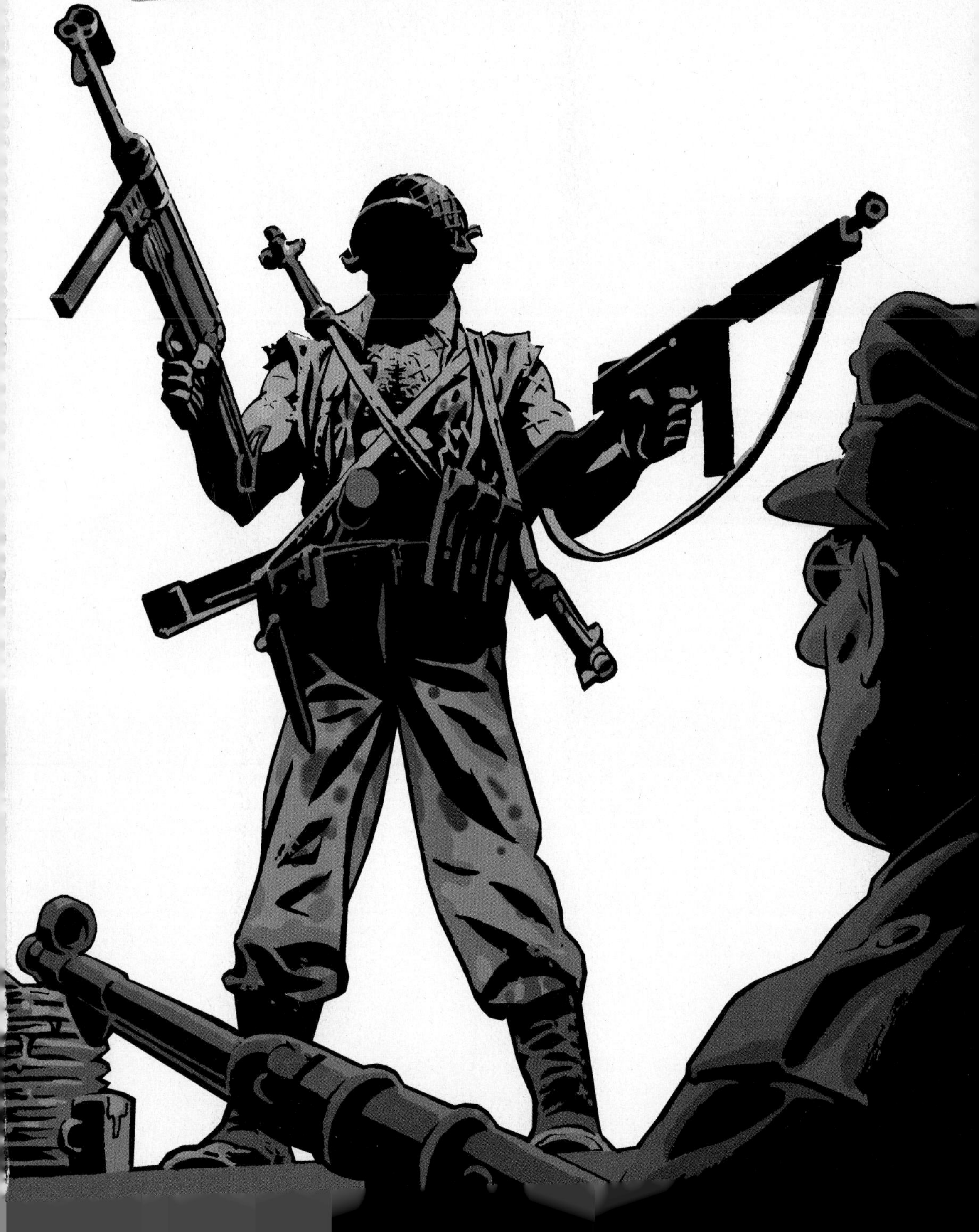

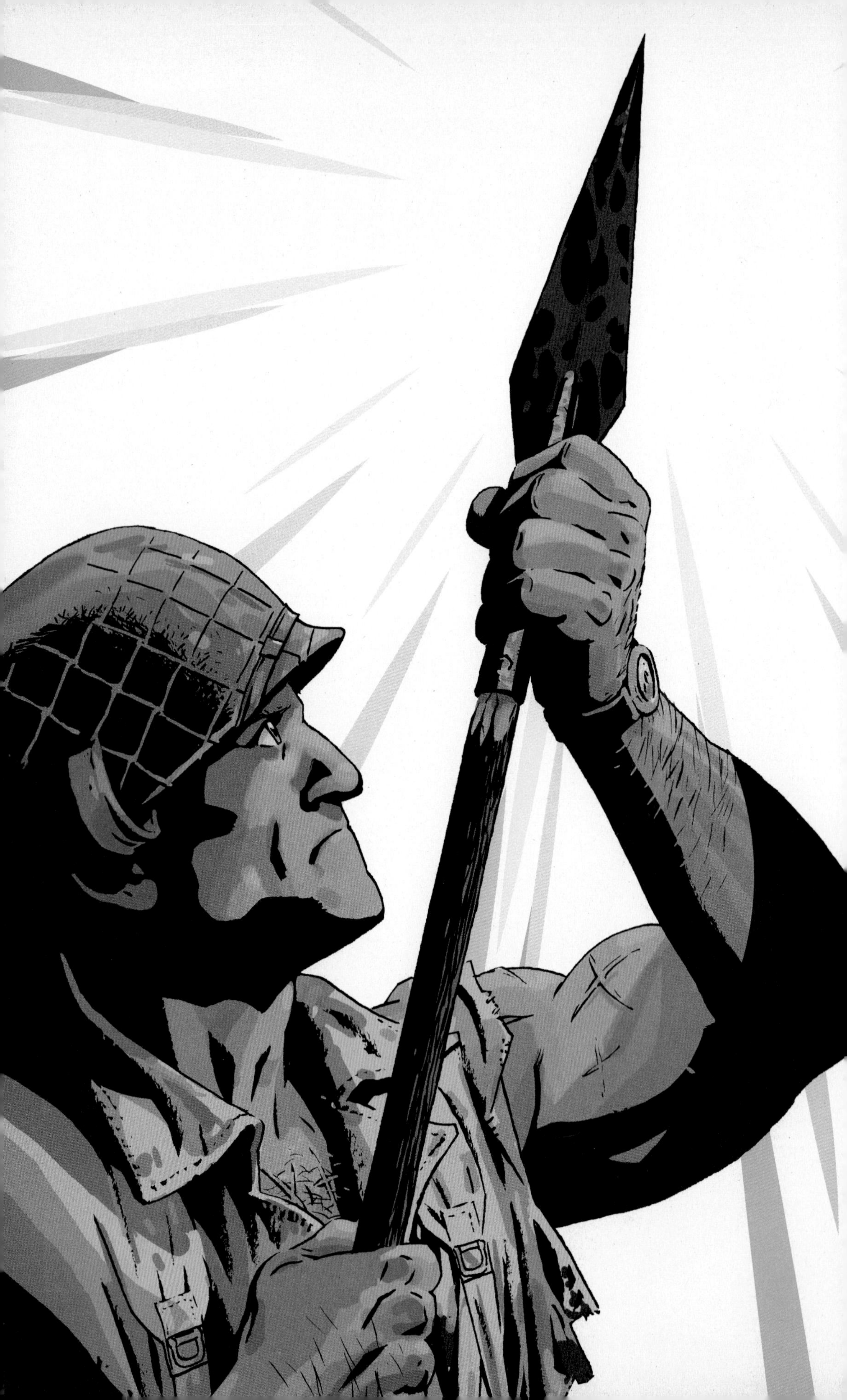

Peter J. Tomasi *story and words*   **Peter Snejbjerg** *artist*

Bjarne Hansen *colorist*   **Ken Lopez** • **Rob Leigh** *letterers*

LIGHT BRIGADE

Peter Snejbjerg with **Bjarne Hansen** *original covers*

The Light Brigade created by
Peter J. Tomasi *and* Peter Snejbjerg

DEDICATIONS

To my wife, Deborah, and my son, Alexander,
for their luminous presence and open hearts.

To my mother and father,
who gave me my love of story and history.
— *Peter J. Tomasi*

For my dad, Poul Snejbjerg
— *Peter Snejbjerg*

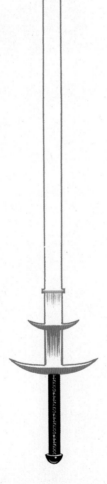

Dan DiDio *Senior VP-Executive Editor*
Joey Cavalieri *Editor-original series*
Harvey Richards *Assistant Editor-original series*
Anton Kawasaki *Editor-collected edition*
Robbin Brosterman *Senior Art Director*
Paul Levitz *President & Publisher*
Georg Brewer *VP-Design & DC Direct Creative*
Richard Bruning *Senior VP-Creative Director*
Patrick Caldon *Executive VP-Finance & Operations*
Chris Caramalis *VP-Finance*
John Cunningham *VP-Marketing*
Terri Cunningham *VP-Managing Editor*
Stephanie Fierman *Senior VP-Sales & Marketing*
Alison Gill *VP-Manufacturing*
Rich Johnson *VP-Book Trade Sales*
Hank Kanalz *VP-General Manager, WildStorm*
Lillian Laserson *Senior VP & General Counsel*
Jim Lee *Editorial Director-WildStorm*
Paula Lowitt *Senior VP-Business & Legal Affairs*
David McKillips *VP-Advertising & Custom Publishing*
John Nee *VP-Business Development*
Gregory Noveck *Senior VP-Creative Affairs*
Cheryl Rubin *Senior VP-Brand Management*
Jeff Trojan *VP-Business Development, DC Direct*
Bob Wayne *VP-Sales*

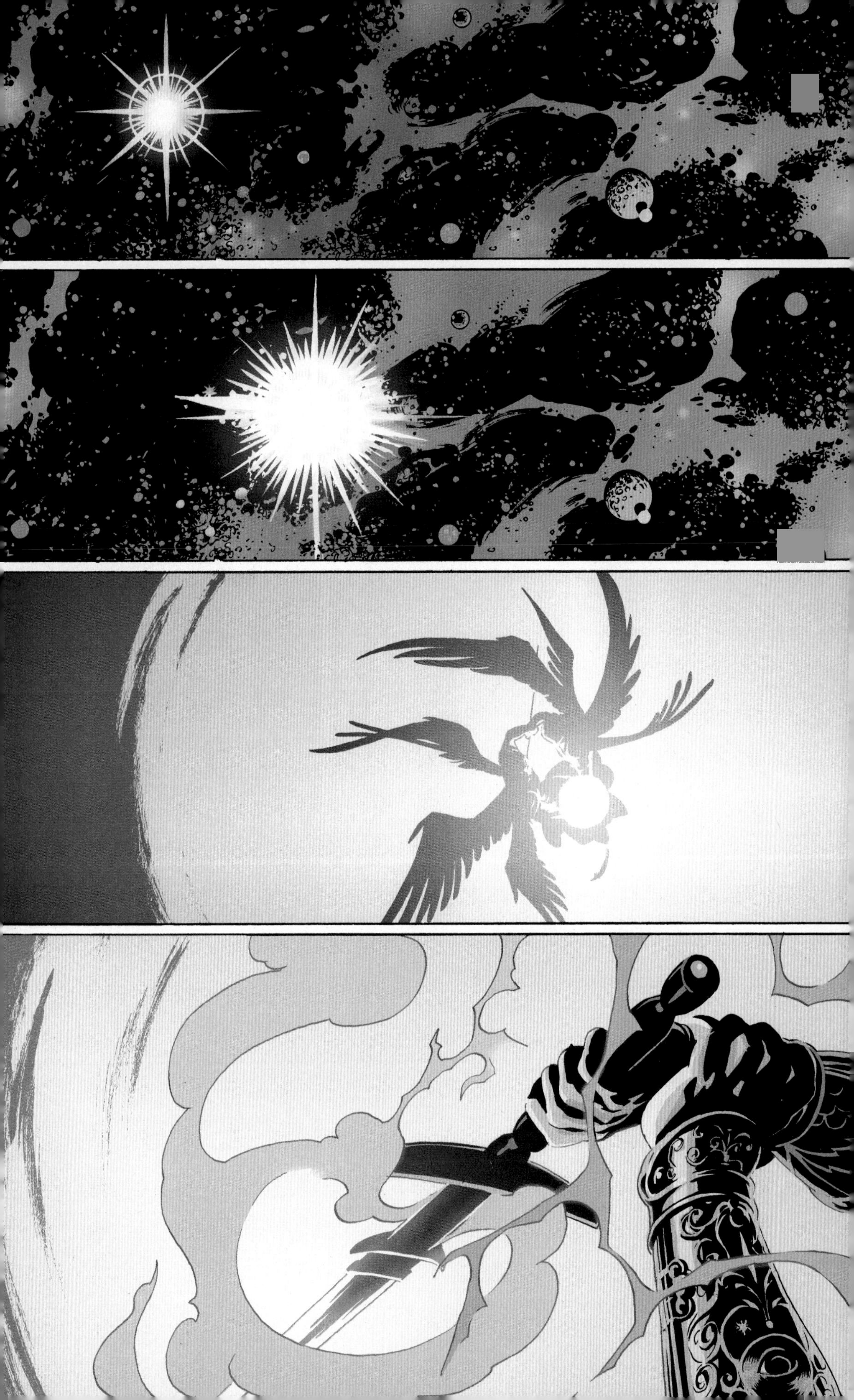

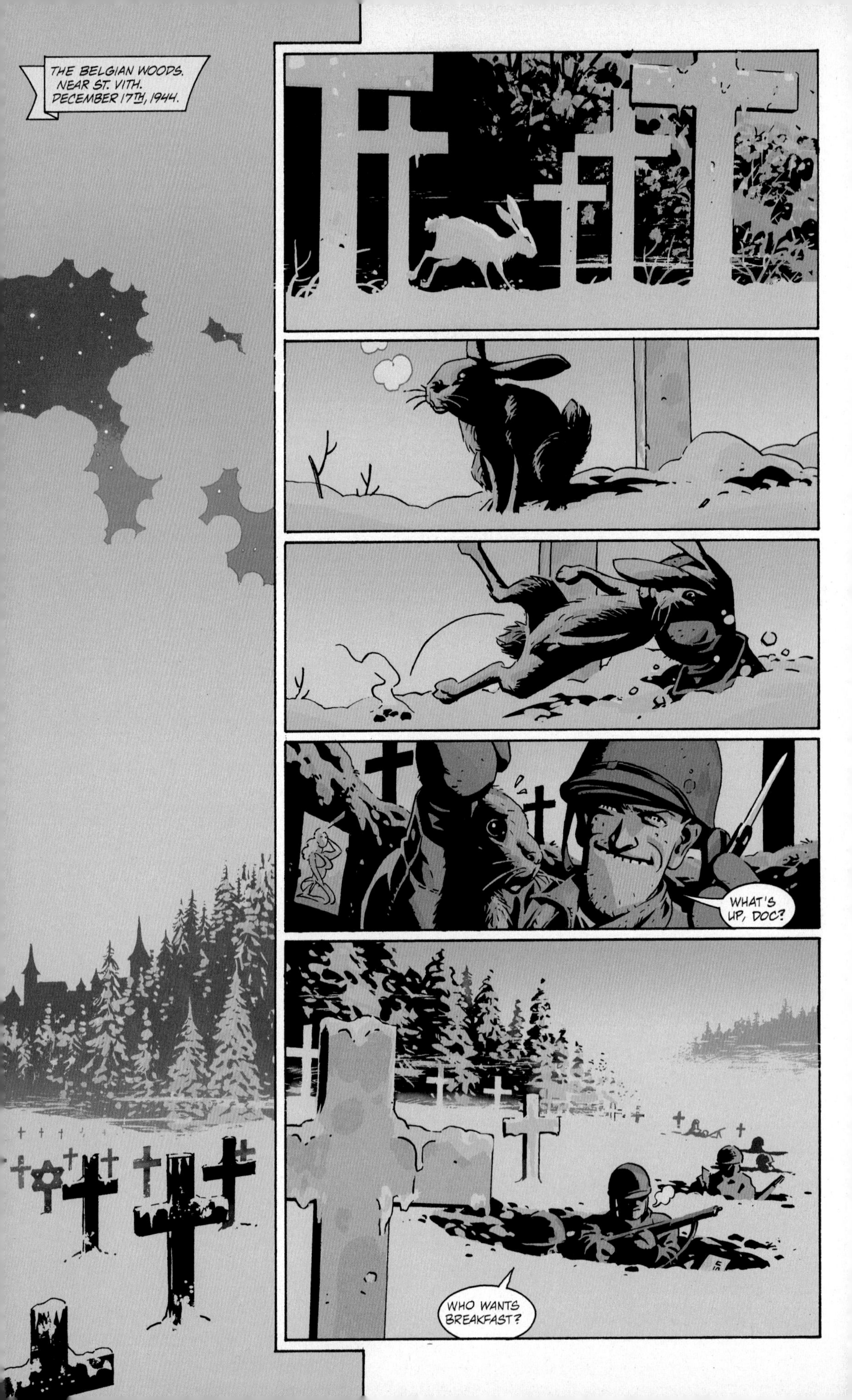
THE BELGIAN WOODS. NEAR ST. VITH. DECEMBER 17TH, 1944.
WHAT'S UP, DOC?
WHO WANTS BREAKFAST?

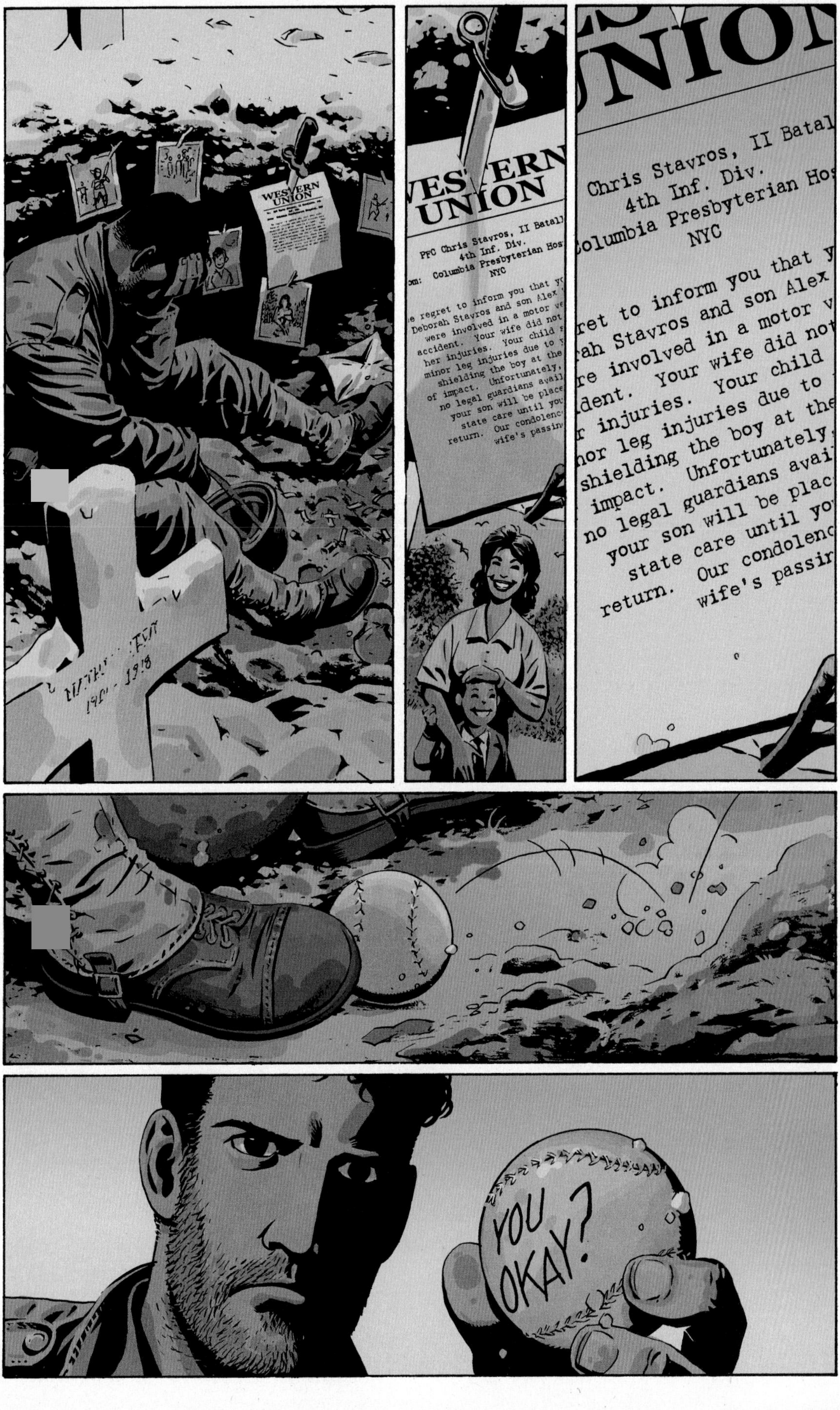
WESTERN UNION
PFC Chris Stavros, II Batal
4th Inf. Div.
om: Columbia Presbyterian Hos
NYC
e regret to inform you that yo
Deborah Stavros and son Alex
were involved in a motor ve
accident. Your wife did not
her injuries. Your child s
minor leg injuries due to y
shielding the boy at the
of impact. Unfortunately,
no legal guardians avail
your son will be place
state care until you
return. Our condolenc
wife's passin
UNION
Chris Stavros, II Batal
4th Inf. Div.
Columbia Presbyterian Hos
NYC
ret to inform you that y
rah Stavros and son Alex
re involved in a motor v
dent. Your wife did not
r injuries. Your child
nor leg injuries due to
shielding the boy at the
impact. Unfortunately,
no legal guardians avai
your son will be plac
state care until yo
return. Our condolenc
wife's passir
YOU OKAY?

A TELEGRAM LIKE THAT--HE SHOULDN'T BE ALONE, ARCH. I'M GONNA GO OVER AND--
STAY PUT. HE'S NOT GOING ANYWHERE, HAL.
HOPE IT DOESN'T SIT IN THE SNOW TOO LONG, IT'LL SCREW UP THE STITCHING.
SHOULD'VE THOUGHT OF THAT BEFORE YOU THREW IT OVER.
MAYBE CHRIS DIDN'T SEE--
POK
MAYBE HE DID.
GOTTA TAKE A DUMP. GIMME SOME PAPER.
JESSE, WHAT THE HELL AM I GONNA DO WITH THREE SHEETS, YOU CHEAP SCREWHEAD?
ONE UP. ONE DOWN. ONE TO POLISH.
LONG WAY TO BERLIN, NICKY.
THIS ONE'S FOR YOU, DAVID.
IT'D BE THE BEGINNING OF THE JUSTICE SOCIETY OF AMERICA. WE'D BE THE FOUNDING MEMBERS.
I MAY READ YOUR COMIC BOOKS, BUT I SURE AS HELL AM NOT PUTTING ONE OF YOUR SHIRTS ON, SIMON.
AND BY THE WAY, SUPERMAN'S NOT IN THE JUSTICE SOCIETY.

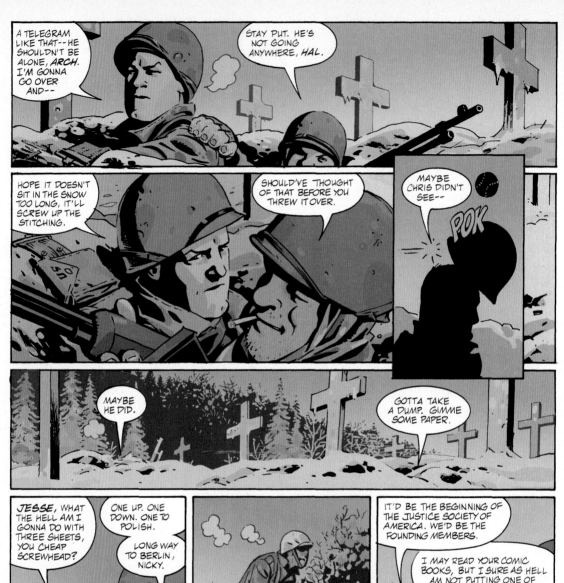

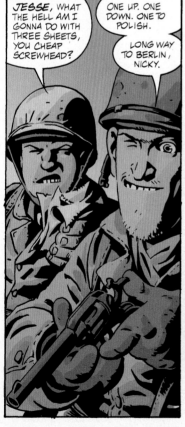

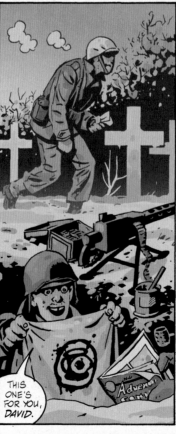

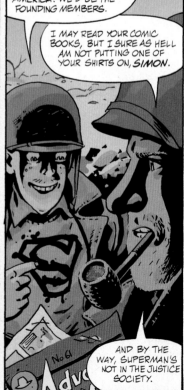

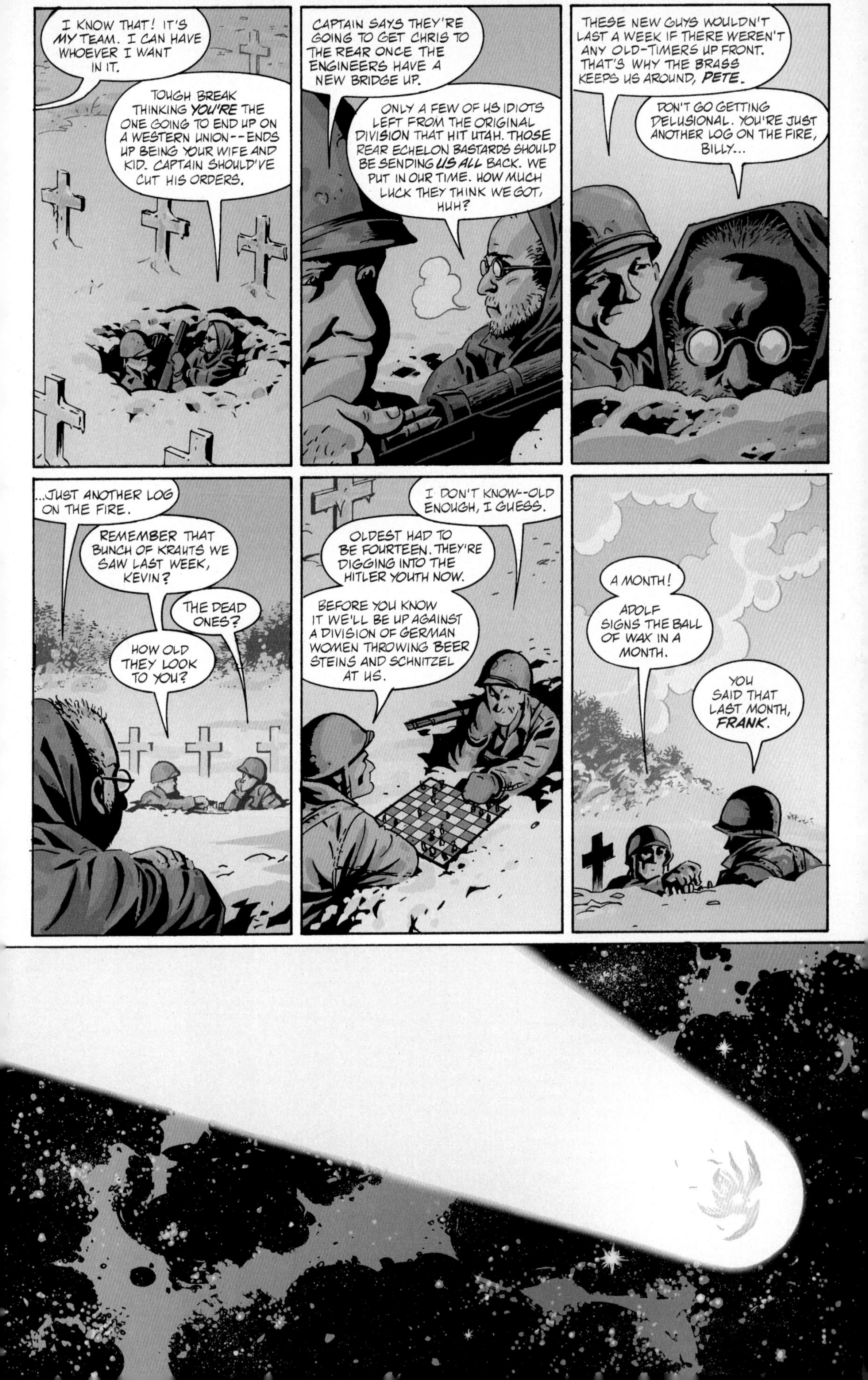
I KNOW THAT! IT'S MY TEAM. I CAN HAVE WHOEVER I WANT IN IT.
TOUGH BREAK THINKING YOU'RE THE ONE GOING TO END UP ON A WESTERN UNION--ENDS UP BEING YOUR WIFE AND KID. CAPTAIN SHOULD'VE CUT HIS ORDERS.
CAPTAIN SAYS THEY'RE GOING TO GET CHRIS TO THE REAR ONCE THE ENGINEERS HAVE A NEW BRIDGE UP.
ONLY A FEW OF US IDIOTS LEFT FROM THE ORIGINAL DIVISION THAT HIT UTAH. THOSE REAR ECHELON BASTARDS SHOULD BE SENDING US ALL BACK. WE PUT IN OUR TIME. HOW MUCH LUCK THEY THINK WE GOT, HUH?
THESE NEW GUYS WOULDN'T LAST A WEEK IF THERE WEREN'T ANY OLD-TIMERS UP FRONT. THAT'S WHY THE BRASS KEEPS US AROUND, PETE.
DON'T GO GETTING DELUSIONAL. YOU'RE JUST ANOTHER LOG ON THE FIRE, BILLY...
...JUST ANOTHER LOG ON THE FIRE.
REMEMBER THAT BUNCH OF KRAUTS WE SAW LAST WEEK, KEVIN?
THE DEAD ONES?
HOW OLD THEY LOOK TO YOU?
I DON'T KNOW--OLD ENOUGH, I GUESS.
OLDEST HAD TO BE FOURTEEN. THEY'RE DIGGING INTO THE HITLER YOUTH NOW.
BEFORE YOU KNOW IT WE'LL BE UP AGAINST A DIVISION OF GERMAN WOMEN THROWING BEER STEINS AND SCHNITZEL AT US.
A MONTH!
ADOLF SIGNS THE BALL OF WAX IN A MONTH.
YOU SAID THAT LAST MONTH, FRANK.

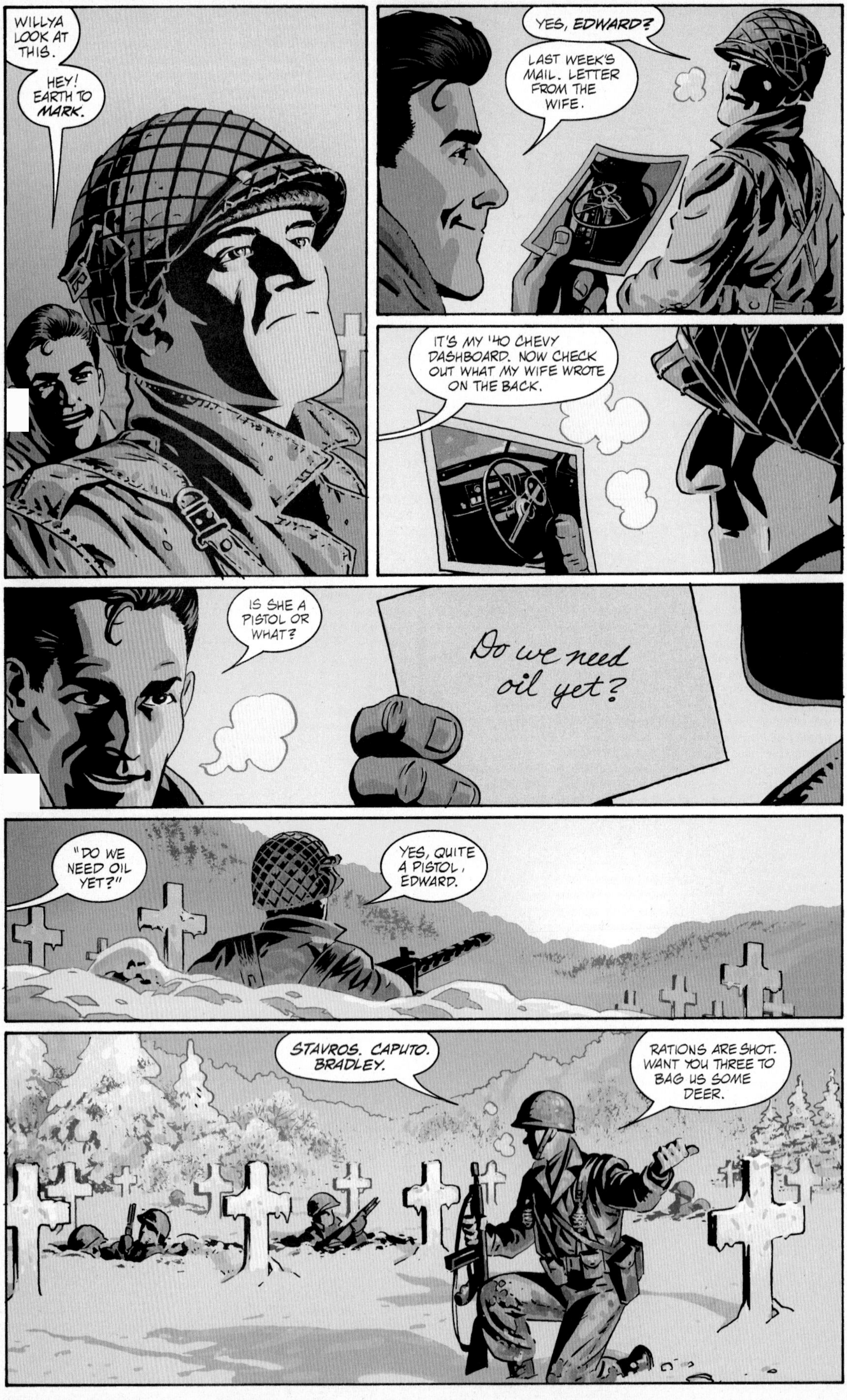
WILLYA LOOK AT THIS.
HEY! EARTH TO MARK.
YES, EDWARD?
LAST WEEK'S MAIL. LETTER FROM THE WIFE.
IT'S MY '40 CHEVY DASHBOARD. NOW CHECK OUT WHAT MY WIFE WROTE ON THE BACK.
IS SHE A PISTOL OR WHAT?
Do we need oil yet?
"DO WE NEED OIL YET?"
YES, QUITE A PISTOL, EDWARD.
STAVROS. CAPUTO. BRADLEY.
RATIONS ARE SHOT. WANT YOU THREE TO BAG US SOME DEER.

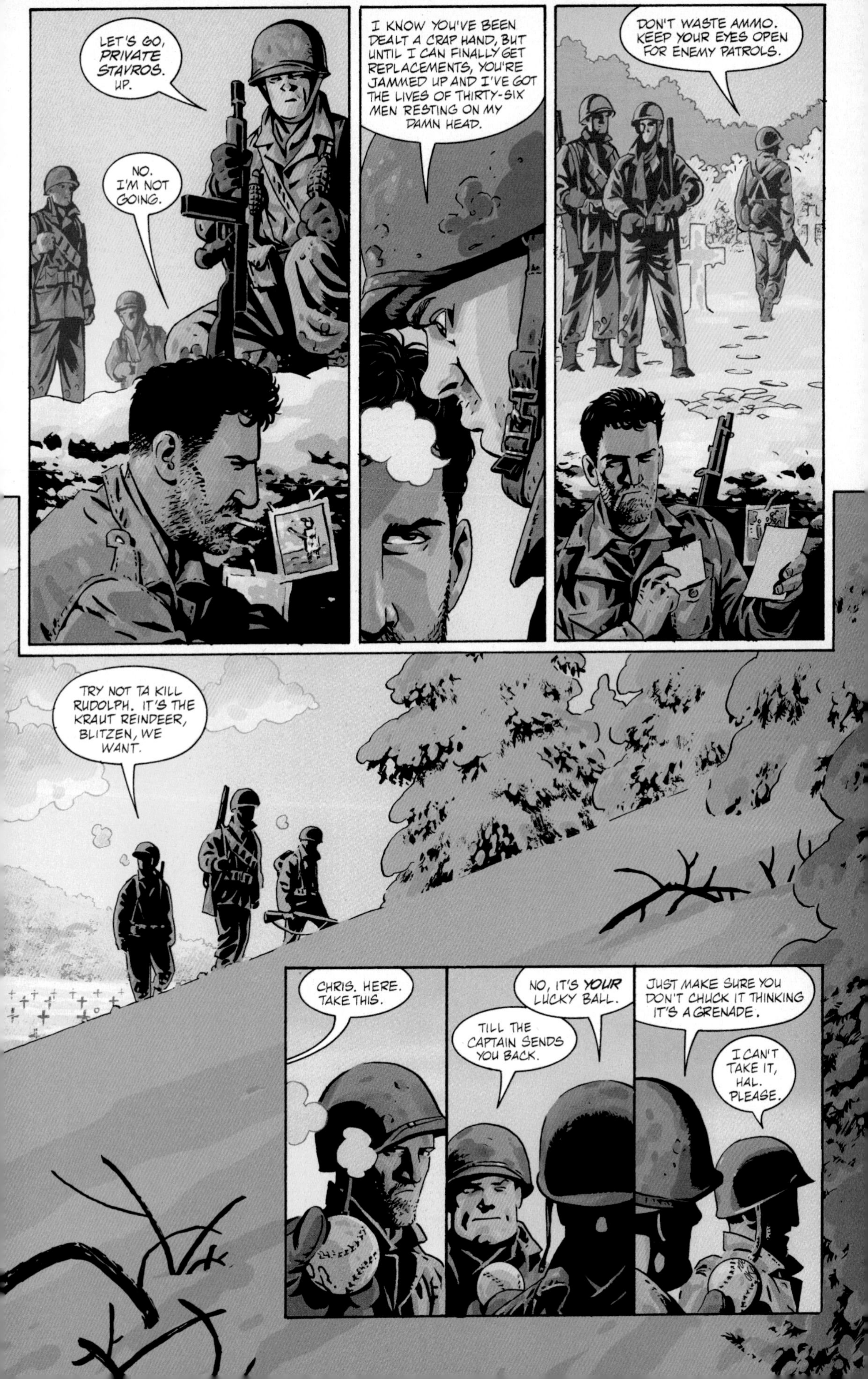
LET'S GO, PRIVATE STAVROS. UP.
NO. I'M NOT GOING.
I KNOW YOU'VE BEEN DEALT A CRAP HAND, BUT UNTIL I CAN FINALLY GET REPLACEMENTS, YOU'RE JAMMED UP AND I'VE GOT THE LIVES OF THIRTY-SIX MEN RESTING ON MY DAMN HEAD.
DON'T WASTE AMMO. KEEP YOUR EYES OPEN FOR ENEMY PATROLS.
TRY NOT TA KILL RUDOLPH. IT'S THE KRAUT REINDEER, BLITZEN, WE WANT.
CHRIS. HERE. TAKE THIS.
NO, IT'S *YOUR* LUCKY BALL.
TILL THE CAPTAIN SENDS YOU BACK.
JUST MAKE SURE YOU DON'T CHUCK IT THINKING IT'S A GRENADE.
I CAN'T TAKE IT, HAL. PLEASE.

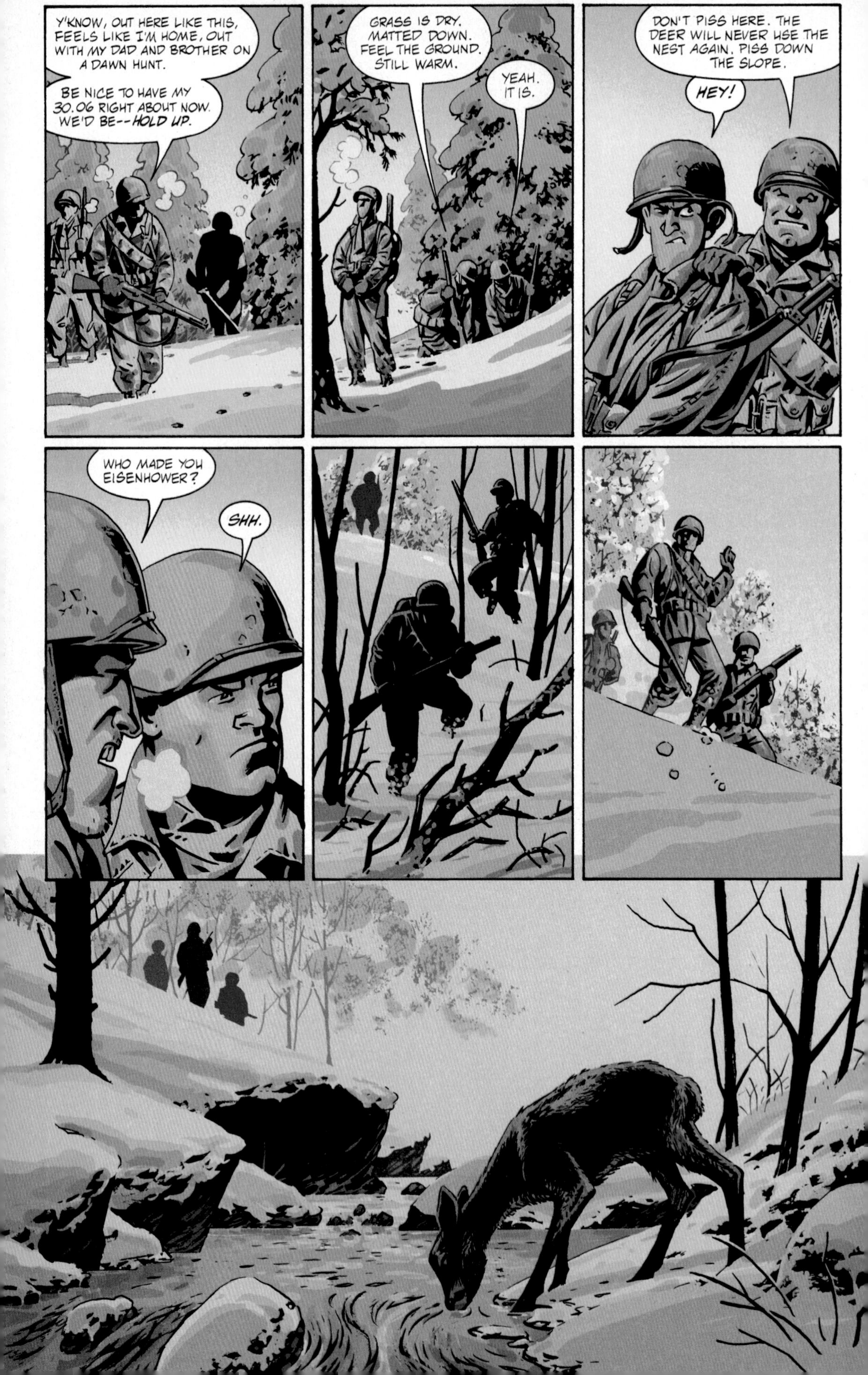
Y'KNOW, OUT HERE LIKE THIS, FEELS LIKE I'M HOME, OUT WITH MY DAD AND BROTHER ON A DAWN HUNT.
BE NICE TO HAVE MY 30.06 RIGHT ABOUT NOW. WE'D BE--HOLD UP.
GRASS IS DRY. MATTED DOWN. FEEL THE GROUND. STILL WARM.
YEAH. IT IS.
DON'T PISS HERE. THE DEER WILL NEVER USE THE NEST AGAIN. PISS DOWN THE SLOPE.
HEY!
WHO MADE YOU EISENHOWER?
SHH.

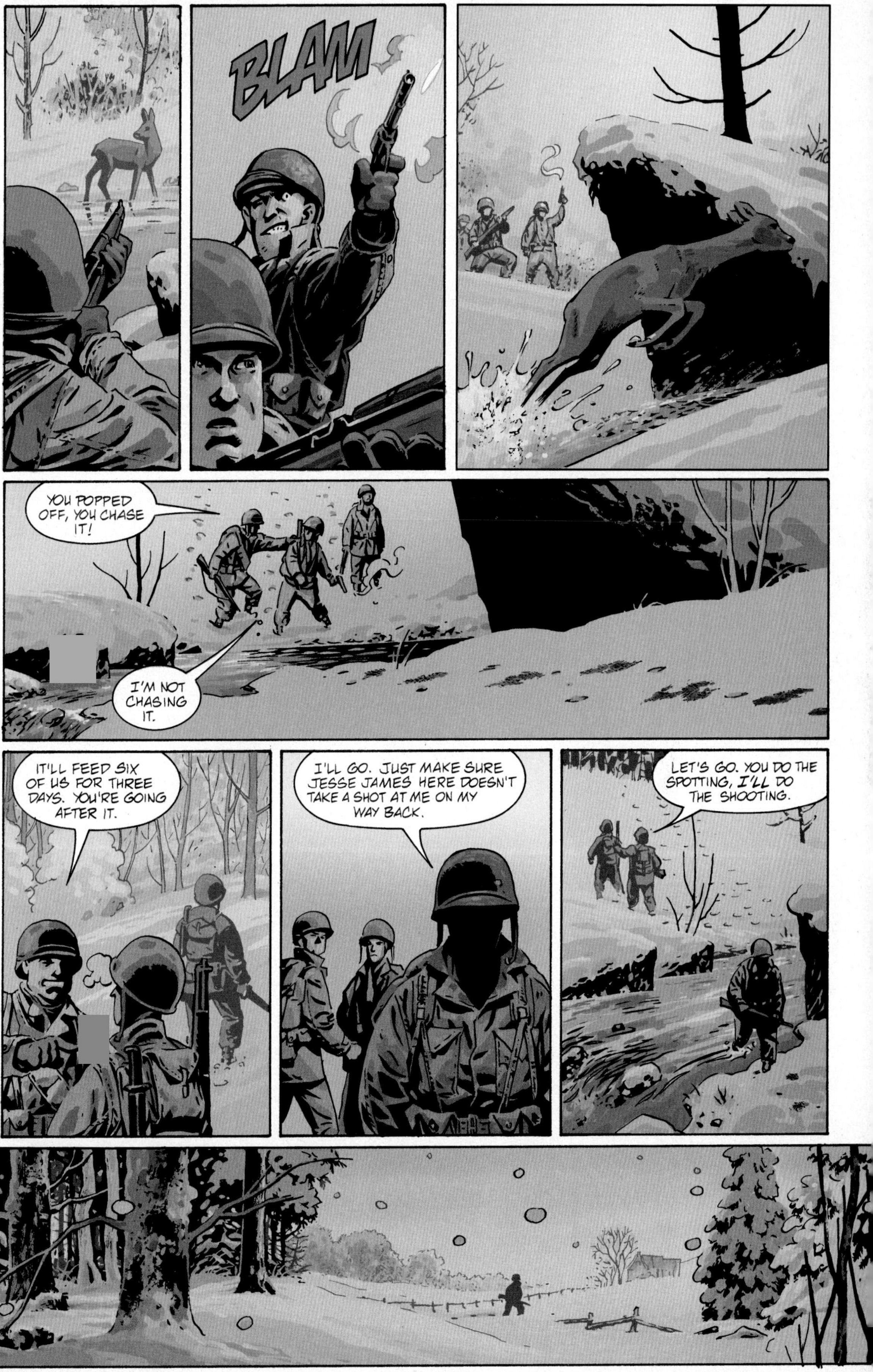
BLAM
YOU POPPED OFF, YOU CHASE IT!
I'M NOT CHASING IT.
IT'LL FEED SIX OF US FOR THREE DAYS. YOU'RE GOING AFTER IT.
I'LL GO. JUST MAKE SURE JESSE JAMES HERE DOESN'T TAKE A SHOT AT ME ON MY WAY BACK.
LET'S GO. YOU DO THE SPOTTING, *I'LL* DO THE SHOOTING.

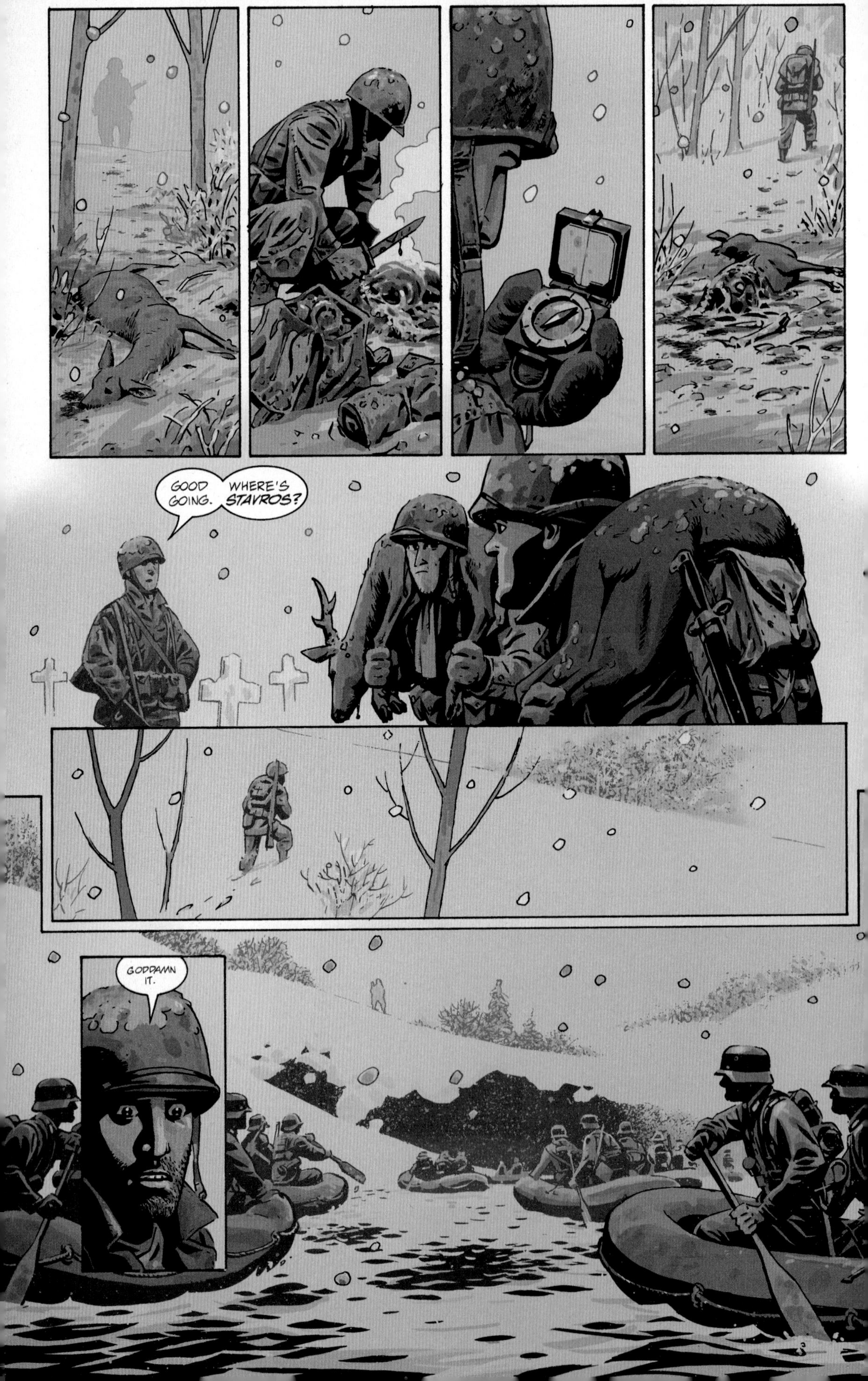
GOOD GOING.
WHERE'S STAVROS?
GODDAMN IT.

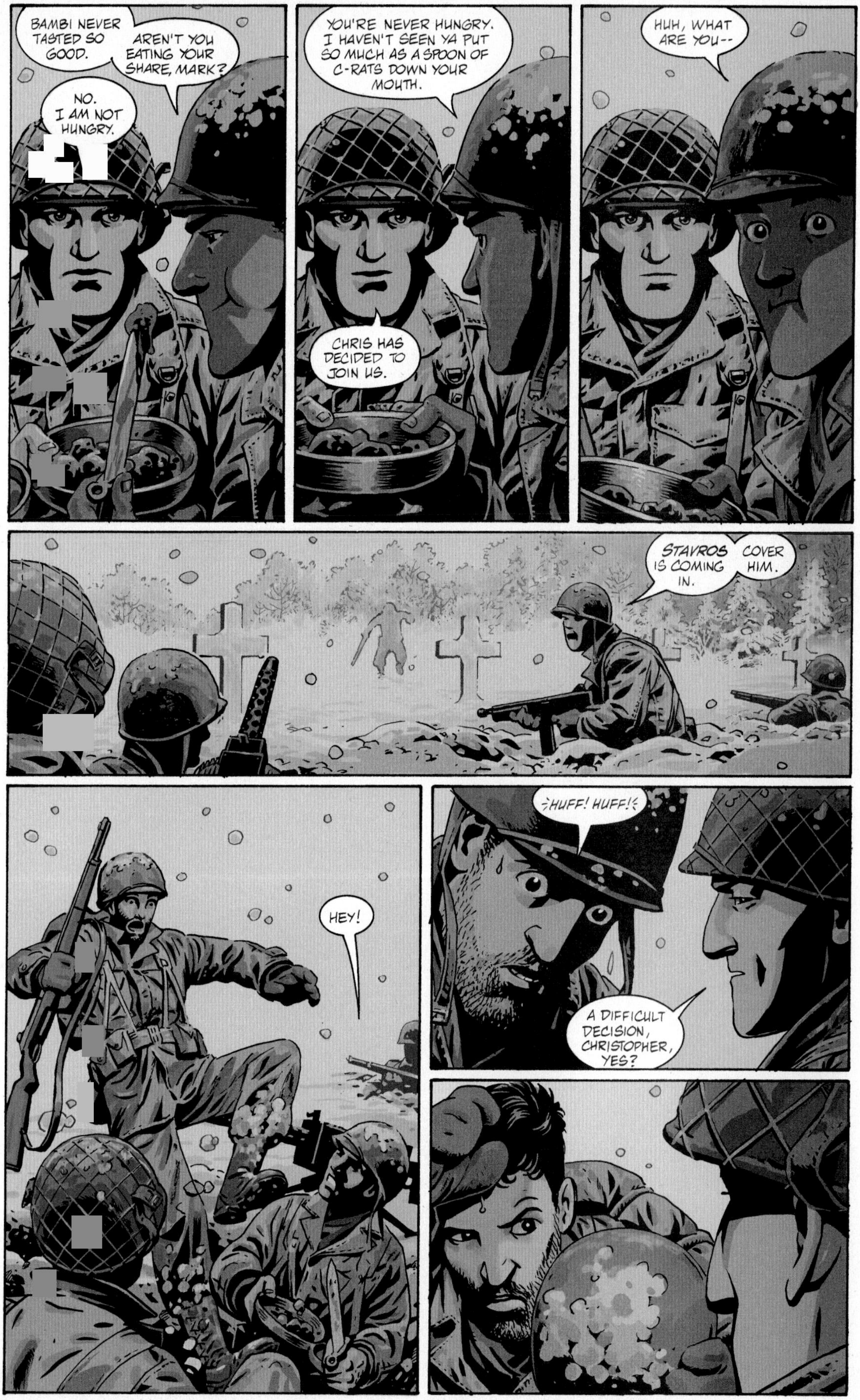
BAMBI NEVER TASTED SO GOOD.
AREN'T YOU EATING YOUR SHARE, MARK?
NO. I AM NOT HUNGRY.
YOU'RE NEVER HUNGRY. I HAVEN'T SEEN YA PUT SO MUCH AS A SPOON OF C-RATS DOWN YOUR MOUTH.
CHRIS HAS DECIDED TO JOIN US.
HUH, WHAT ARE YOU--
STAVROS IS COMING IN.
COVER HIM.
HEY!
HUFF! HUFF!
A DIFFICULT DECISION, CHRISTOPHER, YES?

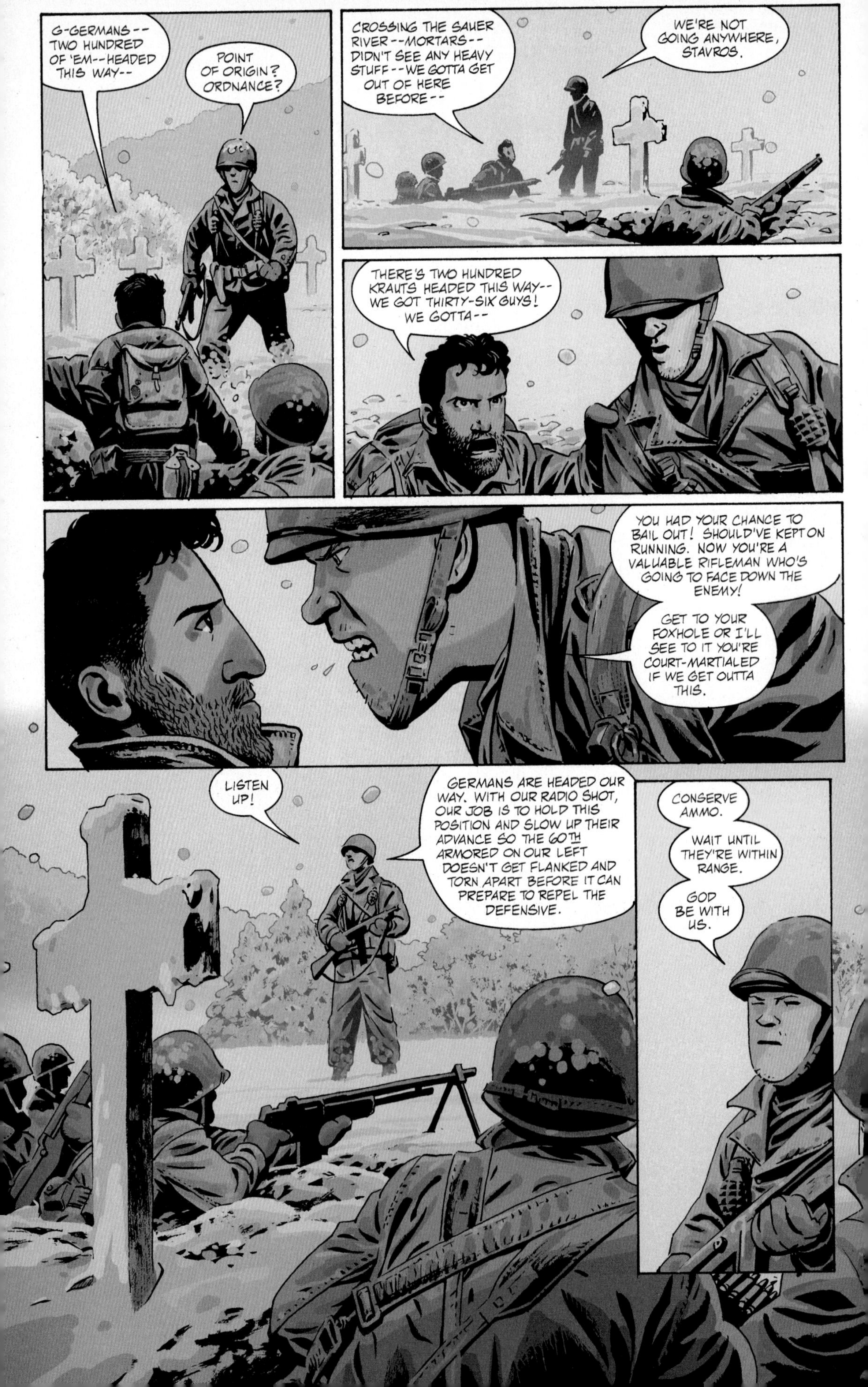
G-GERMANS-- TWO HUNDRED OF 'EM--HEADED THIS WAY--
POINT OF ORIGIN? ORDNANCE?
CROSSING THE SAUER RIVER--MORTARS--DIDN'T SEE ANY HEAVY STUFF--WE GOTTA GET OUT OF HERE BEFORE--
WE'RE NOT GOING ANYWHERE, STAVROS.
THERE'S TWO HUNDRED KRAUTS HEADED THIS WAY--WE GOT THIRTY-SIX GUYS! WE GOTTA--
YOU HAD YOUR CHANCE TO BAIL OUT! SHOULD'VE KEPT ON RUNNING. NOW YOU'RE A VALUABLE RIFLEMAN WHO'S GOING TO FACE DOWN THE ENEMY!
GET TO YOUR FOXHOLE OR I'LL SEE TO IT YOU'RE COURT-MARTIALED IF WE GET OUTTA THIS.
LISTEN UP!
GERMANS ARE HEADED OUR WAY. WITH OUR RADIO SHOT, OUR JOB IS TO HOLD THIS POSITION AND SLOW UP THEIR ADVANCE SO THE 60TH ARMORED ON OUR LEFT DOESN'T GET FLANKED AND TORN APART BEFORE IT CAN PREPARE TO REPEL THE DEFENSIVE.
CONSERVE AMMO.
WAIT UNTIL THEY'RE WITHIN RANGE.
GOD BE WITH US.

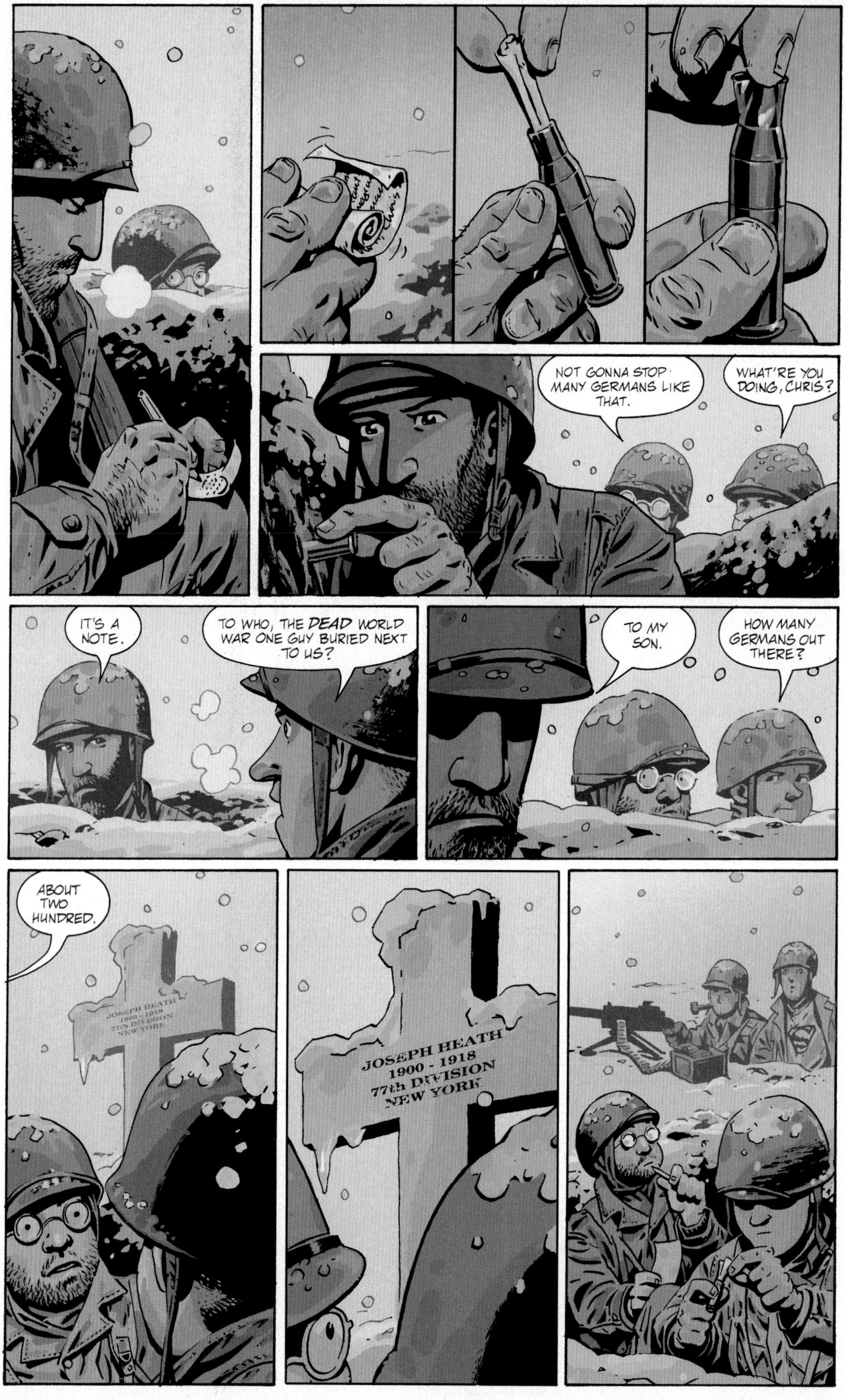
NOT GONNA STOP MANY GERMANS LIKE THAT.
WHAT'RE YOU DOING, CHRIS?
IT'S A NOTE.
TO WHO, THE DEAD WORLD WAR ONE GUY BURIED NEXT TO US?
TO MY SON.
HOW MANY GERMANS OUT THERE?
ABOUT TWO HUNDRED.
JOSEPH HEATH
1900 - 1918
77th DIVISION
NEW YORK
JOSEPH HEATH
1900 - 1918
77th DIVISION
NEW YORK

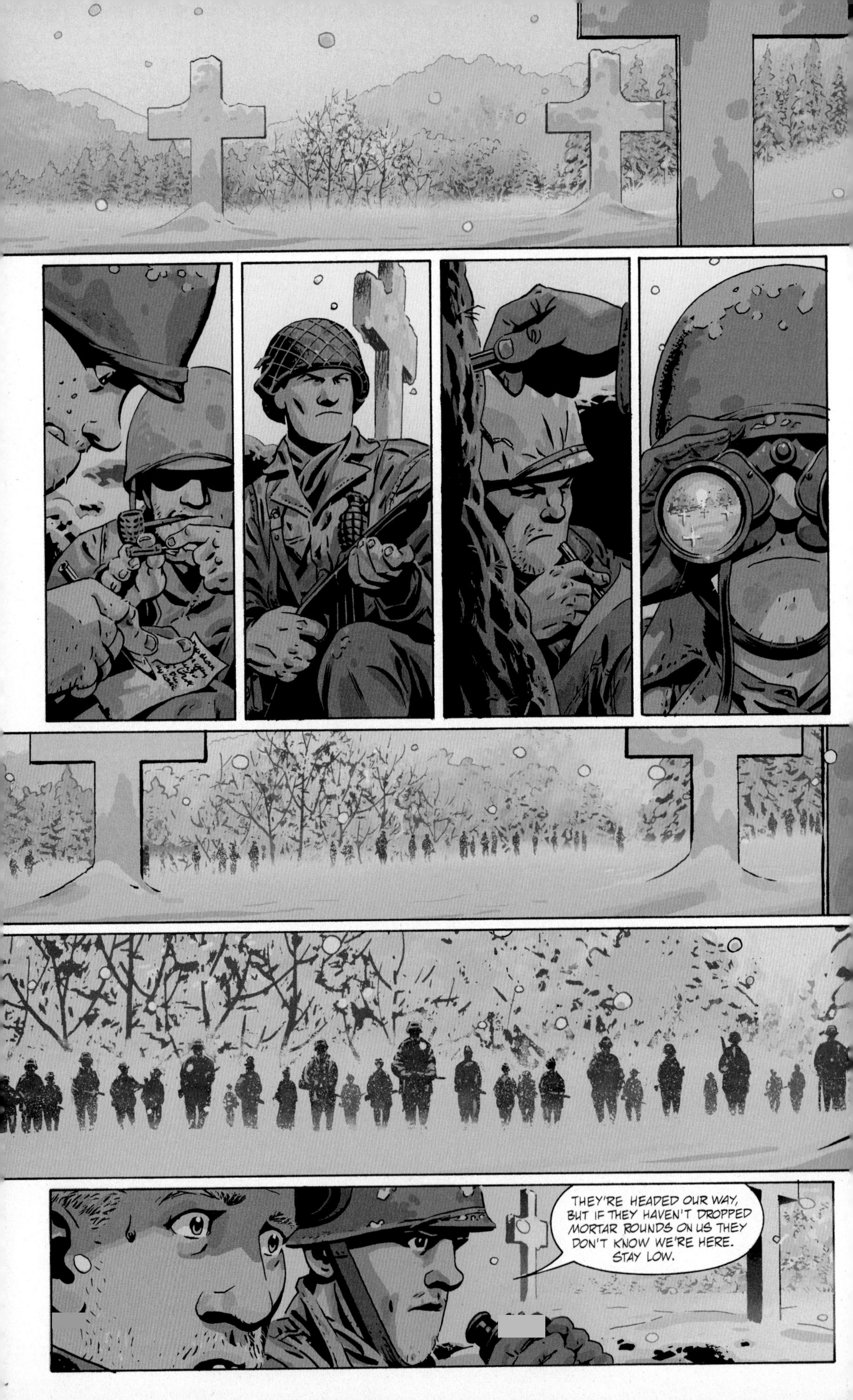
THEY'RE HEADED OUR WAY, BUT IF THEY HAVEN'T DROPPED MORTAR ROUNDS ON US THEY DON'T KNOW WE'RE HERE. STAY LOW.

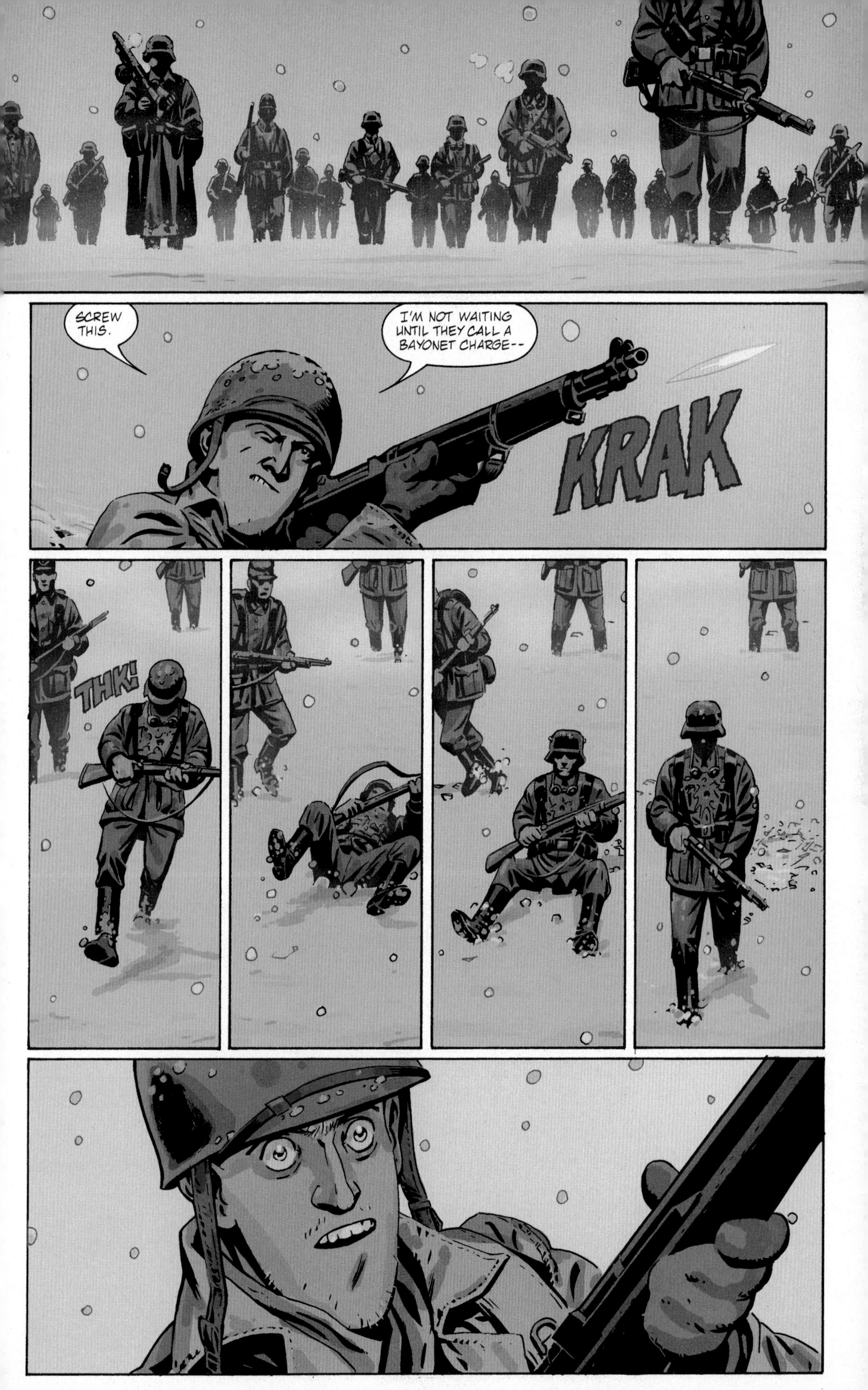
SCREW THIS.
I'M NOT WAITING UNTIL THEY CALL A BAYONET CHARGE--
KRAK
THK!

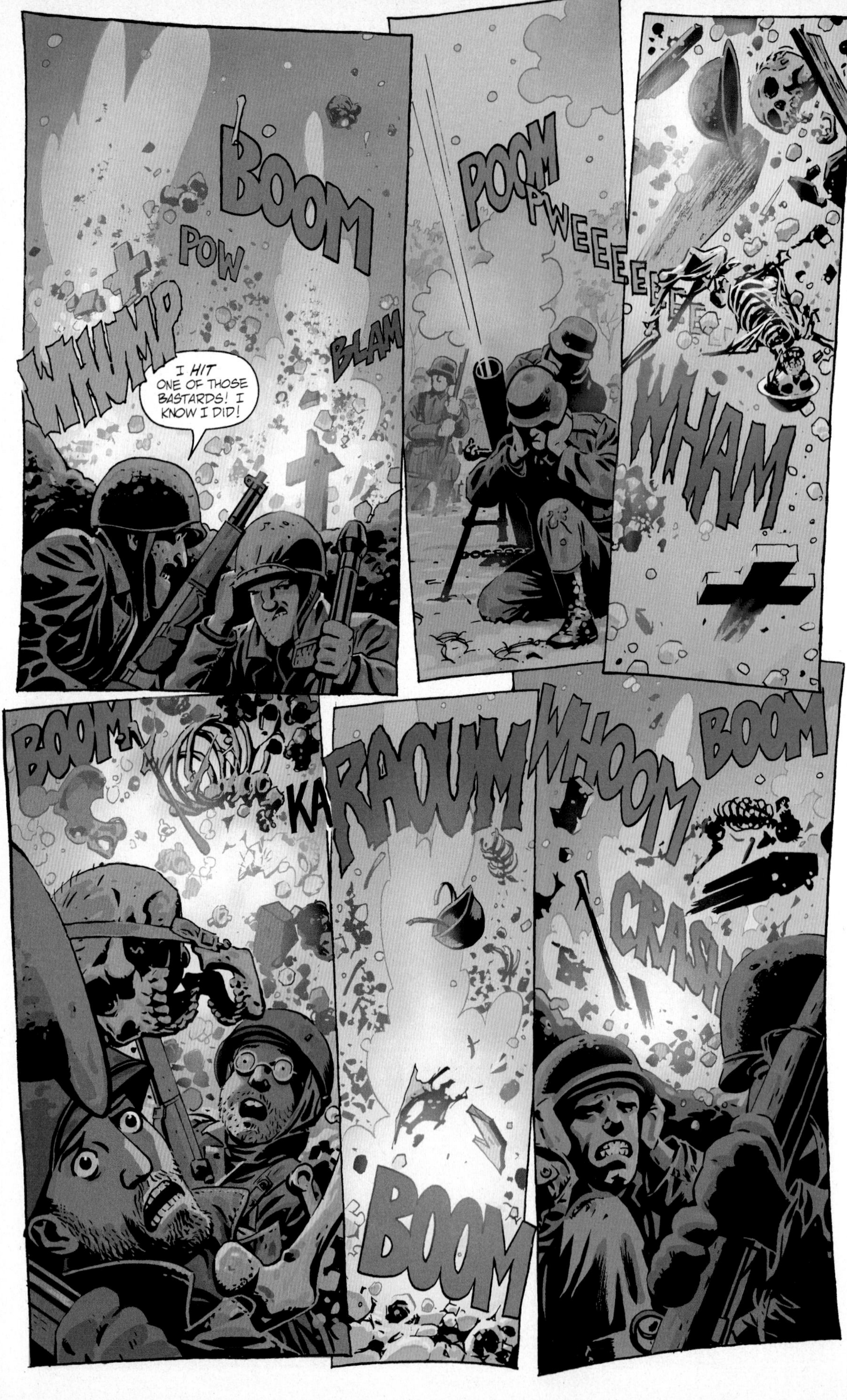

BOOM
POW
WHUMP
BLAM
I HIT ONE OF THOSE BASTARDS! I KNOW I DID!
POOM
PWEEEEEEEEE
WHAM
BOOM
KA
RAOUM
BOOM
WHOOM
BOOM
CRASH

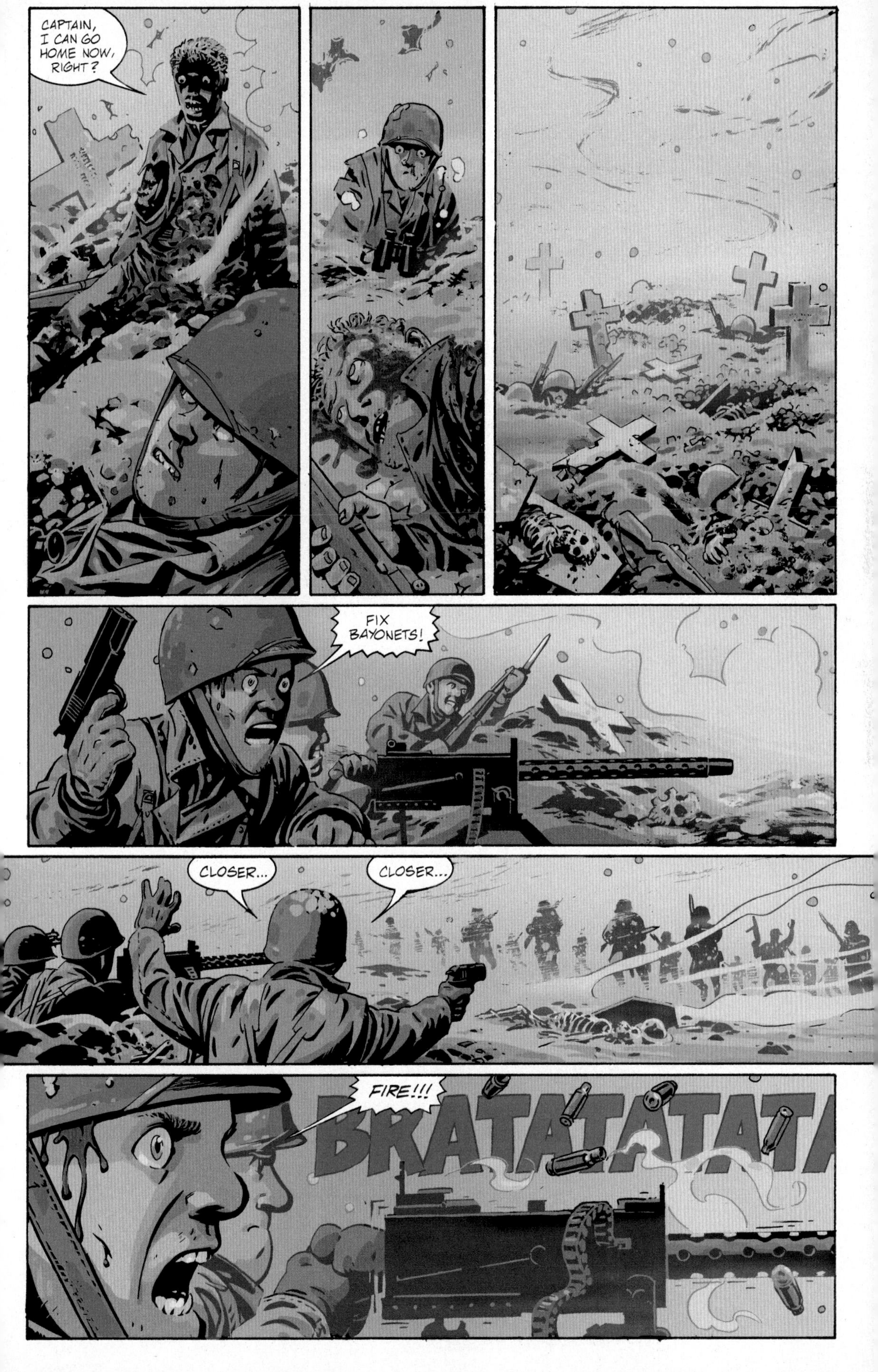
CAPTAIN, I CAN GO HOME NOW, RIGHT?
FIX BAYONETS!
CLOSER...
CLOSER...
FIRE!!!
BRATATATATA

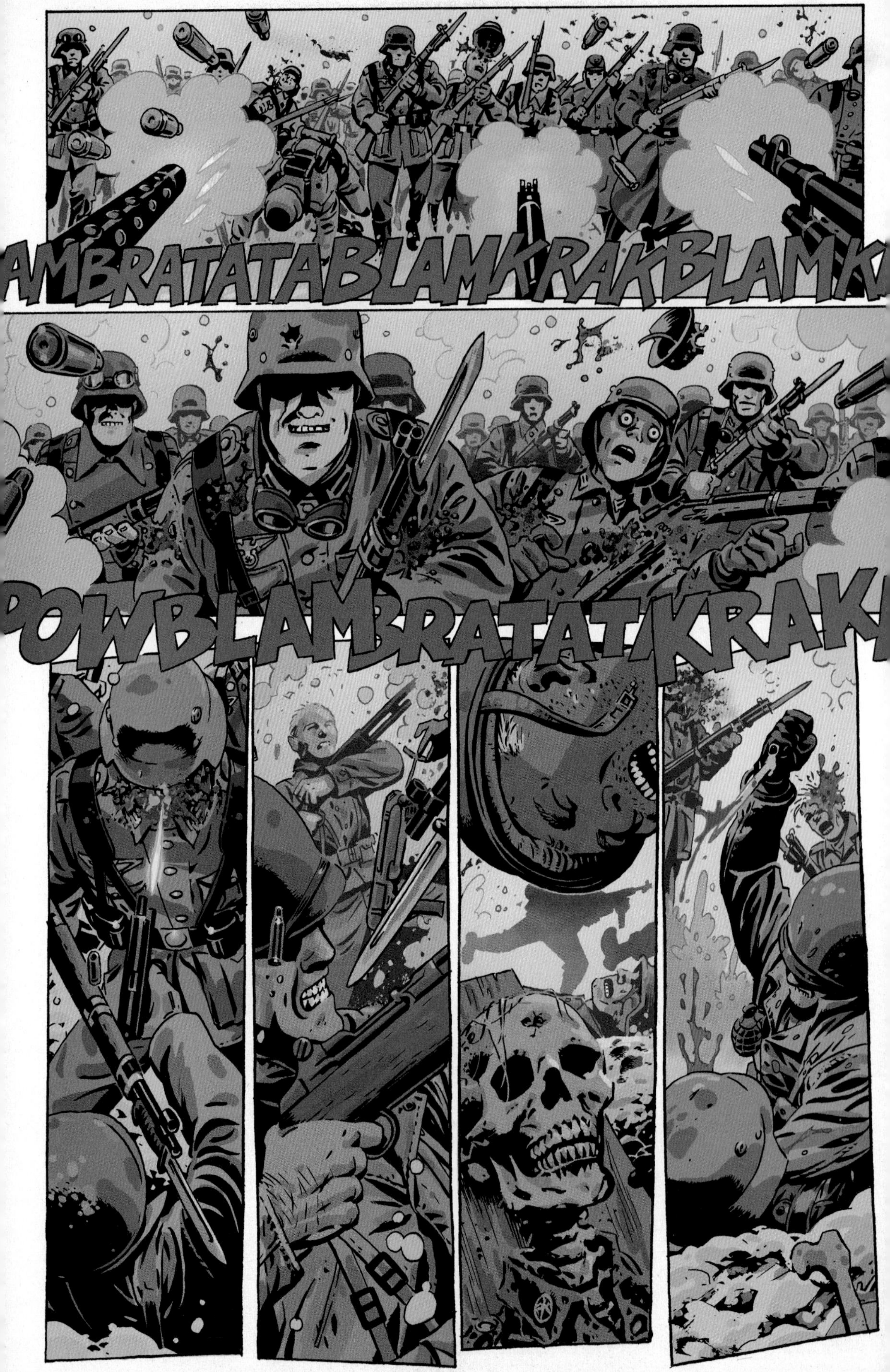
AMBRATATABLAMKRAKBLAMK
POWBLAMBRATATKRAK

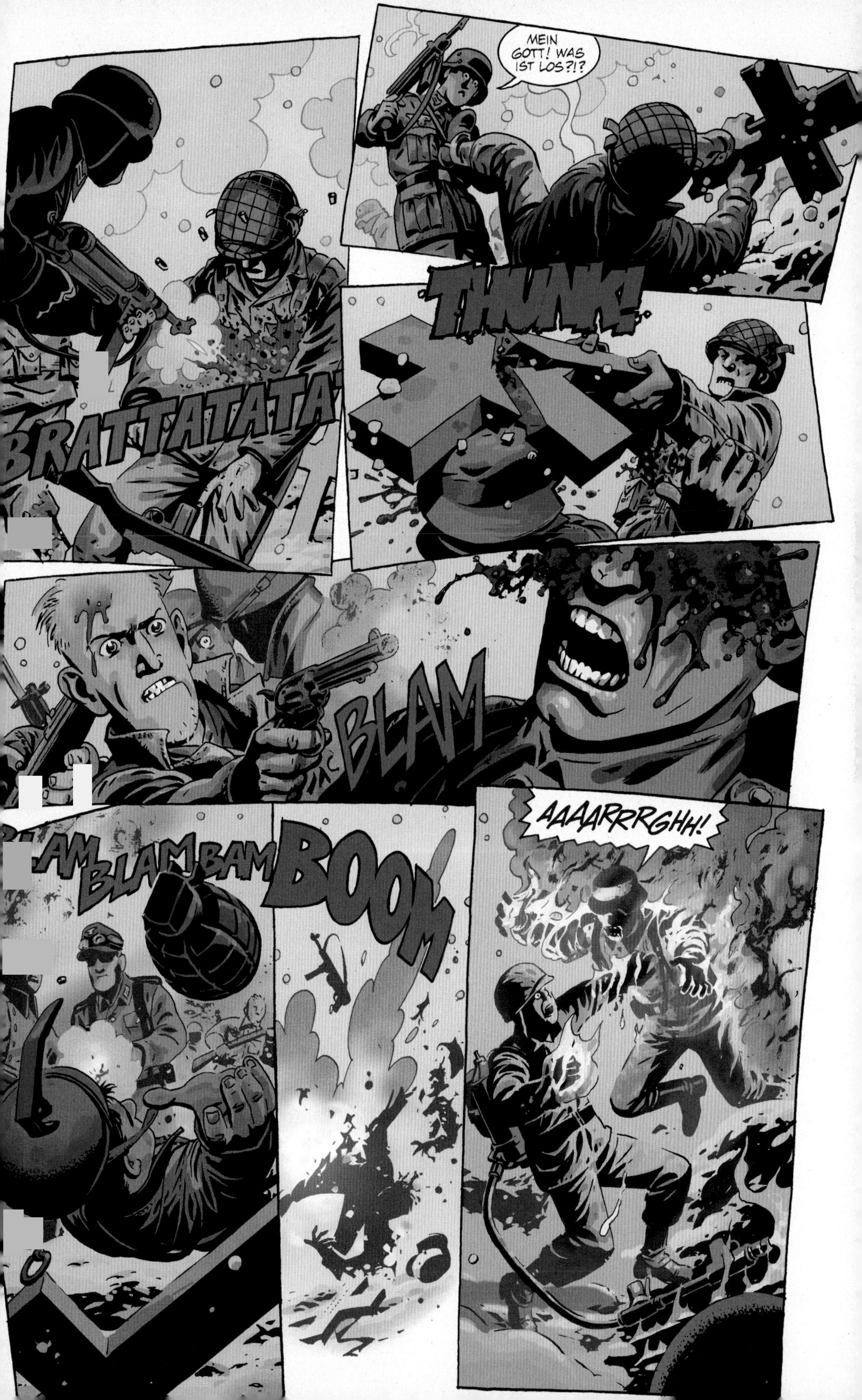
BRATTATATAT
MEIN GOTT! WAS IST LOS?!?
THUNK!
BLAM
BLAM BLAM BLAM BAM
BOOM
AAAARRRGHH!

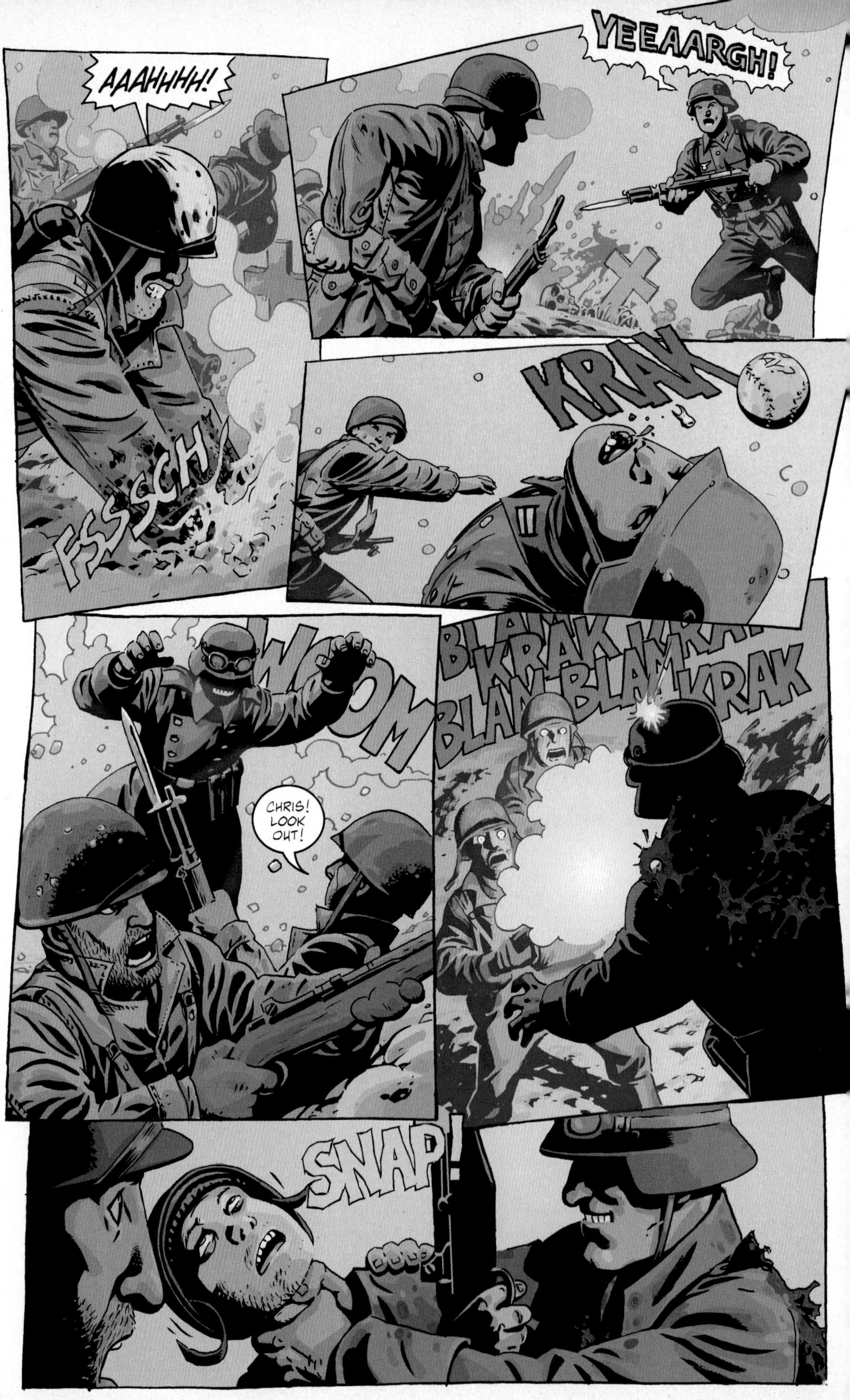

AAAHHHH!
FSSSCH!
YEEAARGH!
KRAK
WOOM
CHRIS! LOOK OUT!
BLAM KRAK
BLAM BLAM KRAK
SNAP!

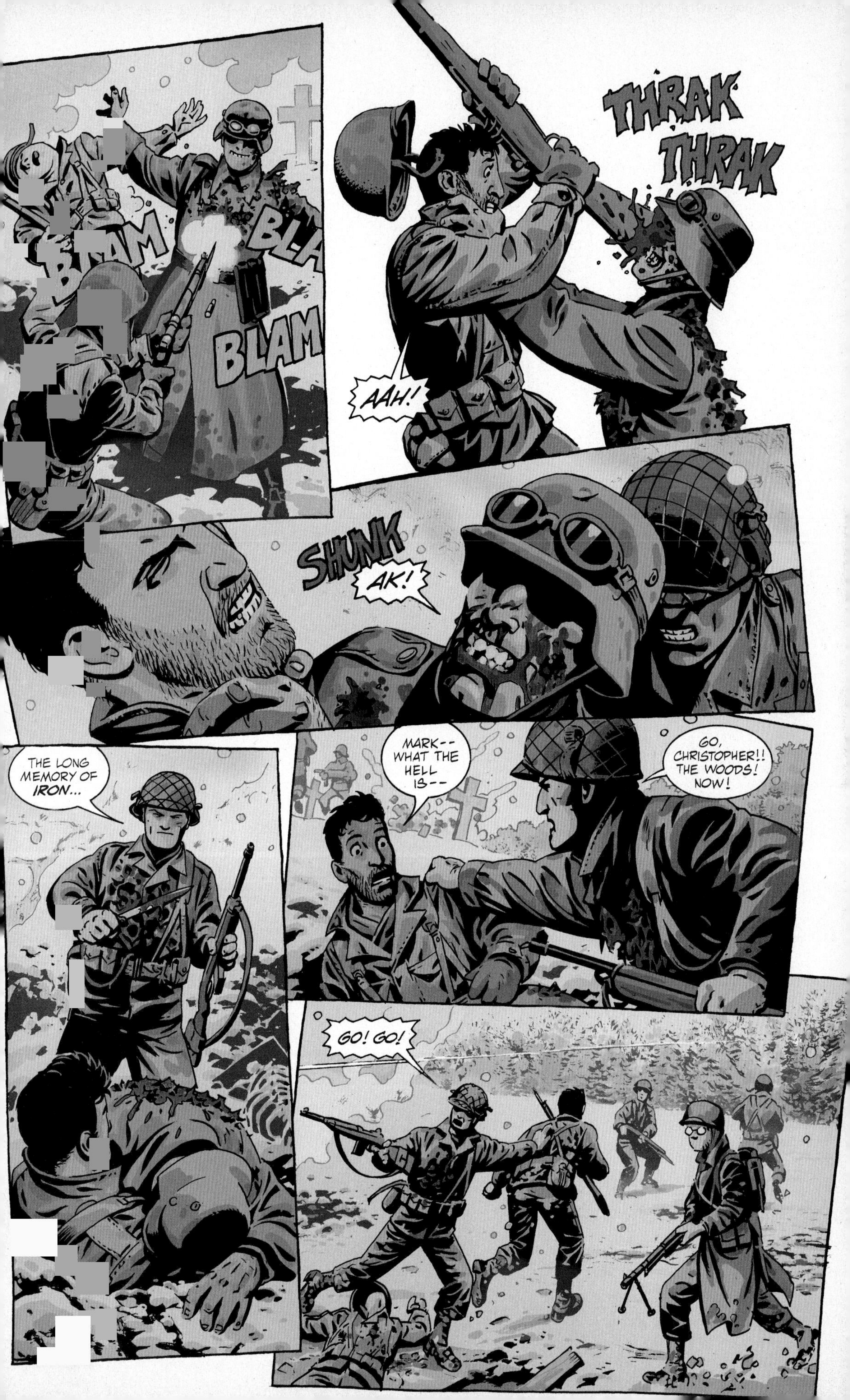
BLAM
BLA
BLAM
THRAK
THRAK
AAH!
SHUNK
AK!
THE LONG MEMORY OF *IRON*...
MARK-- WHAT THE HELL IS--
GO, CHRISTOPHER!! THE WOODS! NOW!
GO! GO!

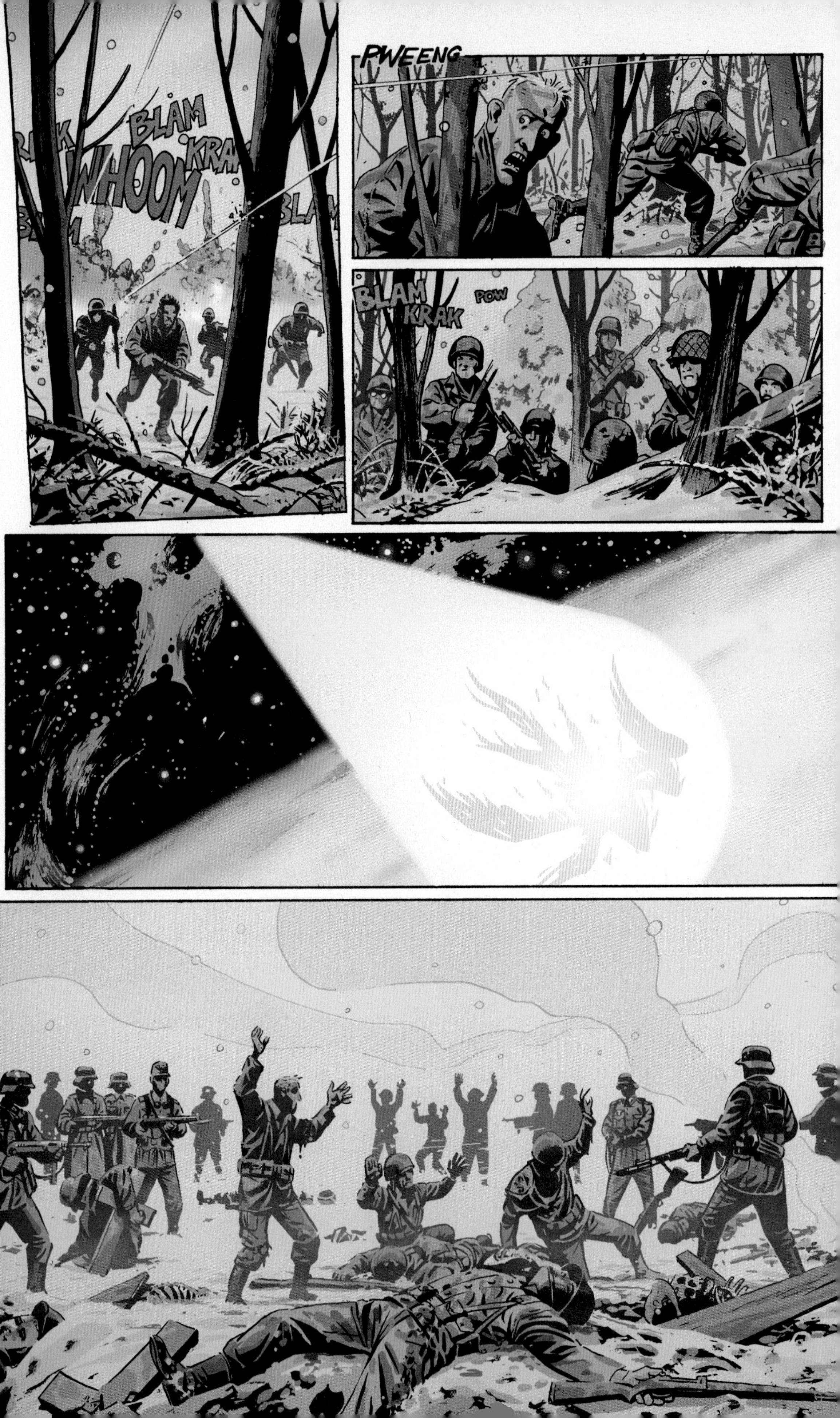
BLAM
KRAK
WHOOM
BLAM
PWEENG
BLAM
KRAK
POW

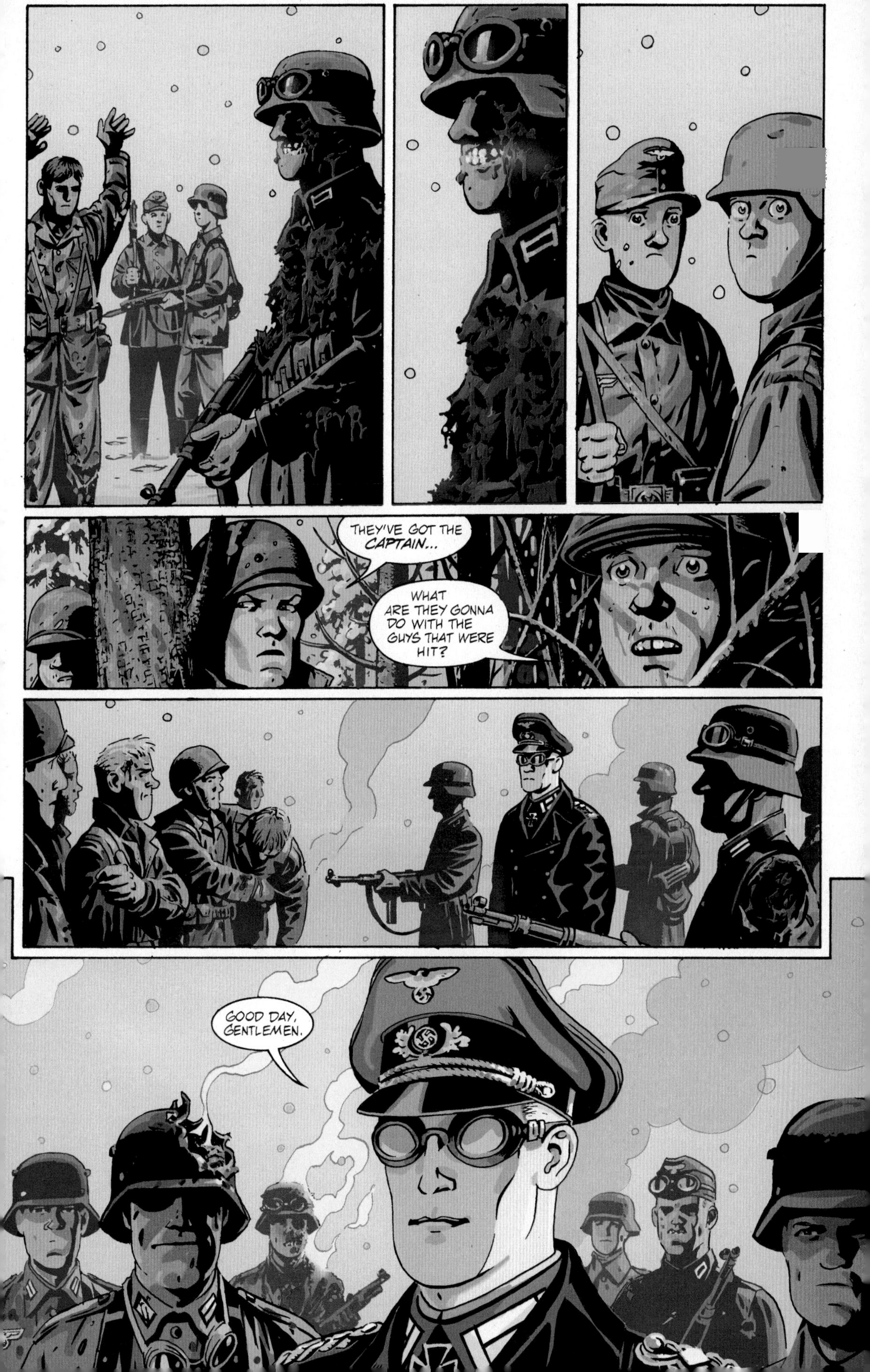
THEY'VE GOT THE CAPTAIN...
WHAT ARE THEY GONNA DO WITH THE GUYS THAT WERE HIT?
GOOD DAY, GENTLEMEN.

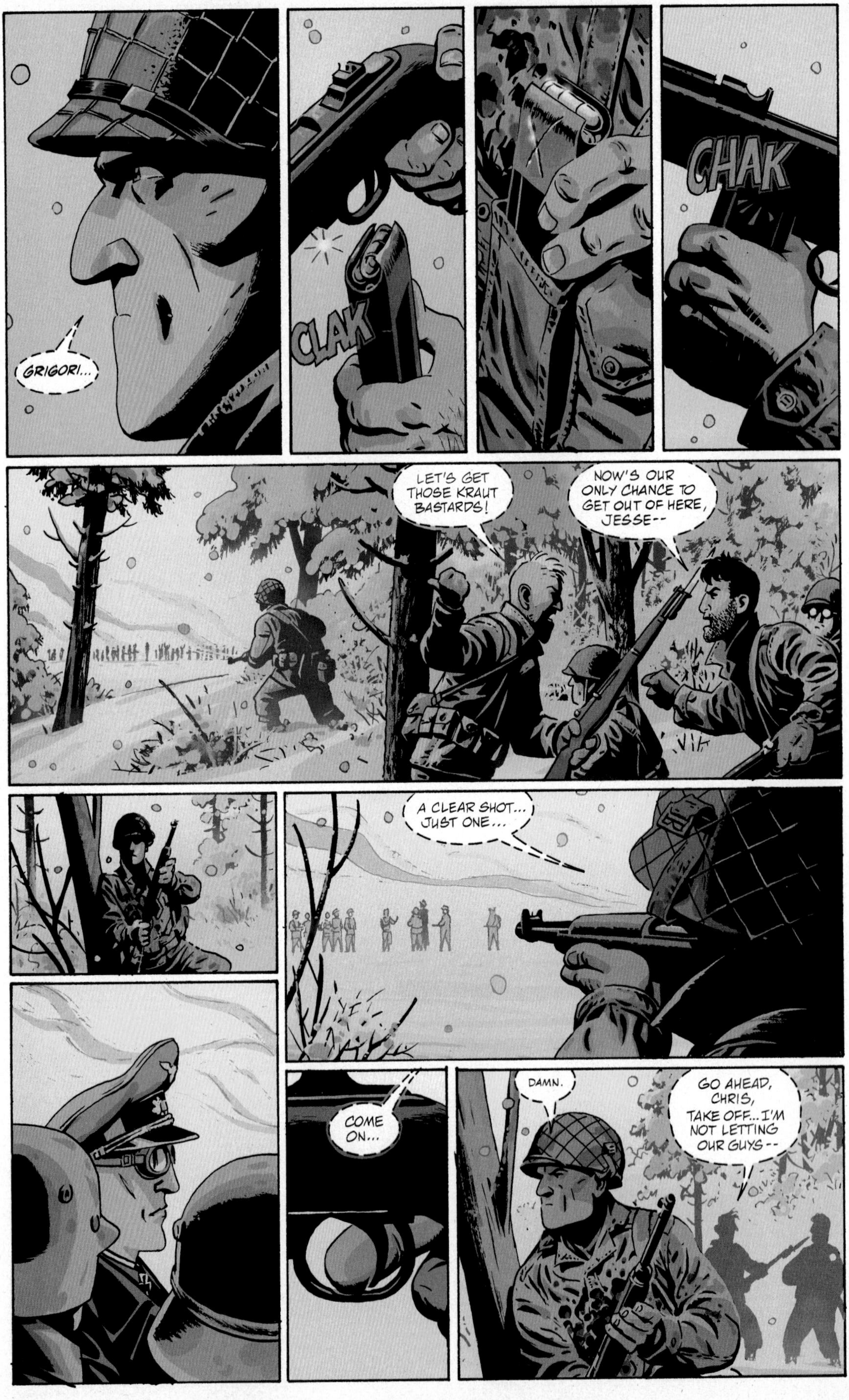
GRIGORI...
CLAK
CHAK
LET'S GET THOSE KRAUT BASTARDS!
NOW'S OUR ONLY CHANCE TO GET OUT OF HERE, JESSE--
A CLEAR SHOT... JUST ONE...
COME ON...
DAMN.
GO AHEAD, CHRIS, TAKE OFF... I'M NOT LETTING OUR GUYS--

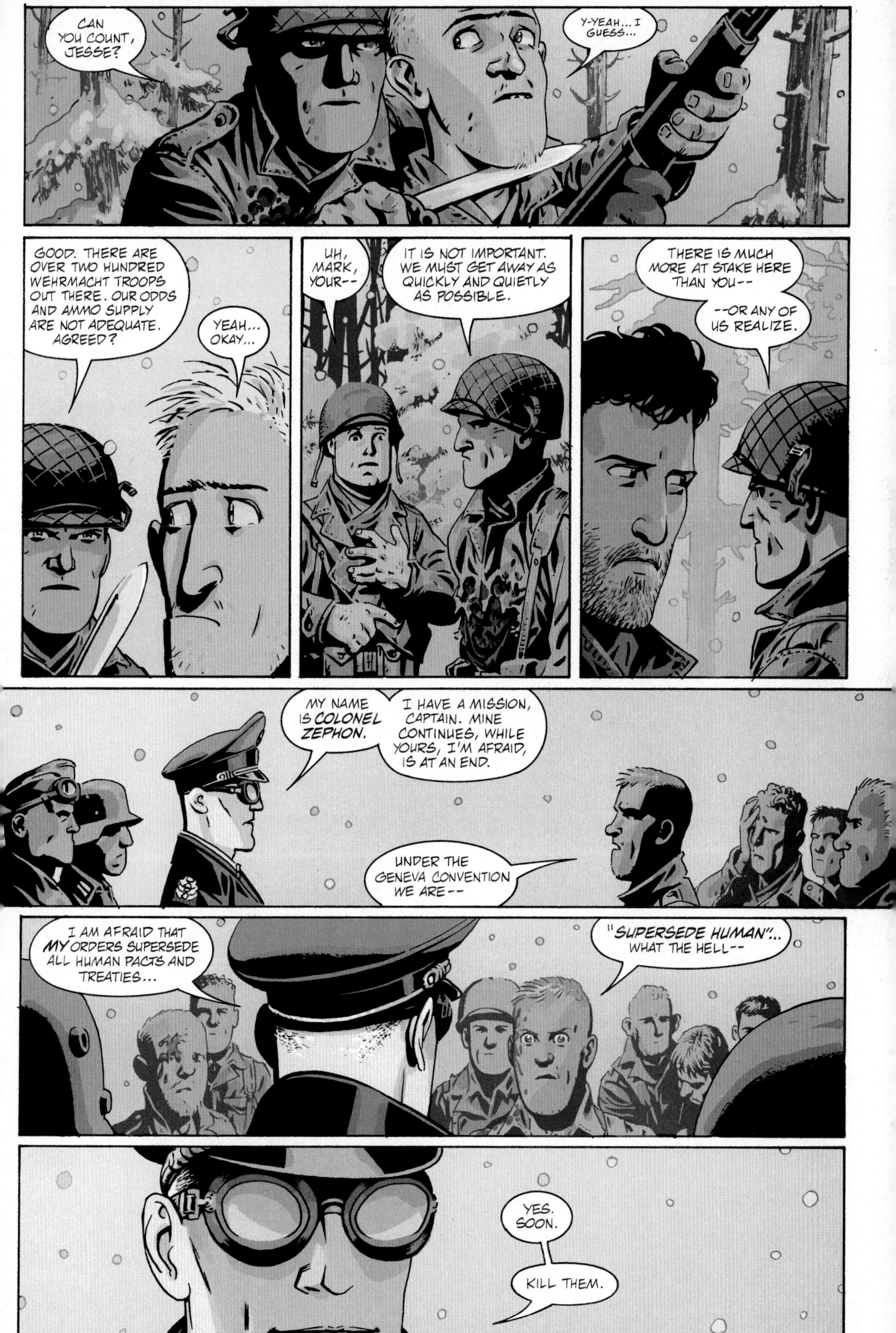
CAN YOU COUNT, JESSE?
Y-YEAH... I GUESS...
GOOD. THERE ARE OVER TWO HUNDRED WEHRMACHT TROOPS OUT THERE. OUR ODDS AND AMMO SUPPLY ARE NOT ADEQUATE. AGREED?
YEAH... OKAY...
UH, MARK, YOUR--
IT IS NOT IMPORTANT. WE MUST GET AWAY AS QUICKLY AND QUIETLY AS POSSIBLE.
THERE IS MUCH MORE AT STAKE HERE THAN YOU--
--OR ANY OF US REALIZE.
MY NAME IS COLONEL ZEPHON.
I HAVE A MISSION, CAPTAIN. MINE CONTINUES, WHILE YOURS, I'M AFRAID, IS AT AN END.
UNDER THE GENEVA CONVENTION WE ARE--
I AM AFRAID THAT MY ORDERS SUPERSEDE ALL HUMAN PACTS AND TREATIES...
"SUPERSEDE HUMAN"... WHAT THE HELL--
YES. SOON.
KILL THEM.

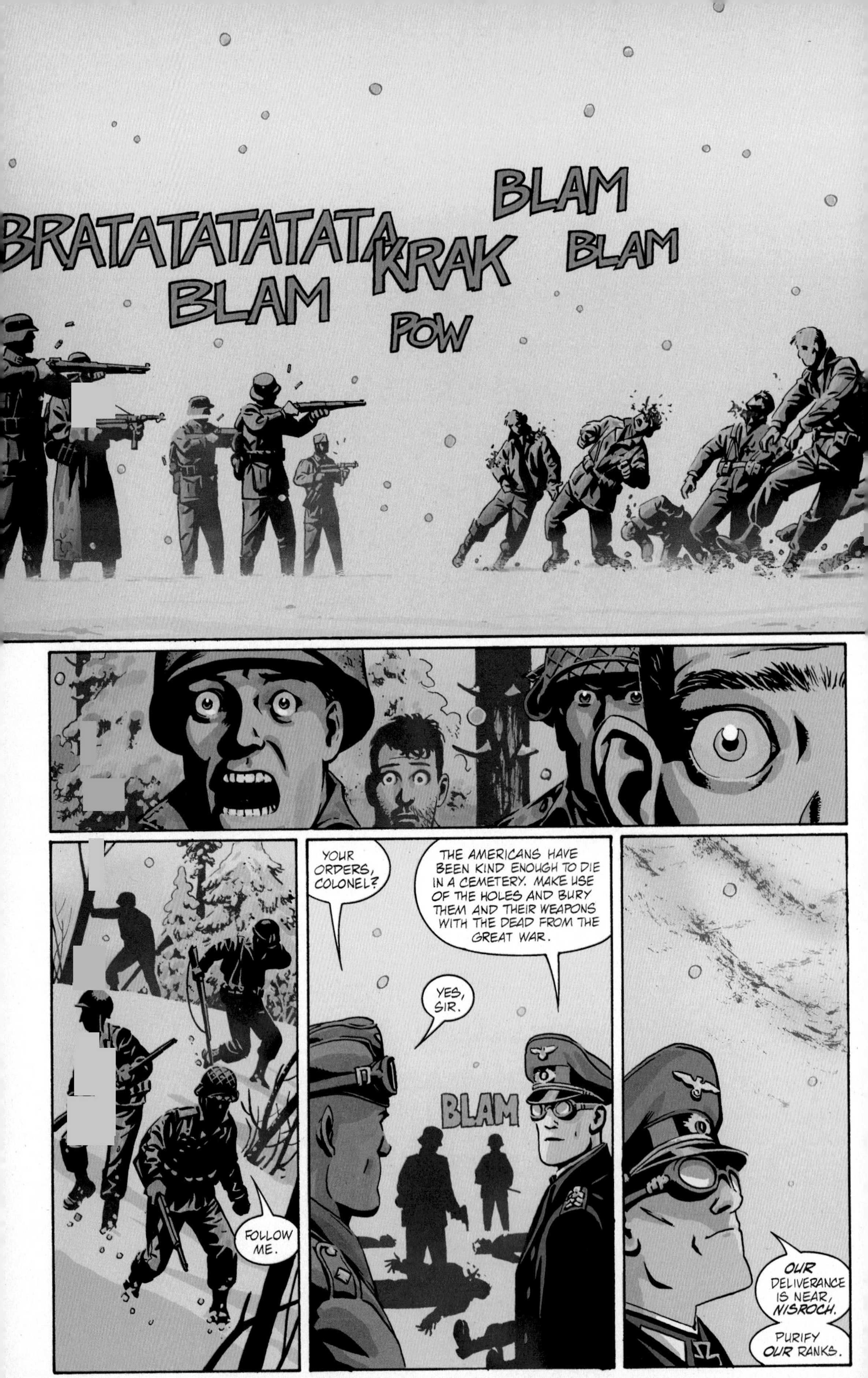
BRATATATATATATA
BLAM
KRAK
BLAM
BLAM
POW
YOUR ORDERS, COLONEL?
THE AMERICANS HAVE BEEN KIND ENOUGH TO DIE IN A CEMETERY. MAKE USE OF THE HOLES AND BURY THEM AND THEIR WEAPONS WITH THE DEAD FROM THE GREAT WAR.
YES, SIR.
BLAM
FOLLOW ME.
OUR DELIVERANCE IS NEAR, NISROCH.
PURIFY OUR RANKS.

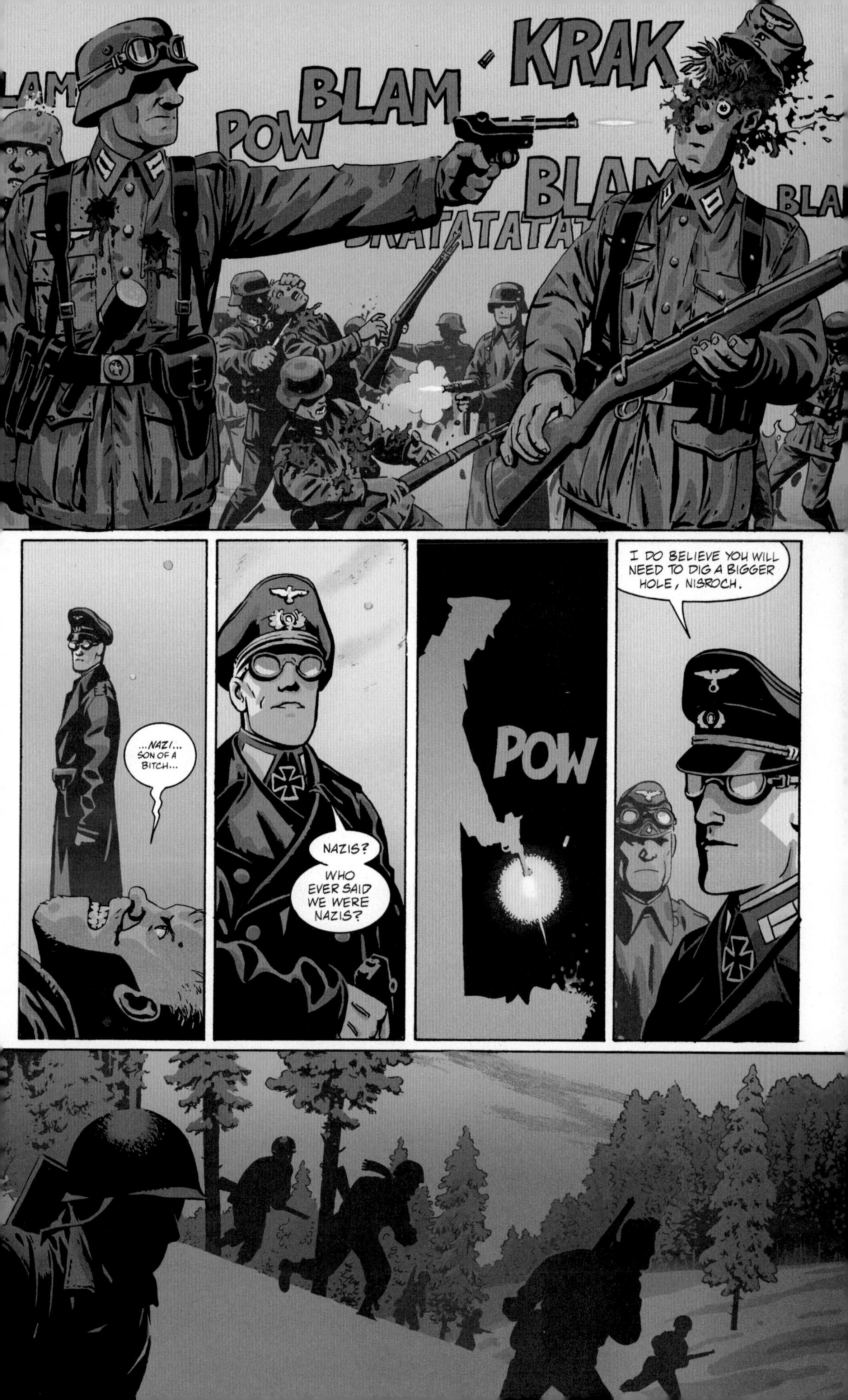

BLAM
KRAK
BLAM
POW
BLAM
BLAM
BRATATATATAT
...NAZI... SON OF A BITCH...
NAZIS? WHO EVER SAID WE WERE NAZIS?
POW
I DO BELIEVE YOU WILL NEED TO DIG A BIGGER HOLE, NISROCH.

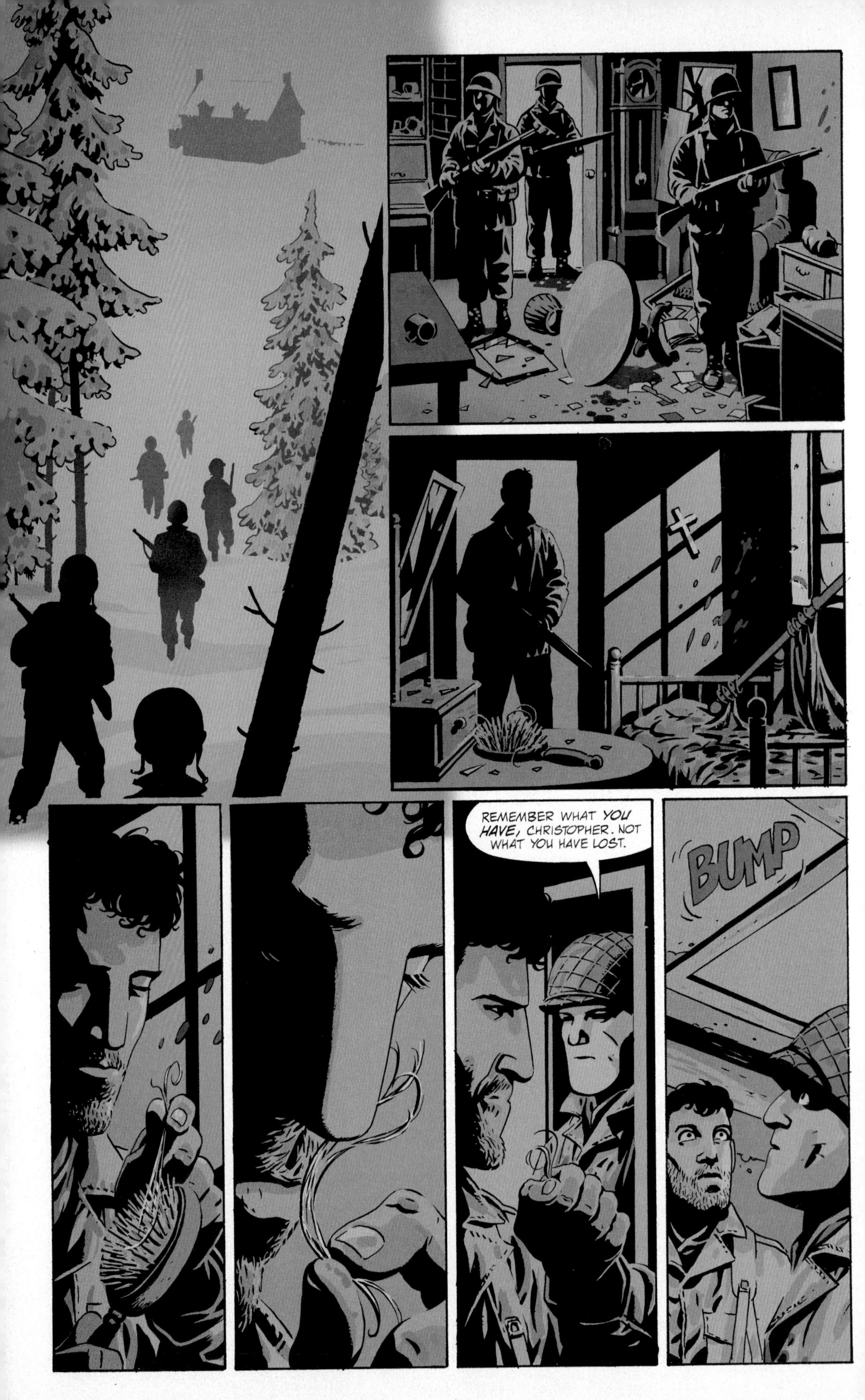
REMEMBER WHAT YOU HAVE, CHRISTOPHER. NOT WHAT YOU HAVE LOST.
BUMP

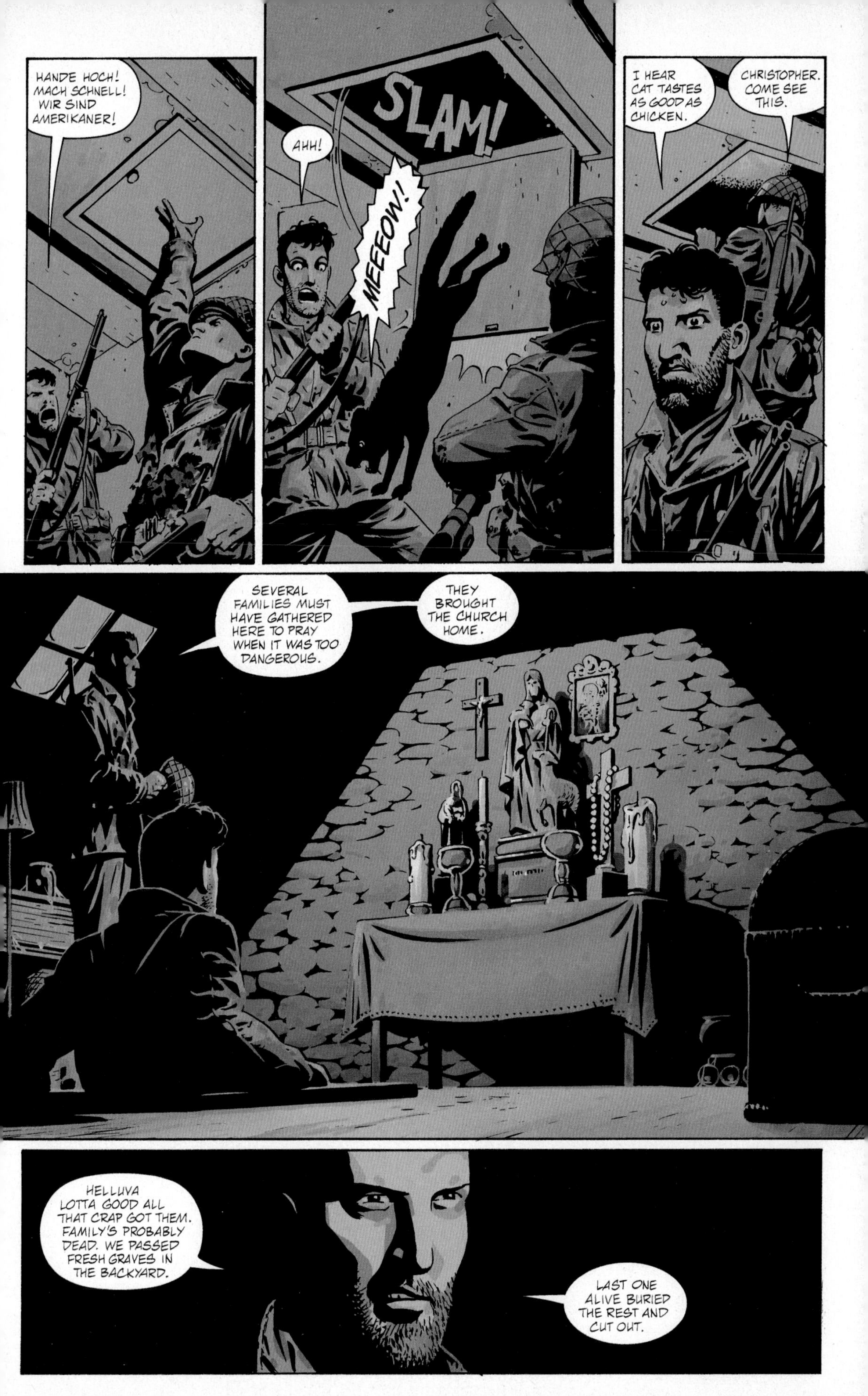
HANDE HOCH! MACH SCHNELL! WIR SIND AMERIKANER!
SLAM!
AHH!
MEEEOW!
I HEAR CAT TASTES AS GOOD AS CHICKEN.
CHRISTOPHER. COME SEE THIS.
SEVERAL FAMILIES MUST HAVE GATHERED HERE TO PRAY WHEN IT WAS TOO DANGEROUS.
THEY BROUGHT THE CHURCH HOME.
HELLUVA LOTTA GOOD ALL THAT CRAP GOT THEM. FAMILY'S PROBABLY DEAD. WE PASSED FRESH GRAVES IN THE BACKYARD.
LAST ONE ALIVE BURIED THE REST AND CUT OUT.

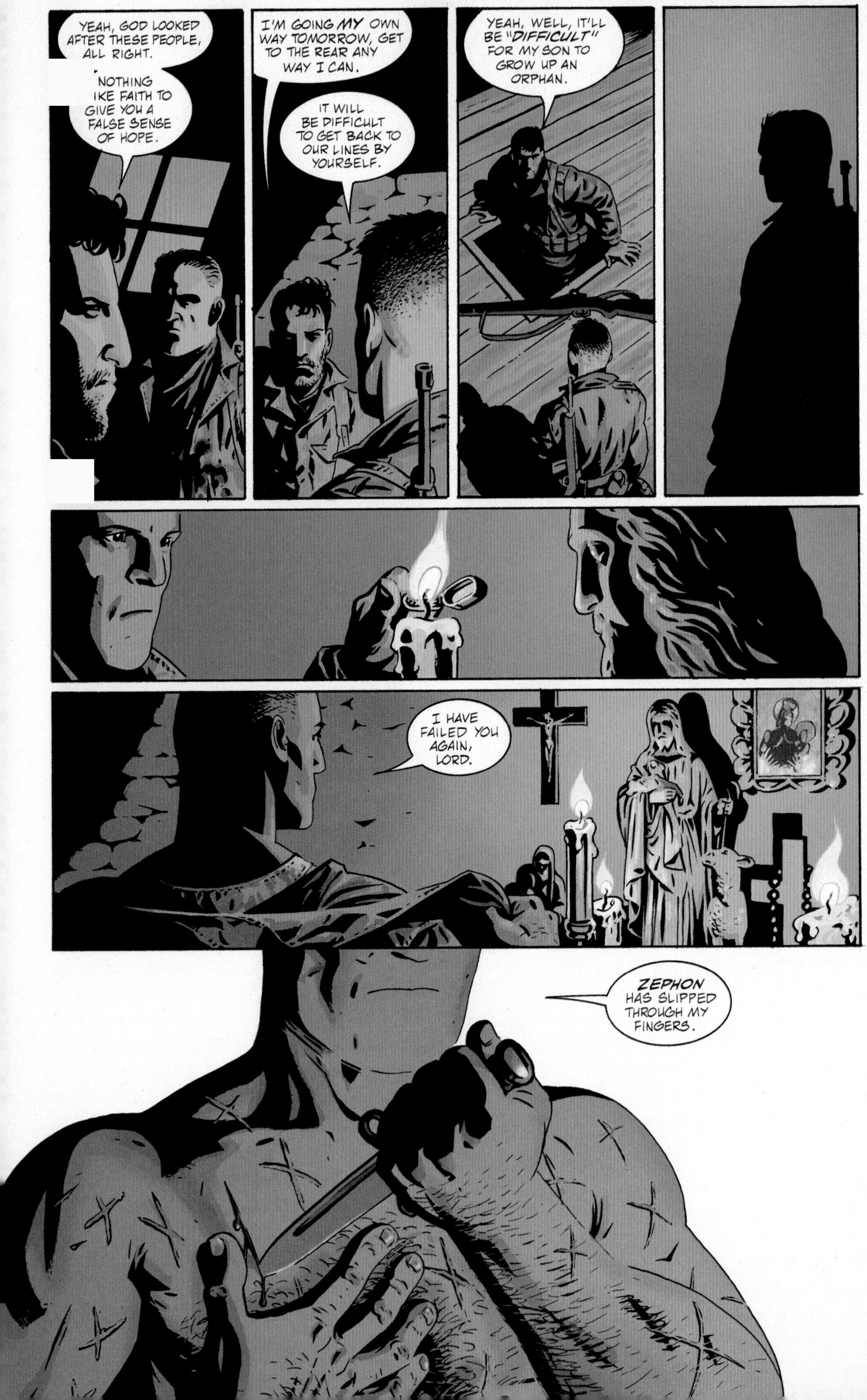
YEAH, GOD LOOKED AFTER THESE PEOPLE, ALL RIGHT.
NOTHING IKE FAITH TO GIVE YOU A FALSE SENSE OF HOPE.
I'M GOING MY OWN WAY TOMORROW, GET TO THE REAR ANY WAY I CAN.
IT WILL BE DIFFICULT TO GET BACK TO OUR LINES BY YOURSELF.
YEAH, WELL, IT'LL BE "DIFFICULT" FOR MY SON TO GROW UP AN ORPHAN.
I HAVE FAILED YOU AGAIN, LORD.
ZEPHON HAS SLIPPED THROUGH MY FINGERS.

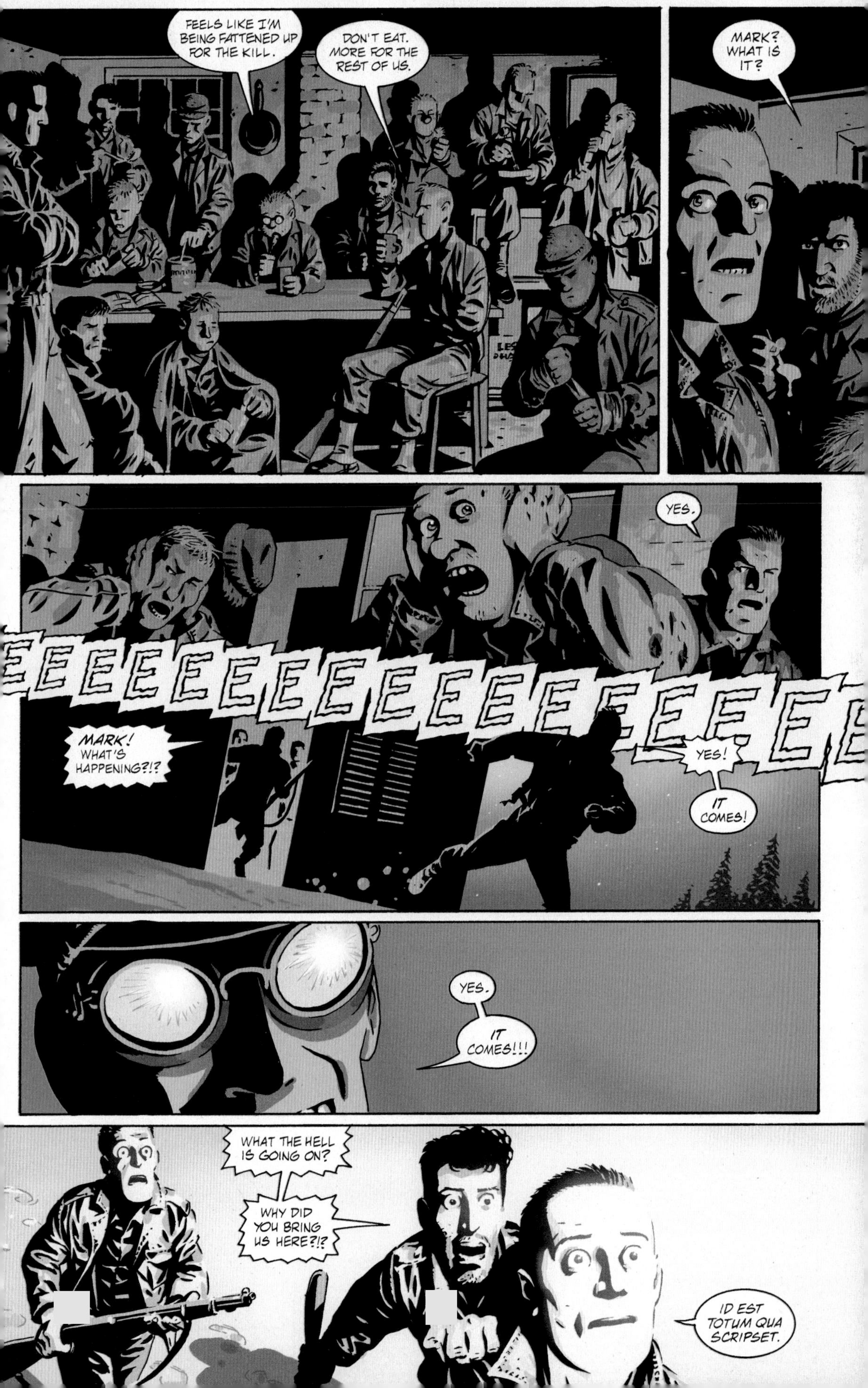
FEELS LIKE I'M BEING FATTENED UP FOR THE KILL.
DON'T EAT. MORE FOR THE REST OF US.
MARK? WHAT IS IT?
YES.
EEEEEEEEEEEEEEEEEE
MARK! WHAT'S HAPPENING?!?
YES!
IT COMES!
YES.
IT COMES!!!
WHAT THE HELL IS GOING ON?
WHY DID YOU BRING US HERE?!?
ID EST TOTUM QUA SCRIPSET.

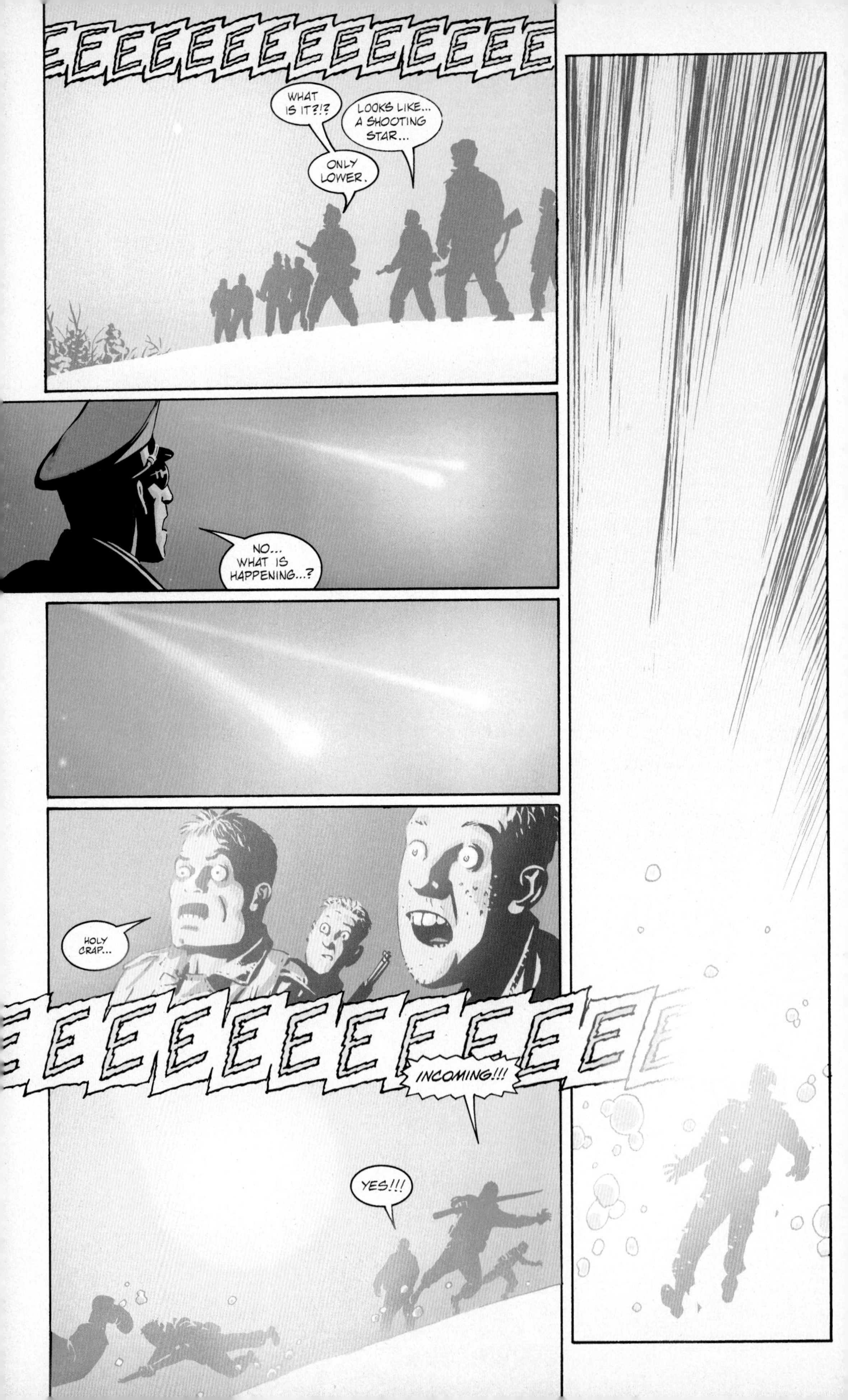
EEEEEEEEEEEEEE
WHAT IS IT?!?
LOOKS LIKE... A SHOOTING STAR...
ONLY LOWER.
NO... WHAT IS HAPPENING...?
HOLY CRAP...
EEEEEEEEEEEE
INCOMING!!!
YES!!!

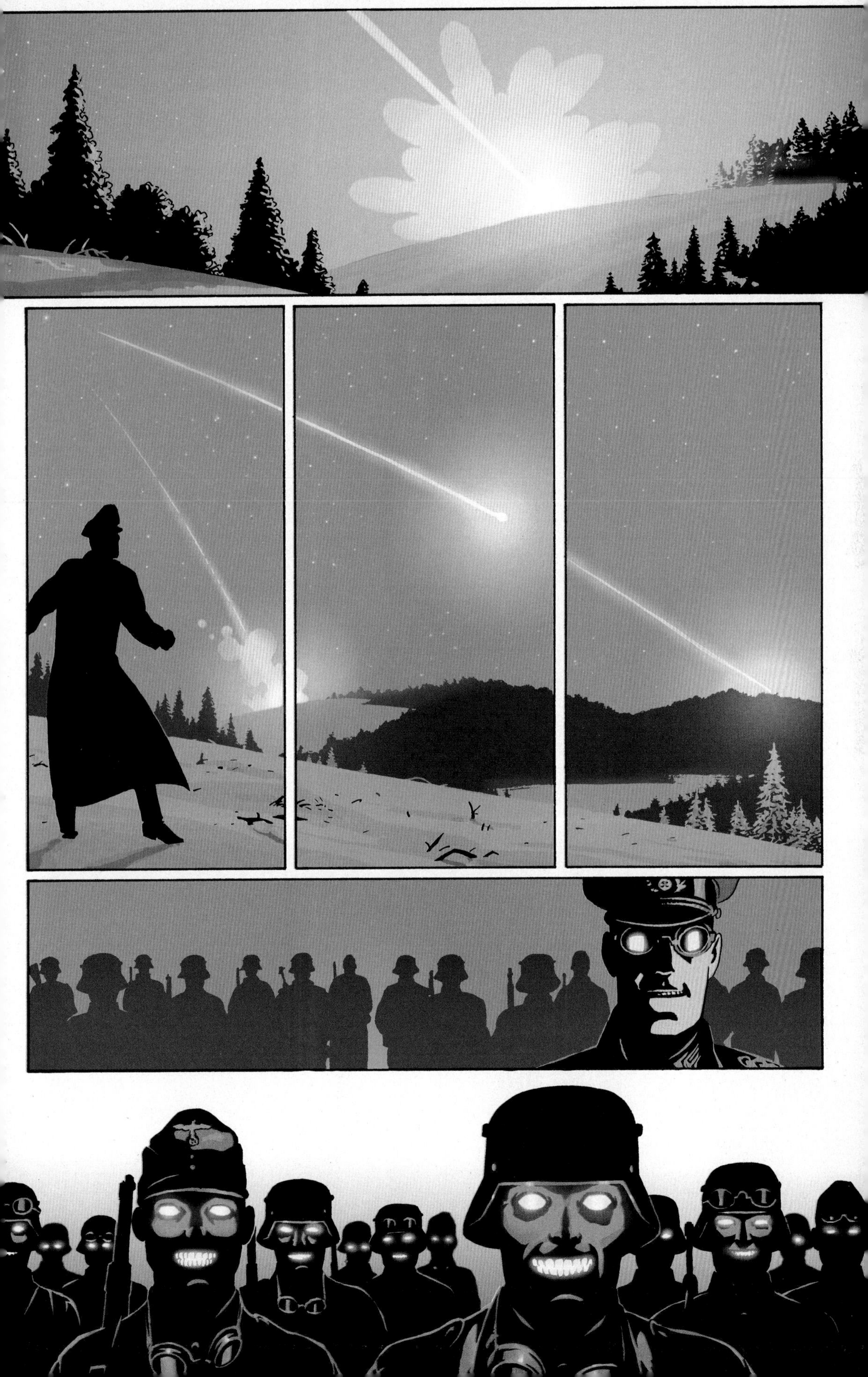

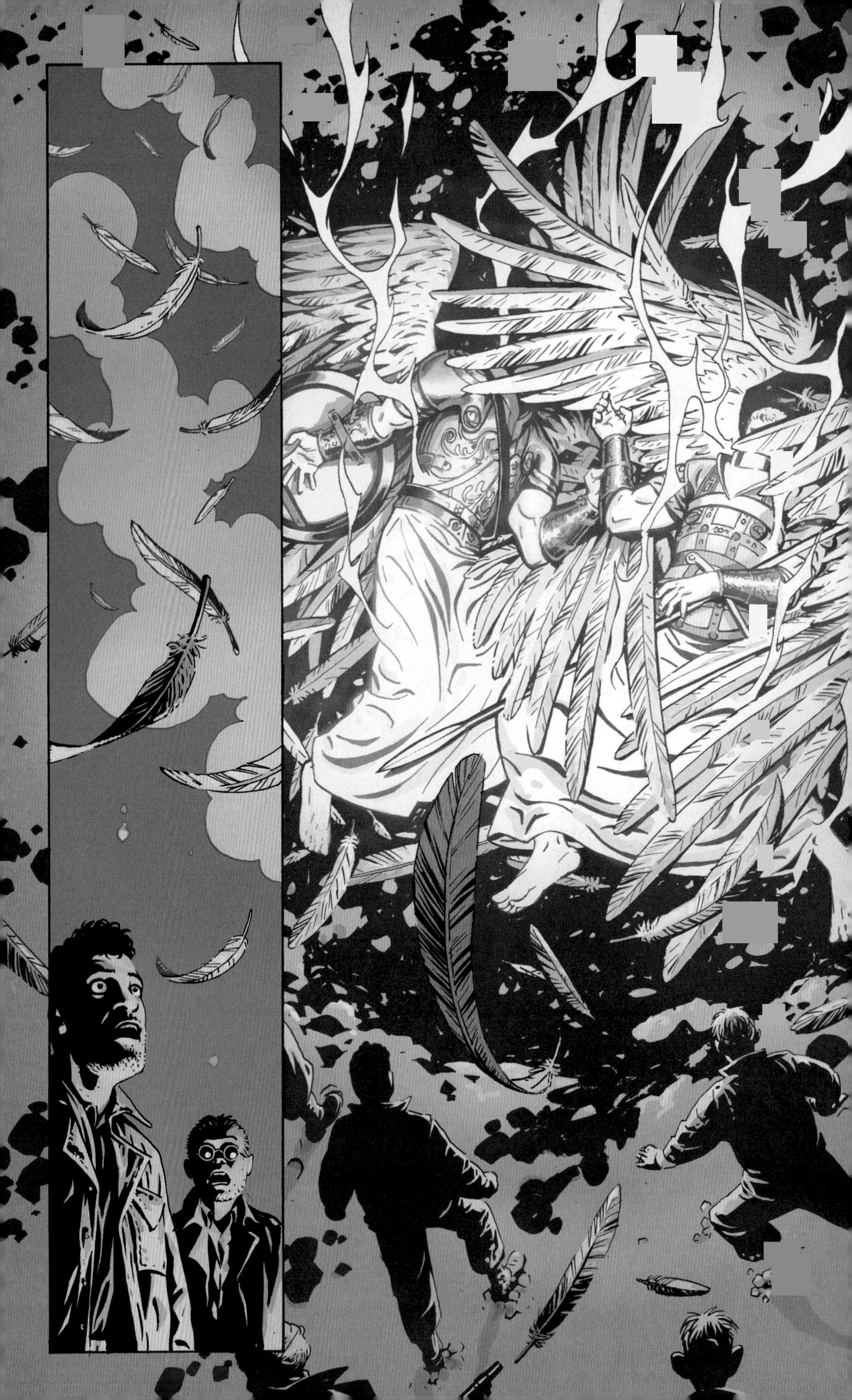

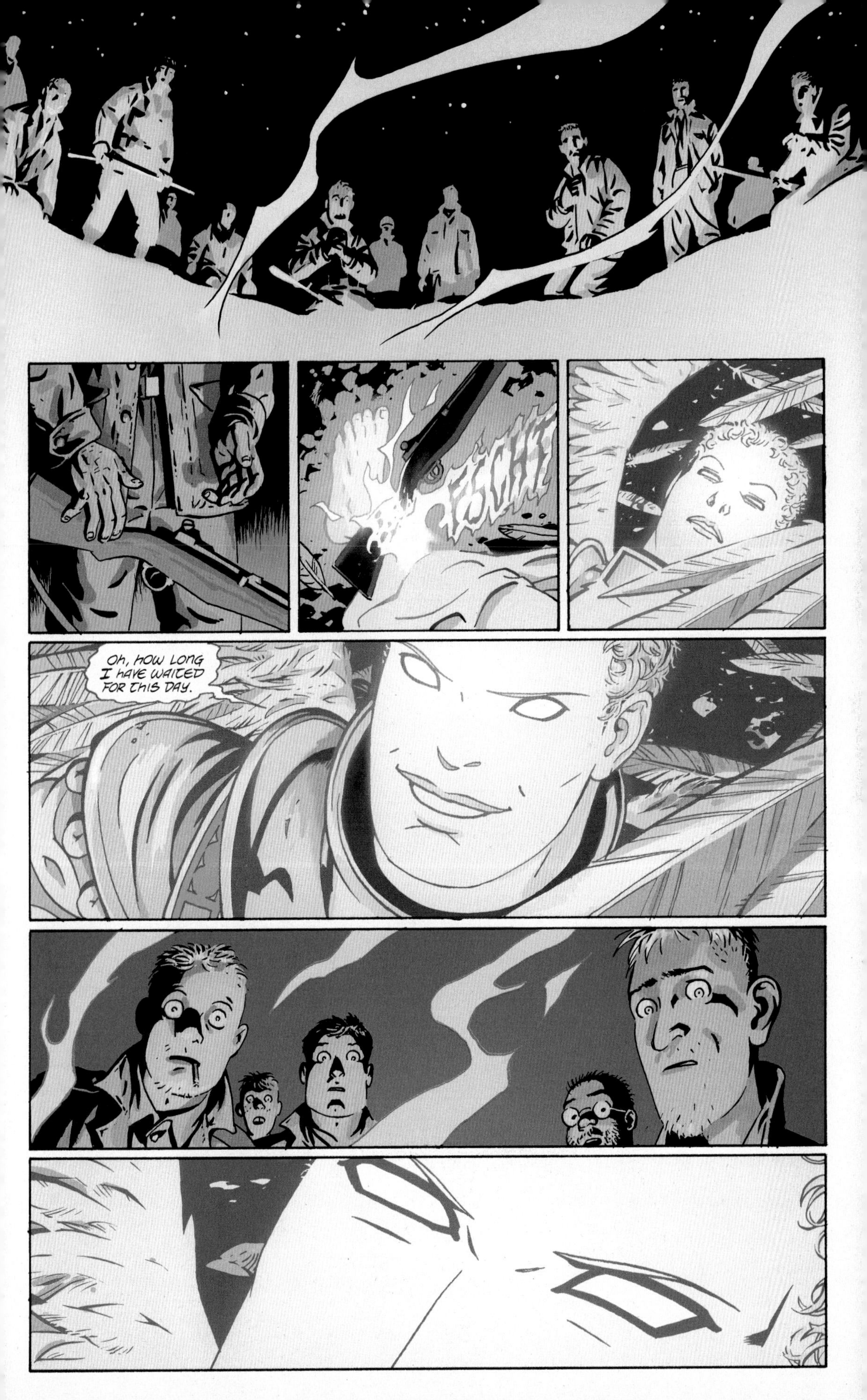
FSCHT
Oh, how long I have waited for this day.

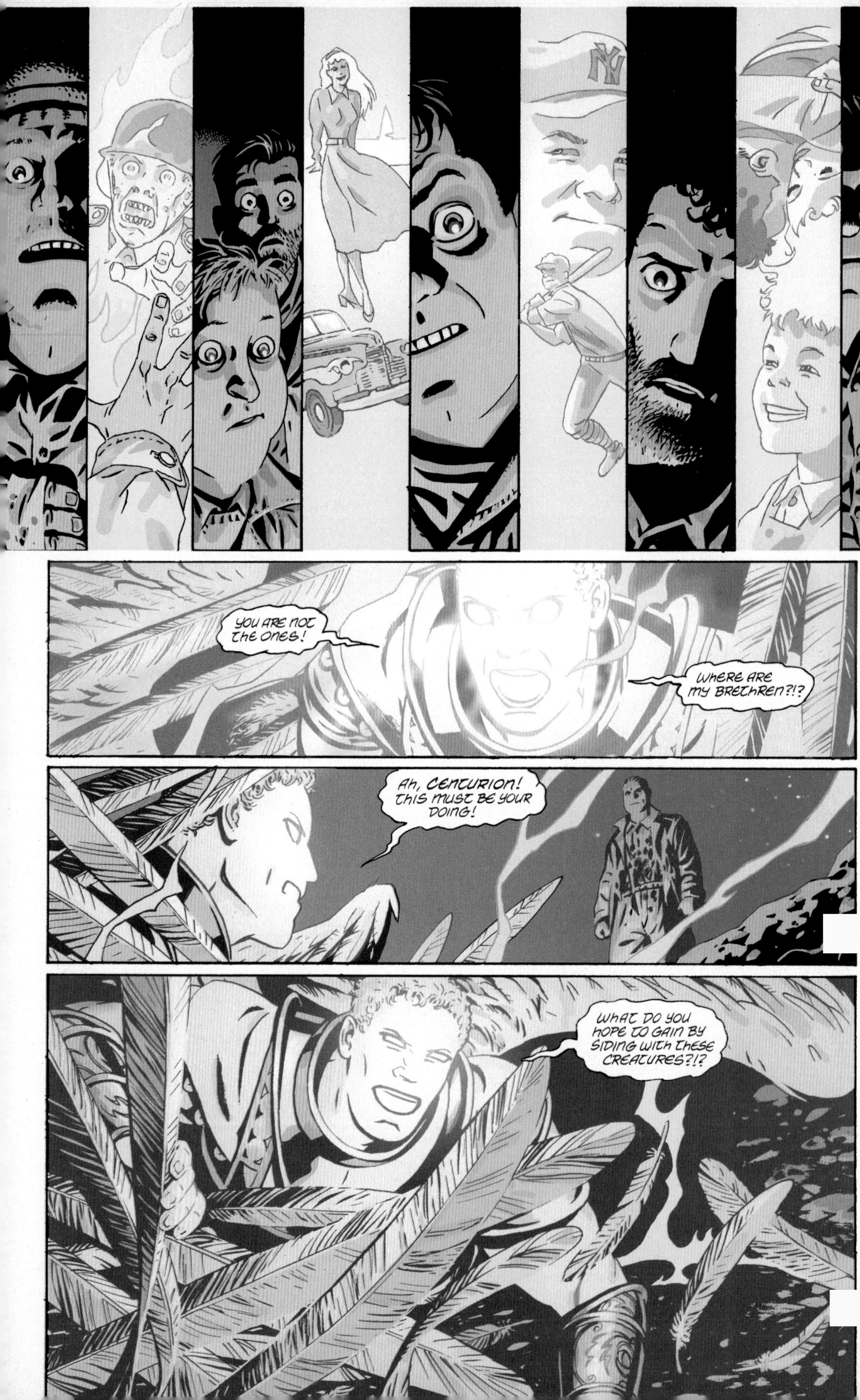
YOU ARE NOT THE ONES!
WHERE ARE MY BRETHREN?!?
AH, CENTURION! THIS MUST BE YOUR DOING!
WHAT DO YOU HOPE TO GAIN BY SIDING WITH THESE CREATURES?!?

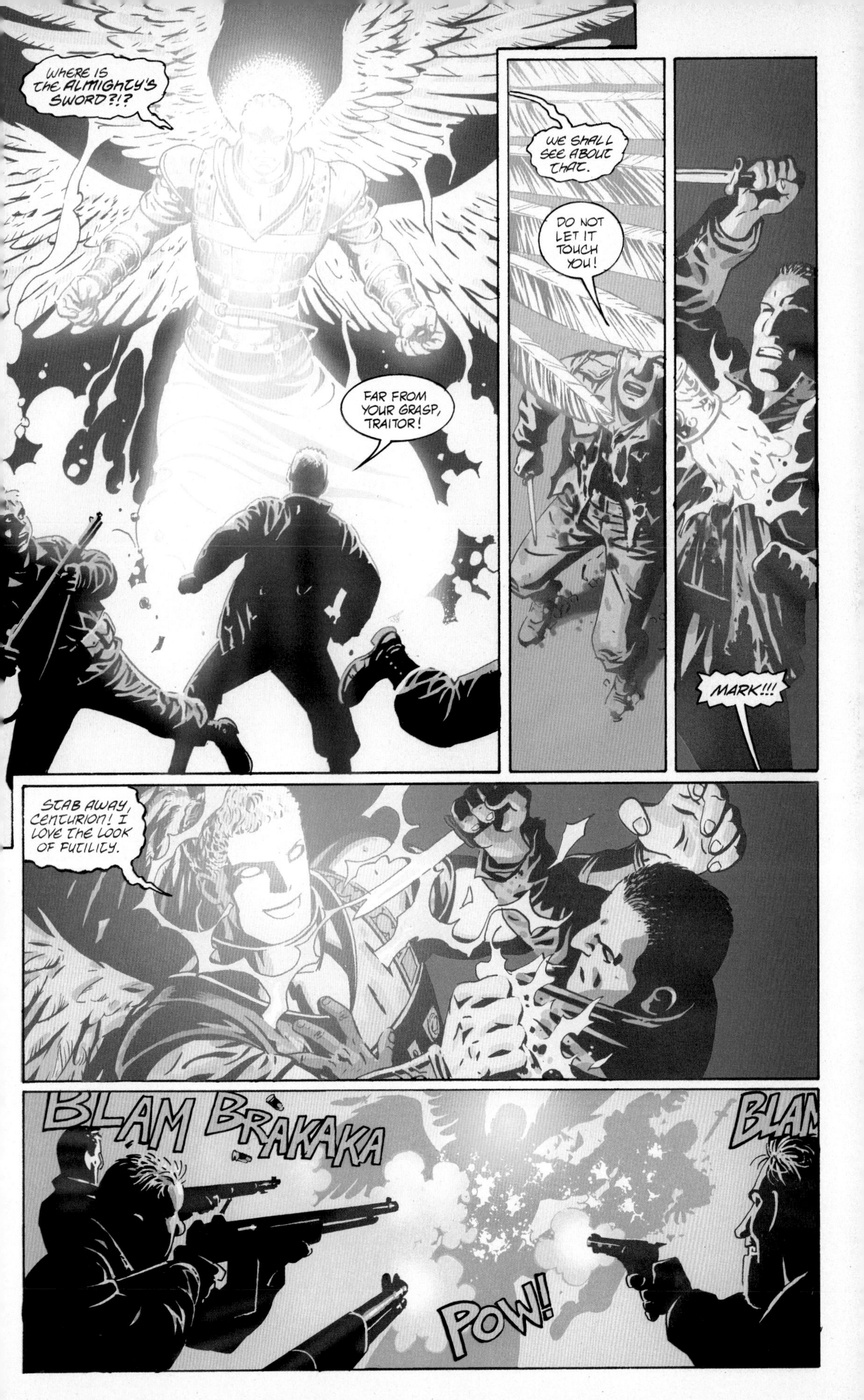
WHERE IS THE ALMIGHTY'S SWORD?!?
FAR FROM YOUR GRASP, TRAITOR!
WE SHALL SEE ABOUT THAT.
DO NOT LET IT TOUCH YOU!
MARK!!!
STAB AWAY, CENTURION! I LOVE THE LOOK OF FUTILITY.
BLAM BRAKAKA
BLAM
POW!

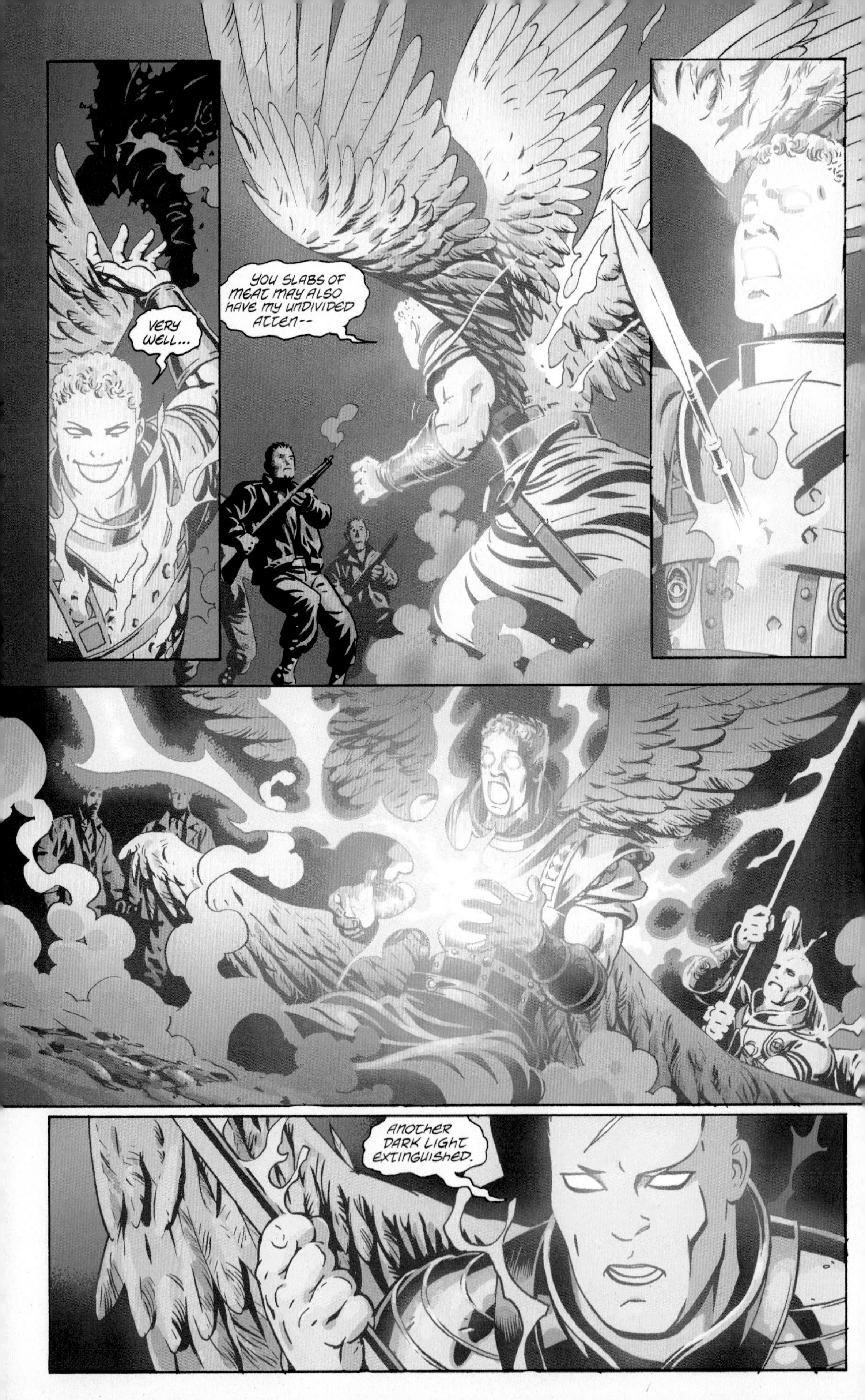
VERY WELL...
YOU SLABS OF MEAT MAY ALSO HAVE MY UNDIVIDED ATTEN--
ANOTHER DARK LIGHT EXTINGUISHED.

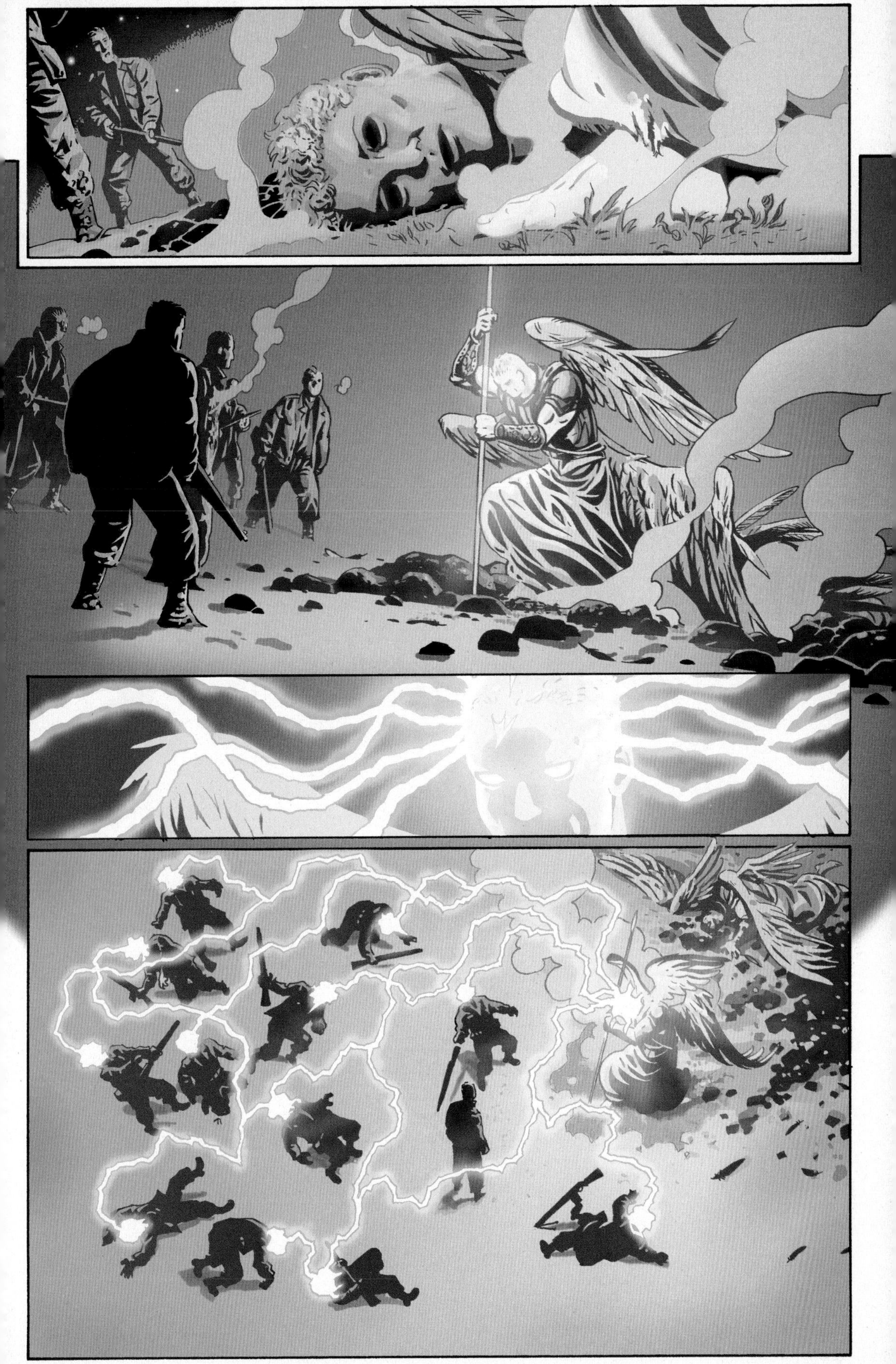

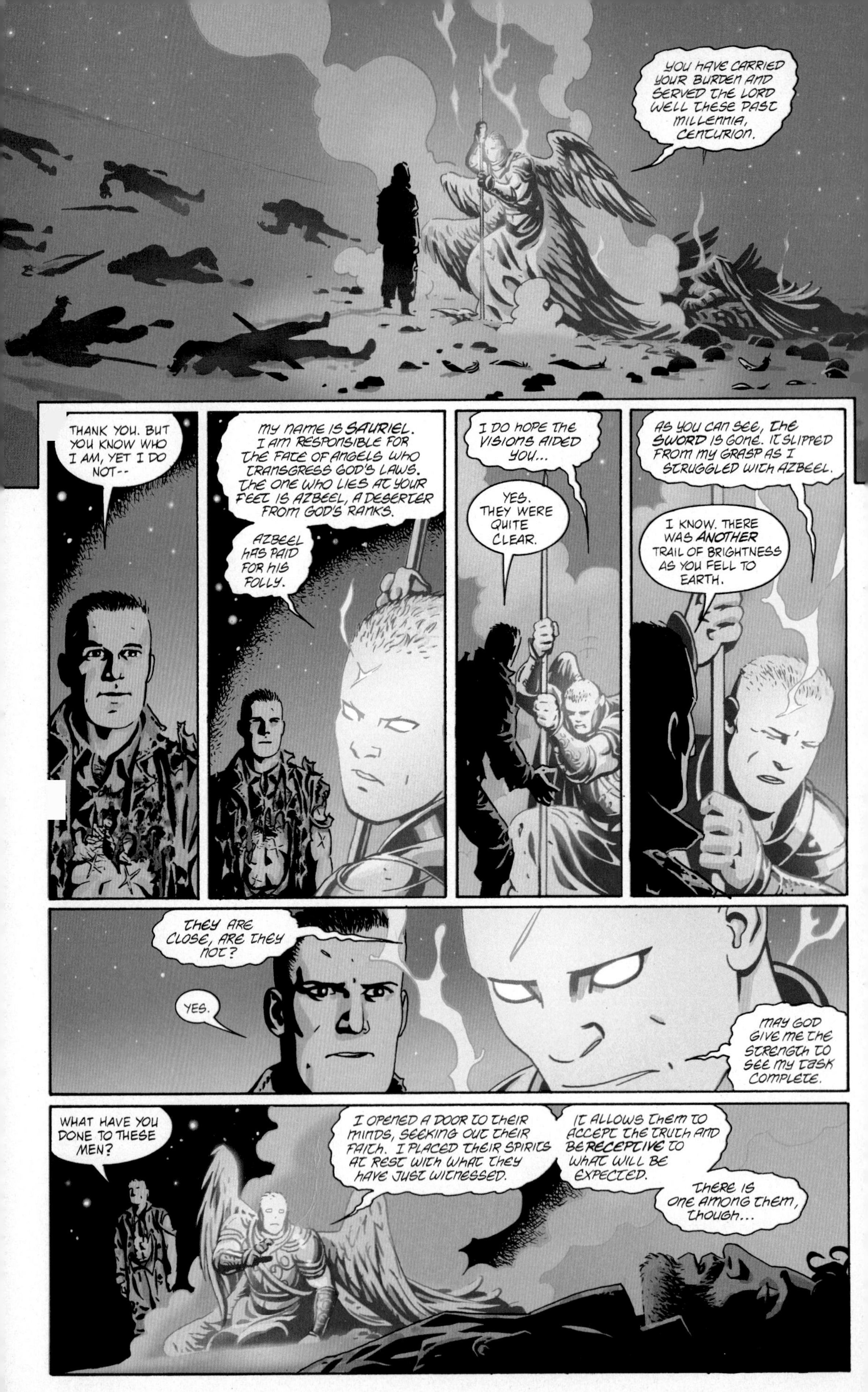
YOU HAVE CARRIED YOUR BURDEN AND SERVED THE LORD WELL THESE PAST MILLENNIA, CENTURION.
THANK YOU. BUT YOU KNOW WHO I AM, YET I DO NOT--
MY NAME IS SAURIEL. I AM RESPONSIBLE FOR THE FATE OF ANGELS WHO TRANSGRESS GOD'S LAWS. THE ONE WHO LIES AT YOUR FEET IS AZBEEL, A DESERTER FROM GOD'S RANKS.
AZBEEL HAS PAID FOR HIS FOLLY.
I DO HOPE THE VISIONS AIDED YOU...
YES. THEY WERE QUITE CLEAR.
AS YOU CAN SEE, THE SWORD IS GONE. IT SLIPPED FROM MY GRASP AS I STRUGGLED WITH AZBEEL.
I KNOW. THERE WAS ANOTHER TRAIL OF BRIGHTNESS AS YOU FELL TO EARTH.
THEY ARE CLOSE, ARE THEY NOT?
YES.
MAY GOD GIVE ME THE STRENGTH TO SEE MY TASK COMPLETE.
WHAT HAVE YOU DONE TO THESE MEN?
I OPENED A DOOR TO THEIR MINDS, SEEKING OUT THEIR FAITH. I PLACED THEIR SPIRITS AT REST WITH WHAT THEY HAVE JUST WITNESSED.
IT ALLOWS THEM TO ACCEPT THE TRUTH AND BE RECEPTIVE TO WHAT WILL BE EXPECTED.
THERE IS ONE AMONG THEM, THOUGH...

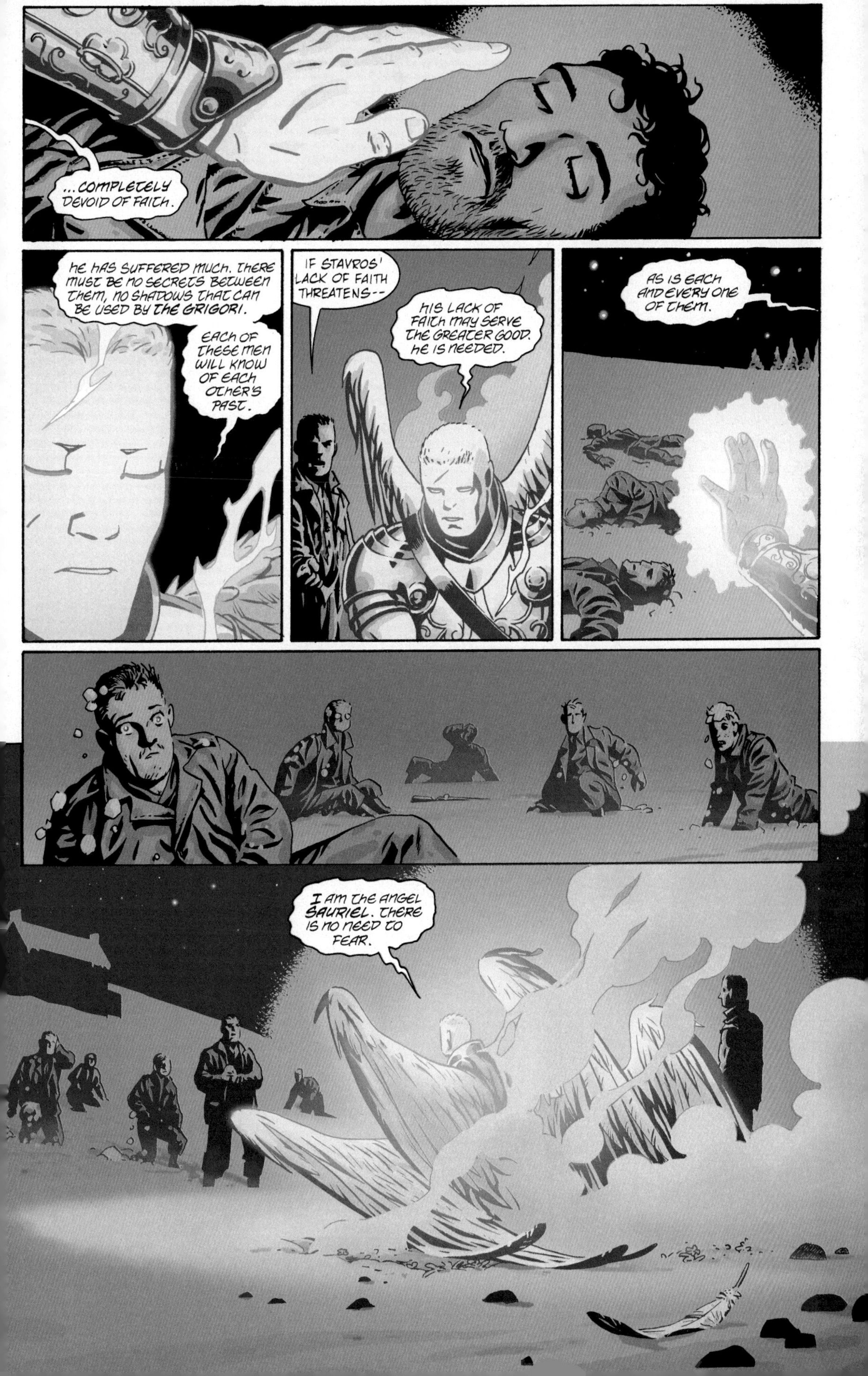

...COMPLETELY DEVOID OF FAITH.
HE HAS SUFFERED MUCH. THERE MUST BE NO SECRETS BETWEEN THEM, NO SHADOWS THAT CAN BE USED BY THE GRIGORI.
EACH OF THESE MEN WILL KNOW OF EACH OTHER'S PAST.
IF STAVROS' LACK OF FAITH THREATENS--
HIS LACK OF FAITH MAY SERVE THE GREATER GOOD. HE IS NEEDED.
AS IS EACH AND EVERY ONE OF THEM.
I AM THE ANGEL SAURIEL. THERE IS NO NEED TO FEAR.

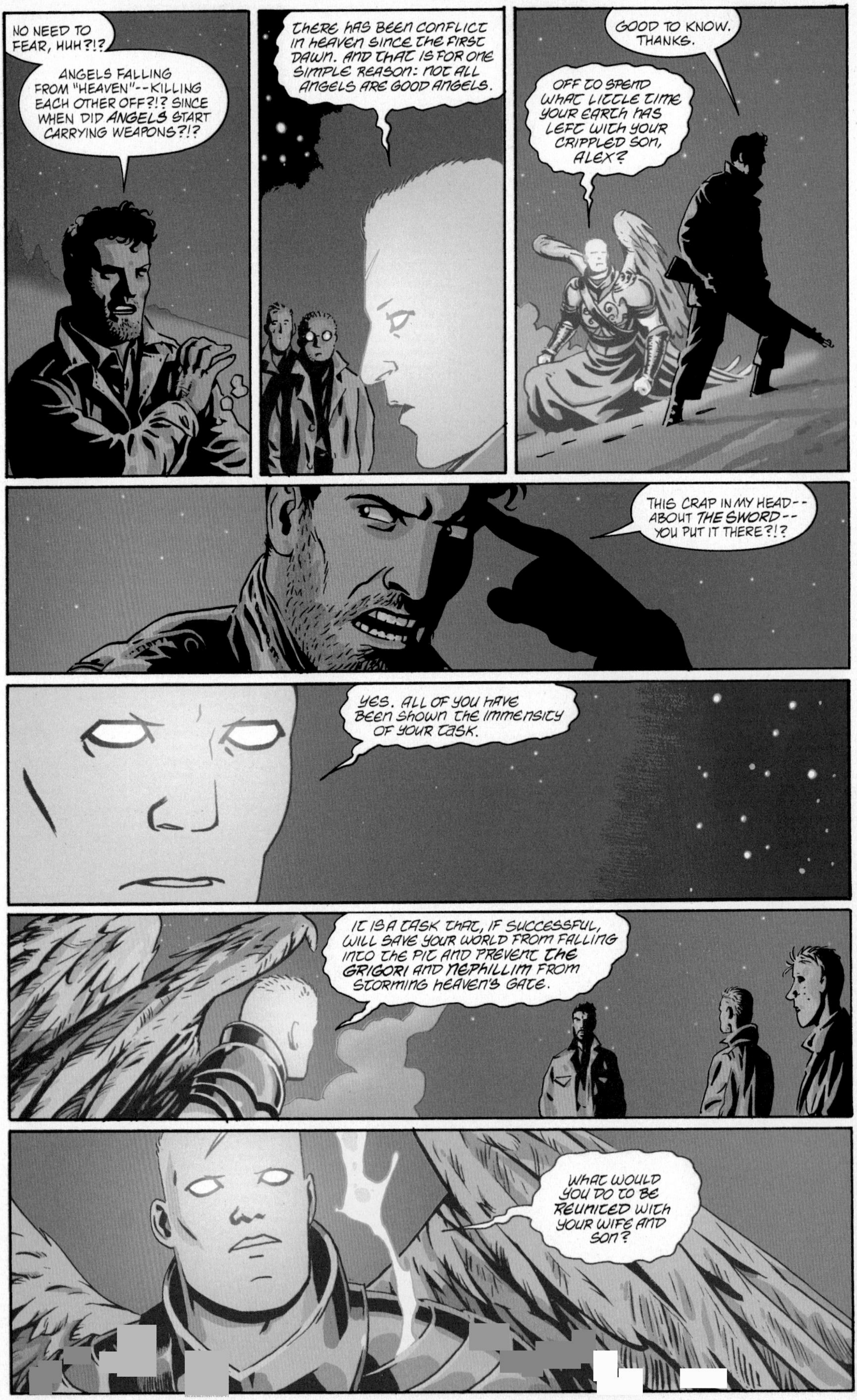
NO NEED TO FEAR, HUH?!?
ANGELS FALLING FROM "HEAVEN"--KILLING EACH OTHER OFF?!? SINCE WHEN DID ANGELS START CARRYING WEAPONS?!?
THERE HAS BEEN CONFLICT IN HEAVEN SINCE THE FIRST DAWN. AND THAT IS FOR ONE SIMPLE REASON: NOT ALL ANGELS ARE GOOD ANGELS.
GOOD TO KNOW. THANKS.
OFF TO SPEND WHAT LITTLE TIME YOUR EARTH HAS LEFT WITH YOUR CRIPPLED SON, ALEX?
THIS CRAP IN MY HEAD--ABOUT THE SWORD--YOU PUT IT THERE?!?
YES. ALL OF YOU HAVE BEEN SHOWN THE IMMENSITY OF YOUR TASK.
IT IS A TASK THAT, IF SUCCESSFUL, WILL SAVE YOUR WORLD FROM FALLING INTO THE PIT AND PREVENT THE GRIGORI AND NEPHILLIM FROM STORMING HEAVEN'S GATE.
WHAT WOULD YOU DO TO BE REUNITED WITH YOUR WIFE AND SON?

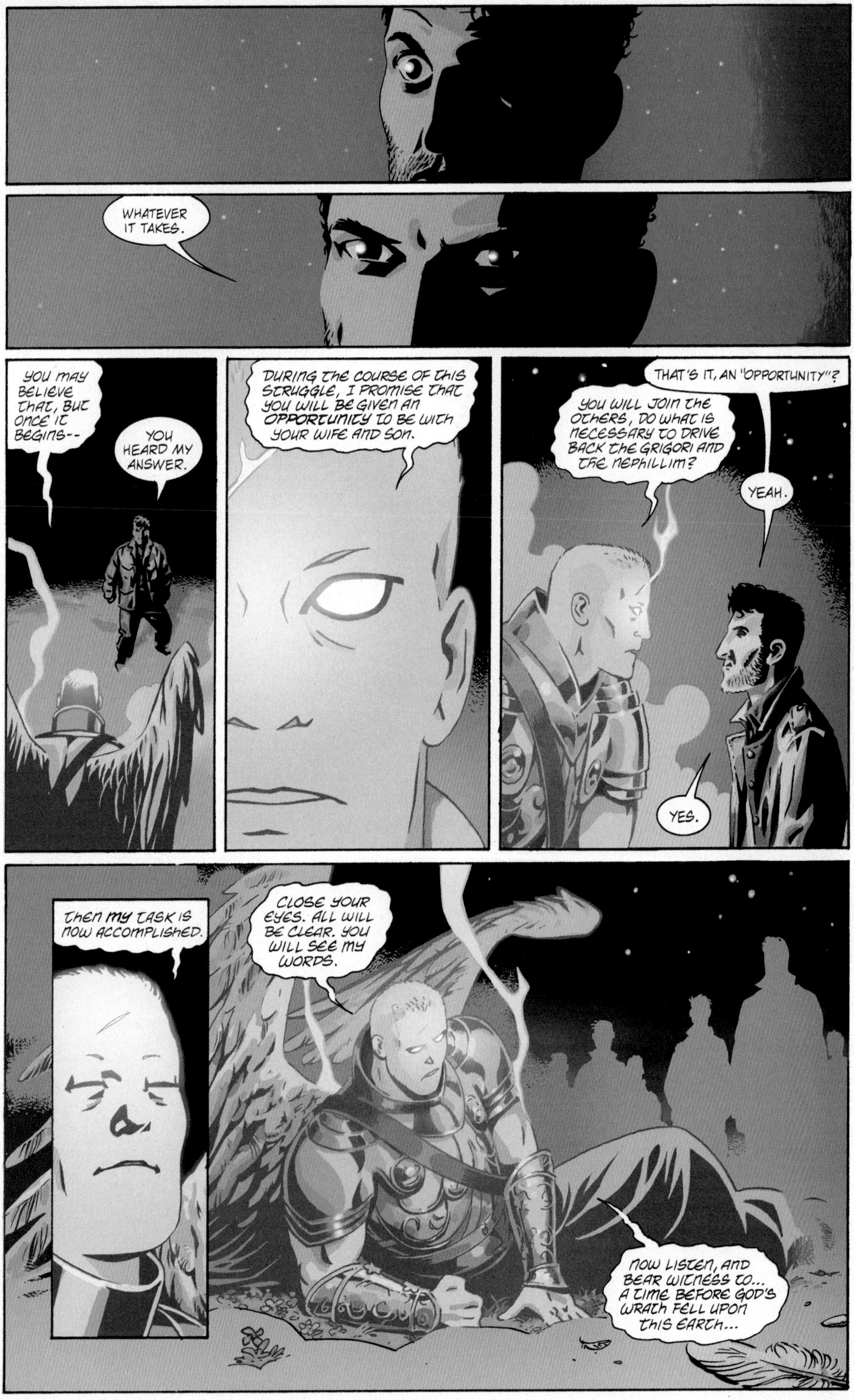
WHATEVER IT TAKES.
YOU MAY BELIEVE THAT, BUT ONCE IT BEGINS--
YOU HEARD MY ANSWER.
DURING THE COURSE OF THIS STRUGGLE, I PROMISE THAT YOU WILL BE GIVEN AN OPPORTUNITY TO BE WITH YOUR WIFE AND SON.
THAT'S IT, AN "OPPORTUNITY"?
YOU WILL JOIN THE OTHERS, DO WHAT IS NECESSARY TO DRIVE BACK THE GRIGORI AND THE NEPHILLIM?
YEAH.
YES.
THEN MY TASK IS NOW ACCOMPLISHED.
CLOSE YOUR EYES. ALL WILL BE CLEAR. YOU WILL SEE MY WORDS.
NOW LISTEN, AND BEAR WITNESS TO... A TIME BEFORE GOD'S WRATH FELL UPON THIS EARTH...

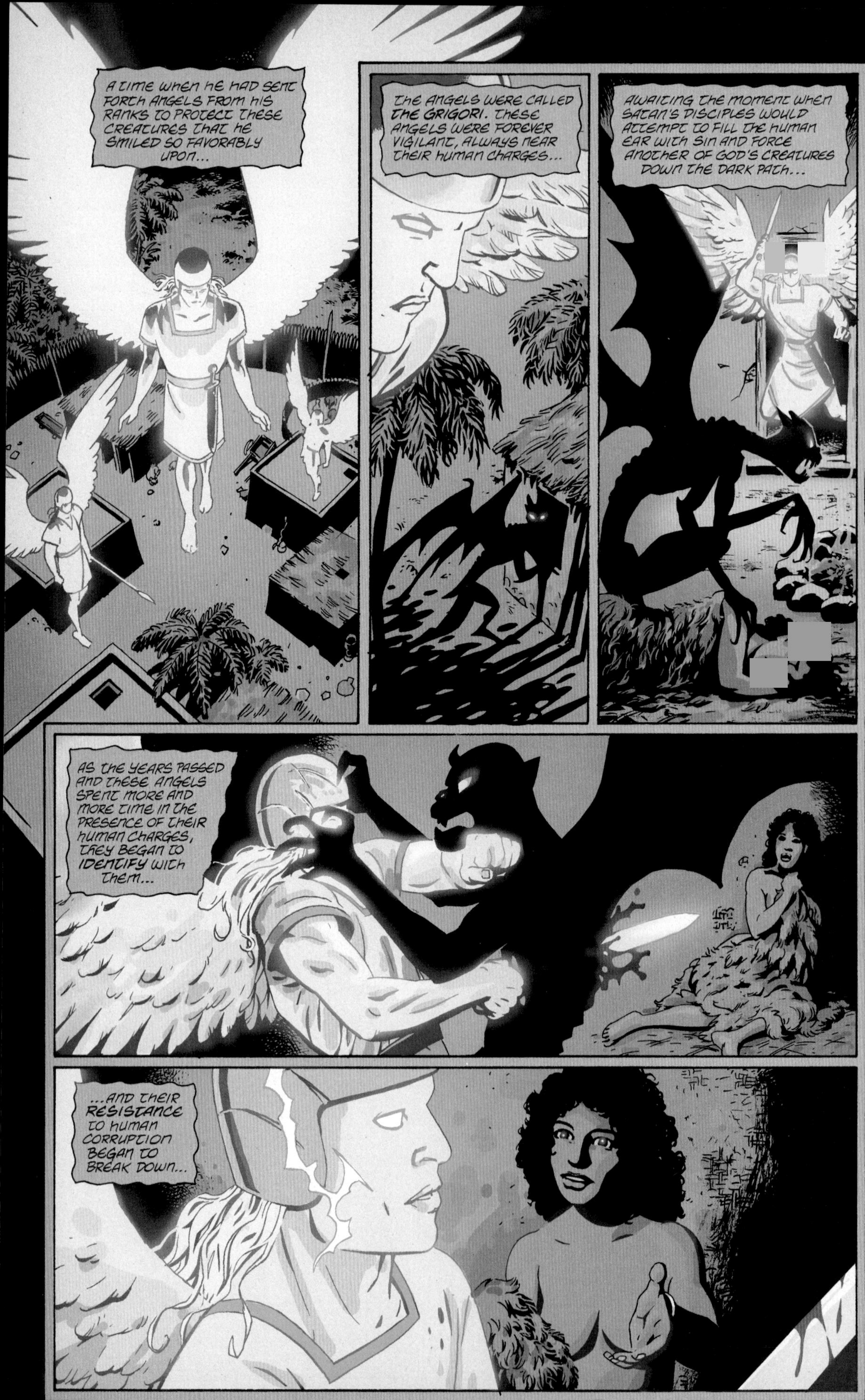
A TIME WHEN HE HAD SENT FORTH ANGELS FROM HIS RANKS TO PROTECT THESE CREATURES THAT HE SMILED SO FAVORABLY UPON...
THE ANGELS WERE CALLED THE GRIGORI. THESE ANGELS WERE FOREVER VIGILANT, ALWAYS NEAR THEIR HUMAN CHARGES...
AWAITING THE MOMENT WHEN SATAN'S DISCIPLES WOULD ATTEMPT TO FILL THE HUMAN EAR WITH SIN AND FORCE ANOTHER OF GOD'S CREATURES DOWN THE DARK PATH...
AS THE YEARS PASSED AND THESE ANGELS SPENT MORE AND MORE TIME IN THE PRESENCE OF THEIR HUMAN CHARGES, THEY BEGAN TO IDENTIFY WITH THEM...
...AND THEIR RESISTANCE TO HUMAN CORRUPTION BEGAN TO BREAK DOWN...

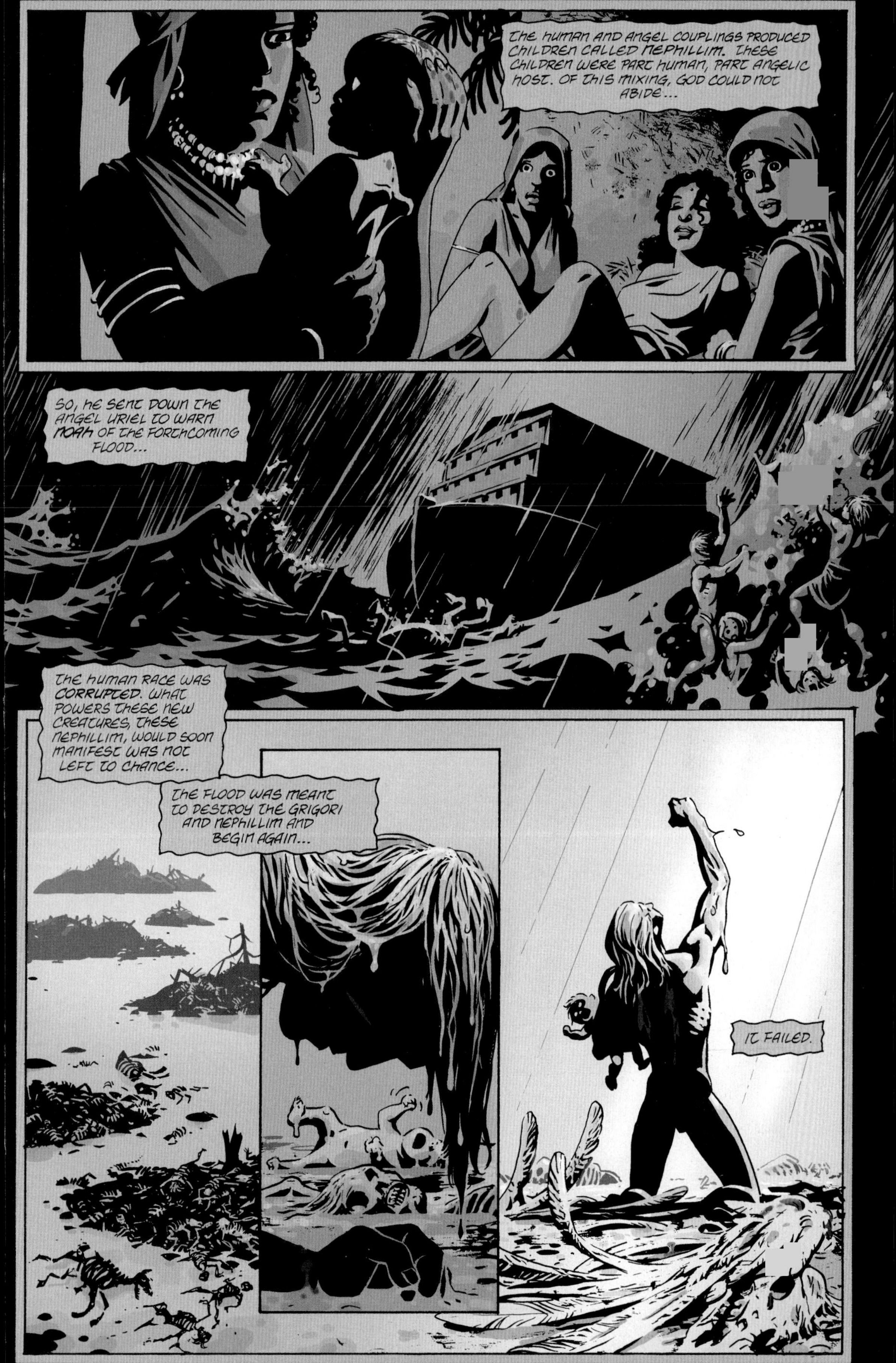
THE HUMAN AND ANGEL COUPLINGS PRODUCED CHILDREN CALLED NEPHILLIM. THESE CHILDREN WERE PART HUMAN, PART ANGELIC HOST. OF THIS MIXING, GOD COULD NOT ABIDE...
SO, HE SENT DOWN THE ANGEL URIEL TO WARN NOAH OF THE FORTHCOMING FLOOD...
THE HUMAN RACE WAS CORRUPTED. WHAT POWERS THESE NEW CREATURES, THESE NEPHILLIM, WOULD SOON MANIFEST WAS NOT LEFT TO CHANCE...
THE FLOOD WAS MEANT TO DESTROY THE GRIGORI AND NEPHILLIM AND BEGIN AGAIN...
IT FAILED.

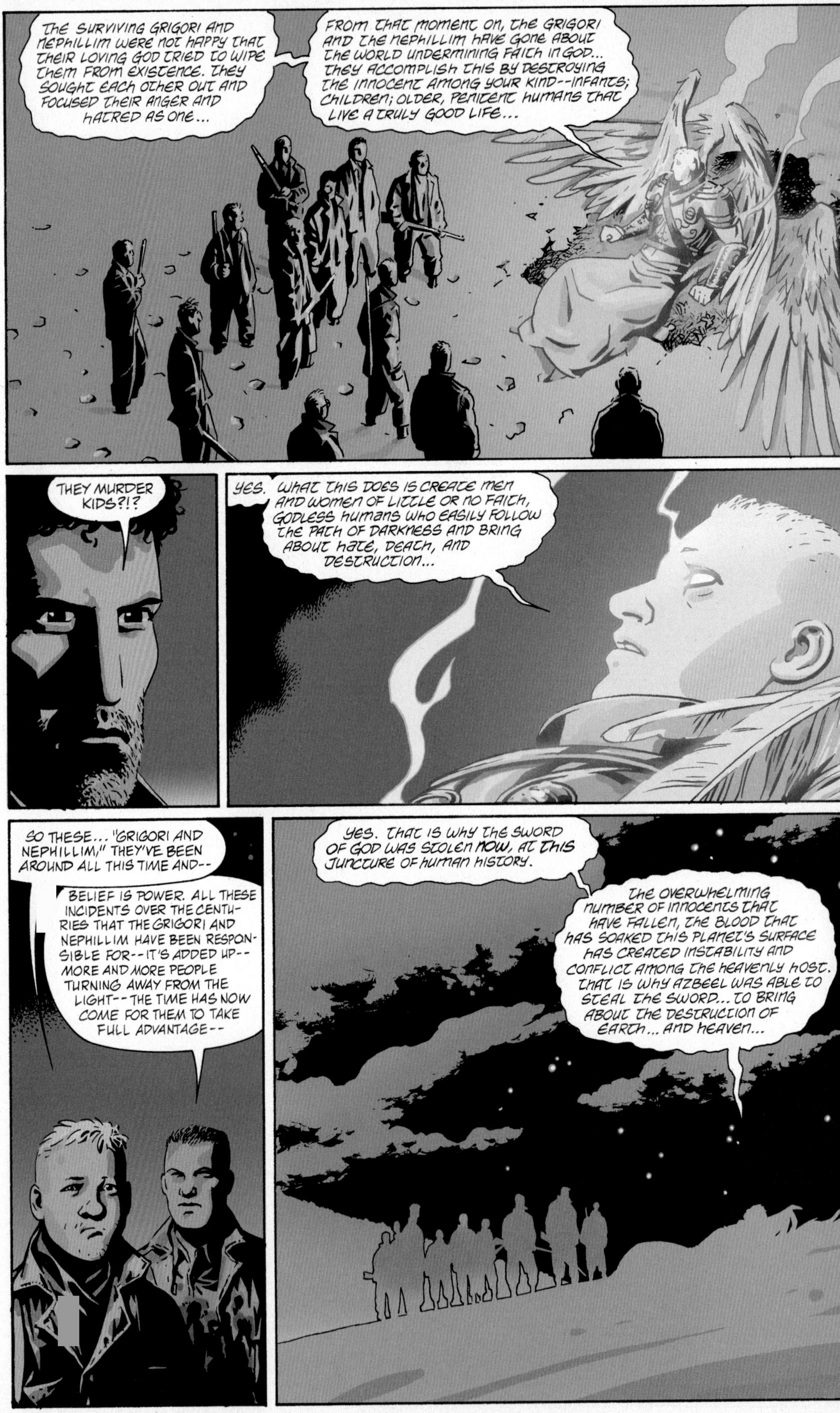
THE SURVIVING GRIGORI AND NEPHILLIM WERE NOT HAPPY THAT THEIR LOVING GOD TRIED TO WIPE THEM FROM EXISTENCE. THEY SOUGHT EACH OTHER OUT AND FOCUSED THEIR ANGER AND HATRED AS ONE...
FROM THAT MOMENT ON, THE GRIGORI AND THE NEPHILLIM HAVE GONE ABOUT THE WORLD UNDERMINING FAITH IN GOD... THEY ACCOMPLISH THIS BY DESTROYING THE INNOCENT AMONG YOUR KIND--INFANTS; CHILDREN; OLDER, PENITENT HUMANS THAT LIVE A TRULY GOOD LIFE...
THEY MURDER KIDS?!?
YES. WHAT THIS DOES IS CREATE MEN AND WOMEN OF LITTLE OR NO FAITH, GODLESS HUMANS WHO EASILY FOLLOW THE PATH OF DARKNESS AND BRING ABOUT HATE, DEATH, AND DESTRUCTION...
SO THESE... "GRIGORI AND NEPHILLIM," THEY'VE BEEN AROUND ALL THIS TIME AND--
BELIEF IS POWER. ALL THESE INCIDENTS OVER THE CENTURIES THAT THE GRIGORI AND NEPHILLIM HAVE BEEN RESPONSIBLE FOR--IT'S ADDED UP--MORE AND MORE PEOPLE TURNING AWAY FROM THE LIGHT--THE TIME HAS NOW COME FOR THEM TO TAKE FULL ADVANTAGE--
YES. THAT IS WHY THE SWORD OF GOD WAS STOLEN NOW, AT THIS JUNCTURE OF HUMAN HISTORY.
THE OVERWHELMING NUMBER OF INNOCENTS THAT HAVE FALLEN, THE BLOOD THAT HAS SOAKED THIS PLANET'S SURFACE HAS CREATED INSTABILITY AND CONFLICT AMONG THE HEAVENLY HOST. THAT IS WHY AZBEEL WAS ABLE TO STEAL THE SWORD... TO BRING ABOUT THE DESTRUCTION OF EARTH... AND HEAVEN...

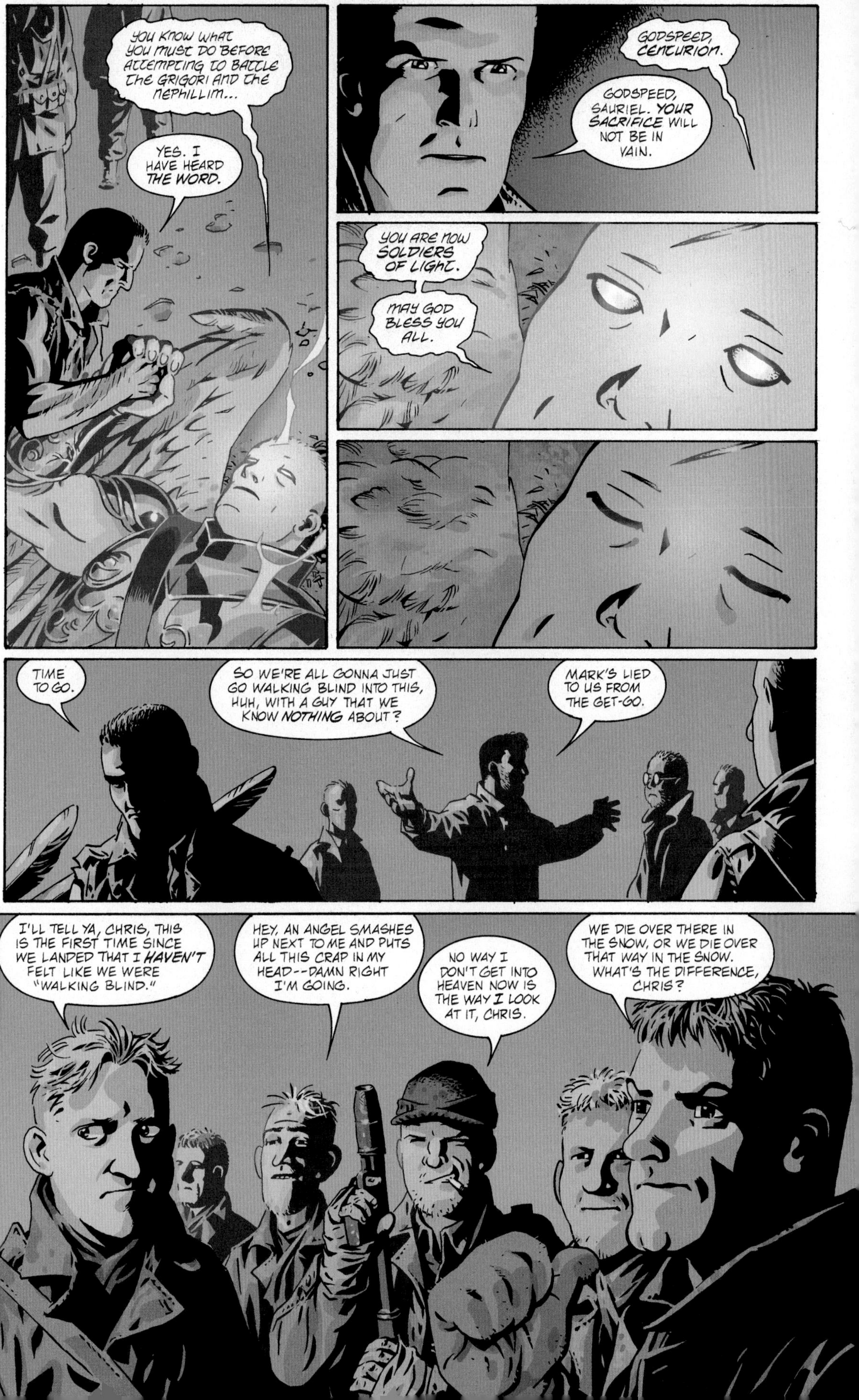
YOU KNOW WHAT YOU MUST DO BEFORE ATTEMPTING TO BATTLE THE GRIGORI AND THE NEPHILLIM...
YES. I HAVE HEARD THE WORD.
GODSPEED, CENTURION.
GODSPEED, SAURIEL. YOUR SACRIFICE WILL NOT BE IN VAIN.
YOU ARE NOW SOLDIERS OF LIGHT.
MAY GOD BLESS YOU ALL.
TIME TO GO.
SO WE'RE ALL GONNA JUST GO WALKING BLIND INTO THIS, HUH, WITH A GUY THAT WE KNOW NOTHING ABOUT?
MARK'S LIED TO US FROM THE GET-GO.
I'LL TELL YA, CHRIS, THIS IS THE FIRST TIME SINCE WE LANDED THAT I HAVEN'T FELT LIKE WE WERE "WALKING BLIND."
HEY, AN ANGEL SMASHES UP NEXT TO ME AND PUTS ALL THIS CRAP IN MY HEAD--DAMN RIGHT I'M GOING.
NO WAY I DON'T GET INTO HEAVEN NOW IS THE WAY I LOOK AT IT, CHRIS.
WE DIE OVER THERE IN THE SNOW, OR WE DIE OVER THAT WAY IN THE SNOW. WHAT'S THE DIFFERENCE, CHRIS?

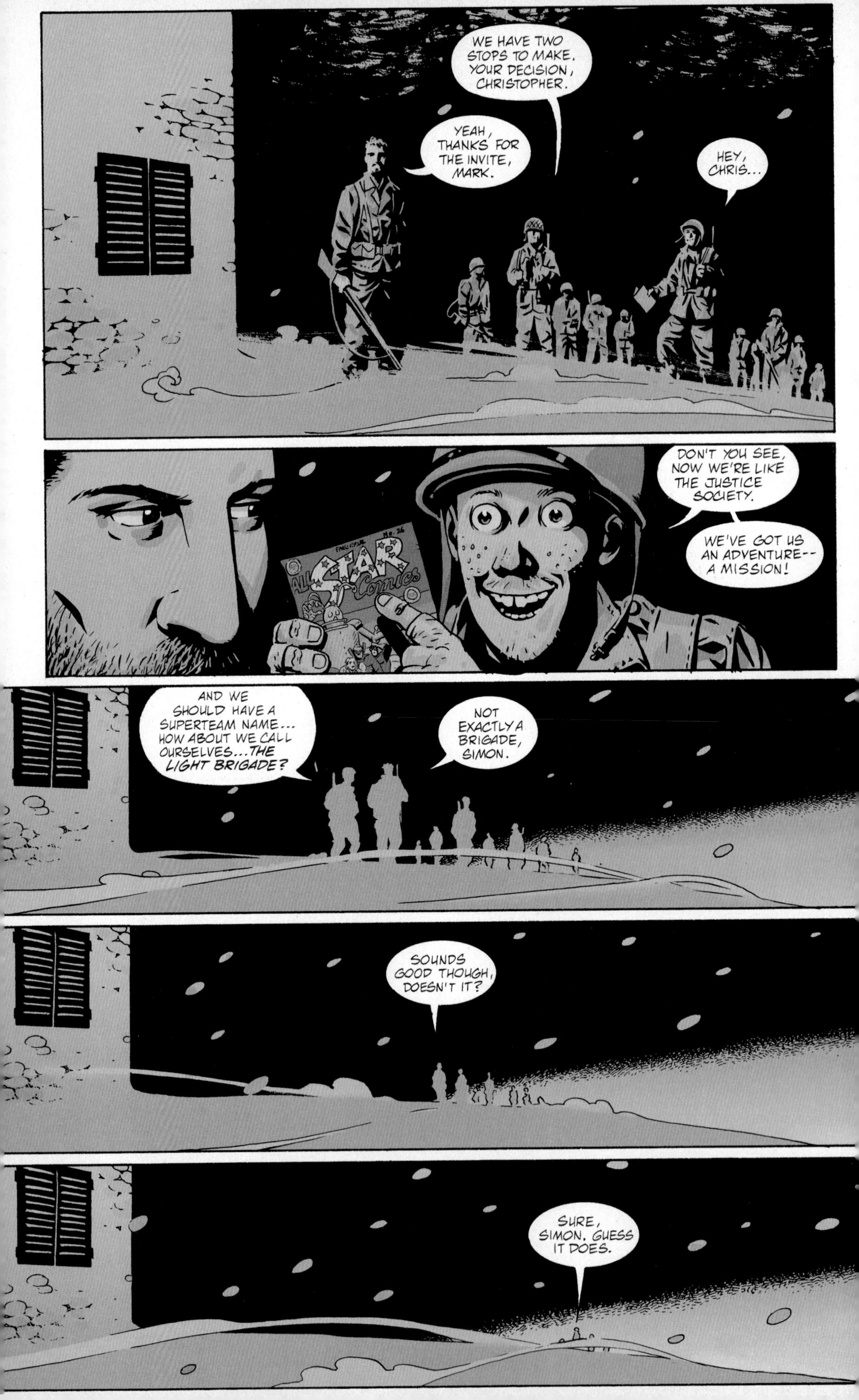
WE HAVE TWO STOPS TO MAKE. YOUR DECISION, CHRISTOPHER.
YEAH, THANKS FOR THE INVITE, MARK.
HEY, CHRIS...
DON'T YOU SEE, NOW WE'RE LIKE THE JUSTICE SOCIETY.
WE'VE GOT US AN ADVENTURE-- A MISSION!
ALL STAR Comics
AND WE SHOULD HAVE A SUPERTEAM NAME... HOW ABOUT WE CALL OURSELVES... THE LIGHT BRIGADE?
NOT EXACTLY A BRIGADE, SIMON.
SOUNDS GOOD THOUGH, DOESN'T IT?
SURE, SIMON. GUESS IT DOES.

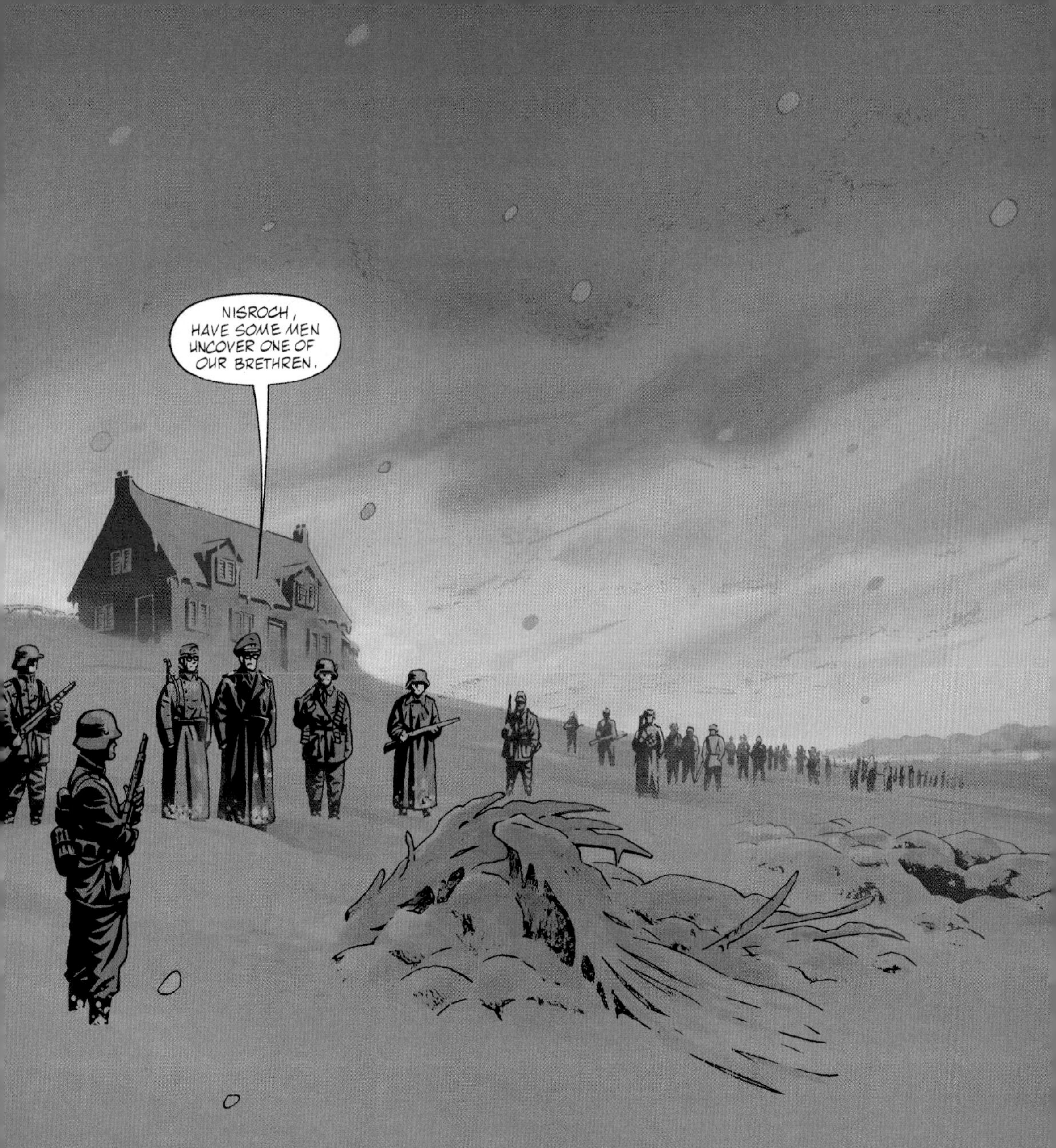
NISROCH, HAVE SOME MEN UNCOVER ONE OF OUR BRETHREN.

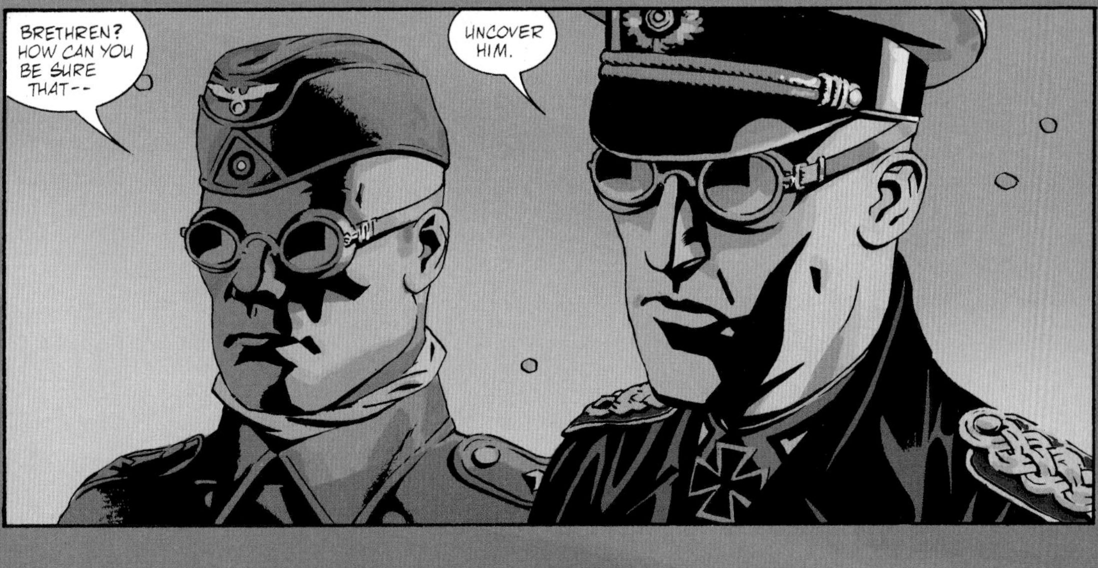
BRETHREN? HOW CAN YOU BE SURE THAT--
UNCOVER HIM.

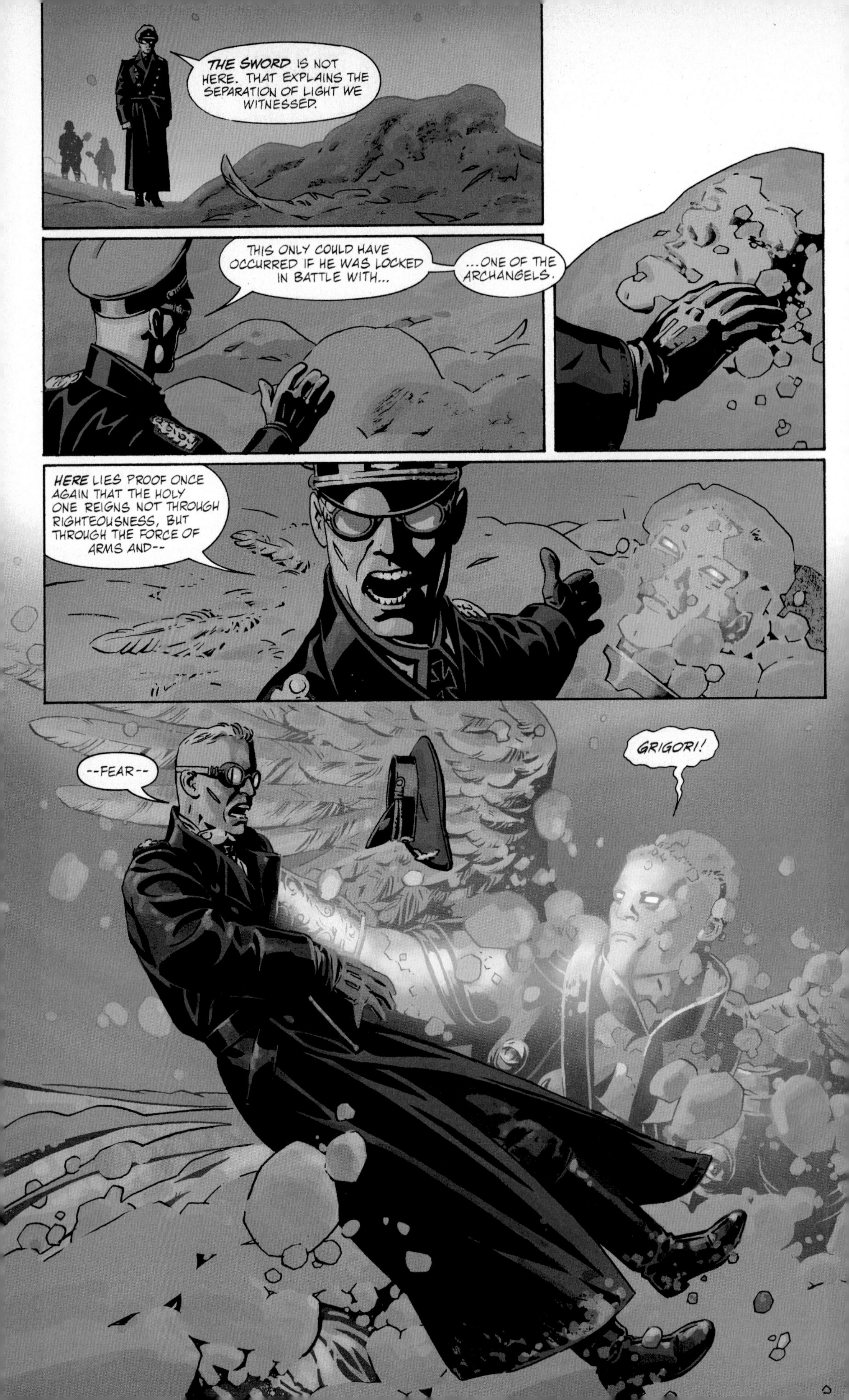
THE SWORD IS NOT HERE. THAT EXPLAINS THE SEPARATION OF LIGHT WE WITNESSED.
THIS ONLY COULD HAVE OCCURRED IF HE WAS LOCKED IN BATTLE WITH...
...ONE OF THE ARCHANGELS.
HERE LIES PROOF ONCE AGAIN THAT THE HOLY ONE REIGNS NOT THROUGH RIGHTEOUSNESS, BUT THROUGH THE FORCE OF ARMS AND--
--FEAR--
GRIGORI!

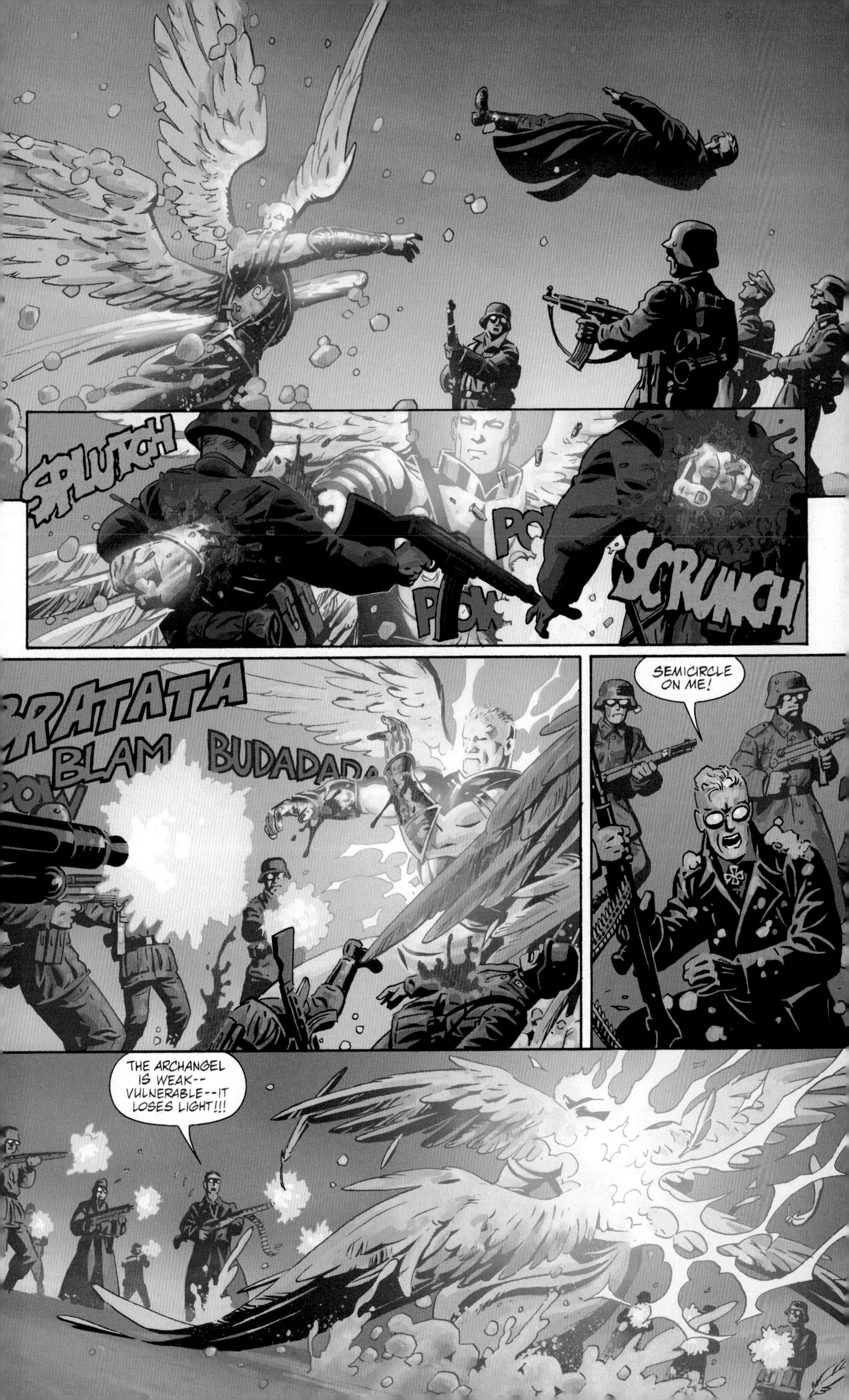
SPLUTCH
SCRUNCH
RATATA
BLAM
BUDADADA
SEMICIRCLE ON ME!
THE ARCHANGEL IS WEAK-- VULNERABLE--IT LOSES LIGHT!!!

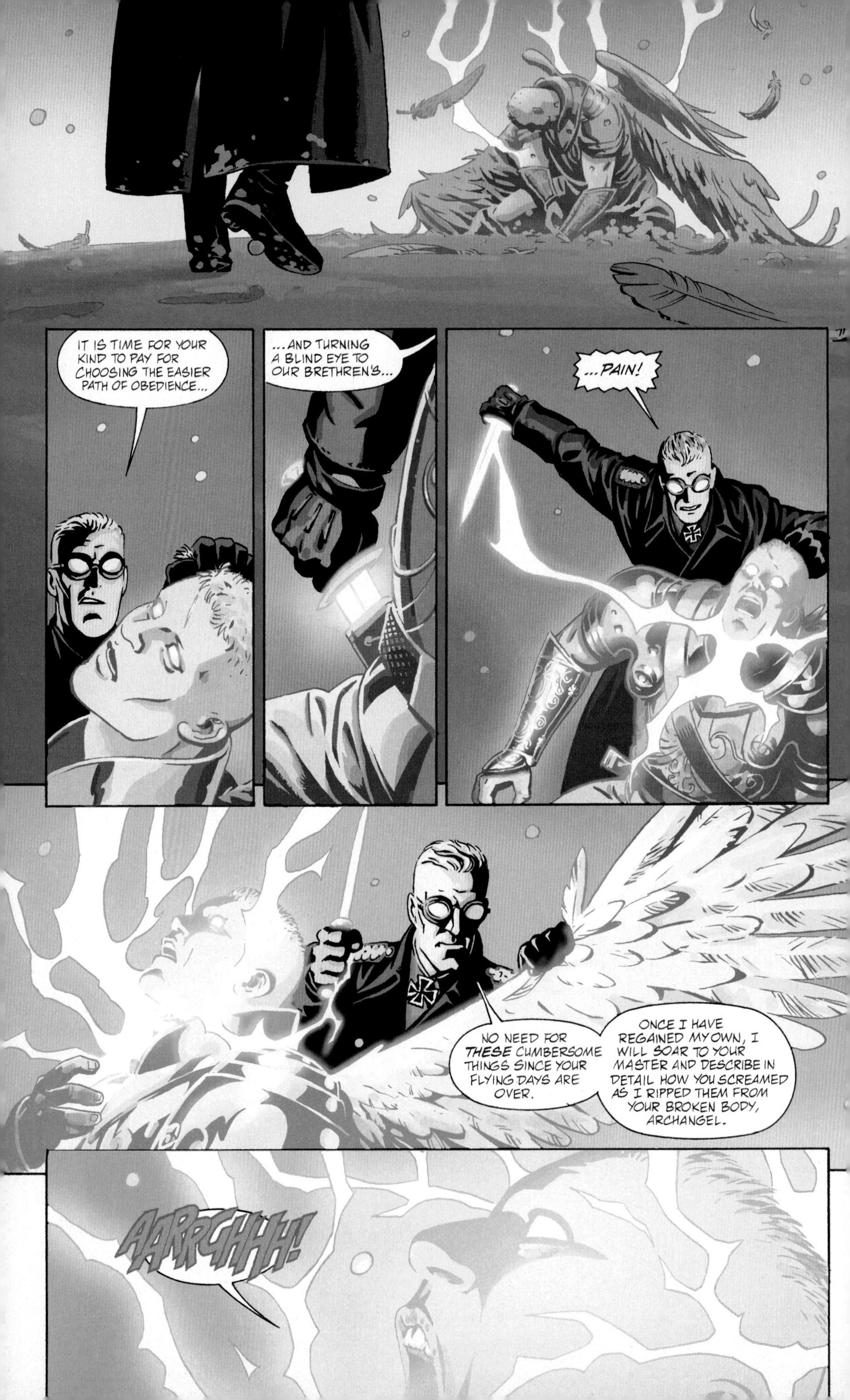
IT IS TIME FOR YOUR KIND TO PAY FOR CHOOSING THE EASIER PATH OF OBEDIENCE...
...AND TURNING A BLIND EYE TO OUR BRETHREN'S...
...PAIN!
NO NEED FOR THESE CUMBERSOME THINGS SINCE YOUR FLYING DAYS ARE OVER.
ONCE I HAVE REGAINED MY OWN, I WILL SOAR TO YOUR MASTER AND DESCRIBE IN DETAIL HOW YOU SCREAMED AS I RIPPED THEM FROM YOUR BROKEN BODY, ARCHANGEL.
AARRGHHH!

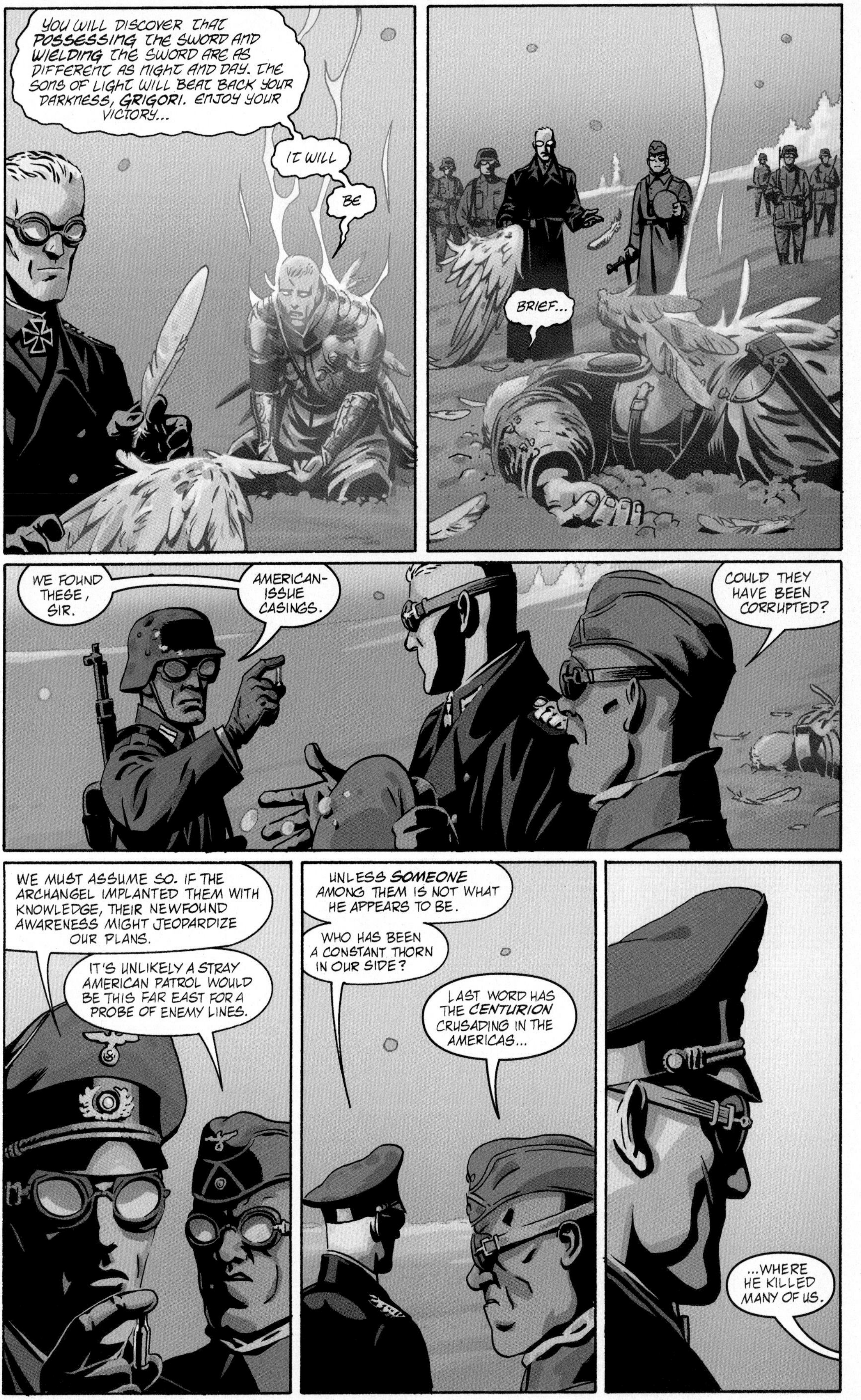
YOU WILL DISCOVER THAT POSSESSING THE SWORD AND WIELDING THE SWORD ARE AS DIFFERENT AS NIGHT AND DAY. THE SONS OF LIGHT WILL BEAT BACK YOUR DARKNESS, GRIGORI. ENJOY YOUR VICTORY...
IT WILL
BE
BRIEF...
WE FOUND THESE, SIR.
AMERICAN-ISSUE CASINGS.
COULD THEY HAVE BEEN CORRUPTED?
WE MUST ASSUME SO. IF THE ARCHANGEL IMPLANTED THEM WITH KNOWLEDGE, THEIR NEWFOUND AWARENESS MIGHT JEOPARDIZE OUR PLANS.
IT'S UNLIKELY A STRAY AMERICAN PATROL WOULD BE THIS FAR EAST FOR A PROBE OF ENEMY LINES.
UNLESS SOMEONE AMONG THEM IS NOT WHAT HE APPEARS TO BE.
WHO HAS BEEN A CONSTANT THORN IN OUR SIDE?
LAST WORD HAS THE CENTURION CRUSADING IN THE AMERICAS...
...WHERE HE KILLED MANY OF US.

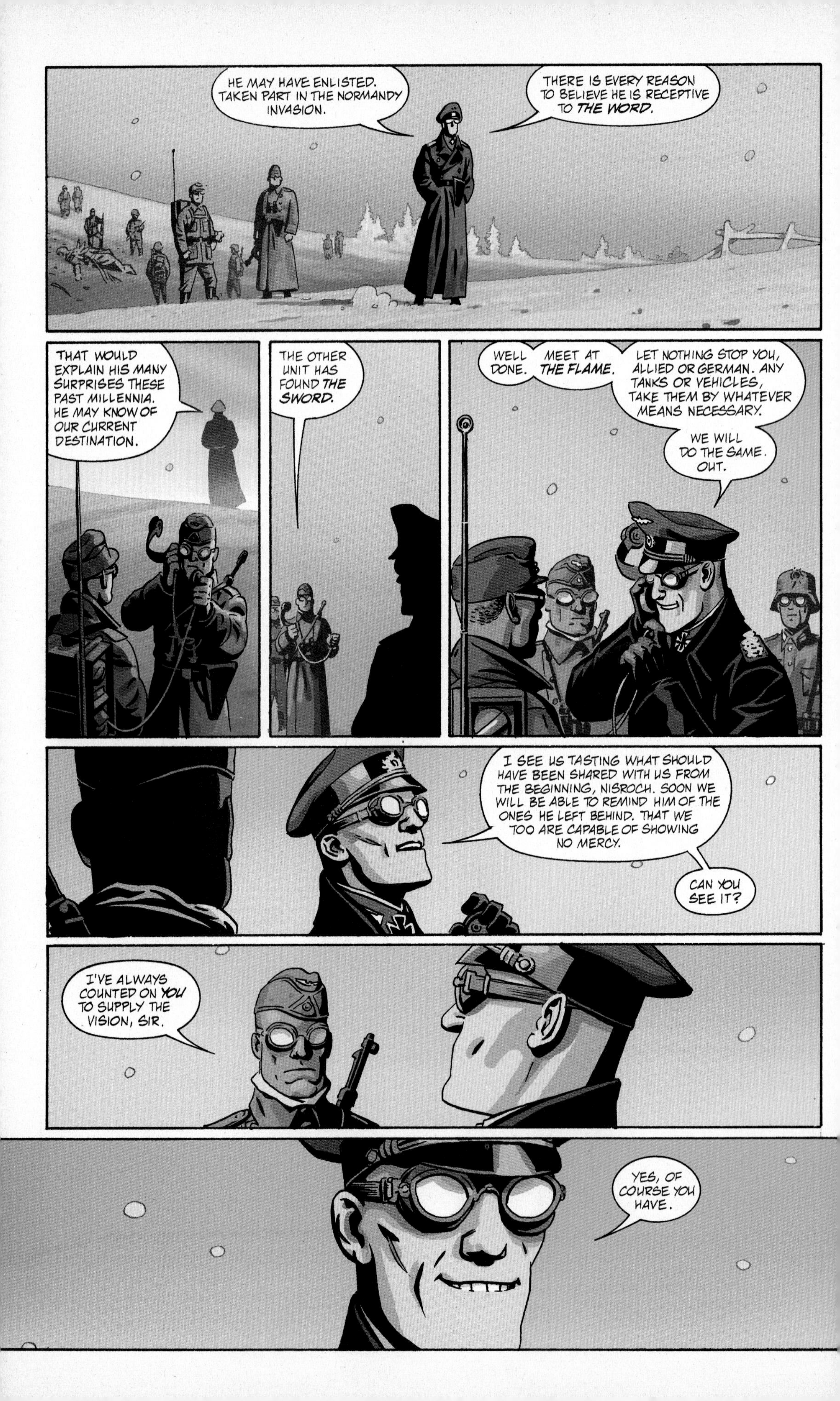

HE MAY HAVE ENLISTED. TAKEN PART IN THE NORMANDY INVASION.
THERE IS EVERY REASON TO BELIEVE HE IS RECEPTIVE TO THE WORD.
THAT WOULD EXPLAIN HIS MANY SURPRISES THESE PAST MILLENNIA. HE MAY KNOW OF OUR CURRENT DESTINATION.
THE OTHER UNIT HAS FOUND THE SWORD.
WELL DONE.
MEET AT THE FLAME.
LET NOTHING STOP YOU, ALLIED OR GERMAN. ANY TANKS OR VEHICLES, TAKE THEM BY WHATEVER MEANS NECESSARY.
WE WILL DO THE SAME. OUT.
I SEE US TASTING WHAT SHOULD HAVE BEEN SHARED WITH US FROM THE BEGINNING, NISROCH. SOON WE WILL BE ABLE TO REMIND HIM OF THE ONES HE LEFT BEHIND. THAT WE TOO ARE CAPABLE OF SHOWING NO MERCY.
CAN YOU SEE IT?
I'VE ALWAYS COUNTED ON YOU TO SUPPLY THE VISION, SIR.
YES, OF COURSE YOU HAVE.

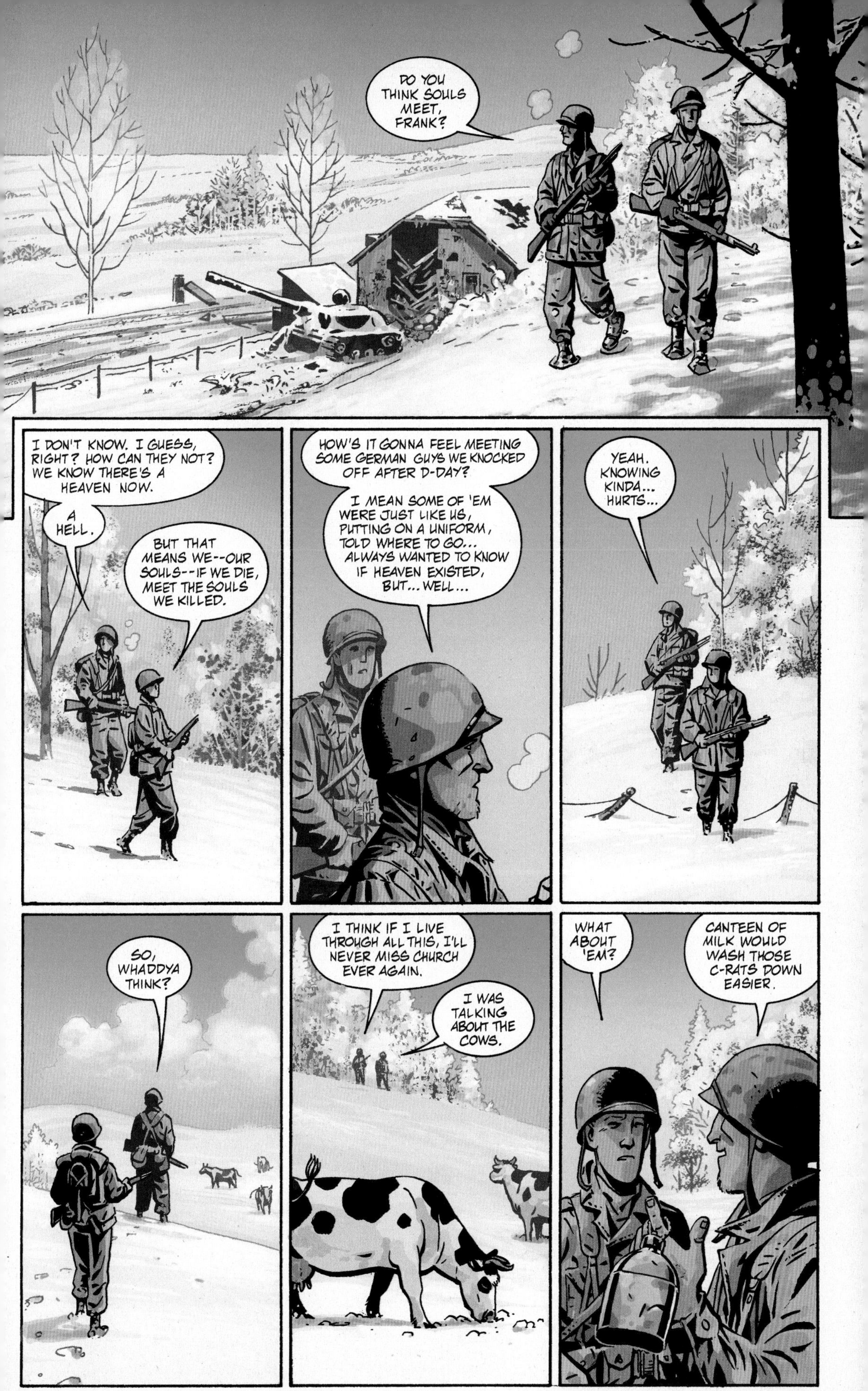
DO YOU THINK SOULS MEET, FRANK?
I DON'T KNOW. I GUESS, RIGHT? HOW CAN THEY NOT? WE KNOW THERE'S A HEAVEN NOW.
A HELL.
BUT THAT MEANS WE--OUR SOULS--IF WE DIE, MEET THE SOULS WE KILLED.
HOW'S IT GONNA FEEL MEETING SOME GERMAN GUYS WE KNOCKED OFF AFTER D-DAY?
I MEAN SOME OF 'EM WERE JUST LIKE US, PUTTING ON A UNIFORM, TOLD WHERE TO GO... ALWAYS WANTED TO KNOW IF HEAVEN EXISTED, BUT... WELL...
YEAH. KNOWING KINDA... HURTS...
SO, WHADDYA THINK?
I THINK IF I LIVE THROUGH ALL THIS, I'LL NEVER MISS CHURCH EVER AGAIN.
I WAS TALKING ABOUT THE COWS.
WHAT ABOUT 'EM?
CANTEEN OF MILK WOULD WASH THOSE C-RATS DOWN EASIER.

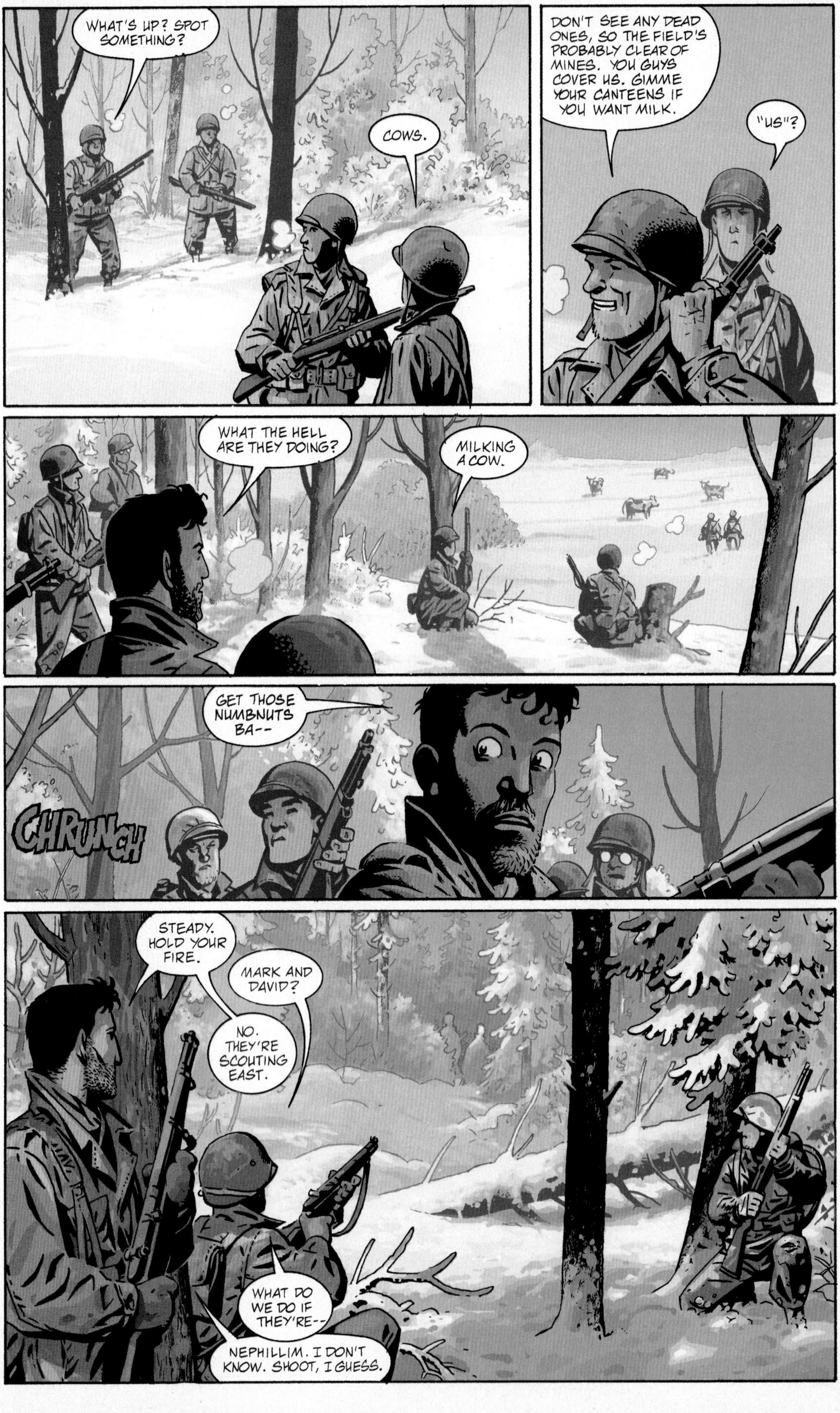
WHAT'S UP? SPOT SOMETHING?
COWS.
DON'T SEE ANY DEAD ONES, SO THE FIELD'S PROBABLY CLEAR OF MINES. YOU GUYS COVER US. GIMME YOUR CANTEENS IF YOU WANT MILK.
"US"?
WHAT THE HELL ARE THEY DOING?
MILKING A COW.
GET THOSE NUMBNUTS BA--
CHRUNCH
STEADY. HOLD YOUR FIRE.
MARK AND DAVID?
NO. THEY'RE SCOUTING EAST.
WHAT DO WE DO IF THEY'RE--
NEPHILLIM. I DON'T KNOW. SHOOT, I GUESS.

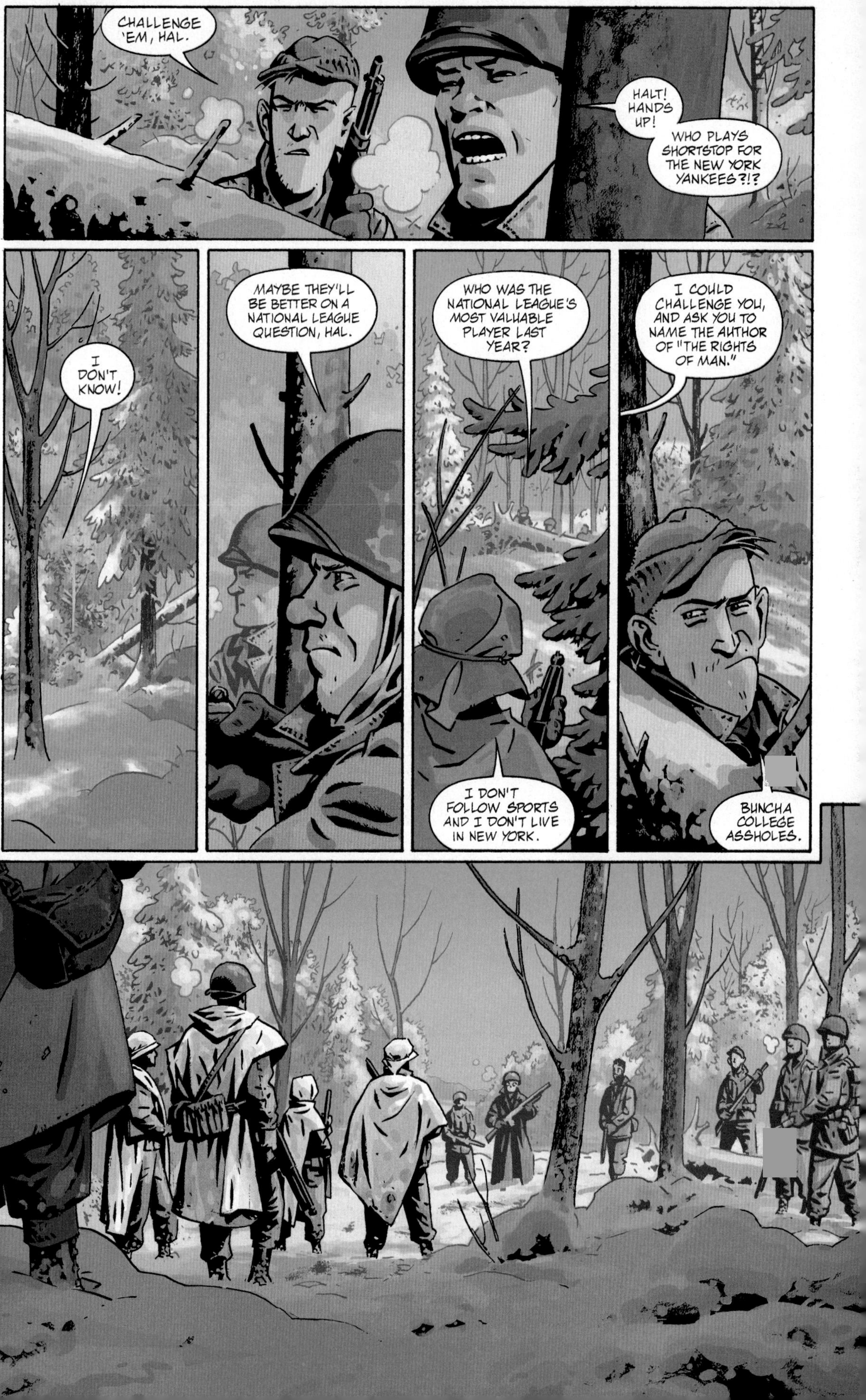
CHALLENGE 'EM, HAL.
HALT! HANDS UP!
WHO PLAYS SHORTSTOP FOR THE NEW YORK YANKEES?!?
I DON'T KNOW!
MAYBE THEY'LL BE BETTER ON A NATIONAL LEAGUE QUESTION, HAL.
WHO WAS THE NATIONAL LEAGUE'S MOST VALUABLE PLAYER LAST YEAR?
I DON'T FOLLOW SPORTS AND I DON'T LIVE IN NEW YORK.
I COULD CHALLENGE YOU, AND ASK YOU TO NAME THE AUTHOR OF "THE RIGHTS OF MAN."
BUNCHA COLLEGE ASSHOLES.

HEY.

GOOD TO SEE SOME FRIENDLY DOGFACES.

IF YOU CAN'T SLEEP ON WHITE SHEETS, I GUESS YOU MIGHT AS WELL WEAR 'EM.

NICE CAMOUFLAGE.

YOU GOT THAT RIGHT.

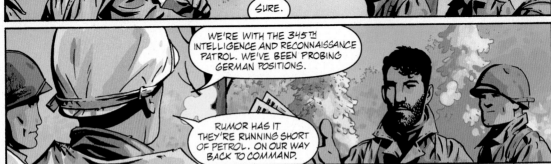

SORRY TO BUST YOUR HUMP, BUT YOU GUYS ARE PRETTY DEEP INTO THE OL' RHINELAND.

YOU HAVE ORDERS?

SURE.

WE'RE WITH THE 345TH INTELLIGENCE AND RECONNAISSANCE PATROL. WE'VE BEEN PROBING GERMAN POSITIONS.

RUMOR HAS IT THEY'RE RUNNING SHORT OF PETROL. ON OUR WAY BACK TO COMMAND.

ALL CHECK OUT CHRIS?

YEP. FINE, HAL. HERE.

NOT TO BUST YOUR HUMP, BUT WHAT ARE YOU GUYS DOING WAY OUT HERE?

LET'S JUST SAY IT'S IMPORTANT TO THE WAR EFFORT AND LEAVE IT AT THAT.

THIS PREOCCUPATION WITH SPORTS...

...WEAVING IT INTO EVERYTHING, PRESUMING EVERYONE YOU MEET KNOWS AS MUCH AS YOU DO.

VERY ANNOYING.

SO'S NOT KNOWING ANYTHING ABOUT BASEBALL.

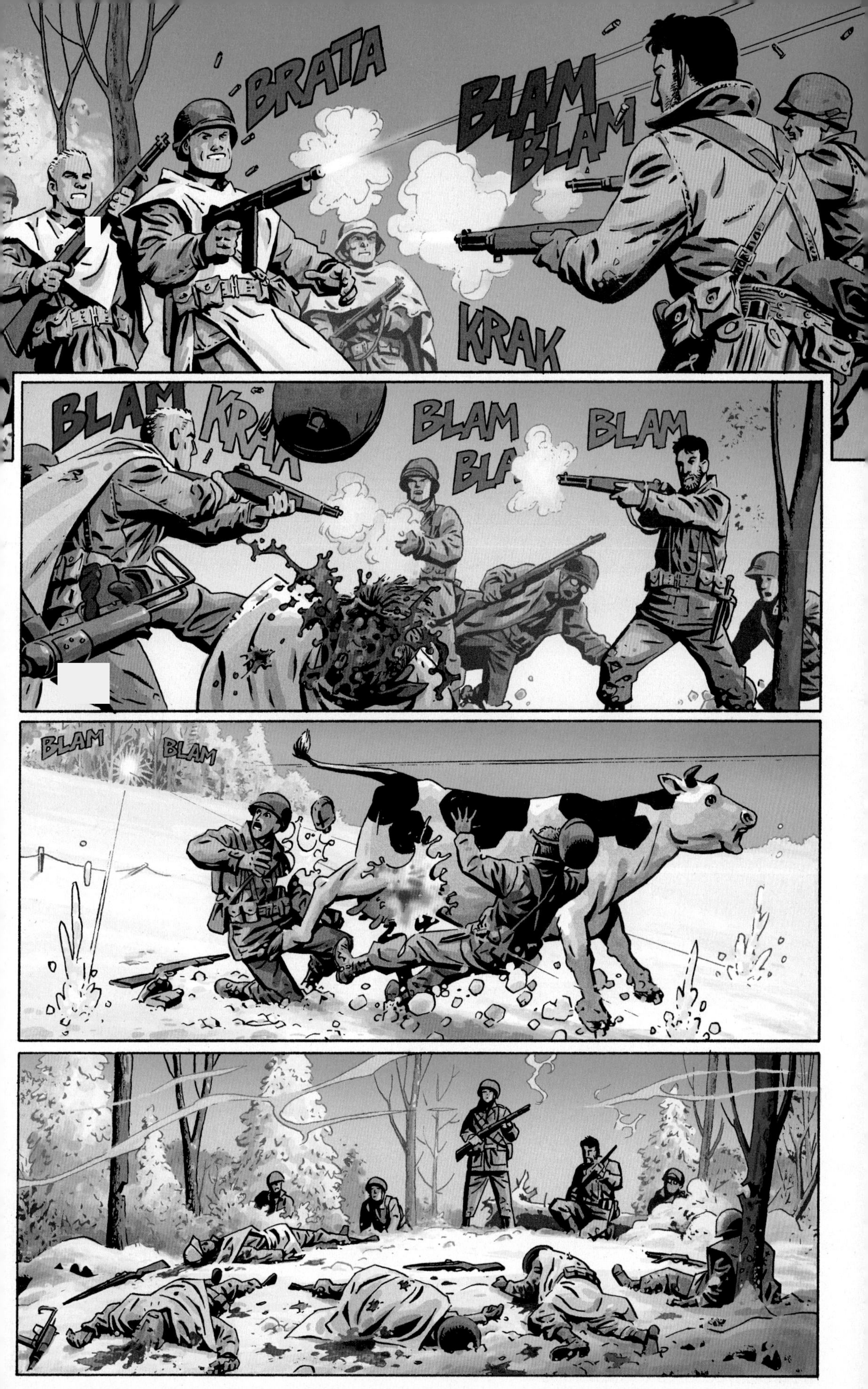
BRATA
BLAM
BLAM
KRAK
BLAM
KRAK
BLAM
BLA
BLAM
BLAM
BLAM

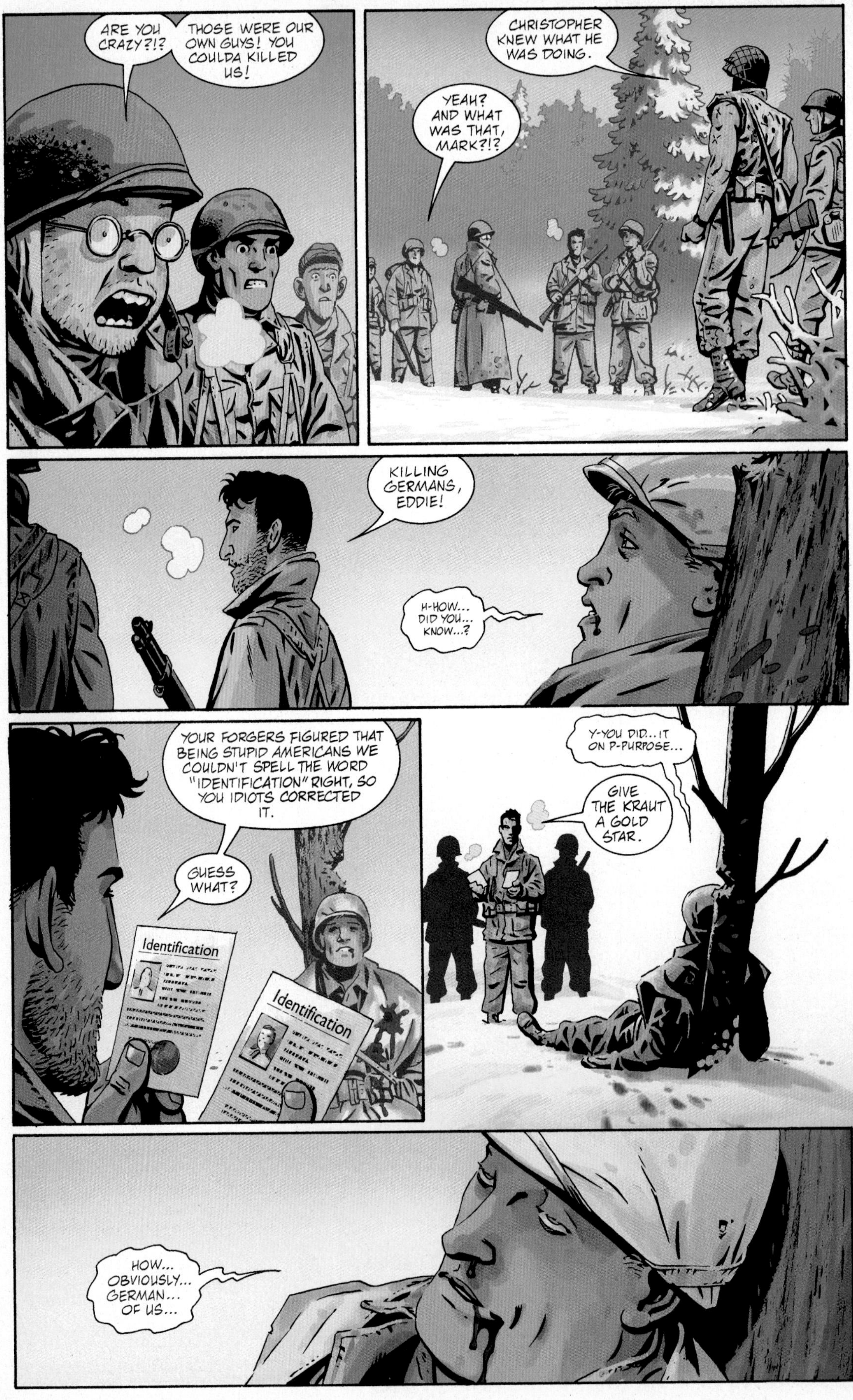
ARE YOU CRAZY?!?
THOSE WERE OUR OWN GUYS! YOU COULDA KILLED US!
CHRISTOPHER KNEW WHAT HE WAS DOING.
YEAH? AND WHAT WAS THAT, MARK?!?
KILLING GERMANS, EDDIE!
H-HOW... DID YOU... KNOW...?
YOUR FORGERS FIGURED THAT BEING STUPID AMERICANS WE COULDN'T SPELL THE WORD "IDENTIFICATION" RIGHT, SO YOU IDIOTS CORRECTED IT.
GUESS WHAT?
Identification
Identification
Y-YOU DID...IT ON P-PURPOSE...
GIVE THE KRAUT A GOLD STAR.
HOW... OBVIOUSLY... GERMAN... OF US...

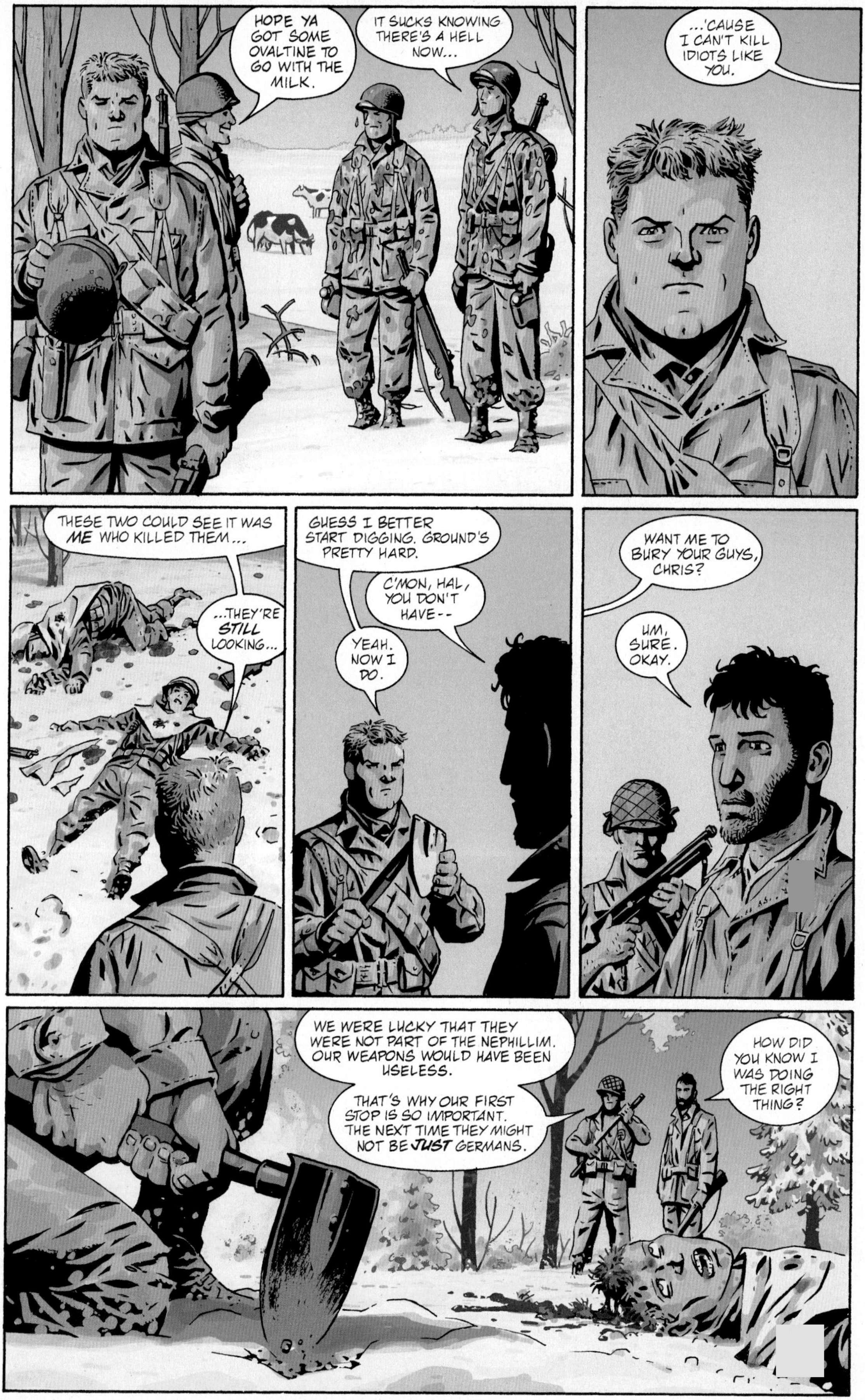
HOPE YA GOT SOME OVALTINE TO GO WITH THE MILK.
IT SUCKS KNOWING THERE'S A HELL NOW...
...'CAUSE I CAN'T KILL IDIOTS LIKE YOU.
THESE TWO COULD SEE IT WAS ME WHO KILLED THEM...
...THEY'RE STILL LOOKING...
GUESS I BETTER START DIGGING. GROUND'S PRETTY HARD.
C'MON, HAL, YOU DON'T HAVE--
YEAH. NOW I DO.
WANT ME TO BURY YOUR GUYS, CHRIS?
UM, SURE. OKAY.
WE WERE LUCKY THAT THEY WERE NOT PART OF THE NEPHILLIM. OUR WEAPONS WOULD HAVE BEEN USELESS.
THAT'S WHY OUR FIRST STOP IS SO IMPORTANT. THE NEXT TIME THEY MIGHT NOT BE JUST GERMANS.
HOW DID YOU KNOW I WAS DOING THE RIGHT THING?

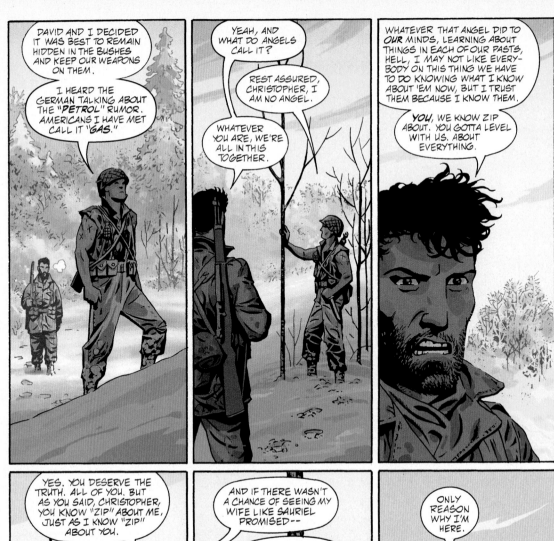

DAVID AND I DECIDED IT WAS BEST TO REMAIN HIDDEN IN THE BUSHES AND KEEP OUR WEAPONS ON THEM.

I HEARD THE GERMAN TALKING ABOUT THE "PETROL" RUMOR. AMERICANS I HAVE MET CALL IT "GAS."

YEAH, AND WHAT DO ANGELS CALL IT?

REST ASSURED, CHRISTOPHER, I AM NO ANGEL.

WHATEVER YOU ARE, WE'RE ALL IN THIS TOGETHER.

WHATEVER THAT ANGEL DID TO OUR MINDS, LEARNING ABOUT THINGS IN EACH OF OUR PASTS, HELL, I MAY NOT LIKE EVERYBODY ON THIS THING WE HAVE TO DO KNOWING WHAT I KNOW ABOUT 'EM NOW, BUT I TRUST THEM BECAUSE I KNOW THEM.

YOU, WE KNOW ZIP ABOUT. YOU GOTTA LEVEL WITH US. ABOUT EVERYTHING.

YES. YOU DESERVE THE TRUTH. ALL OF YOU. BUT AS YOU SAID, CHRISTOPHER, YOU KNOW "ZIP" ABOUT ME, JUST AS I KNOW "ZIP" ABOUT YOU.

YOU KNOW ALL THERE IS TO KNOW. WIFE DEAD. SON ALONE. ME HERE.

AND IF THERE WASN'T A CHANCE OF SEEING MY WIFE LIKE SAURIEL PROMISED--

I DON'T REMEMBER SAURIEL USING THE WORD "PROMISE." IF I RECALL, SAURIEL USED THE WORD "OPPORTUNITY."

ONLY REASON WHY I'M HERE.

TO TAKE IT.

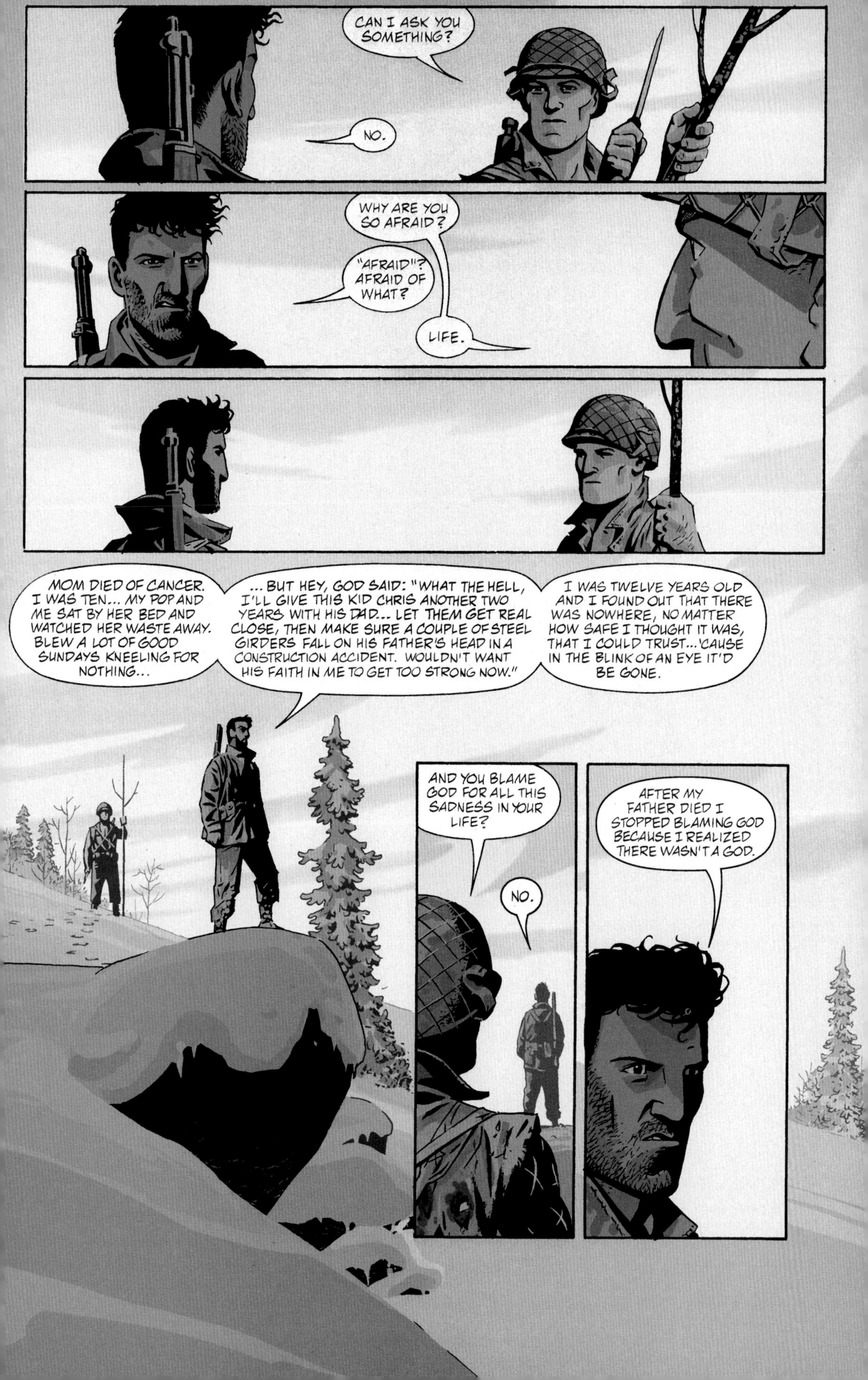
CAN I ASK YOU SOMETHING?
NO.
WHY ARE YOU SO AFRAID?
"AFRAID"? AFRAID OF WHAT?
LIFE.
MOM DIED OF CANCER. I WAS TEN... MY POP AND ME SAT BY HER BED AND WATCHED HER WASTE AWAY. BLEW A LOT OF GOOD SUNDAYS KNEELING FOR NOTHING...
... BUT HEY, GOD SAID: "WHAT THE HELL, I'LL GIVE THIS KID CHRIS ANOTHER TWO YEARS WITH HIS DAD... LET THEM GET REAL CLOSE, THEN MAKE SURE A COUPLE OF STEEL GIRDERS FALL ON HIS FATHER'S HEAD IN A CONSTRUCTION ACCIDENT. WOULDN'T WANT HIS FAITH IN ME TO GET TOO STRONG NOW."
I WAS TWELVE YEARS OLD AND I FOUND OUT THAT THERE WAS NOWHERE, NO MATTER HOW SAFE I THOUGHT IT WAS, THAT I COULD TRUST... 'CAUSE IN THE BLINK OF AN EYE IT'D BE GONE.
AND YOU BLAME GOD FOR ALL THIS SADNESS IN YOUR LIFE?
NO.
AFTER MY FATHER DIED I STOPPED BLAMING GOD BECAUSE I REALIZED THERE WASN'T A GOD.

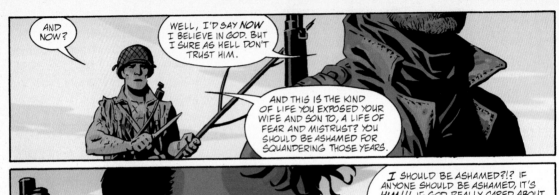

AND NOW?

WELL, I'D SAY *NOW* I BELIEVE IN GOD. BUT I SURE AS HELL DON'T TRUST HIM.

AND THIS IS THE KIND OF LIFE YOU EXPOSED YOUR WIFE AND SON TO, A LIFE OF FEAR AND MISTRUST? YOU SHOULD BE ASHAMED FOR SQUANDERING THOSE YEARS.

***I* SHOULD BE ASHAMED?!? IF ANYONE SHOULD BE ASHAMED, IT'S *HIM!!!* IF GOD REALLY CARED ABOUT US, THIS WAR'D ALL BE OVER AND I'D BE HOME IN MY WIFE'S ARMS. THAT'S HEAVEN, MY FAMILY AROUND ME.**

NOT SOME OTHER PLACE WE SHOULD BE LOOKING FORWARD TO WHEN THEY FINALLY SHOVEL DIRT ON OUR FACES.

SOME "REWARD" FOR TIME WELL SERVED. OUR REWARD'S ALL AROUND US. NOW. WE'VE BEEN LETTING ALL THIS RELIGIOUS CRAP GET IN THE WAY.

FINALLY KNOWING THAT THERE'S A GOD AFTER ALL DOESN'T CHANGE THAT FACT. WE'VE LET SO MANY THINGS GET IN THE WAY... *I'VE* LET SO MANY THINGS GET IN THE WAY...

THINK OF WHAT AWAITS US IF WE CAN DO THE JOB WE HAVE BEEN BLESSED FOR, OF THE CHANGES WE CAN MAKE, CHRISTOPHER.

I'M NOT GONNA GO COUNTING MY MESSIAHS BEFORE THEY'RE HATCHED, MARK.

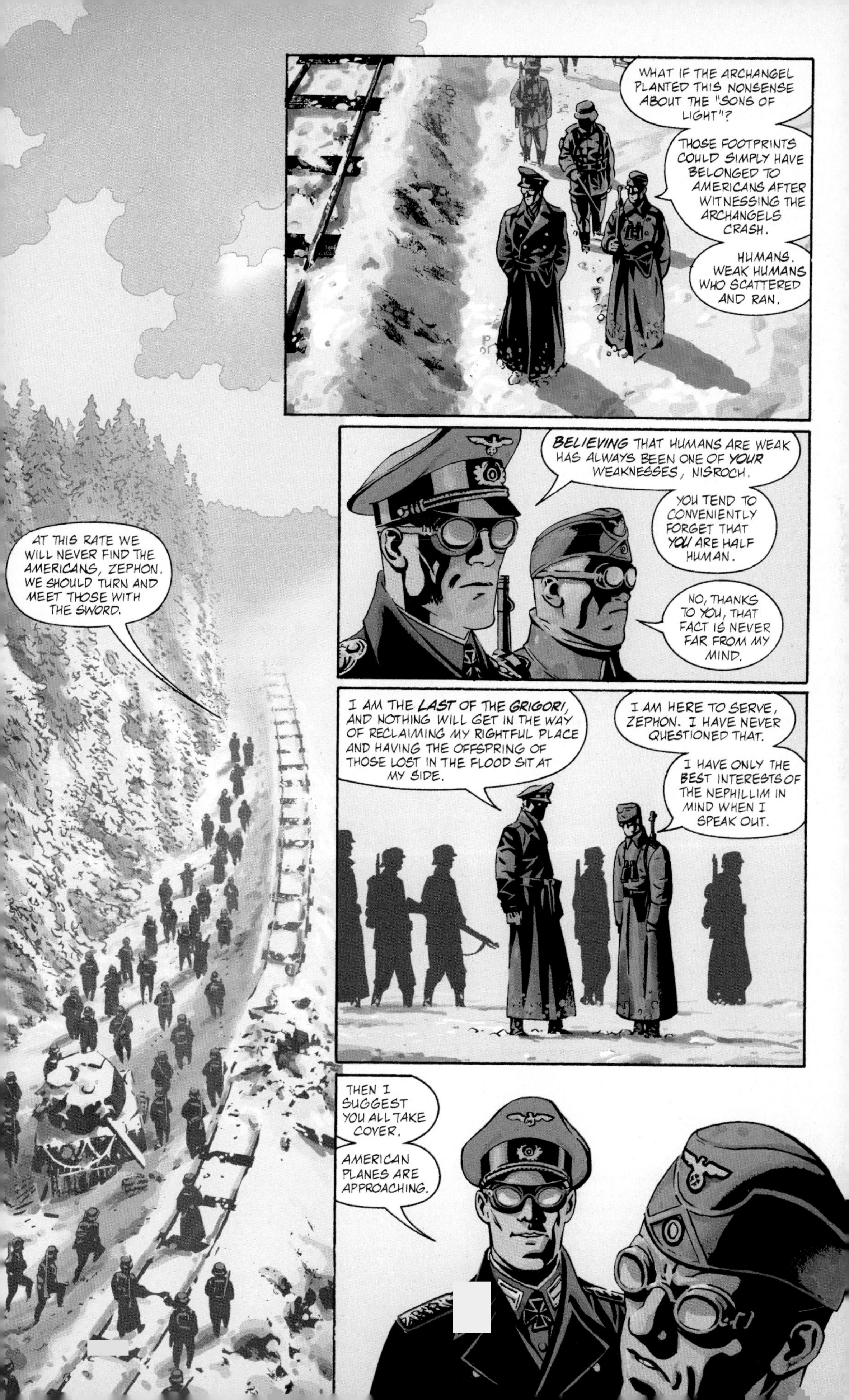
WHAT IF THE ARCHANGEL PLANTED THIS NONSENSE ABOUT THE "SONS OF LIGHT"?
THOSE FOOTPRINTS COULD SIMPLY HAVE BELONGED TO AMERICANS AFTER WITNESSING THE ARCHANGELS CRASH.
HUMANS. WEAK HUMANS WHO SCATTERED AND RAN.
BELIEVING THAT HUMANS ARE WEAK HAS ALWAYS BEEN ONE OF YOUR WEAKNESSES, NISROCH.
YOU TEND TO CONVENIENTLY FORGET THAT YOU ARE HALF HUMAN.
NO, THANKS TO YOU, THAT FACT IS NEVER FAR FROM MY MIND.
AT THIS RATE WE WILL NEVER FIND THE AMERICANS, ZEPHON. WE SHOULD TURN AND MEET THOSE WITH THE SWORD.
I AM THE LAST OF THE GRIGORI, AND NOTHING WILL GET IN THE WAY OF RECLAIMING MY RIGHTFUL PLACE AND HAVING THE OFFSPRING OF THOSE LOST IN THE FLOOD SIT AT MY SIDE.
I AM HERE TO SERVE, ZEPHON. I HAVE NEVER QUESTIONED THAT.
I HAVE ONLY THE BEST INTERESTS OF THE NEPHILLIM IN MIND WHEN I SPEAK OUT.
THEN I SUGGEST YOU ALL TAKE COVER.
AMERICAN PLANES ARE APPROACHING.

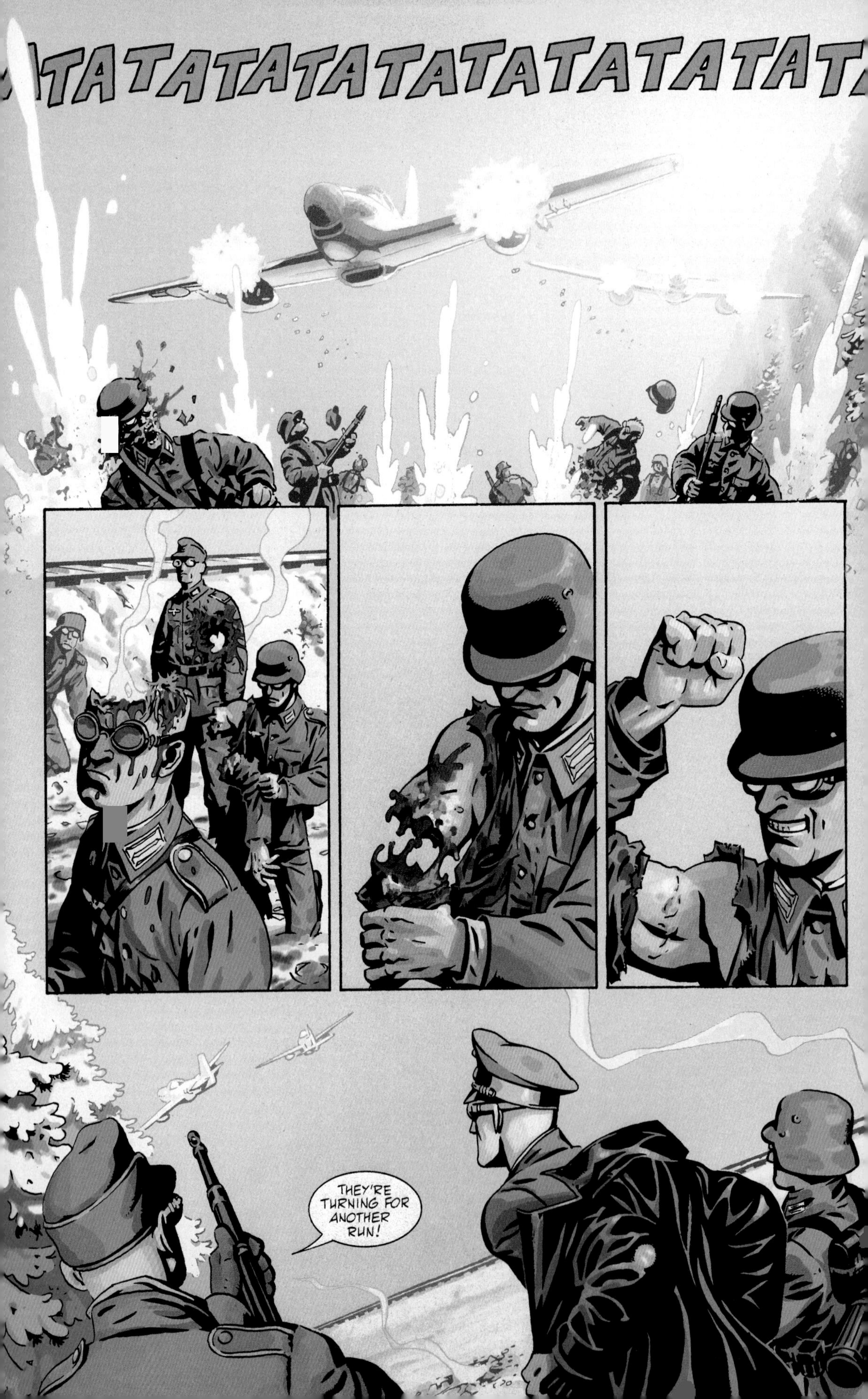
TATATATATATATATATATATA
THEY'RE TURNING FOR ANOTHER RUN!

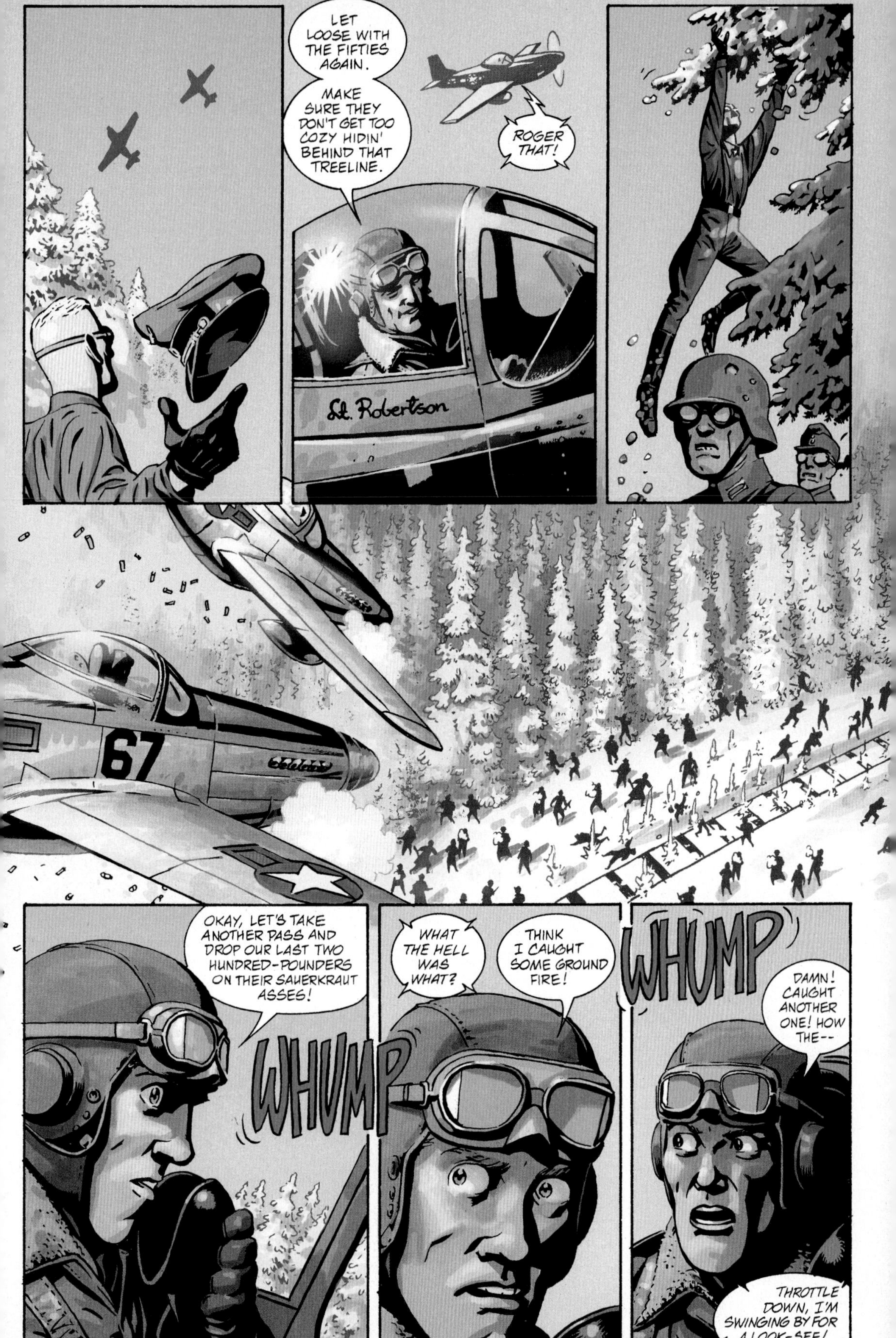
LET LOOSE WITH THE FIFTIES AGAIN.
MAKE SURE THEY DON'T GET TOO COZY HIDIN' BEHIND THAT TREELINE.
ROGER THAT!
Lt. Robertson
67
OKAY, LET'S TAKE ANOTHER PASS AND DROP OUR LAST TWO HUNDRED-POUNDERS ON THEIR SAUERKRAUT ASSES!
WHUMP
WHAT THE HELL WAS WHAT?
THINK I CAUGHT SOME GROUND FIRE!
WHUMP
DAMN! CAUGHT ANOTHER ONE! HOW THE--
THROTTLE DOWN, I'M SWINGING BY FOR A LOOK-SEE!

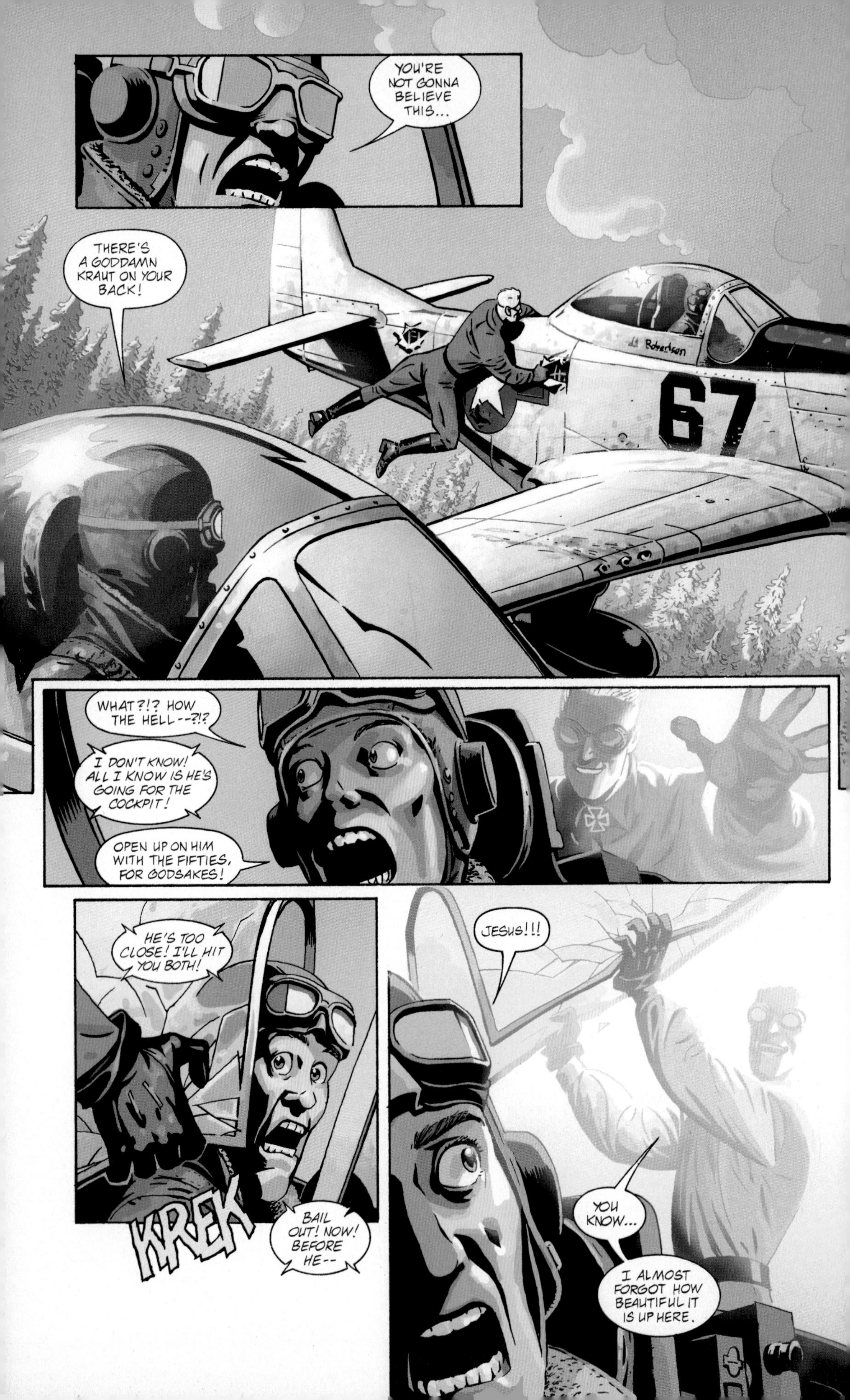
YOU'RE NOT GONNA BELIEVE THIS...
THERE'S A GODDAMN KRAUT ON YOUR BACK!
Robertson
67
WHAT?!? HOW THE HELL--?!?
I DON'T KNOW! ALL I KNOW IS HE'S GOING FOR THE COCKPIT!
OPEN UP ON HIM WITH THE FIFTIES, FOR GODSAKES!
HE'S TOO CLOSE! I'LL HIT YOU BOTH!
KREK
BAIL OUT! NOW! BEFORE HE--
JESUS!!!
YOU KNOW...
I ALMOST FORGOT HOW BEAUTIFUL IT IS UP HERE.

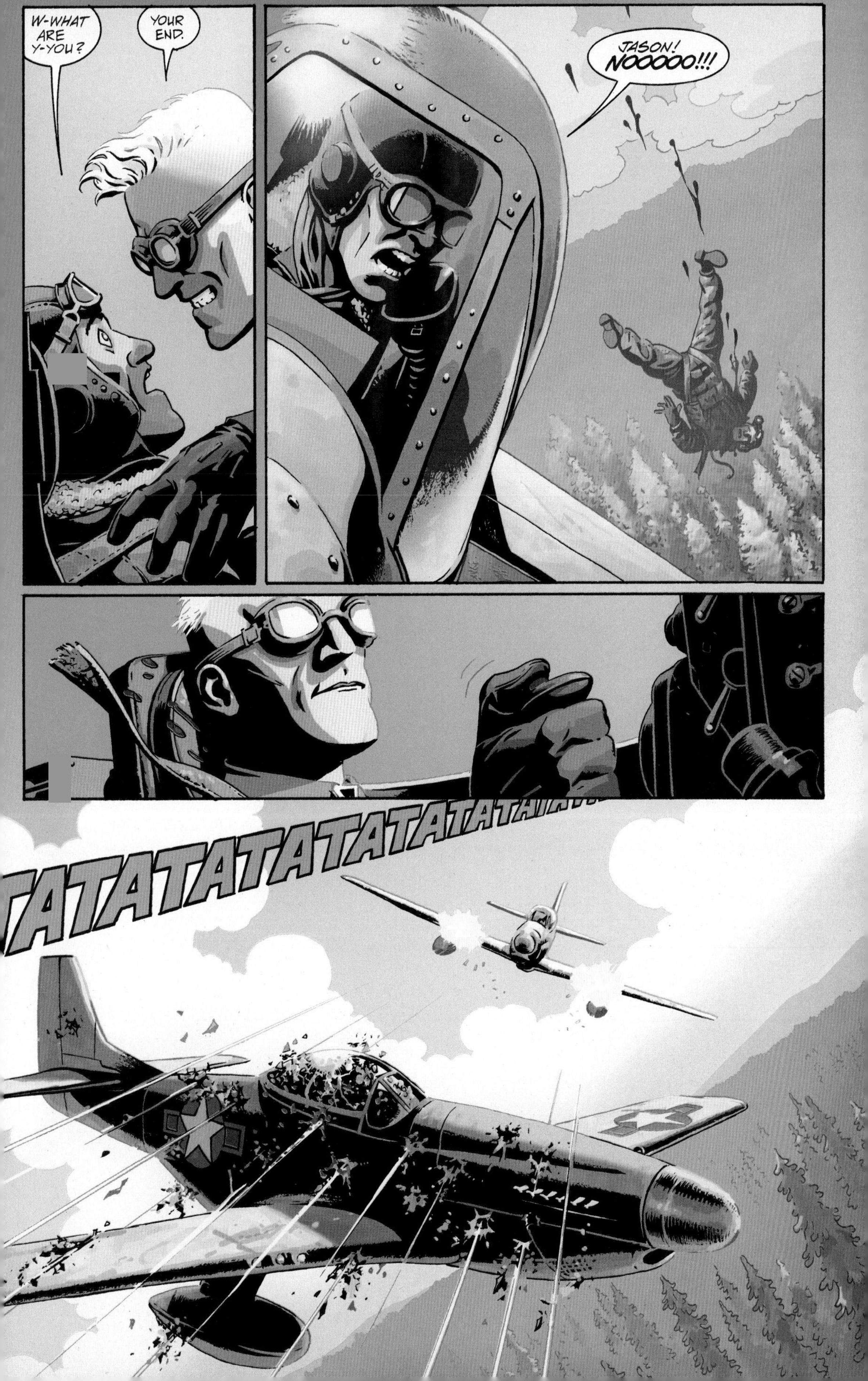
W-WHAT ARE Y-YOU?
YOUR END.
JASON! NOOOOO!!!
TATATATATATATATATA

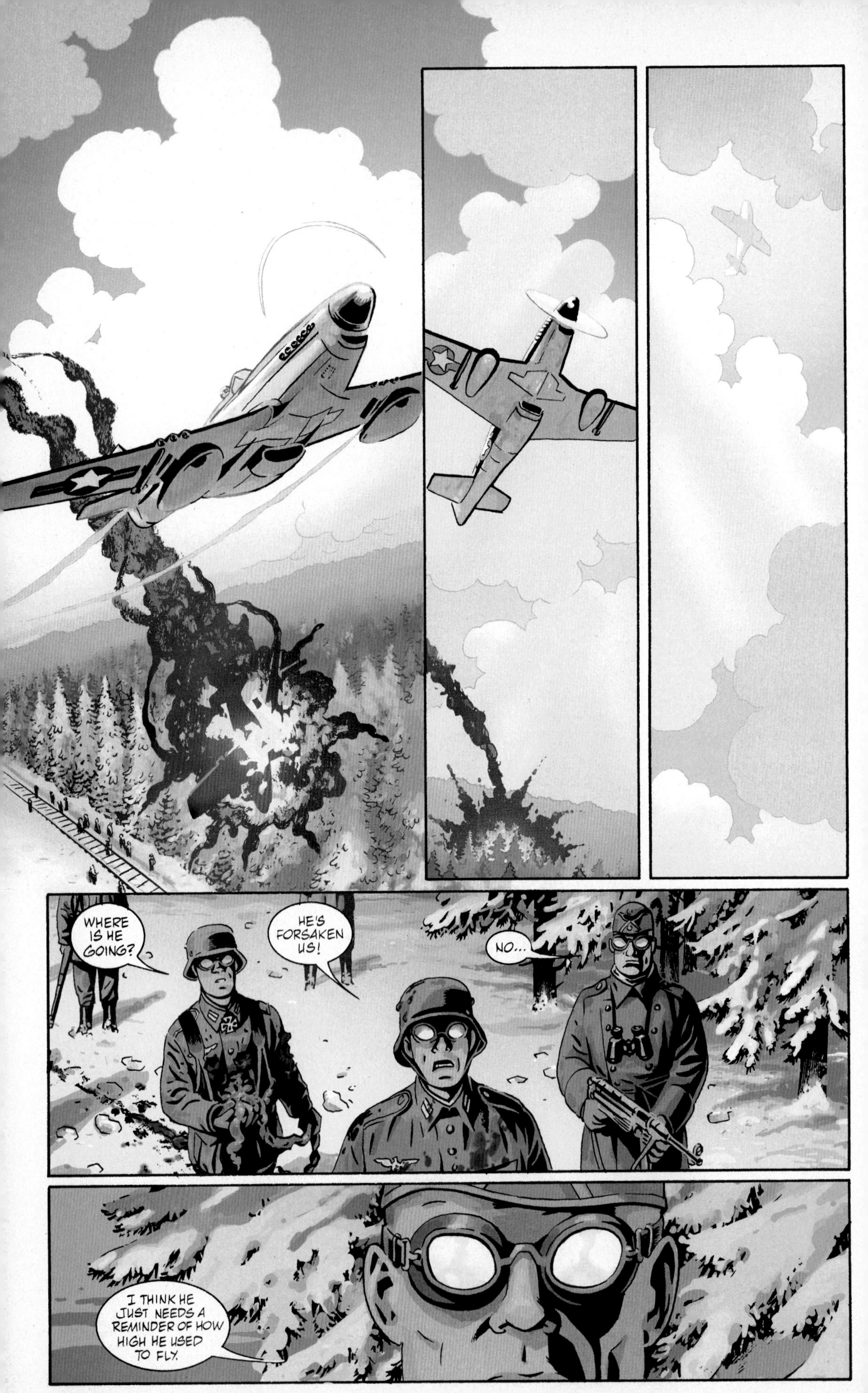
WHERE IS HE GOING?
HE'S FORSAKEN US!
NO...
I THINK HE JUST NEEDS A REMINDER OF HOW HIGH HE USED TO FLY.

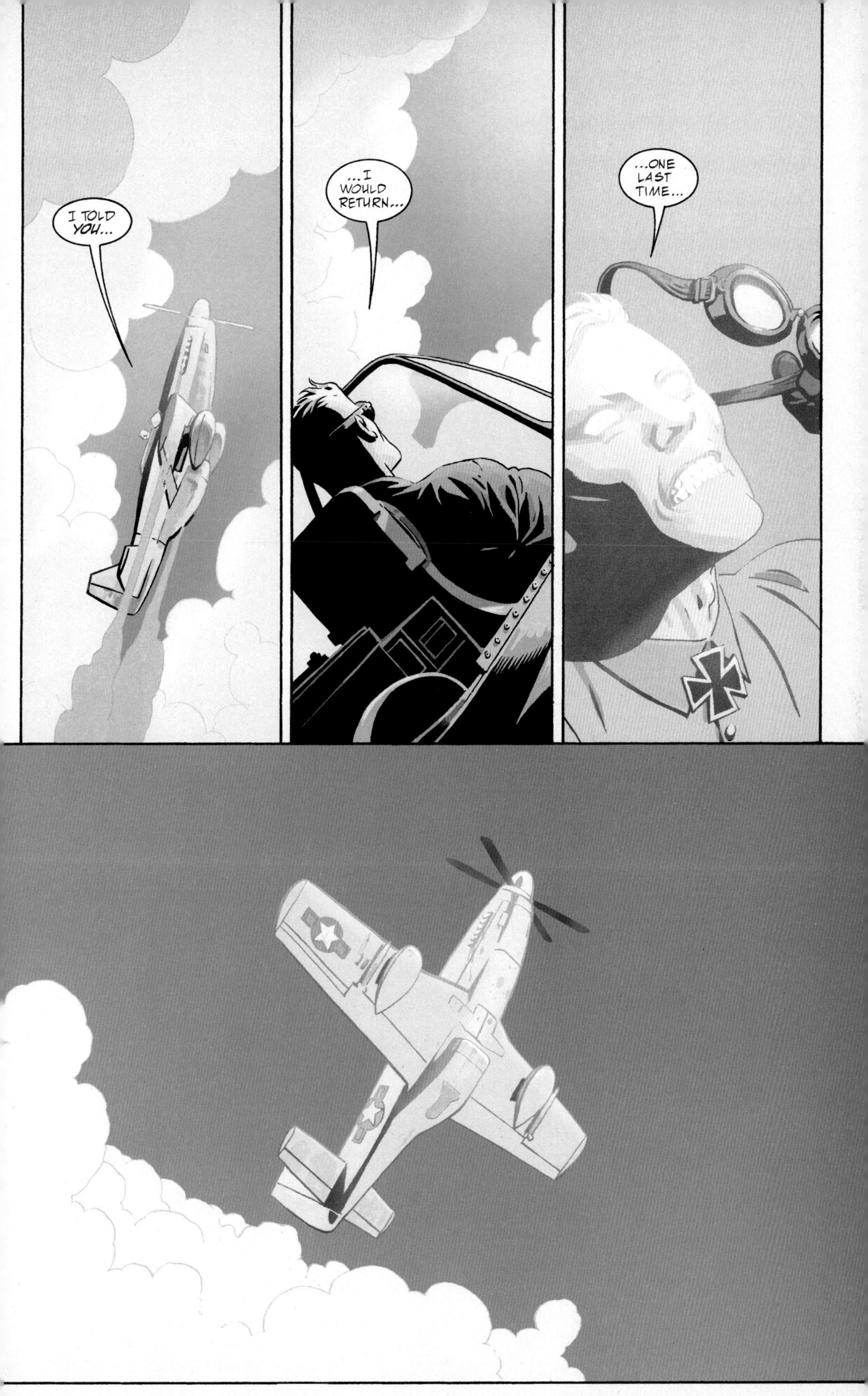
I TOLD YOU...
...I WOULD RETURN...
...ONE LAST TIME...

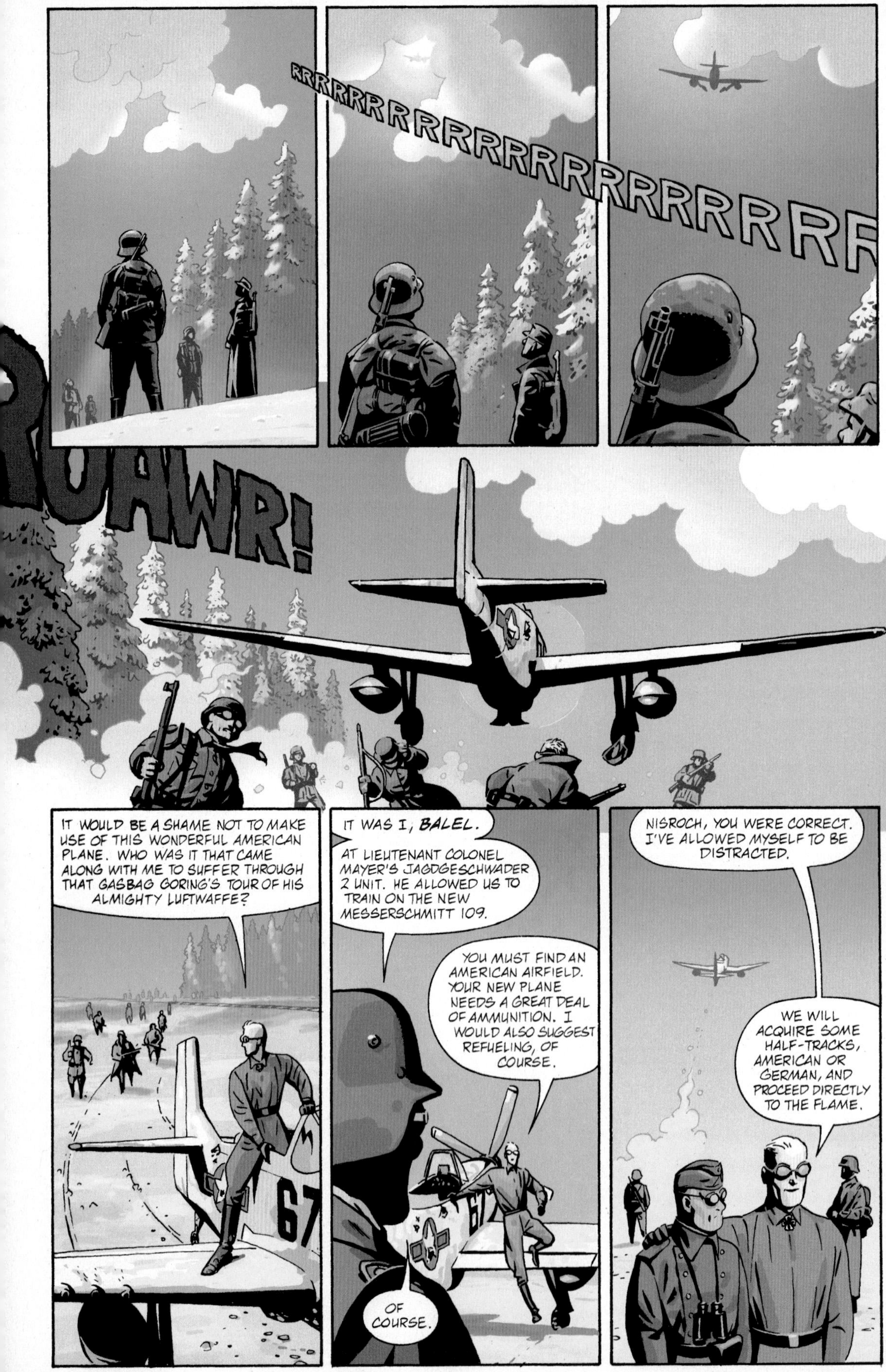
RRRRRRRRRRRRRRRRRRRRRRR
ROAWR!
IT WOULD BE A SHAME NOT TO MAKE USE OF THIS WONDERFUL AMERICAN PLANE. WHO WAS IT THAT CAME ALONG WITH ME TO SUFFER THROUGH THAT GASBAG GORING'S TOUR OF HIS ALMIGHTY LUFTWAFFE?
IT WAS I, BALEL.
AT LIEUTENANT COLONEL MAYER'S JAGDGESCHWADER 2 UNIT. HE ALLOWED US TO TRAIN ON THE NEW MESSERSCHMITT 109.
YOU MUST FIND AN AMERICAN AIRFIELD. YOUR NEW PLANE NEEDS A GREAT DEAL OF AMMUNITION. I WOULD ALSO SUGGEST REFUELING, OF COURSE.
OF COURSE.
NISROCH, YOU WERE CORRECT. I'VE ALLOWED MYSELF TO BE DISTRACTED.
WE WILL ACQUIRE SOME HALF-TRACKS, AMERICAN OR GERMAN, AND PROCEED DIRECTLY TO THE FLAME.
67

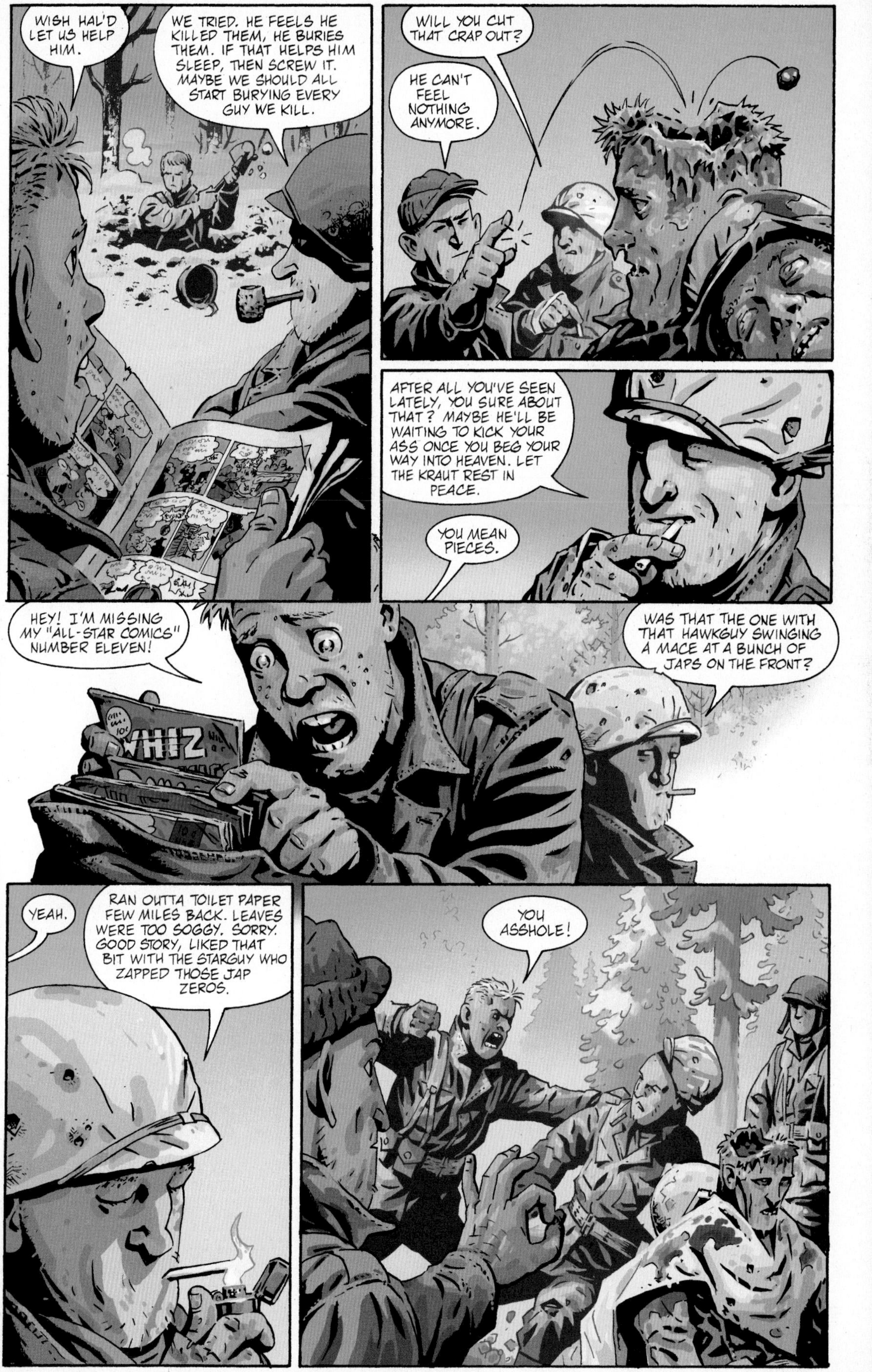

WISH HAL'D LET US HELP HIM.
WE TRIED. HE FEELS HE KILLED THEM, HE BURIES THEM. IF THAT HELPS HIM SLEEP, THEN SCREW IT. MAYBE WE SHOULD ALL START BURYING EVERY GUY WE KILL.
WILL YOU CUT THAT CRAP OUT?
HE CAN'T FEEL NOTHING ANYMORE.
AFTER ALL YOU'VE SEEN LATELY, YOU SURE ABOUT THAT? MAYBE HE'LL BE WAITING TO KICK YOUR ASS ONCE YOU BEG YOUR WAY INTO HEAVEN. LET THE KRAUT REST IN PEACE.
YOU MEAN PIECES.
HEY! I'M MISSING MY "ALL-STAR COMICS" NUMBER ELEVEN!
WAS THAT THE ONE WITH THAT HAWKGUY SWINGING A MACE AT A BUNCH OF JAPS ON THE FRONT?
WHIZ
YEAH.
RAN OUTTA TOILET PAPER FEW MILES BACK. LEAVES WERE TOO SOGGY. SORRY. GOOD STORY, LIKED THAT BIT WITH THE STARGUY WHO ZAPPED THOSE JAP ZEROS.
YOU ASSHOLE!

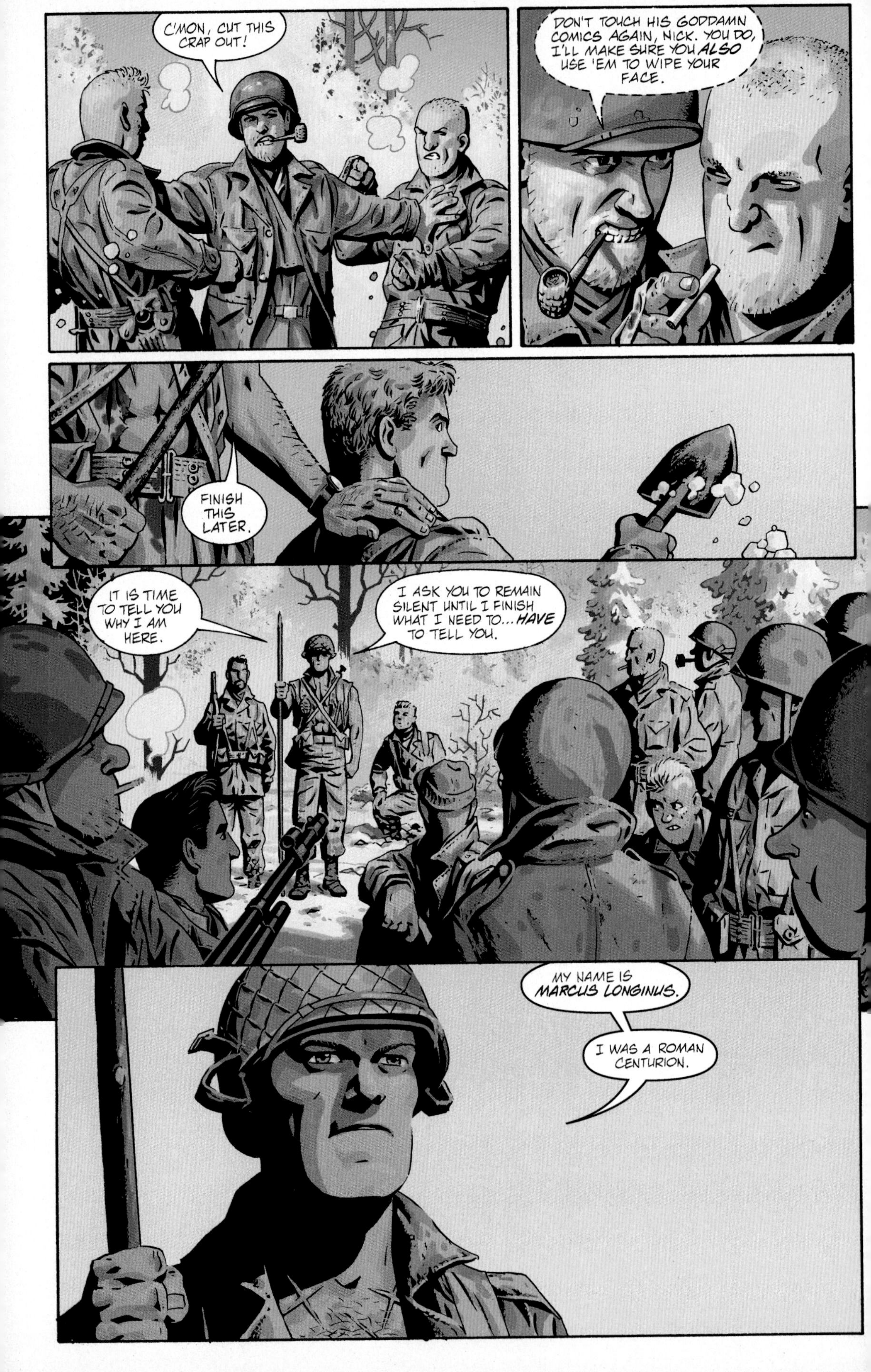
C'MON, CUT THIS CRAP OUT!
DON'T TOUCH HIS GODDAMN COMICS AGAIN, NICK. YOU DO, I'LL MAKE SURE YOU ALSO USE 'EM TO WIPE YOUR FACE.
FINISH THIS LATER.
IT IS TIME TO TELL YOU WHY I AM HERE.
I ASK YOU TO REMAIN SILENT UNTIL I FINISH WHAT I NEED TO... HAVE TO TELL YOU.
MY NAME IS MARCUS LONGINUS.
I WAS A ROMAN CENTURION.

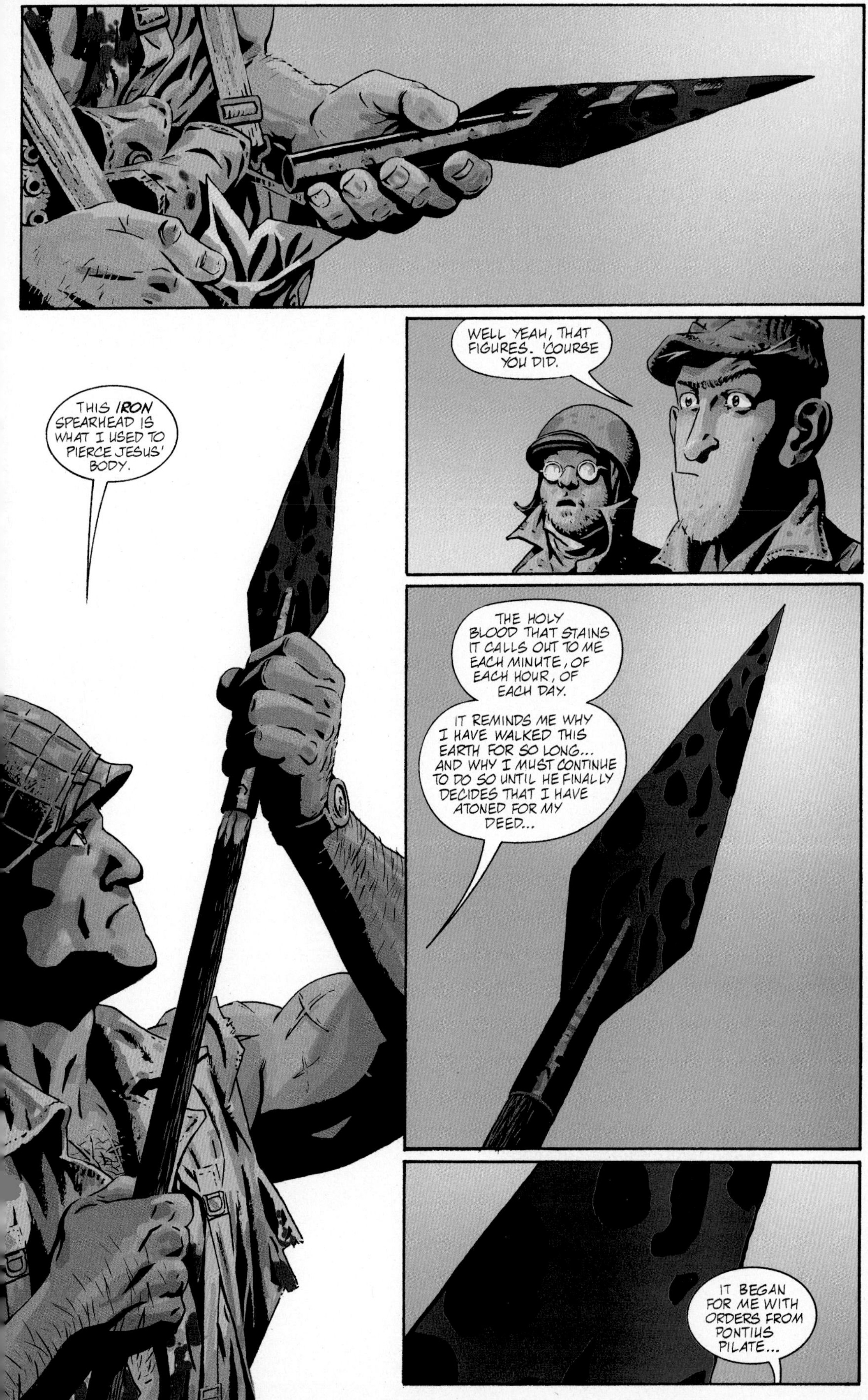
THIS IRON SPEARHEAD IS WHAT I USED TO PIERCE JESUS' BODY.
WELL YEAH, THAT FIGURES. 'COURSE YOU DID.
THE HOLY BLOOD THAT STAINS IT CALLS OUT TO ME EACH MINUTE, OF EACH HOUR, OF EACH DAY.
IT REMINDS ME WHY I HAVE WALKED THIS EARTH FOR SO LONG... AND WHY I MUST CONTINUE TO DO SO UNTIL HE FINALLY DECIDES THAT I HAVE ATONED FOR MY DEED...
IT BEGAN FOR ME WITH ORDERS FROM PONTIUS PILATE...

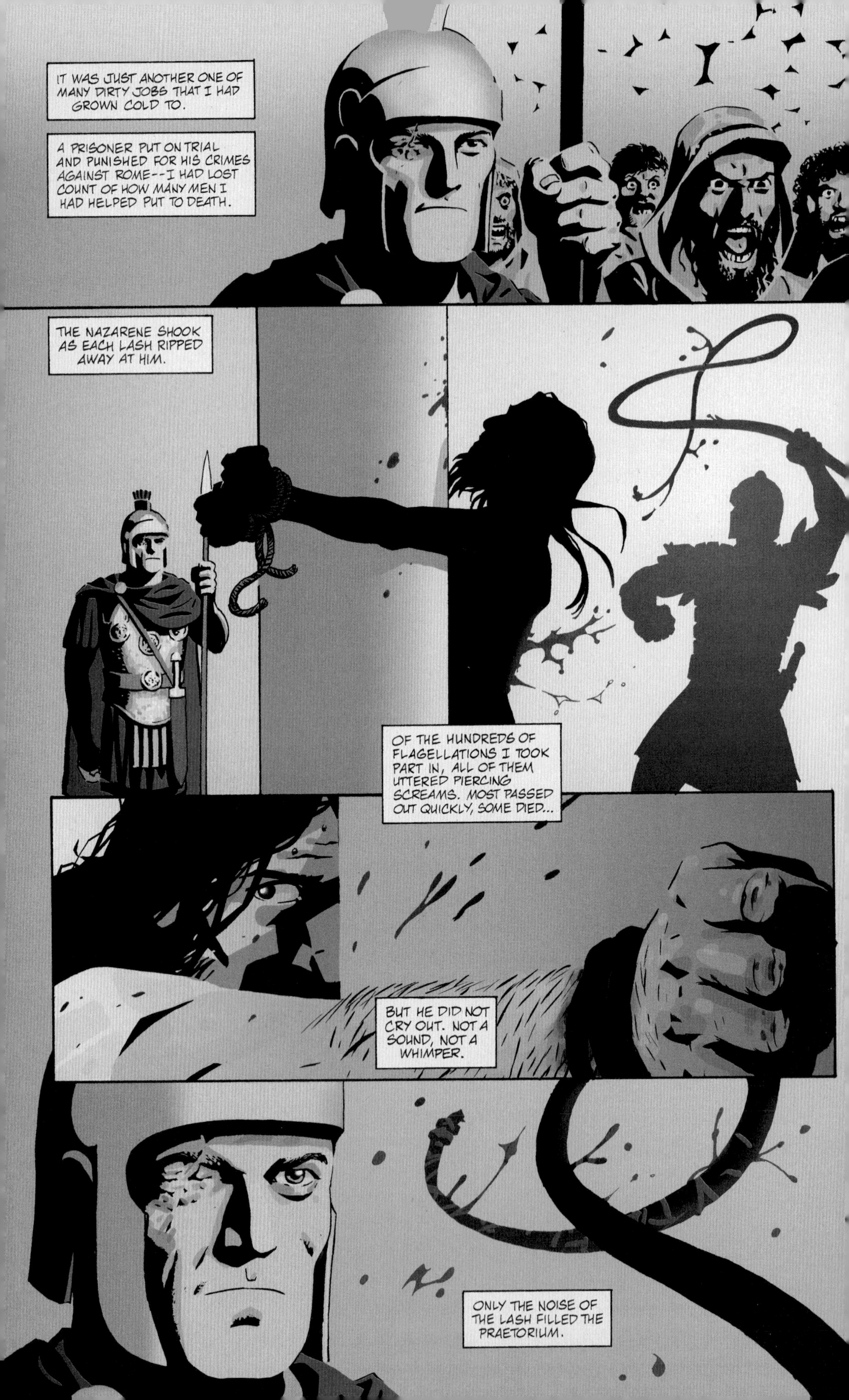
IT WAS JUST ANOTHER ONE OF MANY DIRTY JOBS THAT I HAD GROWN COLD TO.
A PRISONER PUT ON TRIAL AND PUNISHED FOR HIS CRIMES AGAINST ROME--I HAD LOST COUNT OF HOW MANY MEN I HAD HELPED PUT TO DEATH.
THE NAZARENE SHOOK AS EACH LASH RIPPED AWAY AT HIM.
OF THE HUNDREDS OF FLAGELLATIONS I TOOK PART IN, ALL OF THEM UTTERED PIERCING SCREAMS. MOST PASSED OUT QUICKLY, SOME DIED...
BUT HE DID NOT CRY OUT. NOT A SOUND, NOT A WHIMPER.
ONLY THE NOISE OF THE LASH FILLED THE PRAETORIUM.

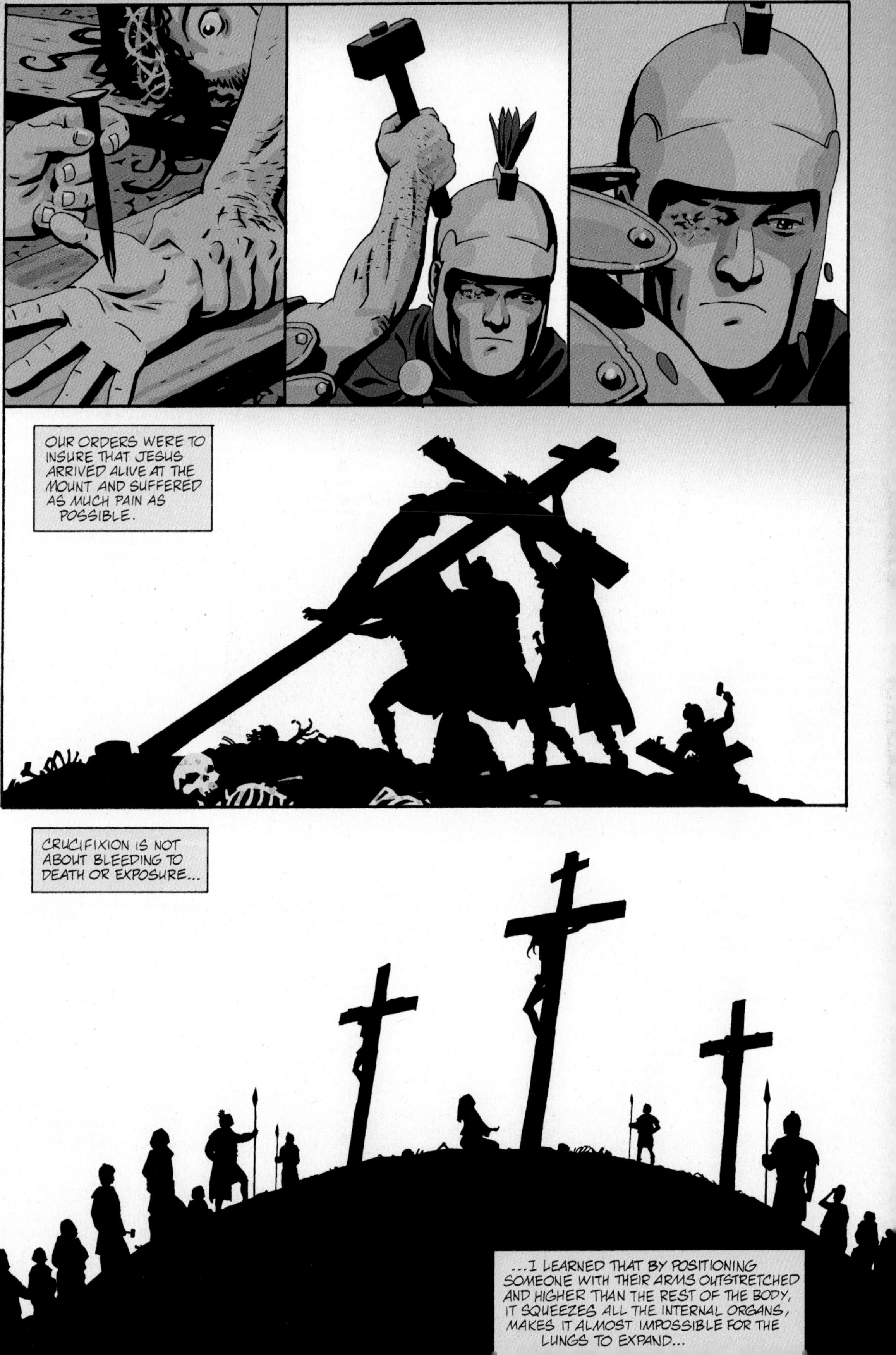
OUR ORDERS WERE TO INSURE THAT JESUS ARRIVED ALIVE AT THE MOUNT AND SUFFERED AS MUCH PAIN AS POSSIBLE.
CRUCIFIXION IS NOT ABOUT BLEEDING TO DEATH OR EXPOSURE...
...I LEARNED THAT BY POSITIONING SOMEONE WITH THEIR ARMS OUTSTRETCHED AND HIGHER THAN THE REST OF THE BODY, IT SQUEEZES ALL THE INTERNAL ORGANS, MAKES IT ALMOST IMPOSSIBLE FOR THE LUNGS TO EXPAND...

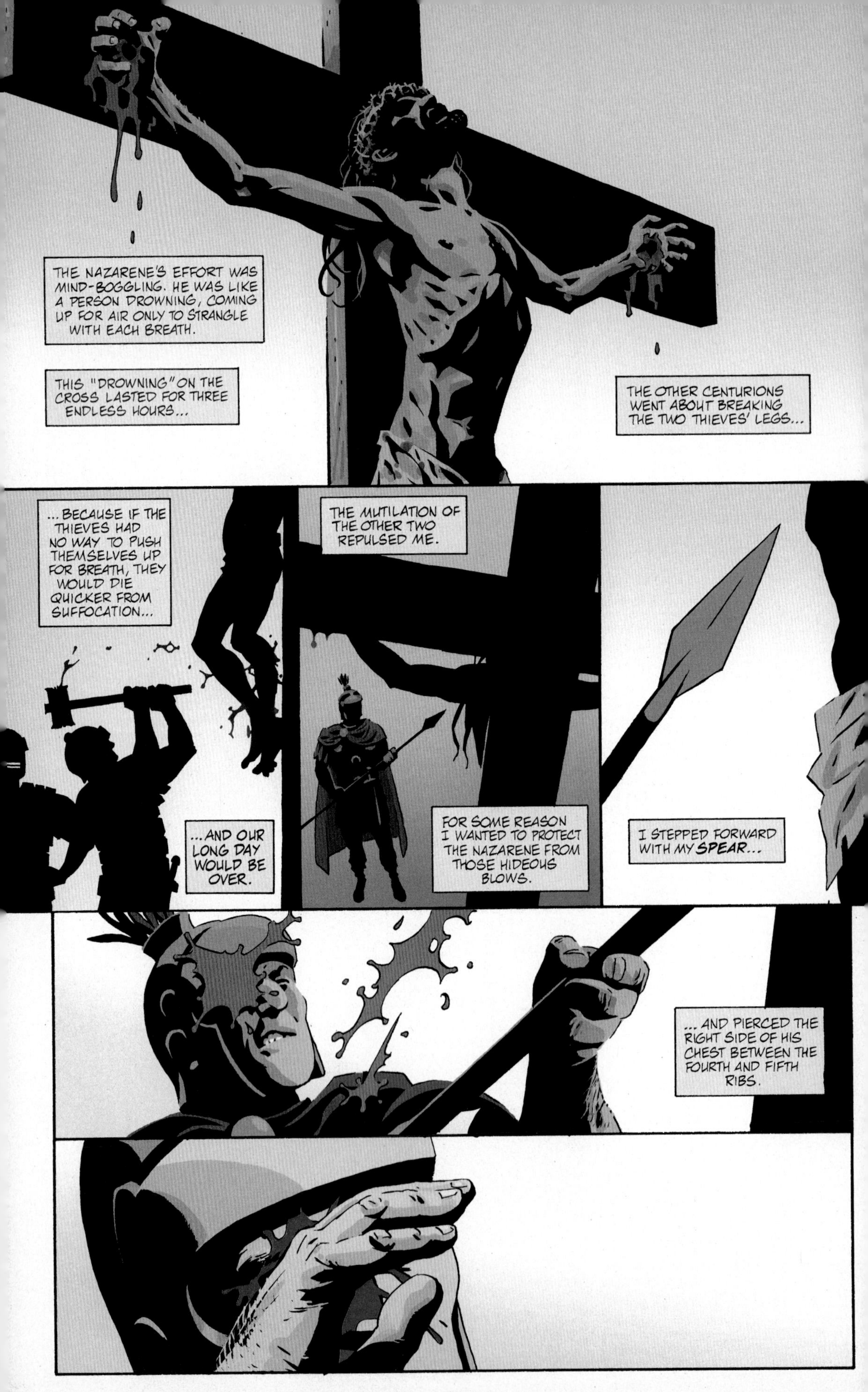
THE NAZARENE'S EFFORT WAS MIND-BOGGLING. HE WAS LIKE A PERSON DROWNING, COMING UP FOR AIR ONLY TO STRANGLE WITH EACH BREATH.
THIS "DROWNING" ON THE CROSS LASTED FOR THREE ENDLESS HOURS...
THE OTHER CENTURIONS WENT ABOUT BREAKING THE TWO THIEVES' LEGS...
...BECAUSE IF THE THIEVES HAD NO WAY TO PUSH THEMSELVES UP FOR BREATH, THEY WOULD DIE QUICKER FROM SUFFOCATION...
...AND OUR LONG DAY WOULD BE OVER.
THE MUTILATION OF THE OTHER TWO REPULSED ME.
FOR SOME REASON I WANTED TO PROTECT THE NAZARENE FROM THOSE HIDEOUS BLOWS.
I STEPPED FORWARD WITH MY SPEAR...
...AND PIERCED THE RIGHT SIDE OF HIS CHEST BETWEEN THE FOURTH AND FIFTH RIBS.

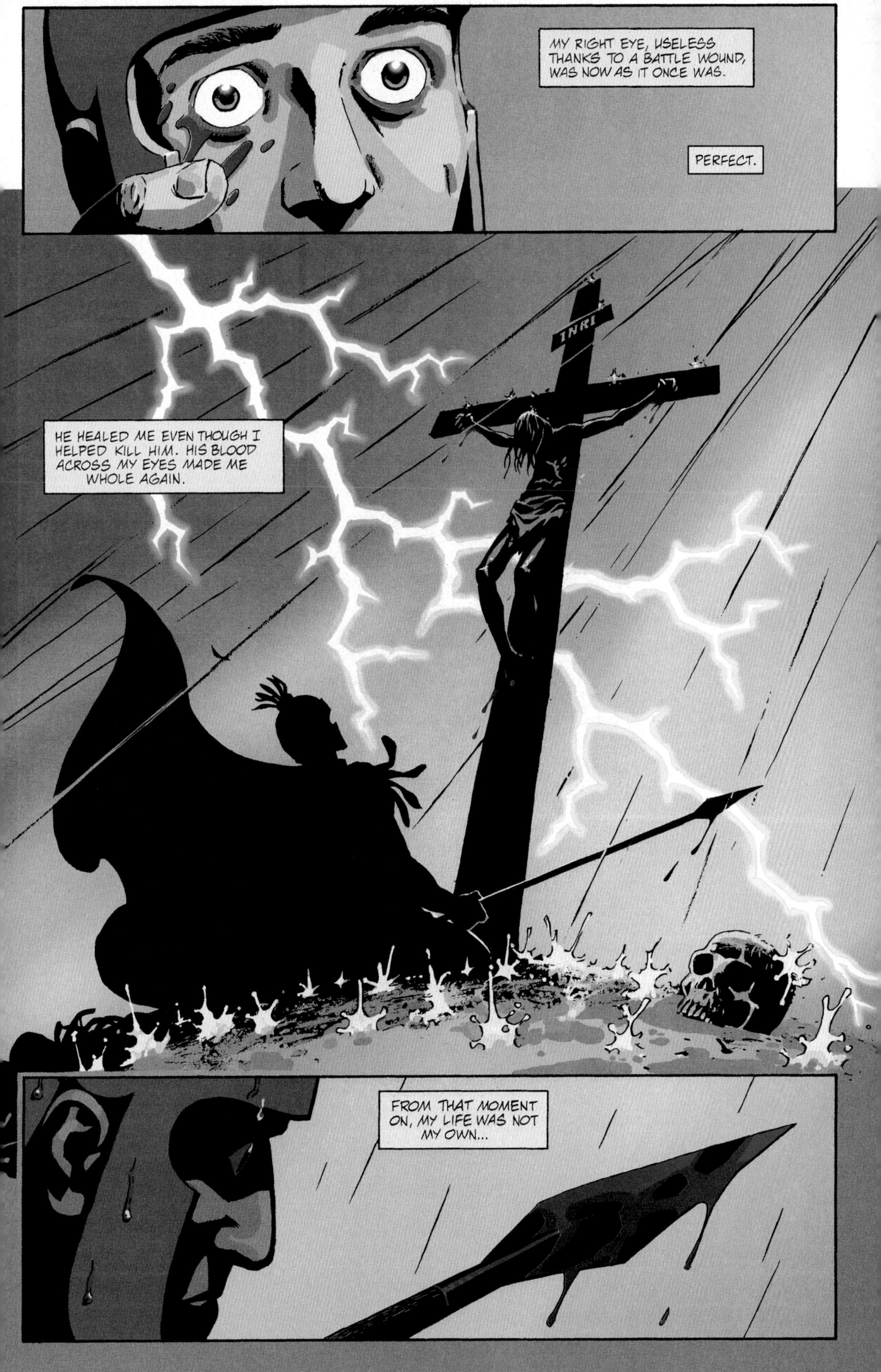
MY RIGHT EYE, USELESS THANKS TO A BATTLE WOUND, WAS NOW AS IT ONCE WAS.
PERFECT.
INRI
HE HEALED ME EVEN THOUGH I HELPED KILL HIM. HIS BLOOD ACROSS MY EYES MADE ME WHOLE AGAIN.
FROM THAT MOMENT ON, MY LIFE WAS NOT MY OWN...

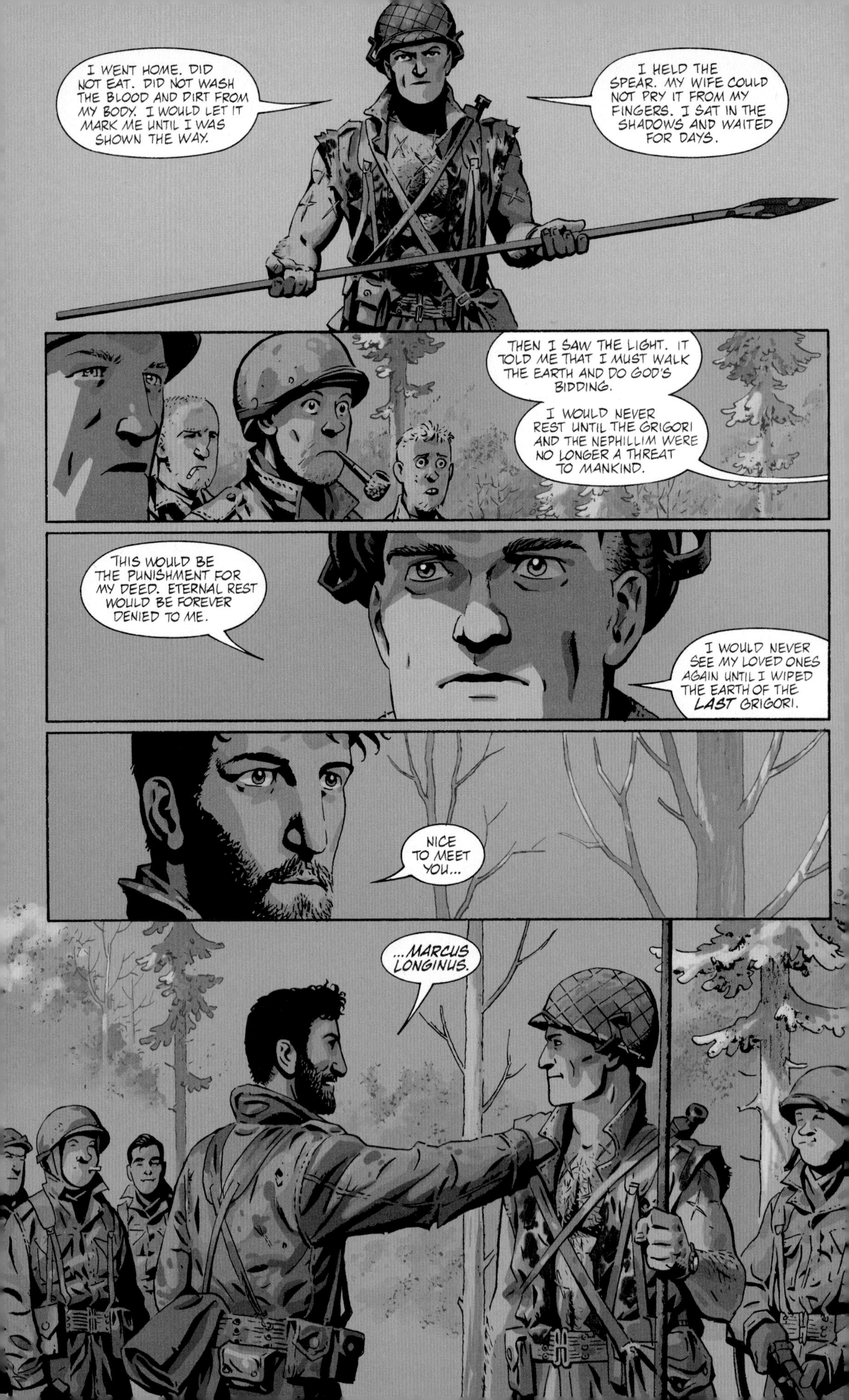
I WENT HOME. DID NOT EAT. DID NOT WASH THE BLOOD AND DIRT FROM MY BODY. I WOULD LET IT MARK ME UNTIL I WAS SHOWN THE WAY.
I HELD THE SPEAR. MY WIFE COULD NOT PRY IT FROM MY FINGERS. I SAT IN THE SHADOWS AND WAITED FOR DAYS.
THEN I SAW THE LIGHT. IT TOLD ME THAT I MUST WALK THE EARTH AND DO GOD'S BIDDING.
I WOULD NEVER REST UNTIL THE GRIGORI AND THE NEPHILLIM WERE NO LONGER A THREAT TO MANKIND.
THIS WOULD BE THE PUNISHMENT FOR MY DEED. ETERNAL REST WOULD BE FOREVER DENIED TO ME.
I WOULD NEVER SEE MY LOVED ONES AGAIN UNTIL I WIPED THE EARTH OF THE *LAST* GRIGORI.
NICE TO MEET YOU...
...*MARCUS LONGINUS.*

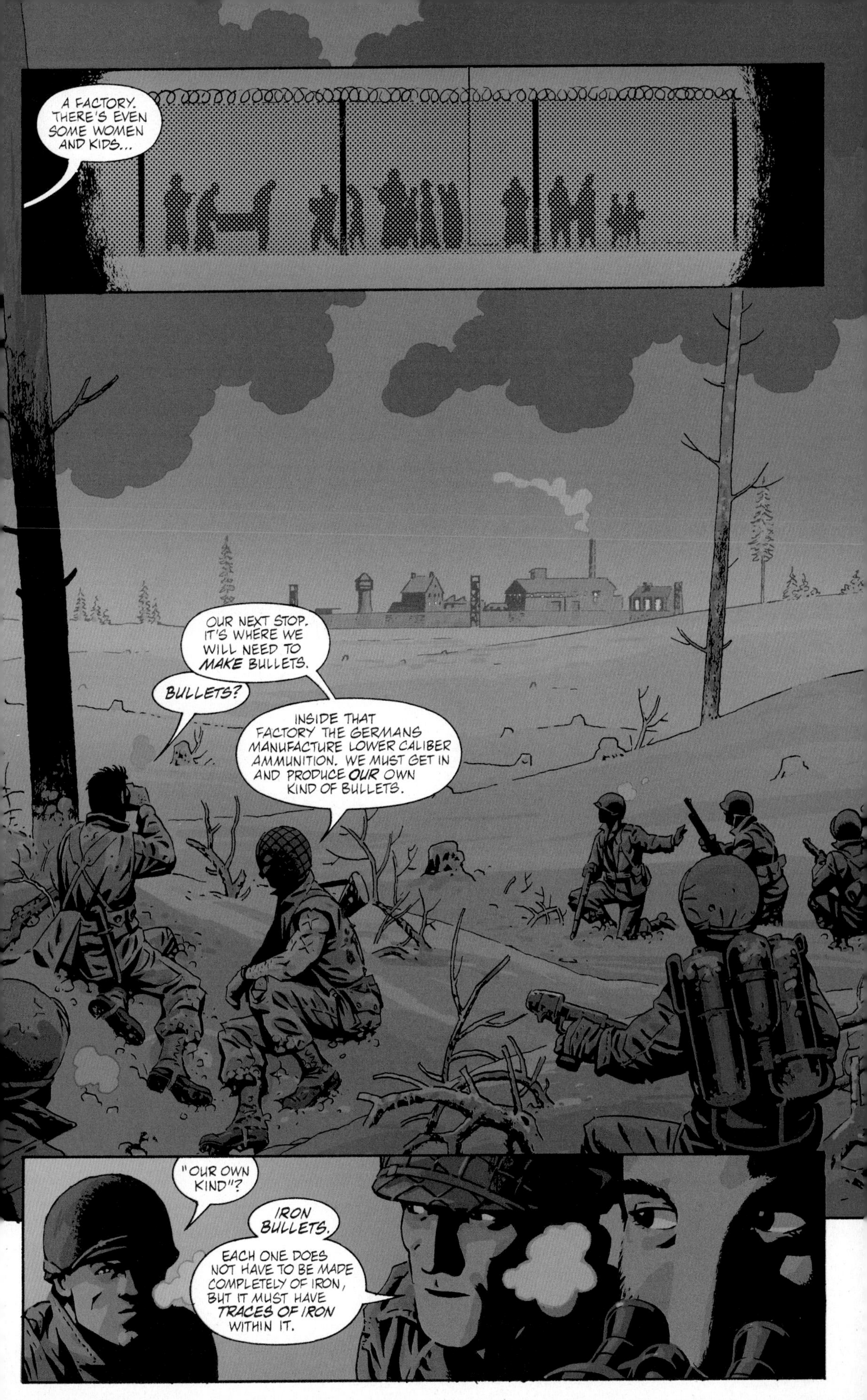
A FACTORY. THERE'S EVEN SOME WOMEN AND KIDS...
OUR NEXT STOP. IT'S WHERE WE WILL NEED TO MAKE BULLETS.
BULLETS?
INSIDE THAT FACTORY THE GERMANS MANUFACTURE LOWER CALIBER AMMUNITION. WE MUST GET IN AND PRODUCE OUR OWN KIND OF BULLETS.
"OUR OWN KIND"?
IRON BULLETS.
EACH ONE DOES NOT HAVE TO BE MADE COMPLETELY OF IRON, BUT IT MUST HAVE TRACES OF IRON WITHIN IT.

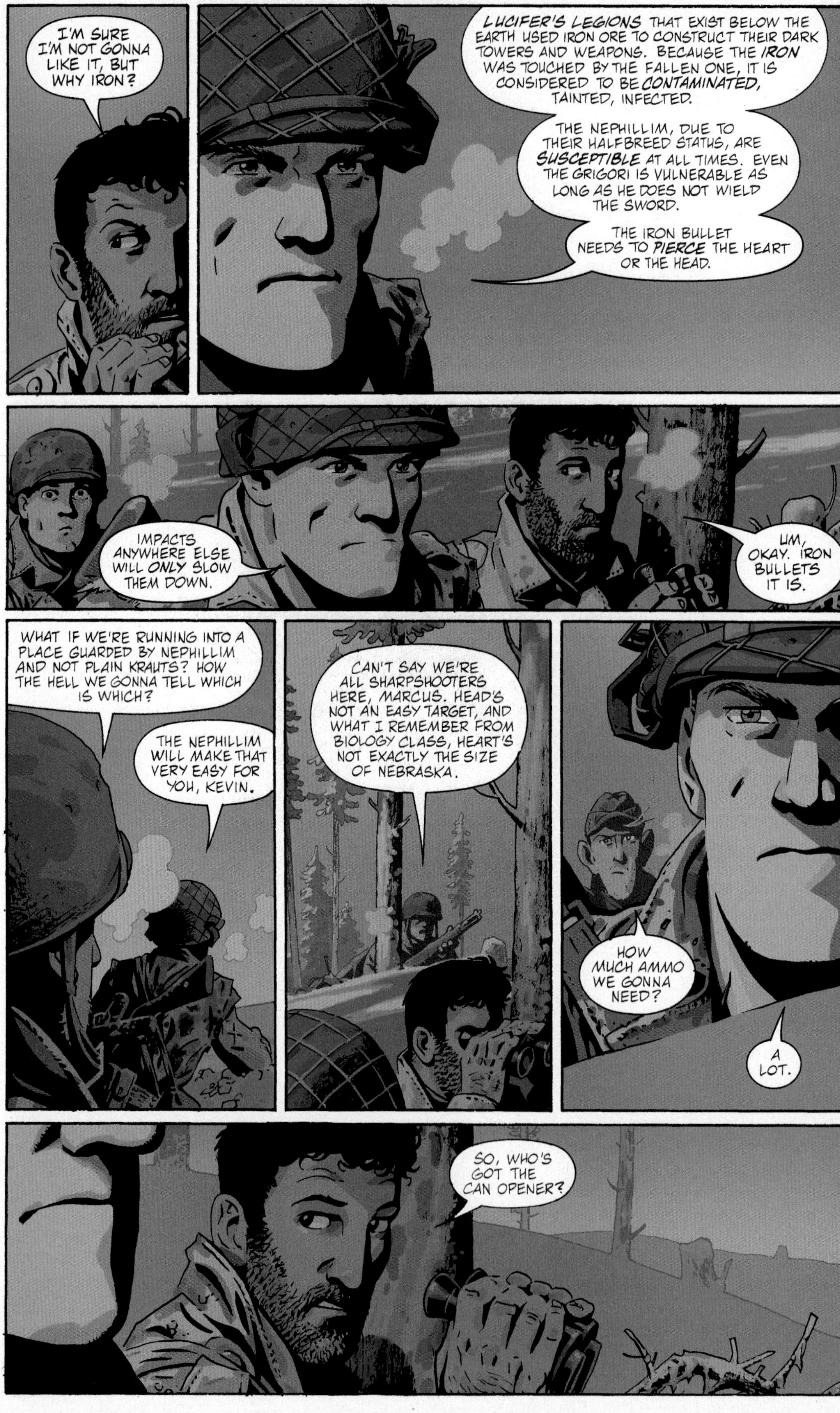
I'M SURE I'M NOT GONNA LIKE IT, BUT WHY IRON?
LUCIFER'S LEGIONS THAT EXIST BELOW THE EARTH USED IRON ORE TO CONSTRUCT THEIR DARK TOWERS AND WEAPONS. BECAUSE THE IRON WAS TOUCHED BY THE FALLEN ONE, IT IS CONSIDERED TO BE CONTAMINATED, TAINTED, INFECTED.
THE NEPHILLIM, DUE TO THEIR HALFBREED STATUS, ARE SUSCEPTIBLE AT ALL TIMES. EVEN THE GRIGORI IS VULNERABLE AS LONG AS HE DOES NOT WIELD THE SWORD.
THE IRON BULLET NEEDS TO PIERCE THE HEART OR THE HEAD.
IMPACTS ANYWHERE ELSE WILL ONLY SLOW THEM DOWN.
UM, OKAY. IRON BULLETS IT IS.
WHAT IF WE'RE RUNNING INTO A PLACE GUARDED BY NEPHILLIM AND NOT PLAIN KRAUTS? HOW THE HELL WE GONNA TELL WHICH IS WHICH?
THE NEPHILLIM WILL MAKE THAT VERY EASY FOR YOU, KEVIN.
CAN'T SAY WE'RE ALL SHARPSHOOTERS HERE, MARCUS. HEAD'S NOT AN EASY TARGET, AND WHAT I REMEMBER FROM BIOLOGY CLASS, HEART'S NOT EXACTLY THE SIZE OF NEBRASKA.
HOW MUCH AMMO WE GONNA NEED?
A LOT.
SO, WHO'S GOT THE CAN OPENER?

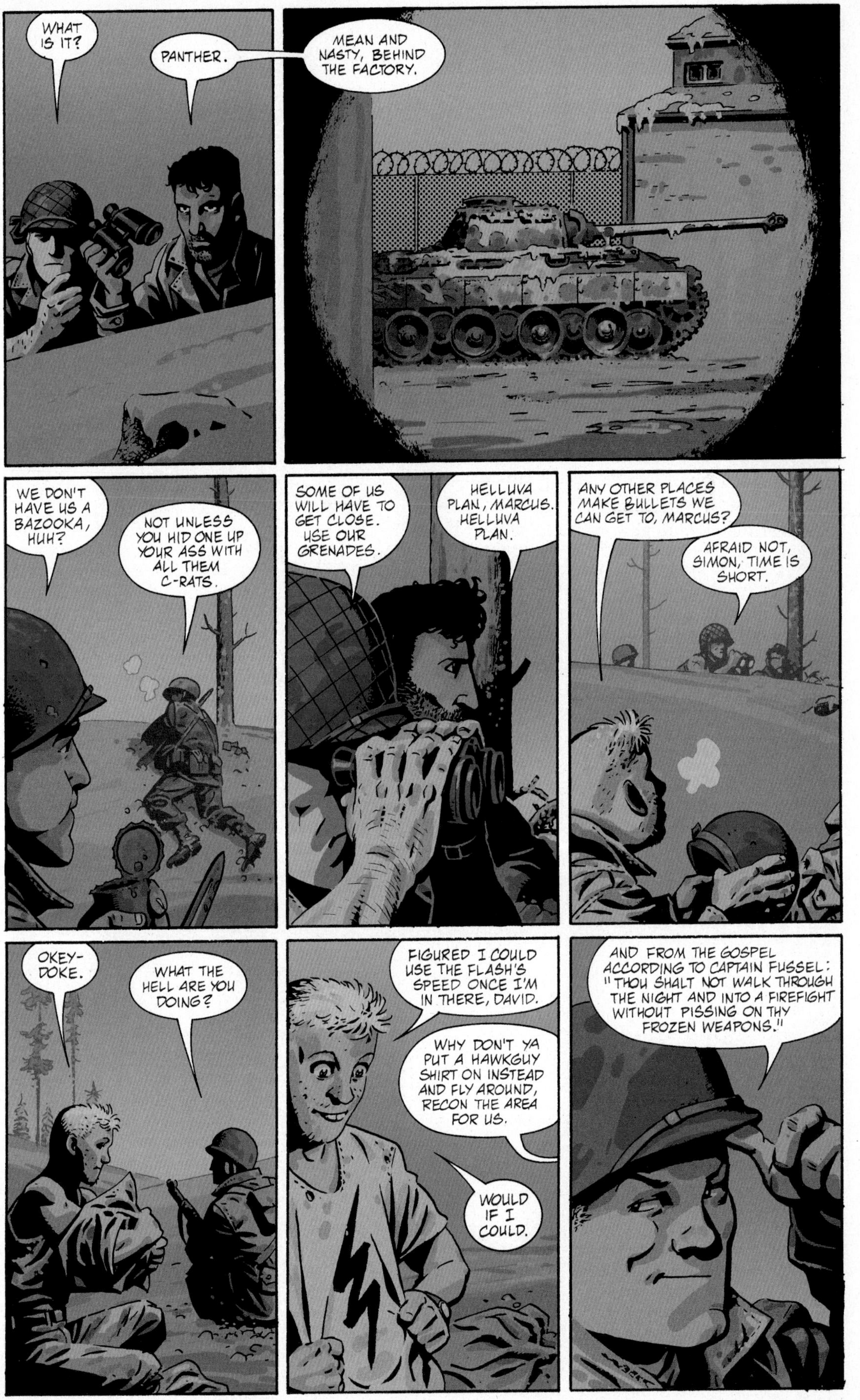
WHAT IS IT?
PANTHER.
MEAN AND NASTY, BEHIND THE FACTORY.
WE DON'T HAVE US A BAZOOKA, HUH?
NOT UNLESS YOU HID ONE UP YOUR ASS WITH ALL THEM C-RATS.
SOME OF US WILL HAVE TO GET CLOSE. USE OUR GRENADES.
HELLUVA PLAN, MARCUS. HELLUVA PLAN.
ANY OTHER PLACES MAKE BULLETS WE CAN GET TO, MARCUS?
AFRAID NOT, SIMON, TIME IS SHORT.
OKEY-DOKE.
WHAT THE HELL ARE YOU DOING?
FIGURED I COULD USE THE FLASH'S SPEED ONCE I'M IN THERE, DAVID.
WHY DON'T YA PUT A HAWKGUY SHIRT ON INSTEAD AND FLY AROUND, RECON THE AREA FOR US.
WOULD IF I COULD.
AND FROM THE GOSPEL ACCORDING TO CAPTAIN FUSSEL: "THOU SHALT NOT WALK THROUGH THE NIGHT AND INTO A FIREFIGHT WITHOUT PISSING ON THY FROZEN WEAPONS."

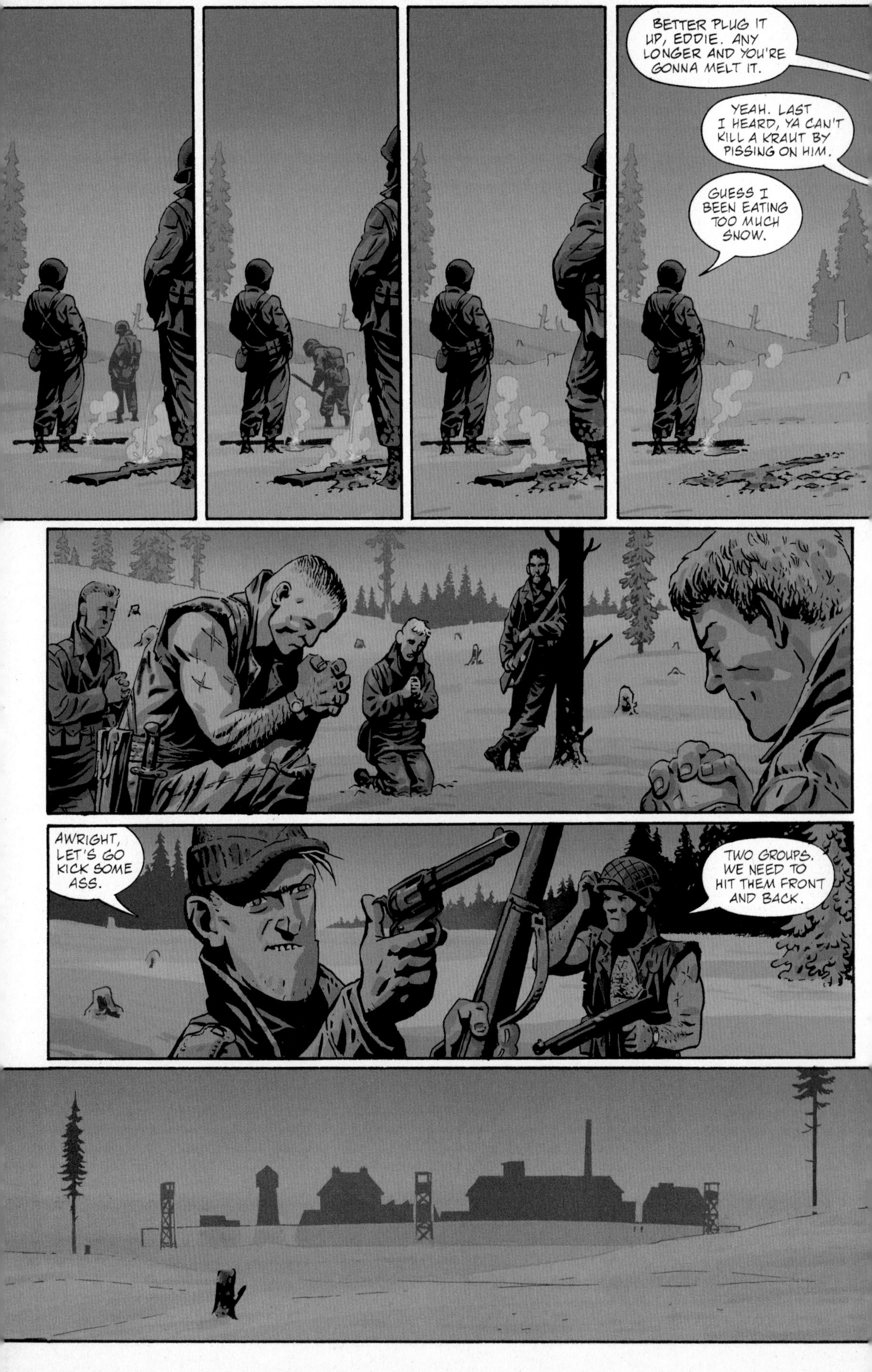
BETTER PLUG IT UP, EDDIE. ANY LONGER AND YOU'RE GONNA MELT IT.
YEAH. LAST I HEARD, YA CAN'T KILL A KRAUT BY PISSING ON HIM.
GUESS I BEEN EATING TOO MUCH SNOW.
AWRIGHT, LET'S GO KICK SOME ASS.
TWO GROUPS. WE NEED TO HIT THEM FRONT AND BACK.

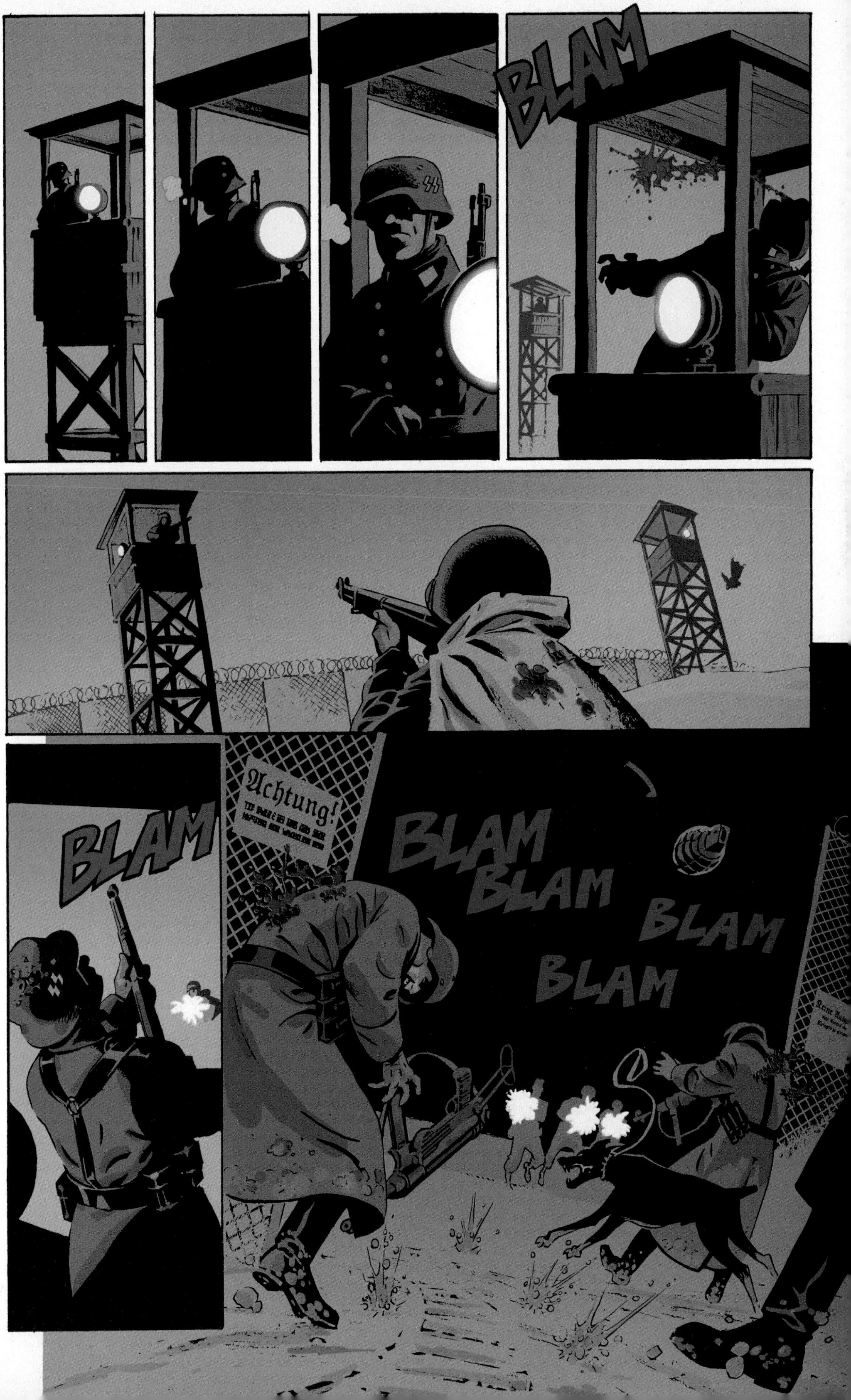
BLAM
BLAM
Achtung!
BLAM
BLAM
BLAM
BLAM

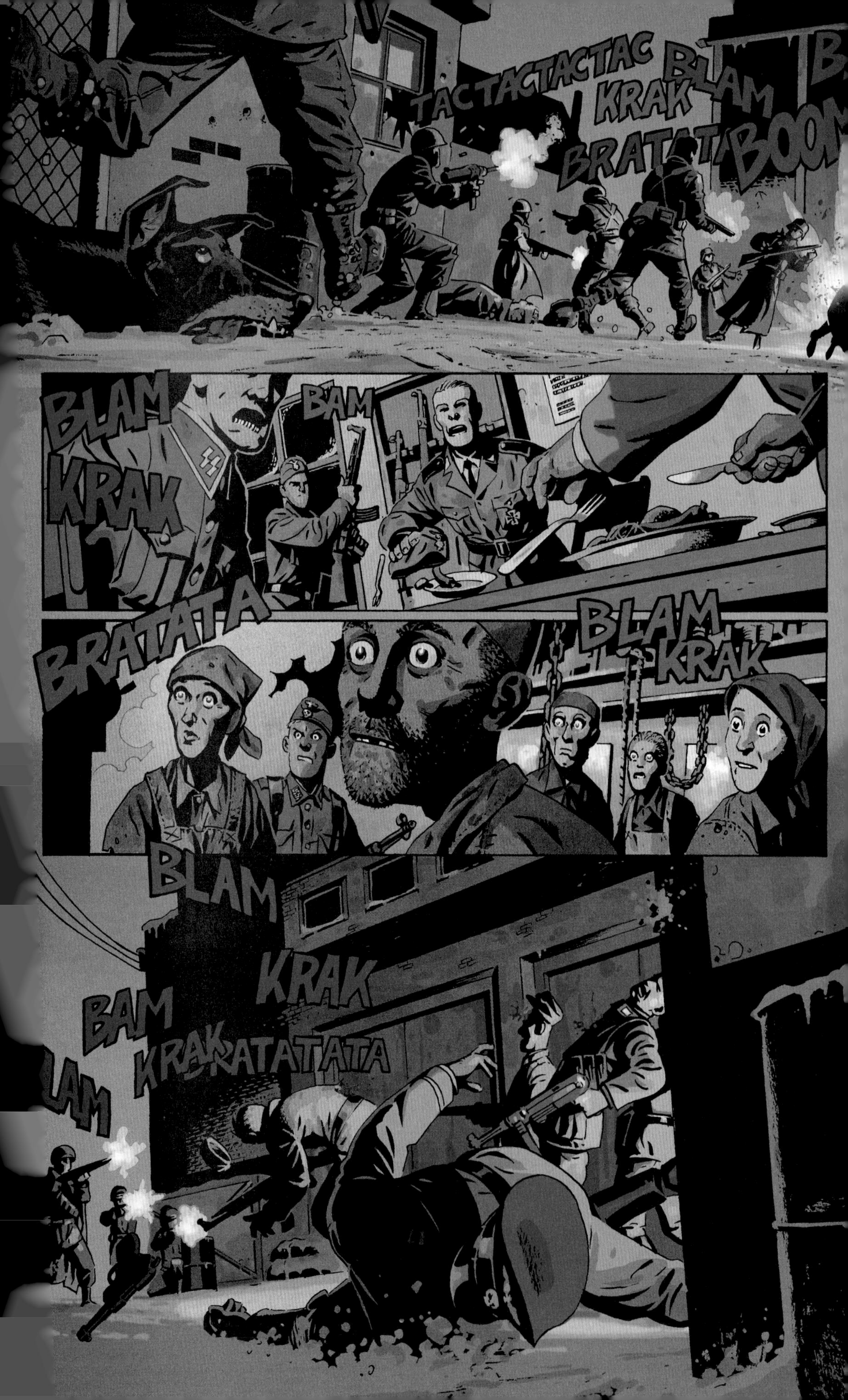
TACTACTACTAC
BLAM
KRAK
BLAM
BRATAT
BOOM
BLAM
BAM
KRAK
BRATATA
BLAM
KRAK
BLAM
KRAK
BAM
KRAKATATATA
LAM

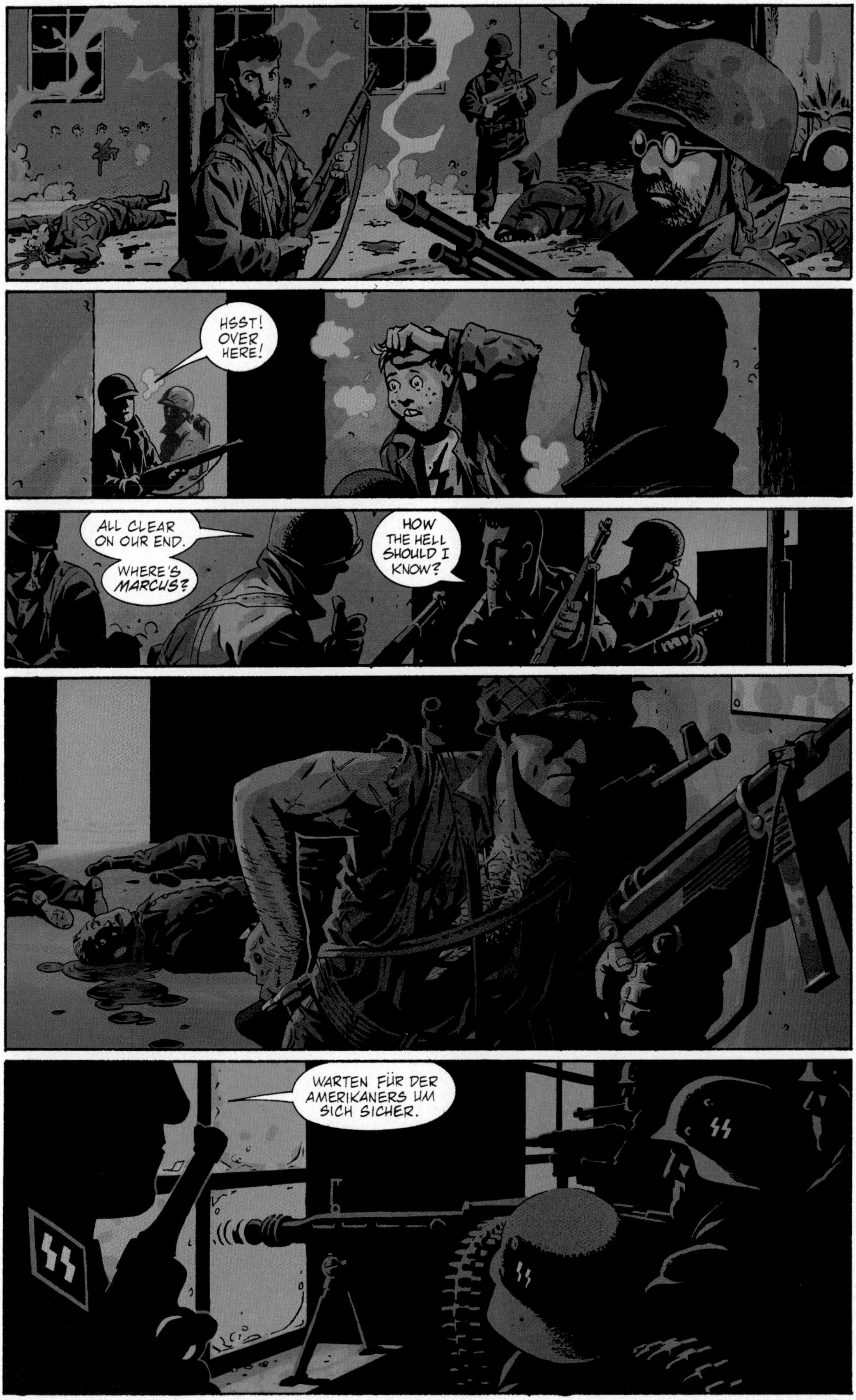
HSST! OVER HERE!
ALL CLEAR ON OUR END.
WHERE'S *MARCUS*?
HOW THE HELL SHOULD I KNOW?
WARTEN FÜR DER AMERIKANERS UM SICH SICHER.

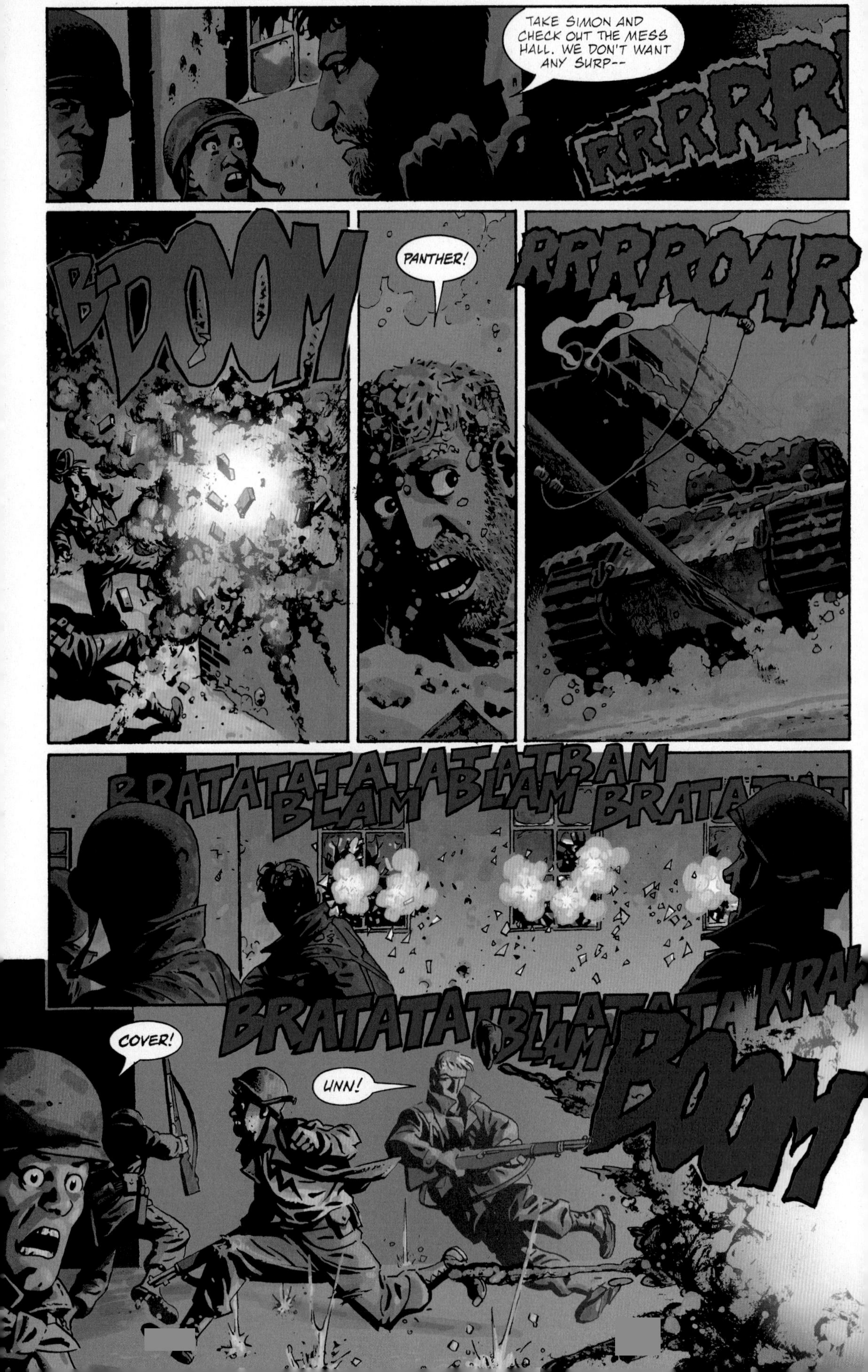
TAKE SIMON AND CHECK OUT THE MESS HALL. WE DON'T WANT ANY SURP--
RRRRR
B-DOOM
PANTHER!
RRRROAR
BRATATATATATATBAM
BLAM BLAM
BRATATAT
BRATATATATATATA KRAK
BLAM
COVER!
UNN!
BOOM

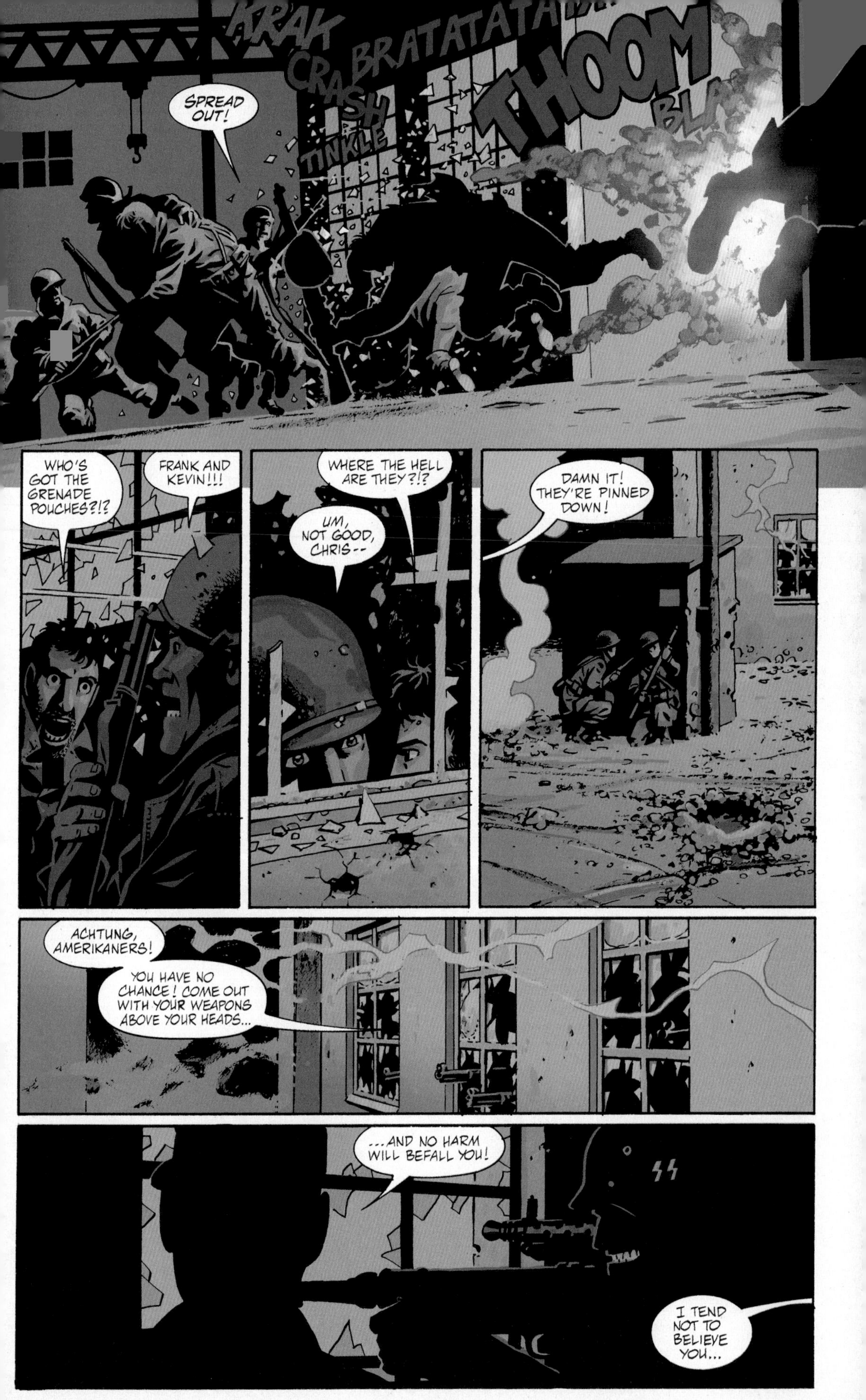
KRAK
CRASH
BRATATATATA
THOOM
BLA
TINKLE
SPREAD OUT!
WHO'S GOT THE GRENADE POUCHES?!?
FRANK AND KEVIN!!!
WHERE THE HELL ARE THEY?!?
UM, NOT GOOD, CHRIS--
DAMN IT! THEY'RE PINNED DOWN!
ACHTUNG, AMERIKANERS!
YOU HAVE NO CHANCE! COME OUT WITH YOUR WEAPONS ABOVE YOUR HEADS...
...AND NO HARM WILL BEFALL YOU!
I TEND NOT TO BELIEVE YOU...

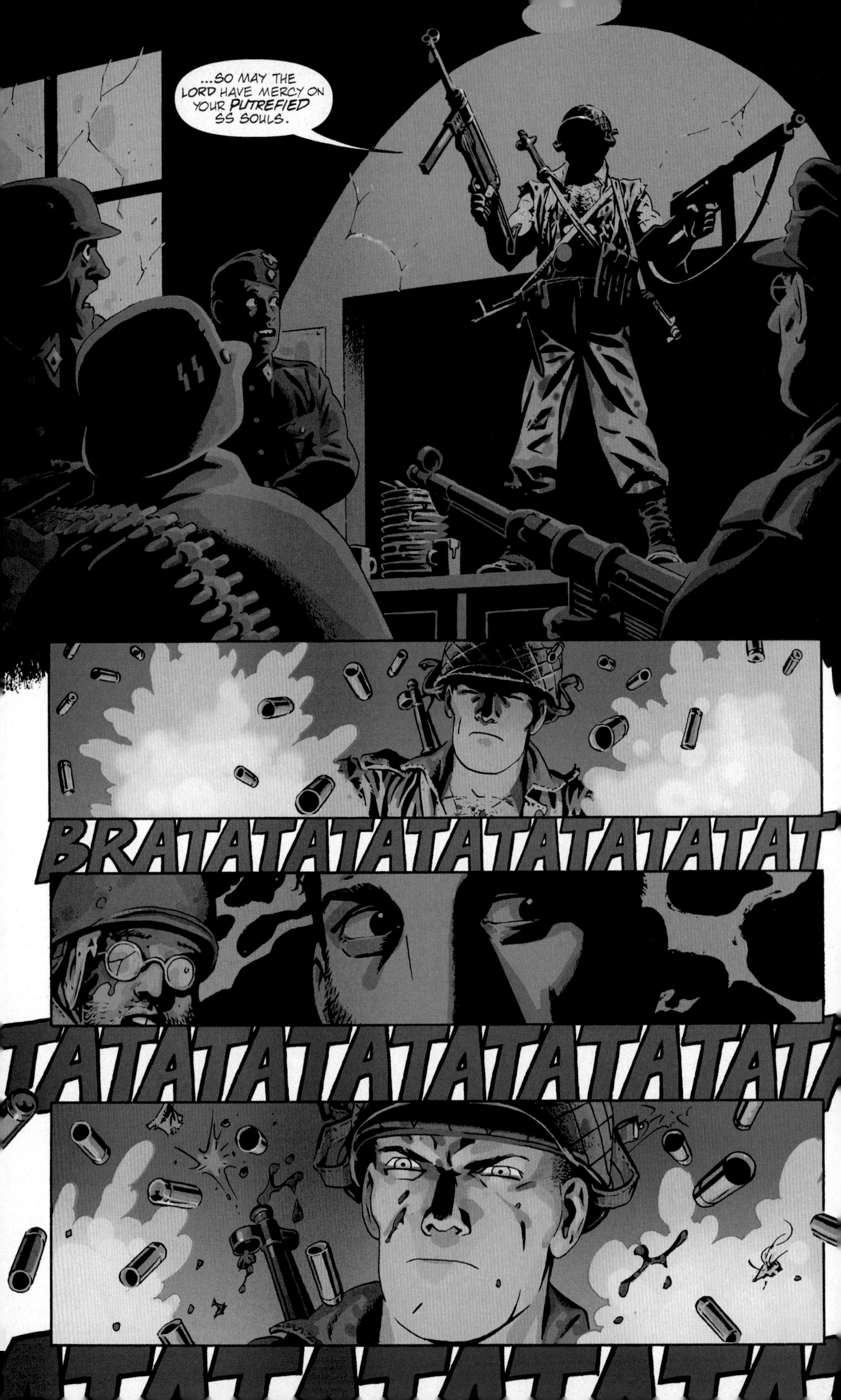
...SO MAY THE LORD HAVE MERCY ON YOUR PUTREFIED SS SOULS.
BRATATATATATATATATATATAT
TATATATATATATATATATATAT
TATATATATATATAT

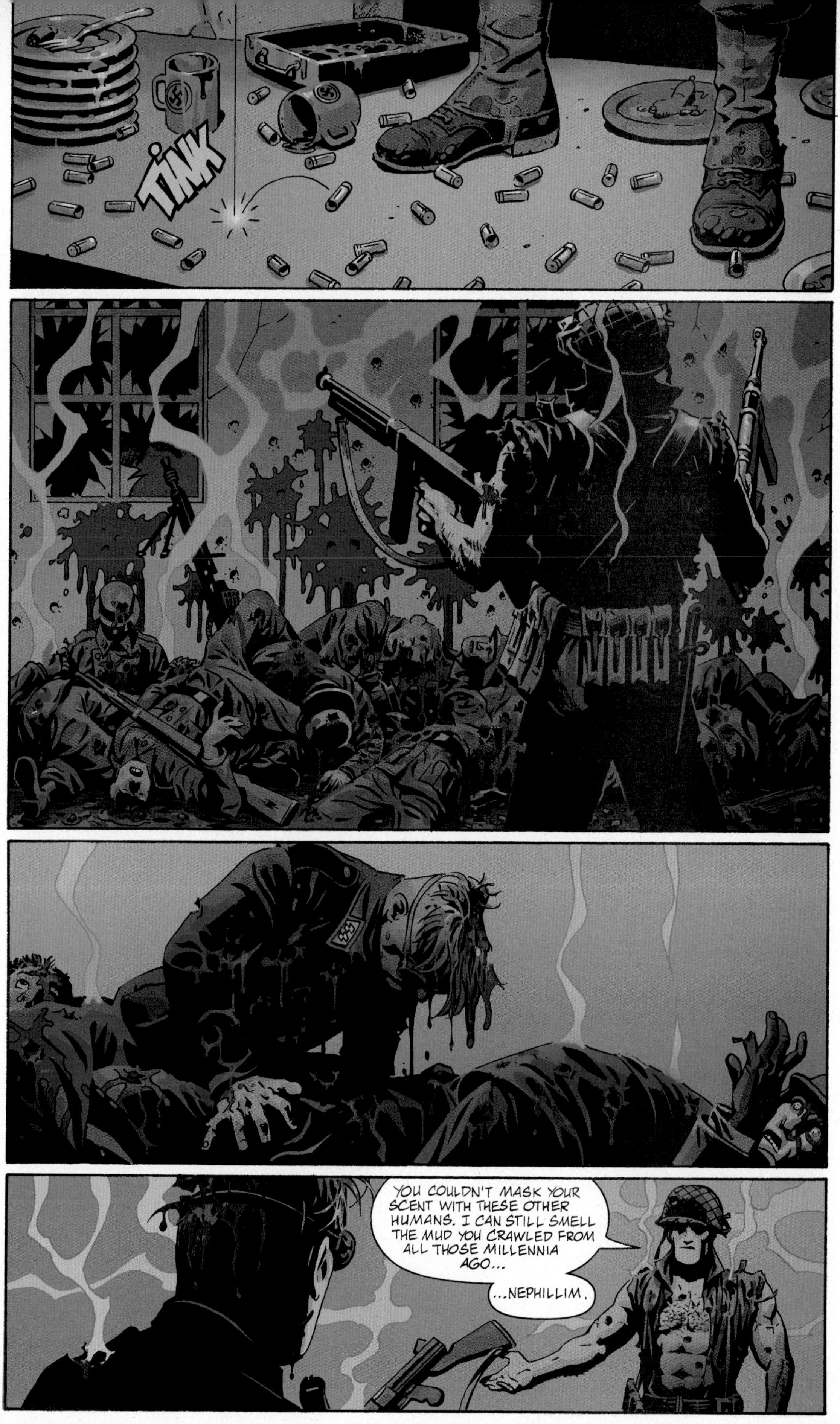
TINK
YOU COULDN'T MASK YOUR SCENT WITH THESE OTHER HUMANS. I CAN STILL SMELL THE MUD YOU CRAWLED FROM ALL THOSE MILLENNIA AGO...
...NEPHILLIM.

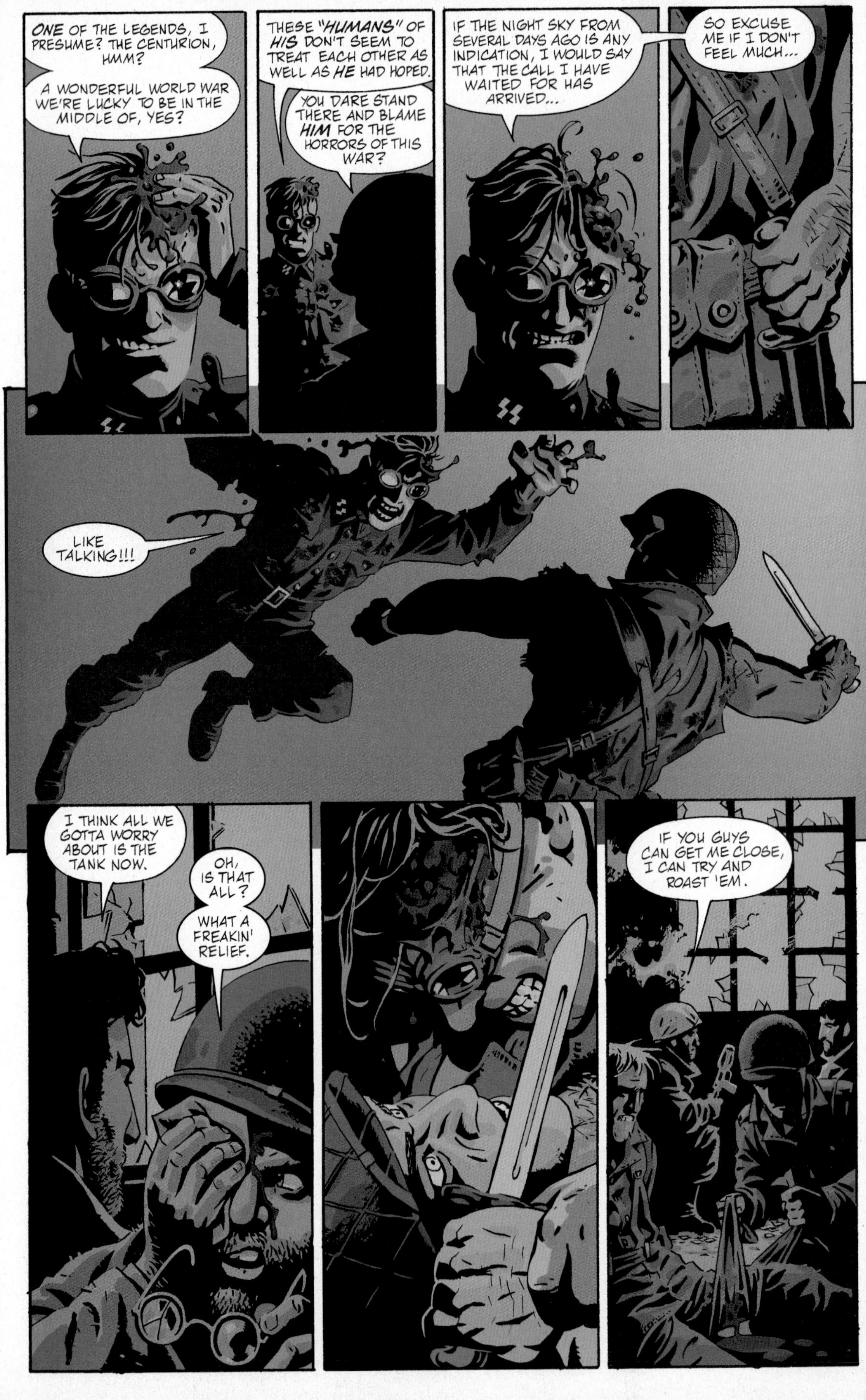
ONE OF THE LEGENDS, I PRESUME? THE CENTURION, HMM?
A WONDERFUL WORLD WAR WE'RE LUCKY TO BE IN THE MIDDLE OF, YES?
THESE "HUMANS" OF HIS DON'T SEEM TO TREAT EACH OTHER AS WELL AS HE HAD HOPED.
YOU DARE STAND THERE AND BLAME HIM FOR THE HORRORS OF THIS WAR?
IF THE NIGHT SKY FROM SEVERAL DAYS AGO IS ANY INDICATION, I WOULD SAY THAT THE CALL I HAVE WAITED FOR HAS ARRIVED...
SO EXCUSE ME IF I DON'T FEEL MUCH...
LIKE TALKING!!!
I THINK ALL WE GOTTA WORRY ABOUT IS THE TANK NOW.
OH, IS THAT ALL?
WHAT A FREAKIN' RELIEF.
IF YOU GUYS CAN GET ME CLOSE, I CAN TRY AND ROAST 'EM.

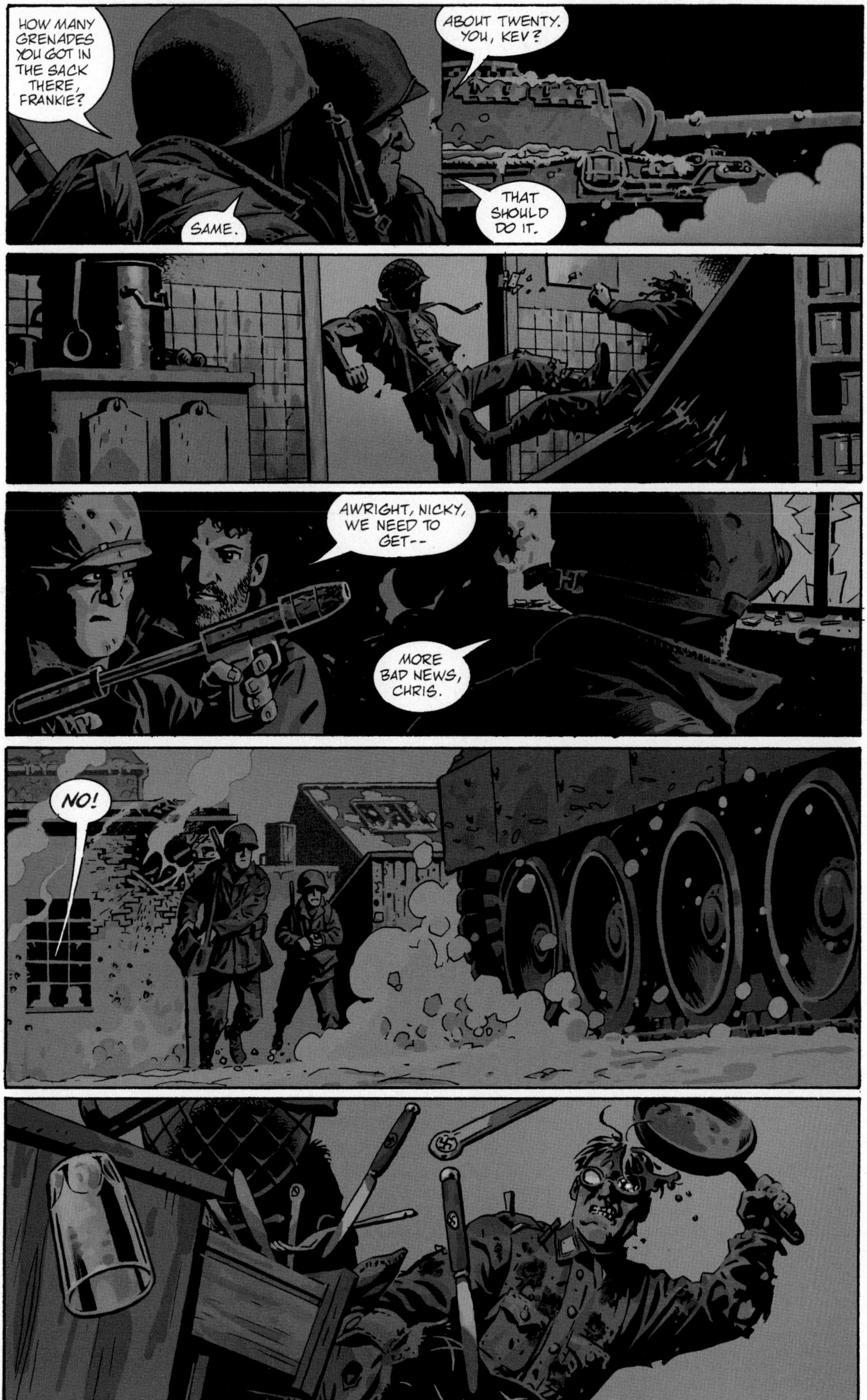
HOW MANY GRENADES YOU GOT IN THE SACK THERE, FRANKIE?
ABOUT TWENTY. YOU, KEV?
SAME.
THAT SHOULD DO IT.
AWRIGHT, NICKY, WE NEED TO GET--
MORE BAD NEWS, CHRIS.
NO!

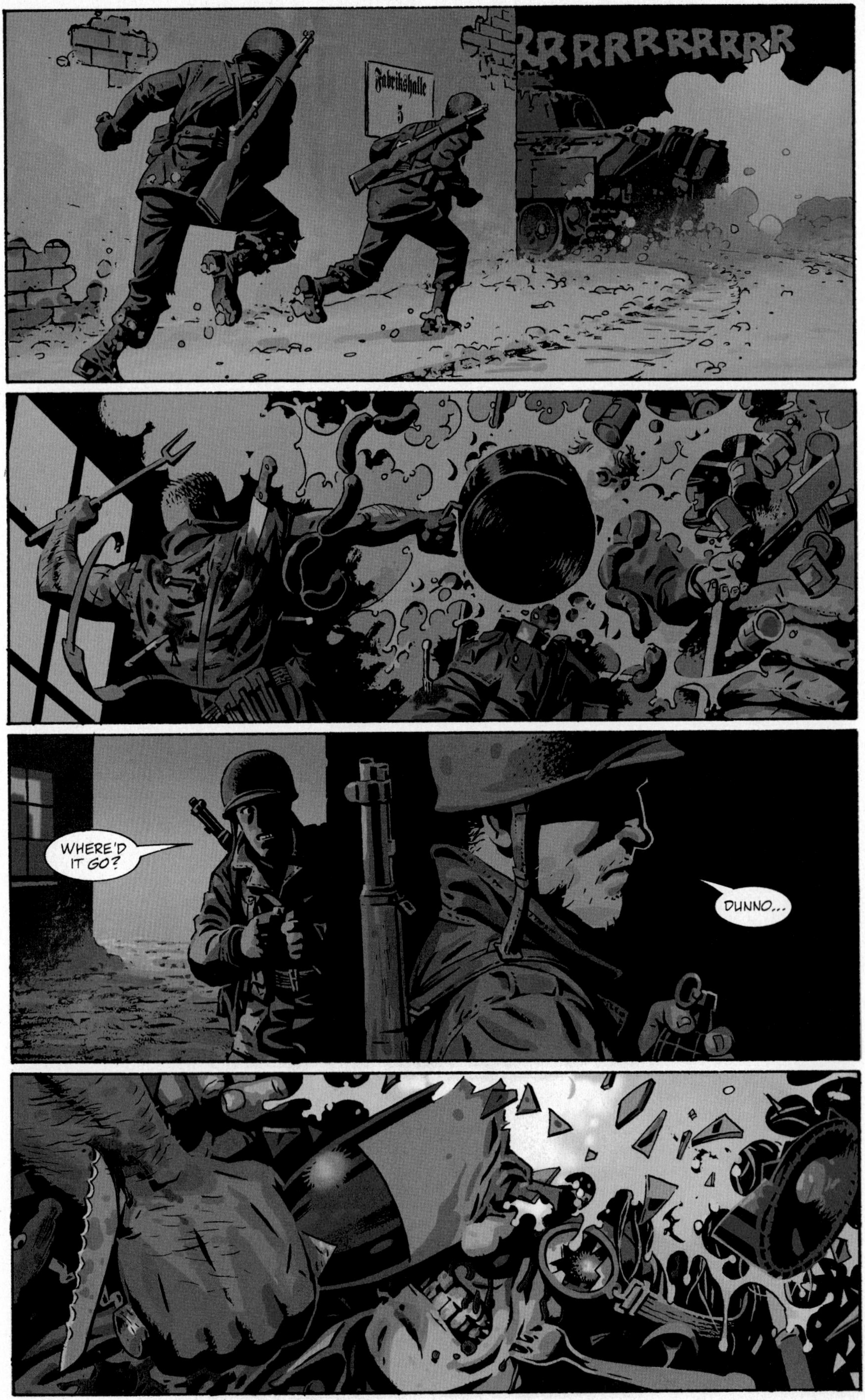
RRRRRRRRRRR
Fabrikshalle
5
WHERE'D IT GO?
DUNNO...

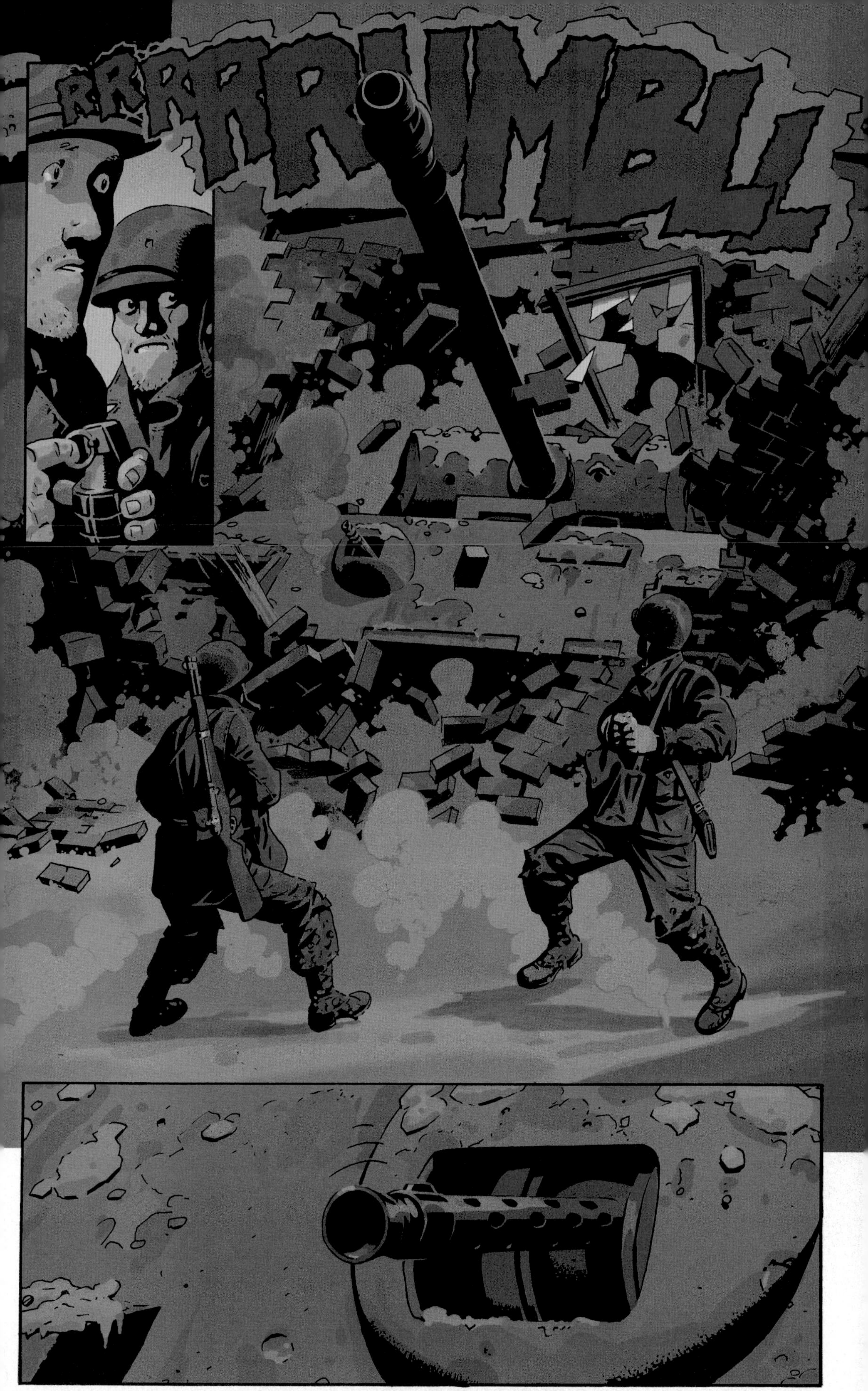
RRRRUMBLL

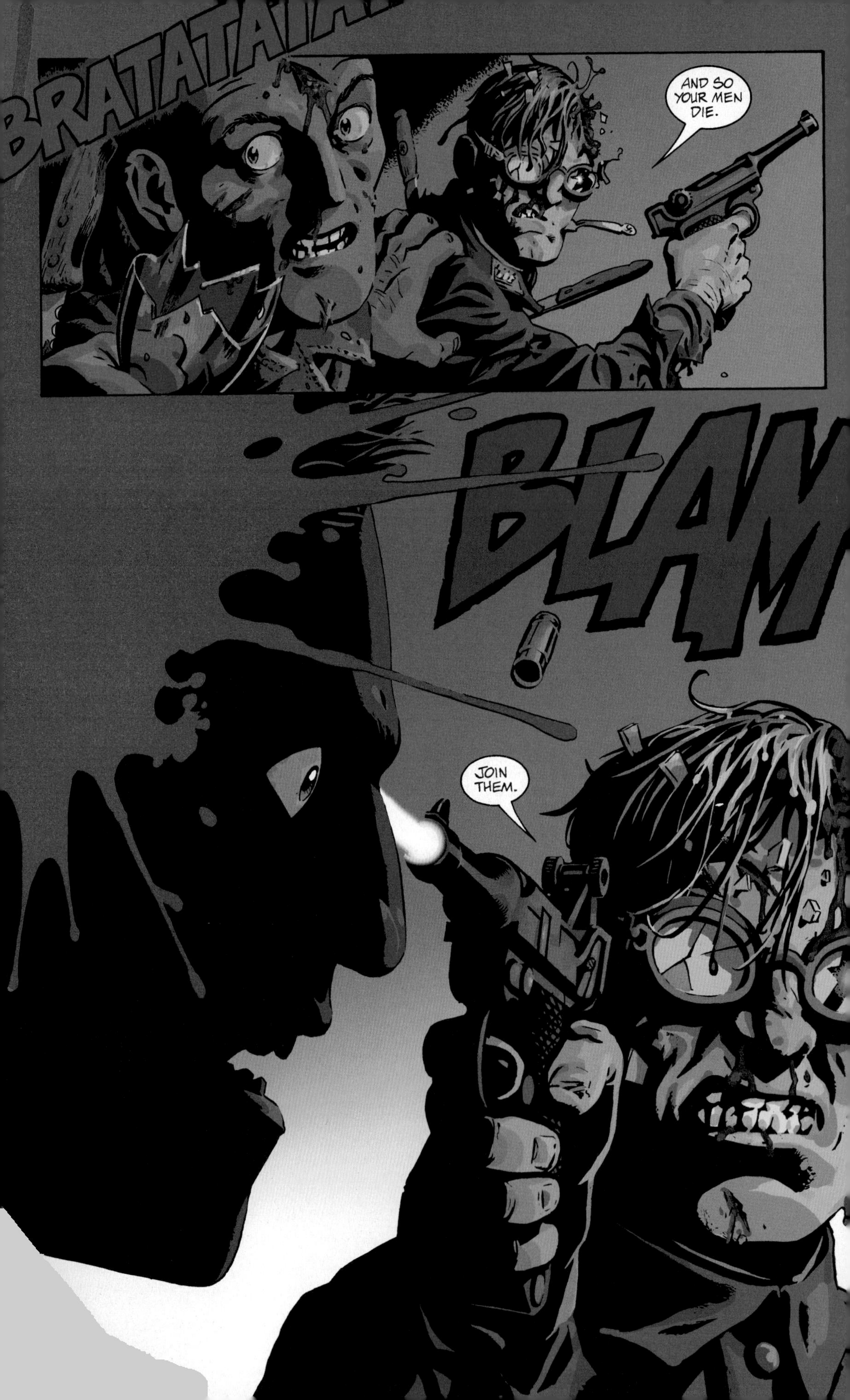
BRATATATA!
AND SO YOUR MEN DIE.
BLAM
JOIN THEM.

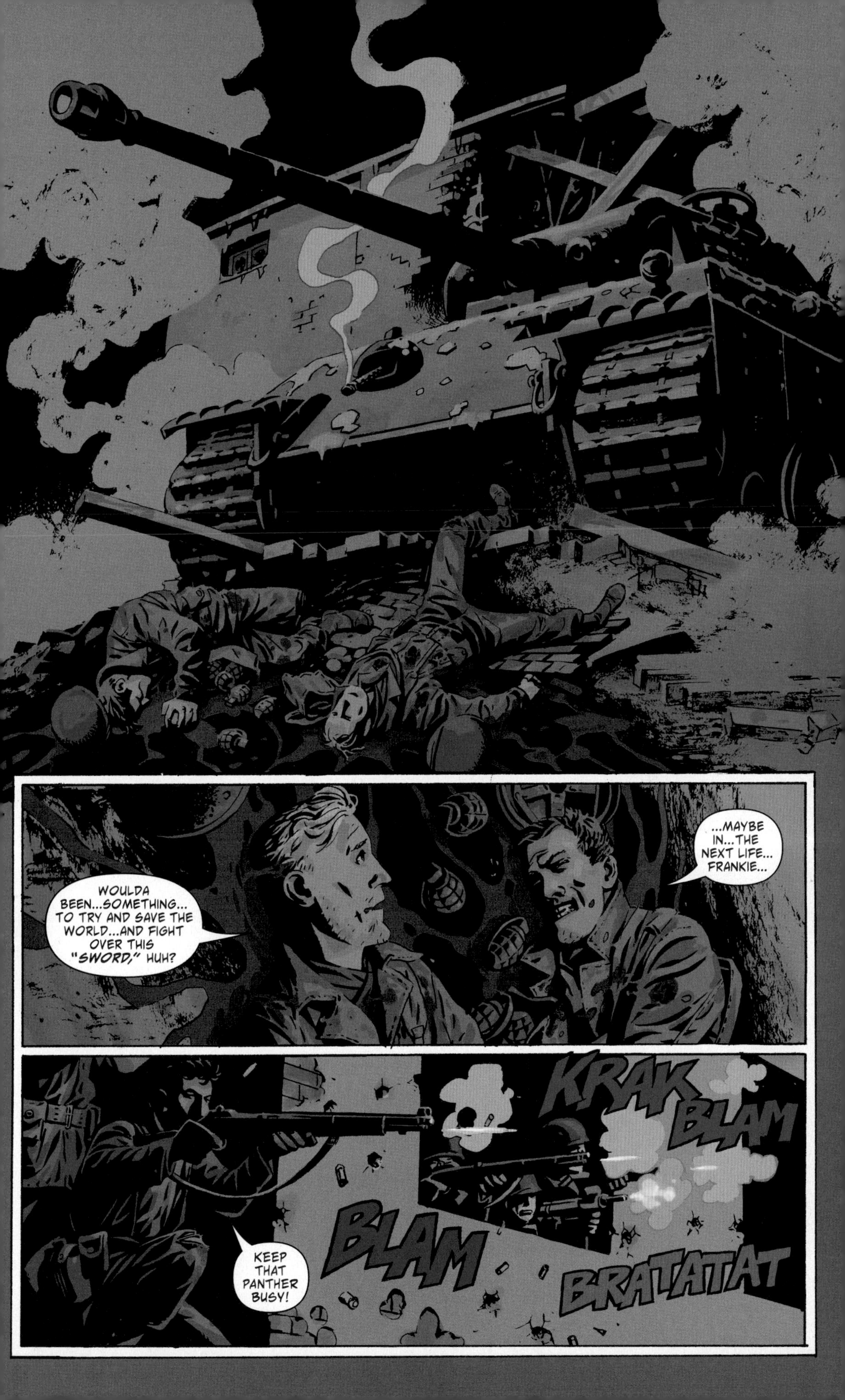
WOULDA BEEN...SOMETHING... TO TRY AND SAVE THE WORLD...AND FIGHT OVER THIS "SWORD," HUH?
...MAYBE IN...THE NEXT LIFE... FRANKIE...
KRAK
BLAM
BLAM
KEEP THAT PANTHER BUSY!
BRATATAT

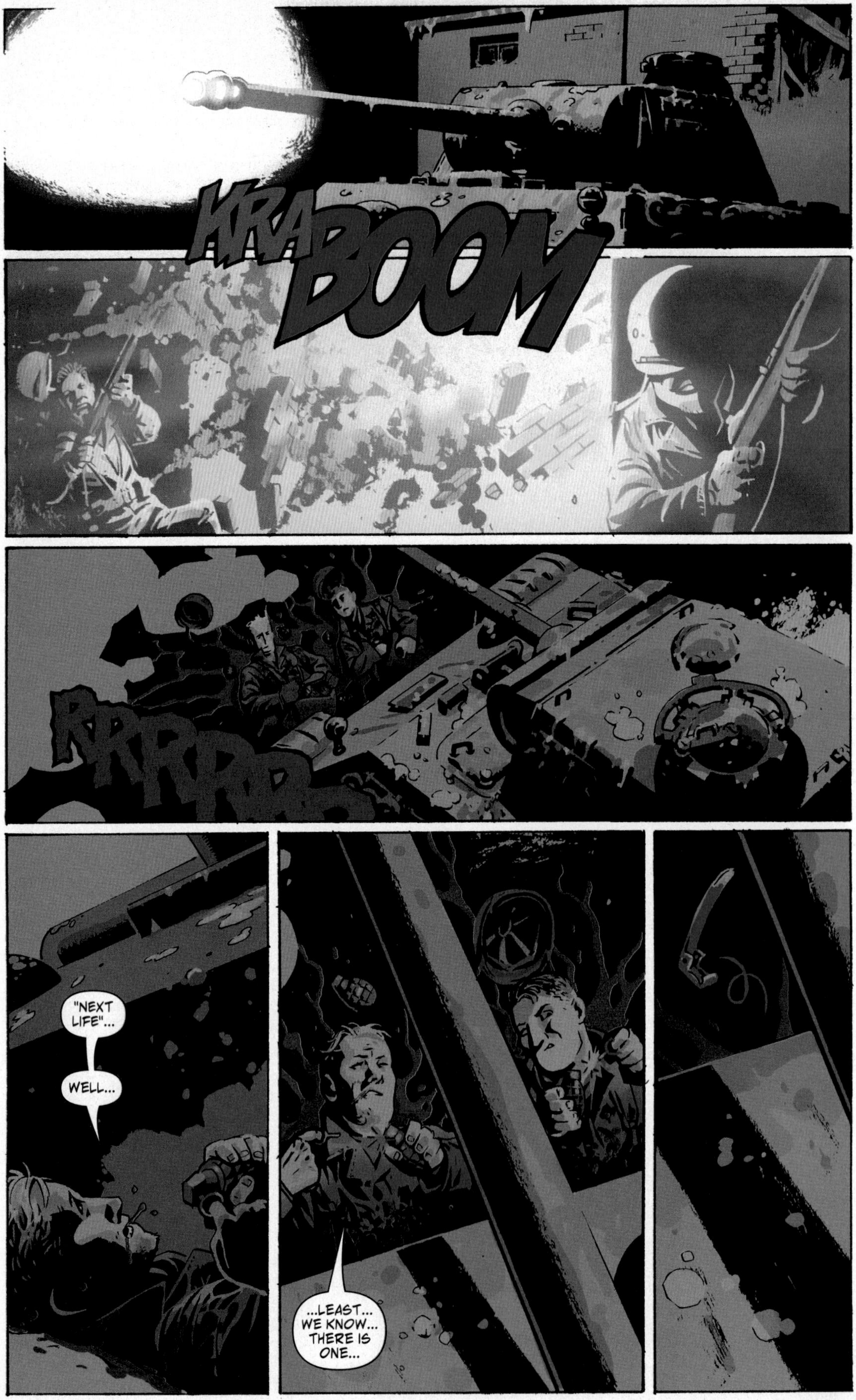
KRA
BOOM
RRRRR
"NEXT LIFE"...
WELL...
...LEAST... WE KNOW... THERE IS ONE...

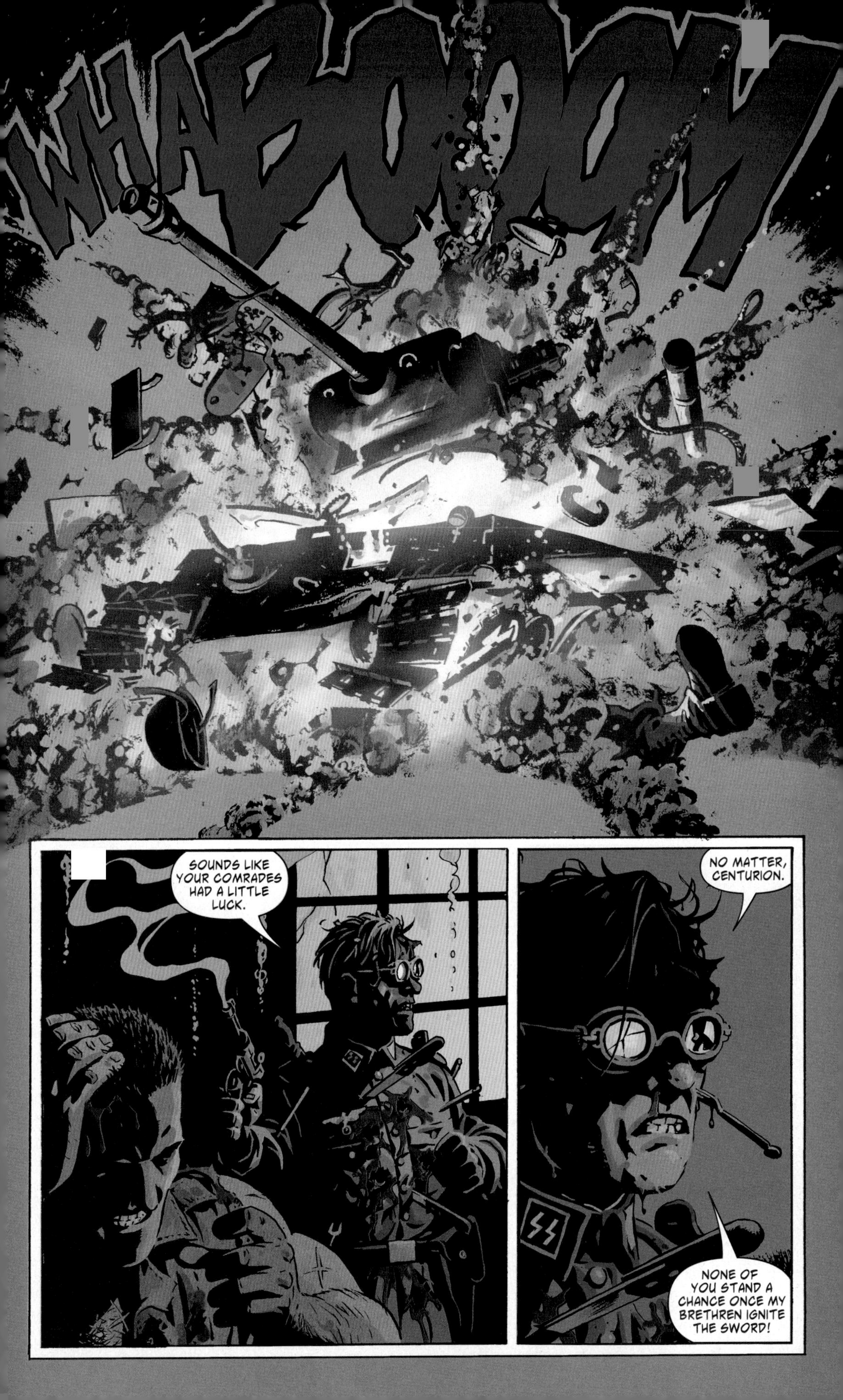
WHABOOOM
SOUNDS LIKE YOUR COMRADES HAD A LITTLE LUCK.
NO MATTER, CENTURION.
NONE OF YOU STAND A CHANCE ONCE MY BRETHREN IGNITE THE SWORD!

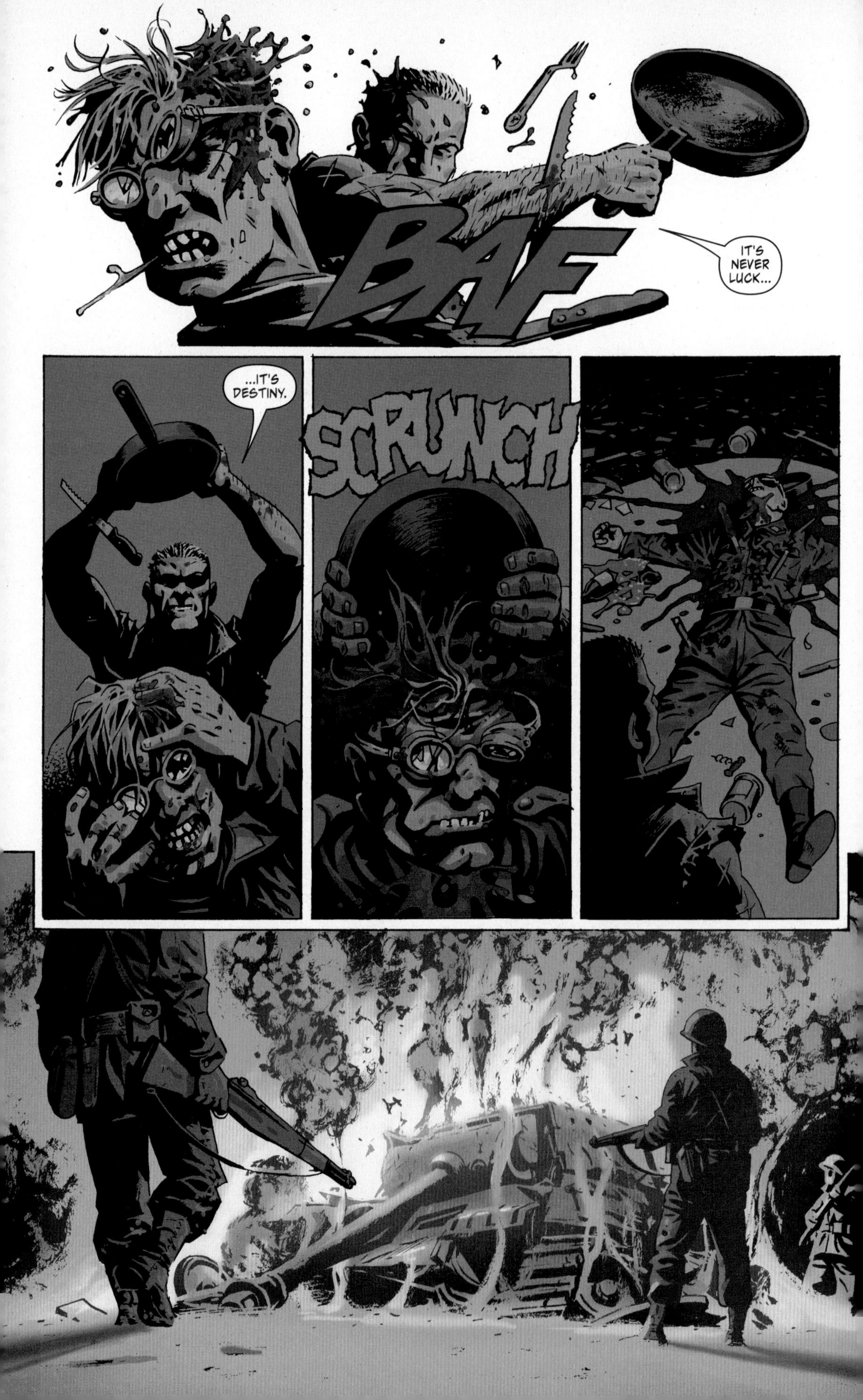
BAF
IT'S NEVER LUCK...
...IT'S DESTINY.
SCRUNCH

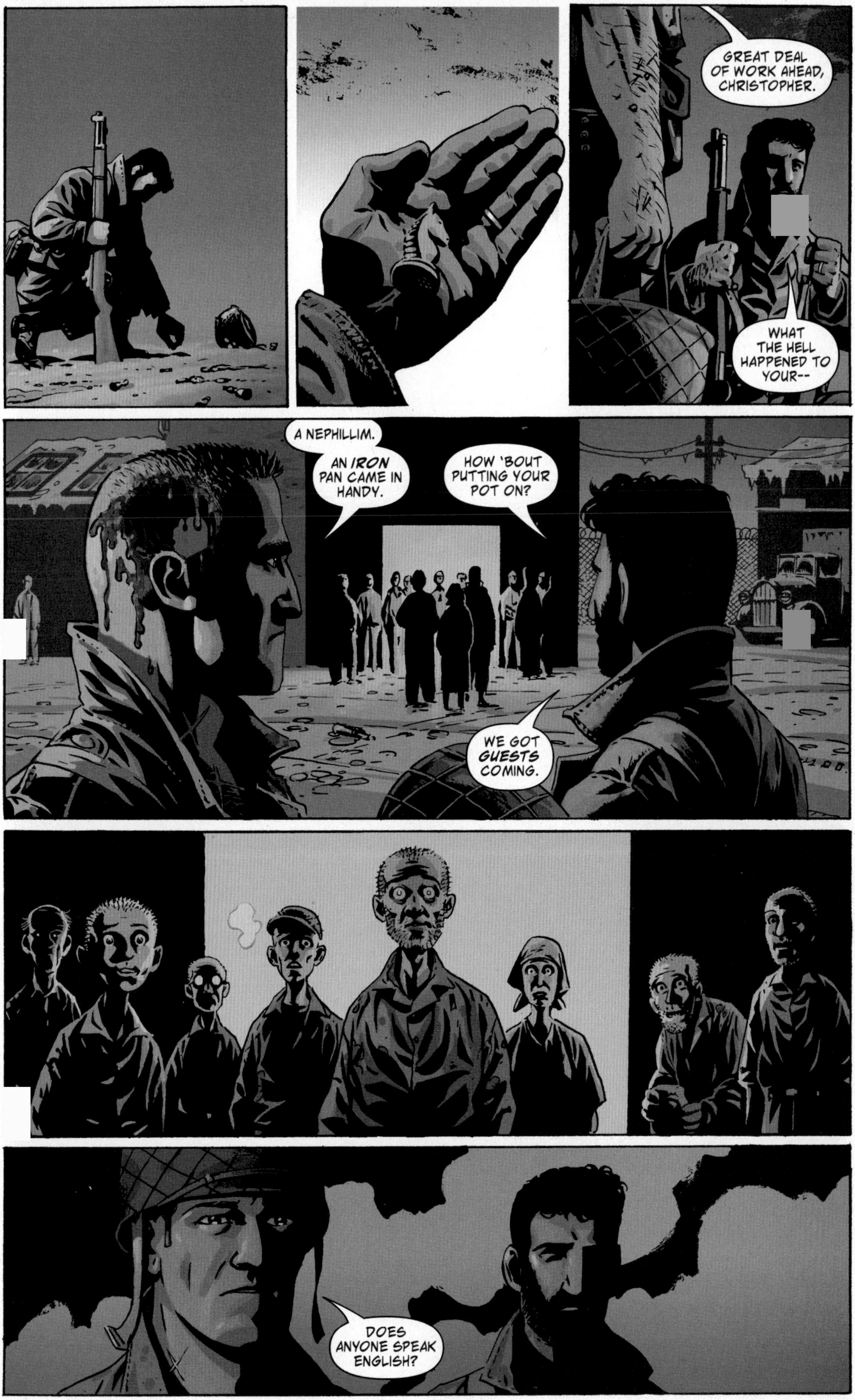
GREAT DEAL OF WORK AHEAD, CHRISTOPHER.
WHAT THE HELL HAPPENED TO YOUR--
A NEPHILLIM.
AN IRON PAN CAME IN HANDY.
HOW 'BOUT PUTTING YOUR POT ON?
WE GOT GUESTS COMING.
DOES ANYONE SPEAK ENGLISH?

I SPEAK ENGLISH. LITTLE BIT.

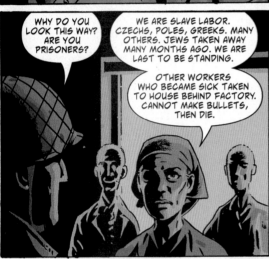

WHY DO YOU LOOK THIS WAY? ARE YOU PRISONERS?

WE ARE SLAVE LABOR. CZECHS, POLES, GREEKS. MANY OTHERS. JEWS TAKEN AWAY MANY MONTHS AGO. WE ARE LAST TO BE STANDING.

OTHER WORKERS WHO BECAME SICK TAKEN TO HOUSE BEHIND FACTORY. CANNOT MAKE BULLETS, THEN DIE.

CAN YOU CONTINUE TO MAKE BULLETS?

THESE BULLETS, THEY ARE FOR YOU AND YOUR SOLDIERS?

YES. SPECIAL BULLETS.

WE WILL GET YOU FOOD. WE WILL HELP YOU IN MAKING THESE BULLETS. BUT, YOU ARE FREE TO GO, IF YOU CHOOSE.

THESE BULLETS, THEY WILL BE USED TO KILL MORE NAZIS?

YEAH. A WHOLE SHITLOAD OF NAZIS.

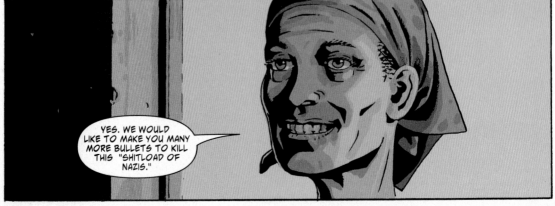

YES. WE WOULD LIKE TO MAKE YOU MANY MORE BULLETS TO KILL THIS "SHITLOAD OF NAZIS."

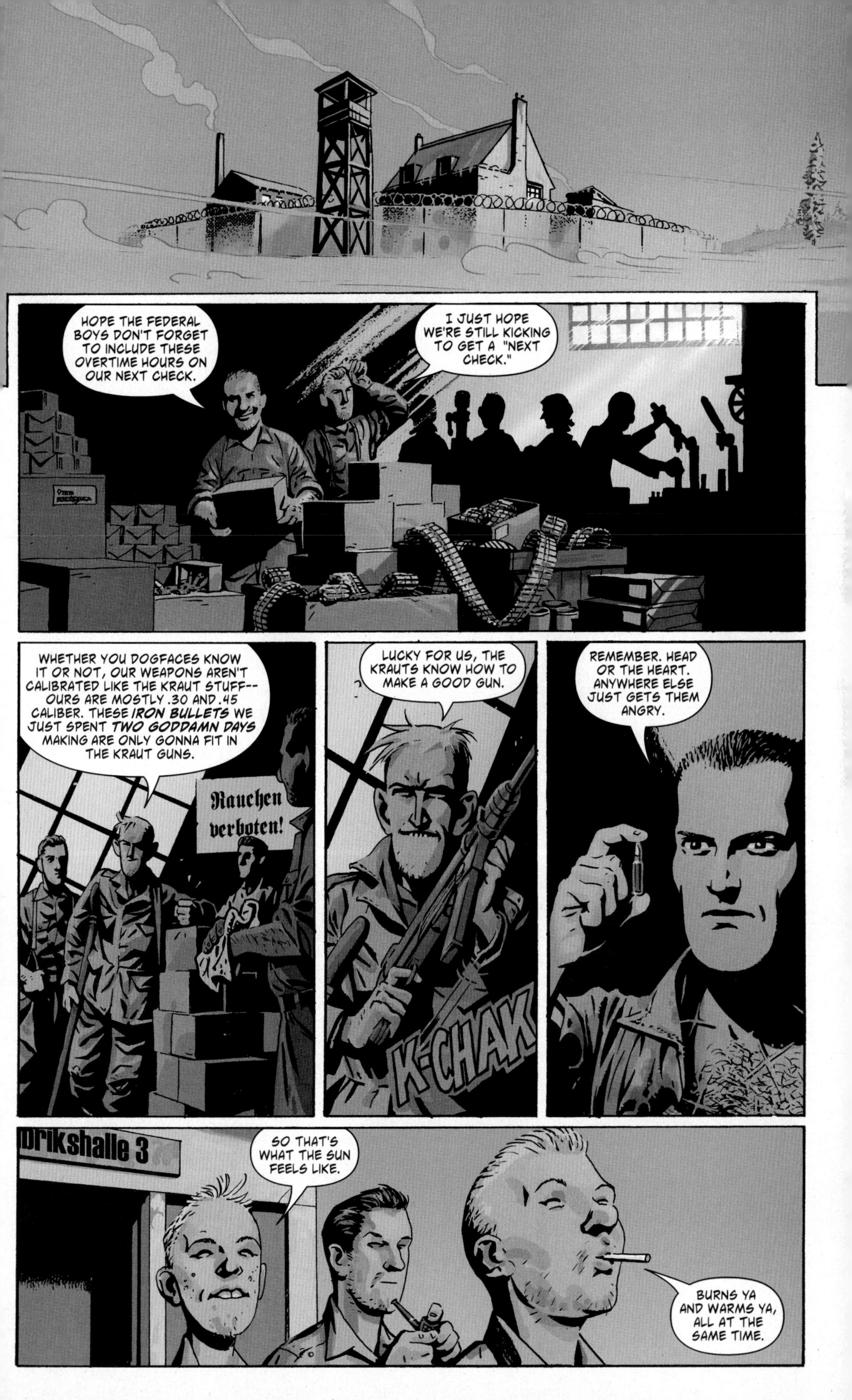
HOPE THE FEDERAL BOYS DON'T FORGET TO INCLUDE THESE OVERTIME HOURS ON OUR NEXT CHECK.
I JUST HOPE WE'RE STILL KICKING TO GET A "NEXT CHECK."
WHETHER YOU DOGFACES KNOW IT OR NOT, OUR WEAPONS AREN'T CALIBRATED LIKE THE KRAUT STUFF-- OURS ARE MOSTLY .30 AND .45 CALIBER. THESE *IRON BULLETS* WE JUST SPENT *TWO GODDAMN DAYS* MAKING ARE ONLY GONNA FIT IN THE KRAUT GUNS.
Rauchen verboten!
LUCKY FOR US, THE KRAUTS KNOW HOW TO MAKE A GOOD GUN.
K-CHAK
REMEMBER. HEAD OR THE HEART. ANYWHERE ELSE JUST GETS THEM ANGRY.
brikshalle 3
SO THAT'S WHAT THE SUN FEELS LIKE.
BURNS YA AND WARMS YA, ALL AT THE SAME TIME.

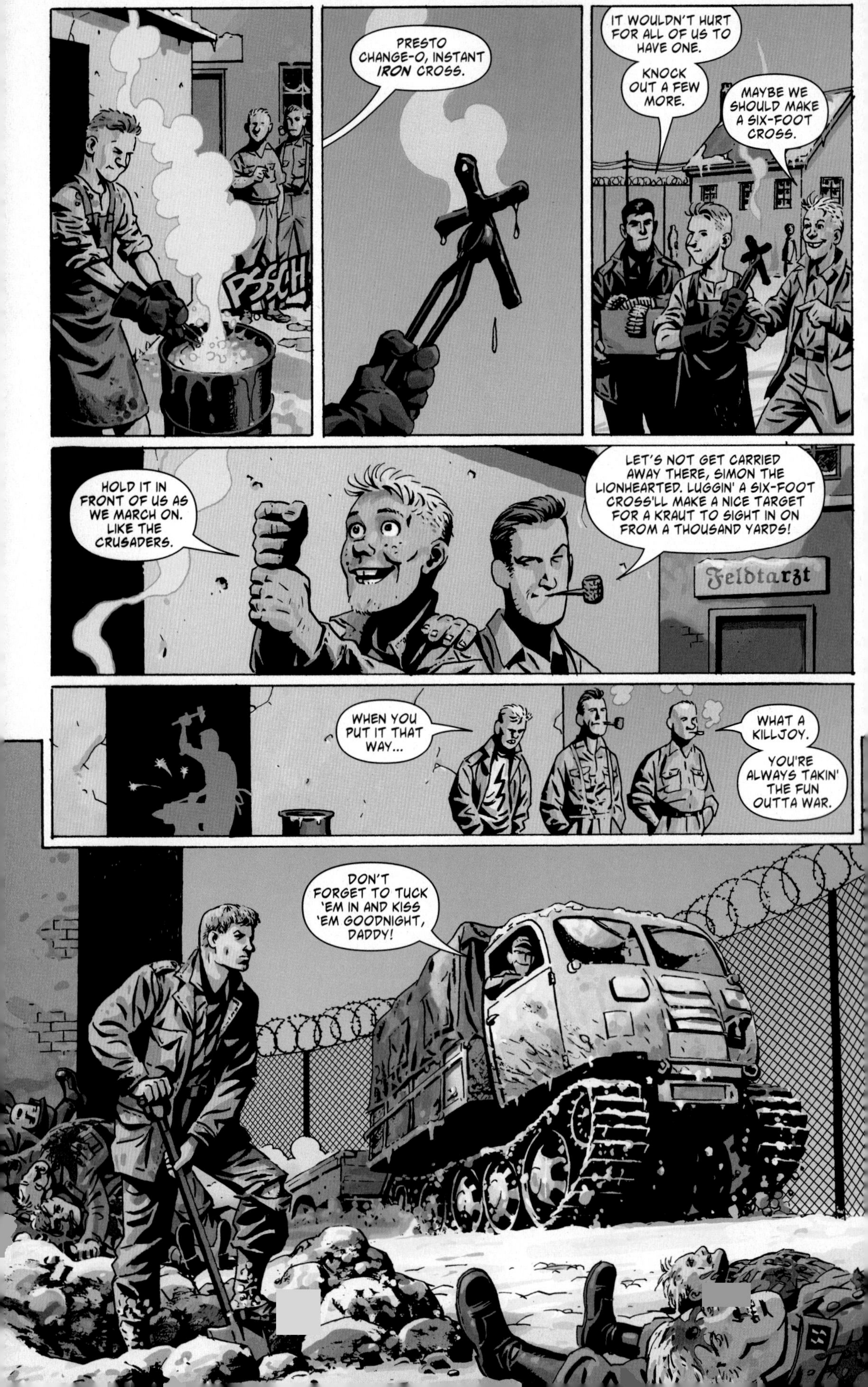
PSSCH
PRESTO CHANGE-O, INSTANT *IRON* CROSS.
IT WOULDN'T HURT FOR ALL OF US TO HAVE ONE.
KNOCK OUT A FEW MORE.
MAYBE WE SHOULD MAKE A SIX-FOOT CROSS.
HOLD IT IN FRONT OF US AS WE MARCH ON. LIKE THE CRUSADERS.
LET'S NOT GET CARRIED AWAY THERE, SIMON THE LIONHEARTED. LUGGIN' A SIX-FOOT CROSS'LL MAKE A NICE TARGET FOR A KRAUT TO SIGHT IN ON FROM A THOUSAND YARDS!
Feldtarzt
WHEN YOU PUT IT THAT WAY...
WHAT A KILLJOY.
YOU'RE ALWAYS TAKIN' THE FUN OUTTA WAR.
DON'T FORGET TO TUCK 'EM IN AND KISS 'EM GOODNIGHT, DADDY!

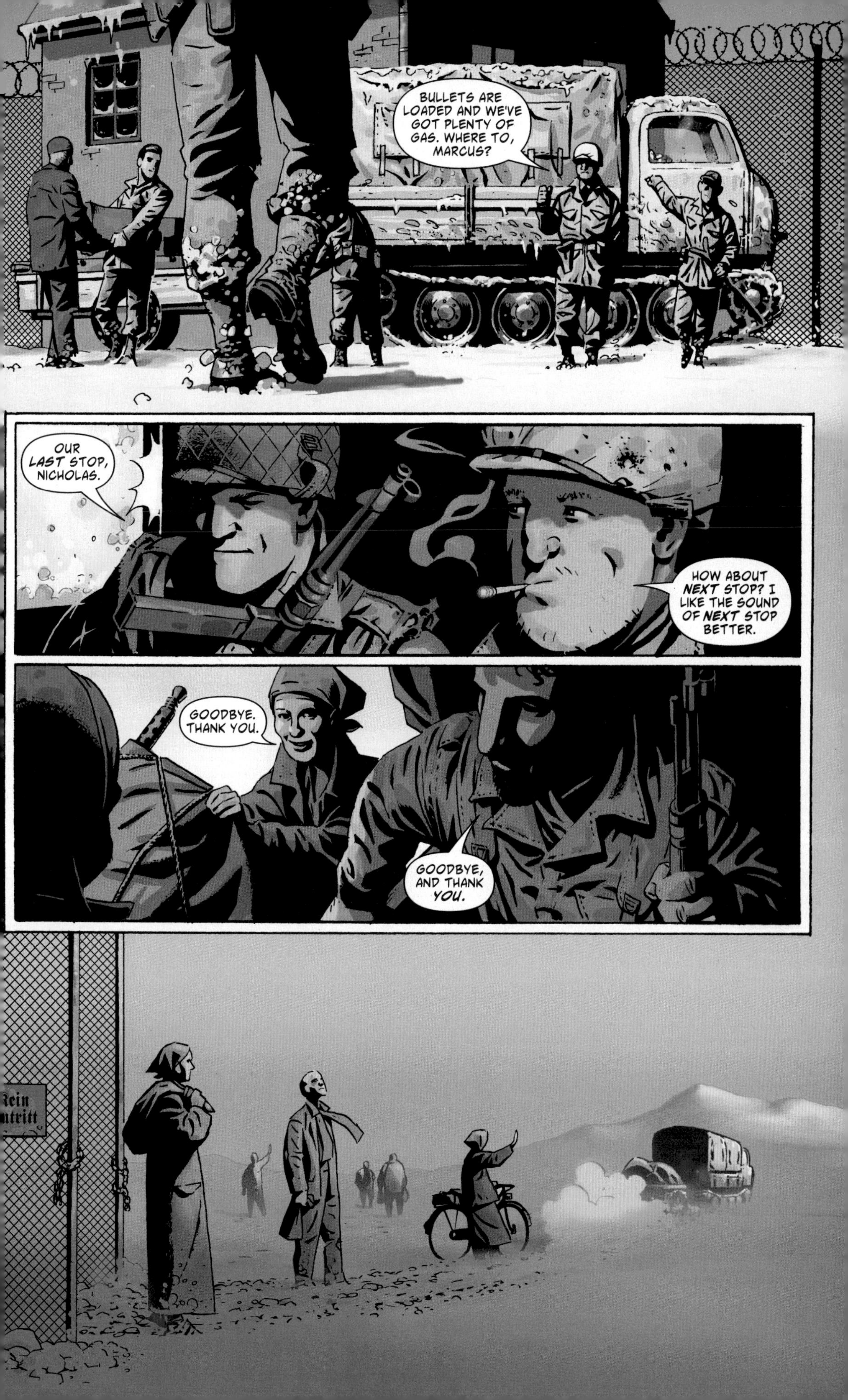
BULLETS ARE LOADED AND WE'VE GOT PLENTY OF GAS. WHERE TO, MARCUS?
OUR LAST STOP, NICHOLAS.
HOW ABOUT NEXT STOP? I LIKE THE SOUND OF NEXT STOP BETTER.
GOODBYE. THANK YOU.
GOODBYE, AND THANK YOU.

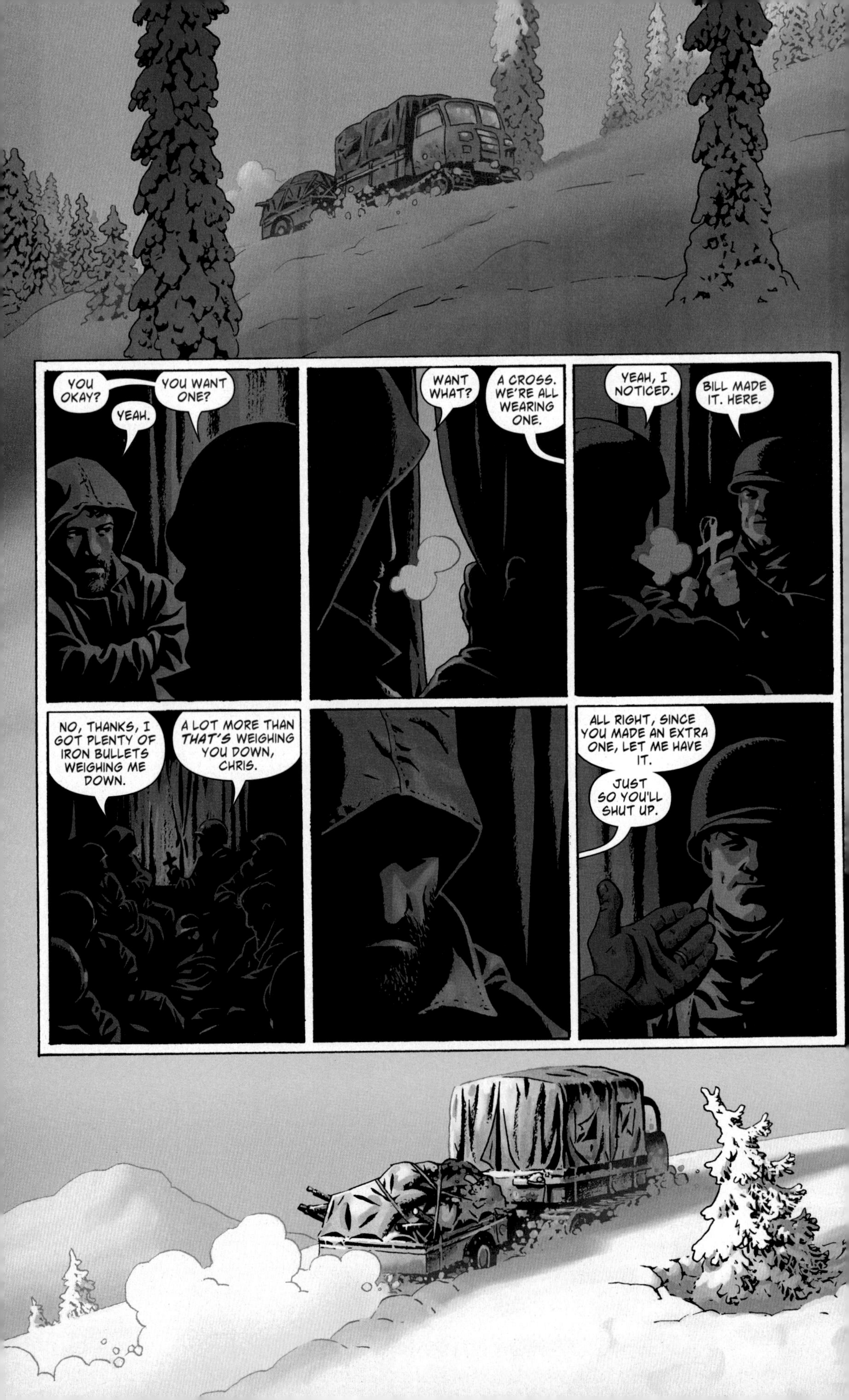
YOU OKAY?
YEAH.
YOU WANT ONE?
WANT WHAT?
A CROSS. WE'RE ALL WEARING ONE.
YEAH, I NOTICED.
BILL MADE IT. HERE.
NO, THANKS, I GOT PLENTY OF IRON BULLETS WEIGHING ME DOWN.
A LOT MORE THAN *THAT'S* WEIGHING YOU DOWN, CHRIS.
ALL RIGHT, SINCE YOU MADE AN EXTRA ONE, LET ME HAVE IT.
JUST SO YOU'LL SHUT UP.

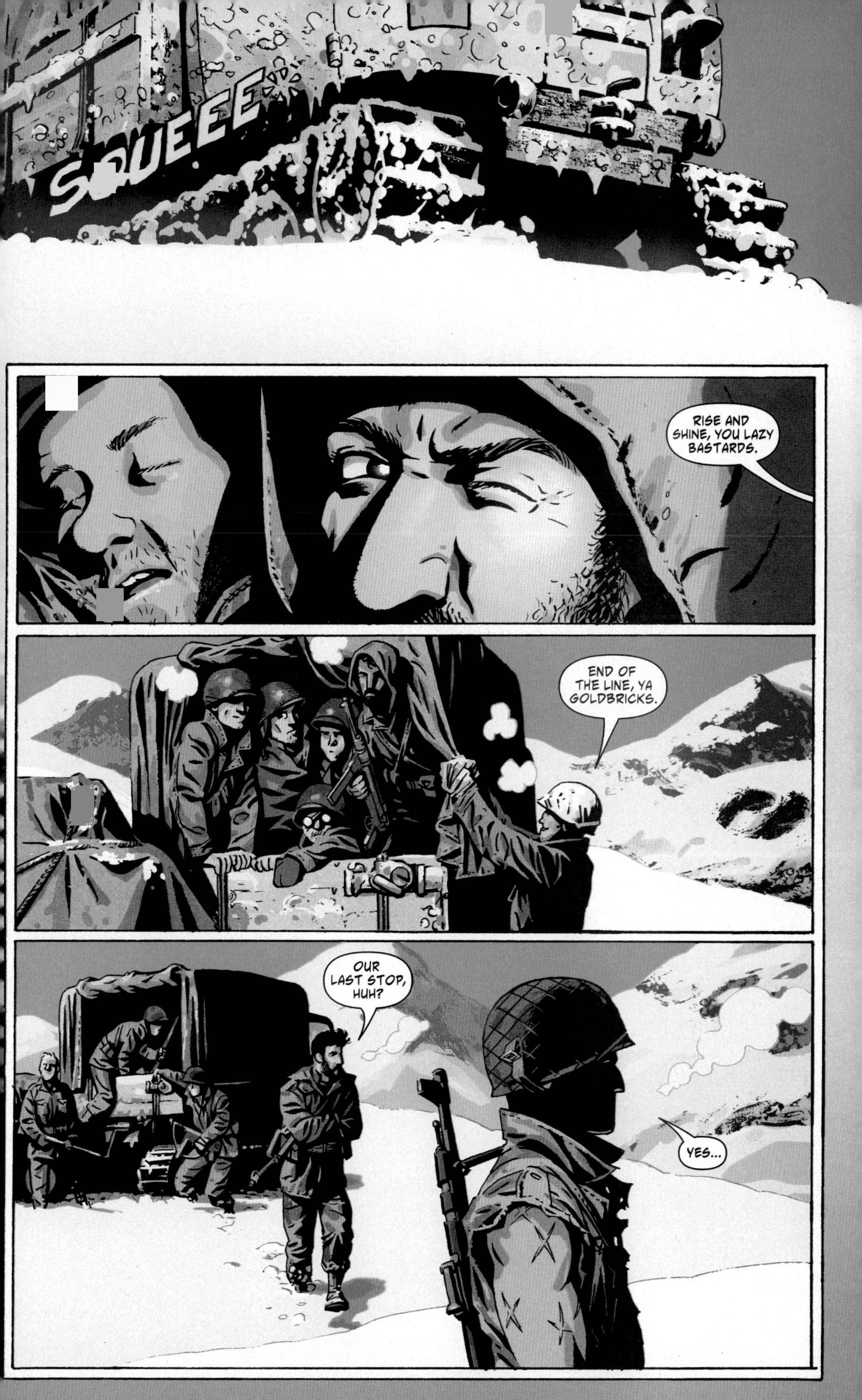
SQUEEE
RISE AND SHINE, YOU LAZY BASTARDS.
END OF THE LINE, YA GOLDBRICKS.
OUR LAST STOP, HUH?
YES...

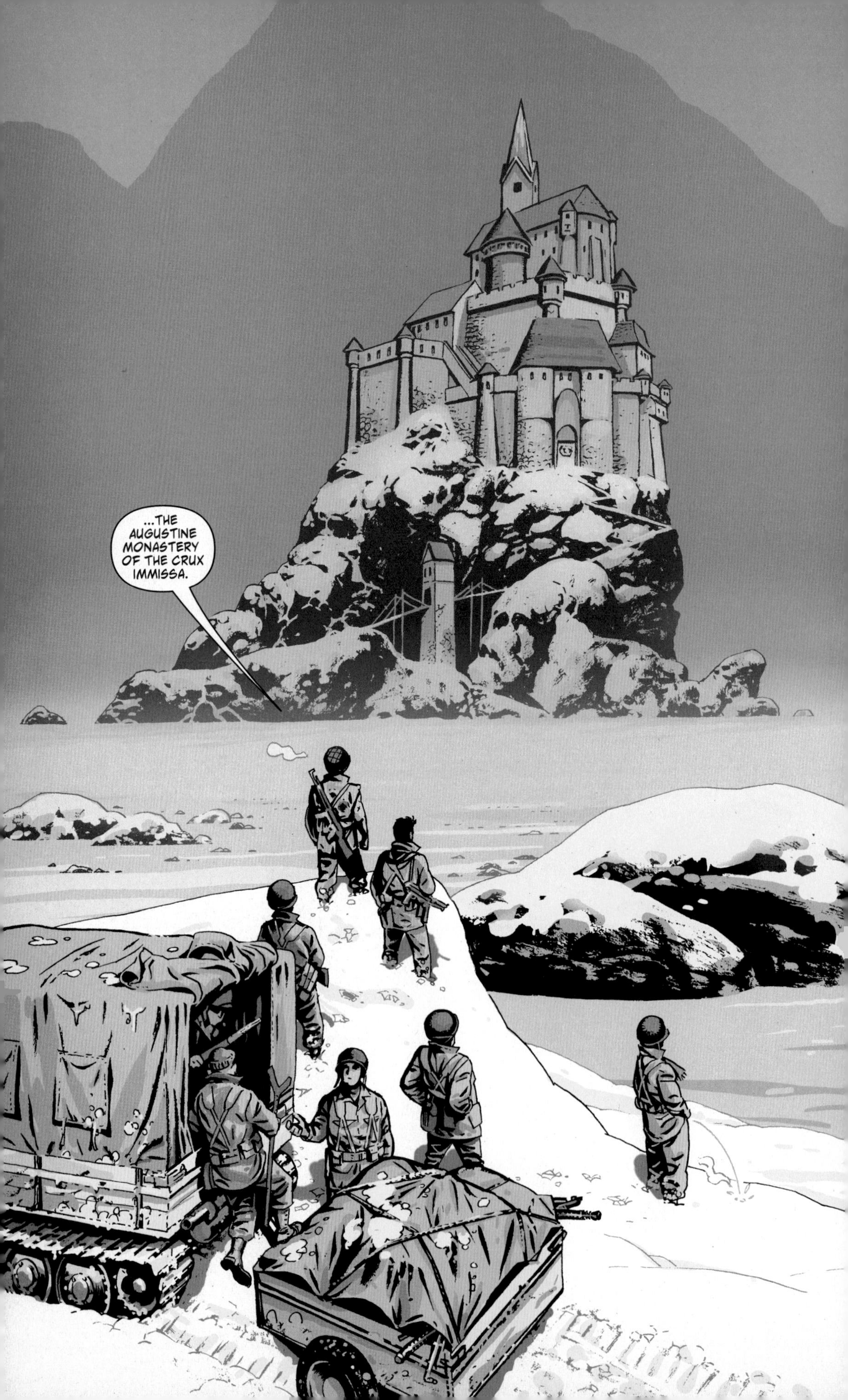
...THE AUGUSTINE MONASTERY OF THE CRUX IMMISSA.

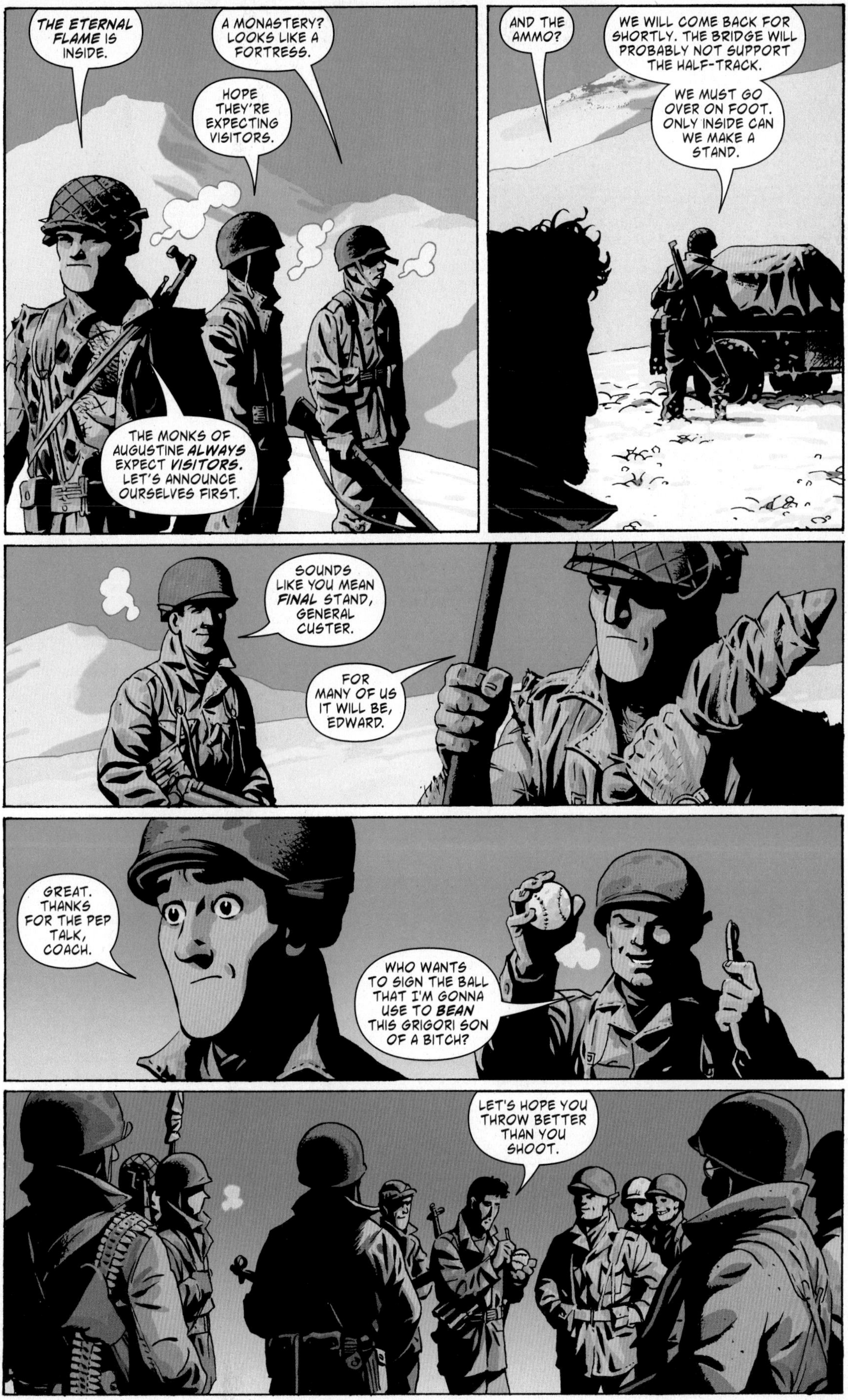
THE ETERNAL FLAME IS INSIDE.
A MONASTERY? LOOKS LIKE A FORTRESS.
HOPE THEY'RE EXPECTING VISITORS.
THE MONKS OF AUGUSTINE ALWAYS EXPECT VISITORS. LET'S ANNOUNCE OURSELVES FIRST.
AND THE AMMO?
WE WILL COME BACK FOR SHORTLY. THE BRIDGE WILL PROBABLY NOT SUPPORT THE HALF-TRACK.
WE MUST GO OVER ON FOOT. ONLY INSIDE CAN WE MAKE A STAND.
SOUNDS LIKE YOU MEAN FINAL STAND, GENERAL CUSTER.
FOR MANY OF US IT WILL BE, EDWARD.
GREAT. THANKS FOR THE PEP TALK, COACH.
WHO WANTS TO SIGN THE BALL THAT I'M GONNA USE TO BEAN THIS GRIGORI SON OF A BITCH?
LET'S HOPE YOU THROW BETTER THAN YOU SHOOT.

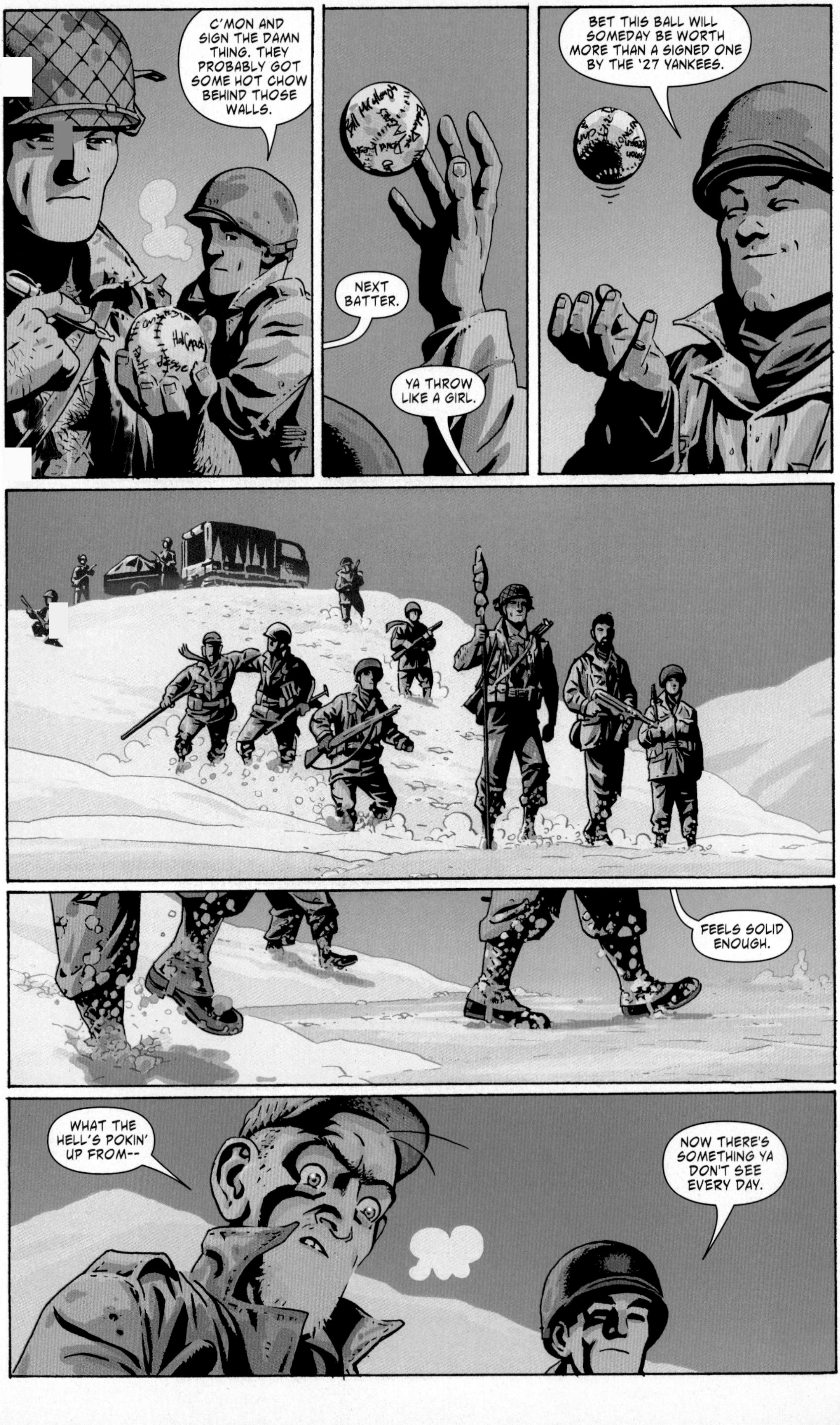
C'MON AND SIGN THE DAMN THING. THEY PROBABLY GOT SOME HOT CHOW BEHIND THOSE WALLS.
NEXT BATTER.
YA THROW LIKE A GIRL.
BET THIS BALL WILL SOMEDAY BE WORTH MORE THAN A SIGNED ONE BY THE '27 YANKEES.
FEELS SOLID ENOUGH.
WHAT THE HELL'S POKIN' UP FROM--
NOW THERE'S SOMETHING YA DON'T SEE EVERY DAY.

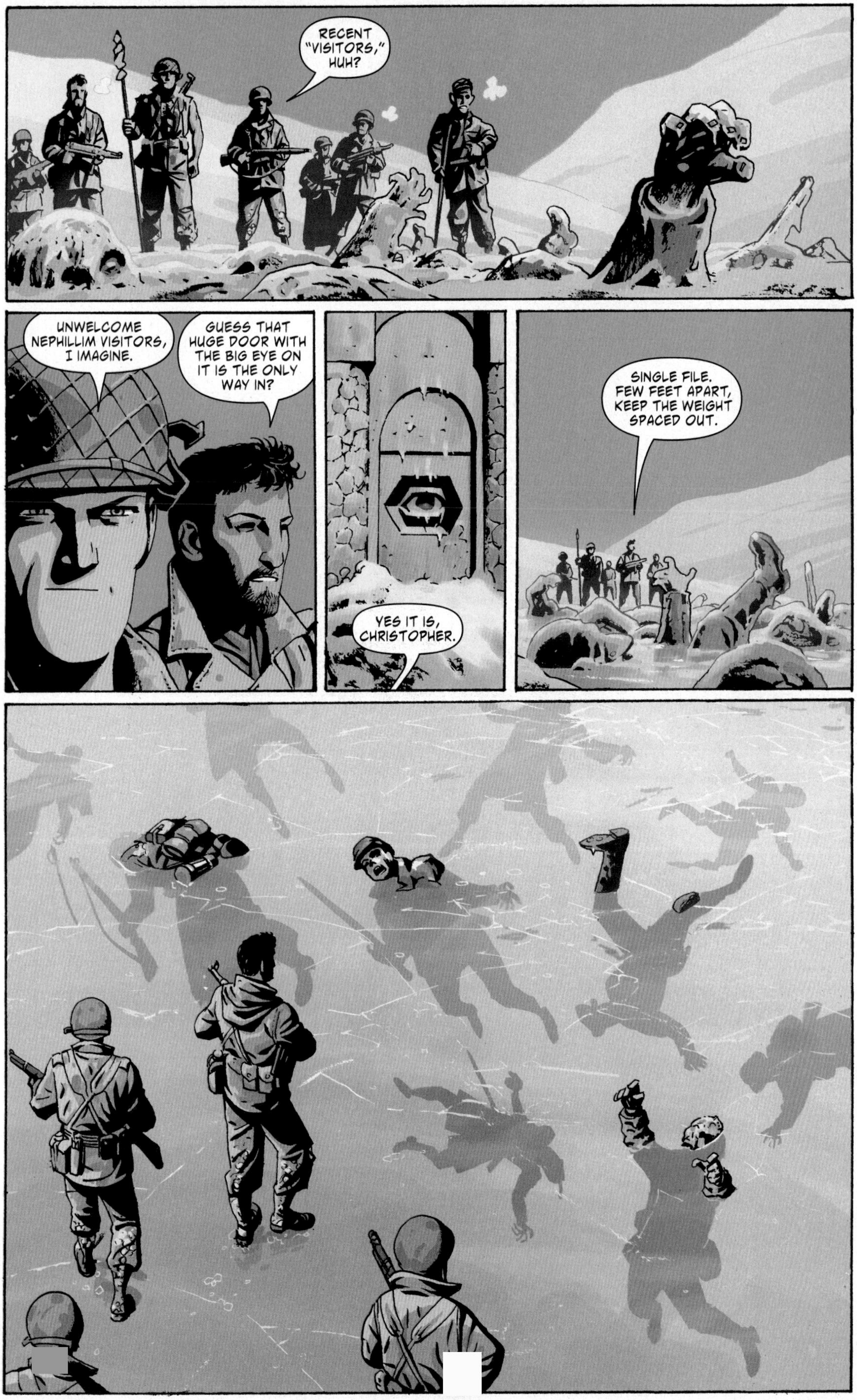
RECENT "VISITORS," HUH?
UNWELCOME NEPHILLIM VISITORS, I IMAGINE.
GUESS THAT HUGE DOOR WITH THE BIG EYE ON IT IS THE ONLY WAY IN?
YES IT IS, CHRISTOPHER.
SINGLE FILE. FEW FEET APART, KEEP THE WEIGHT SPACED OUT.

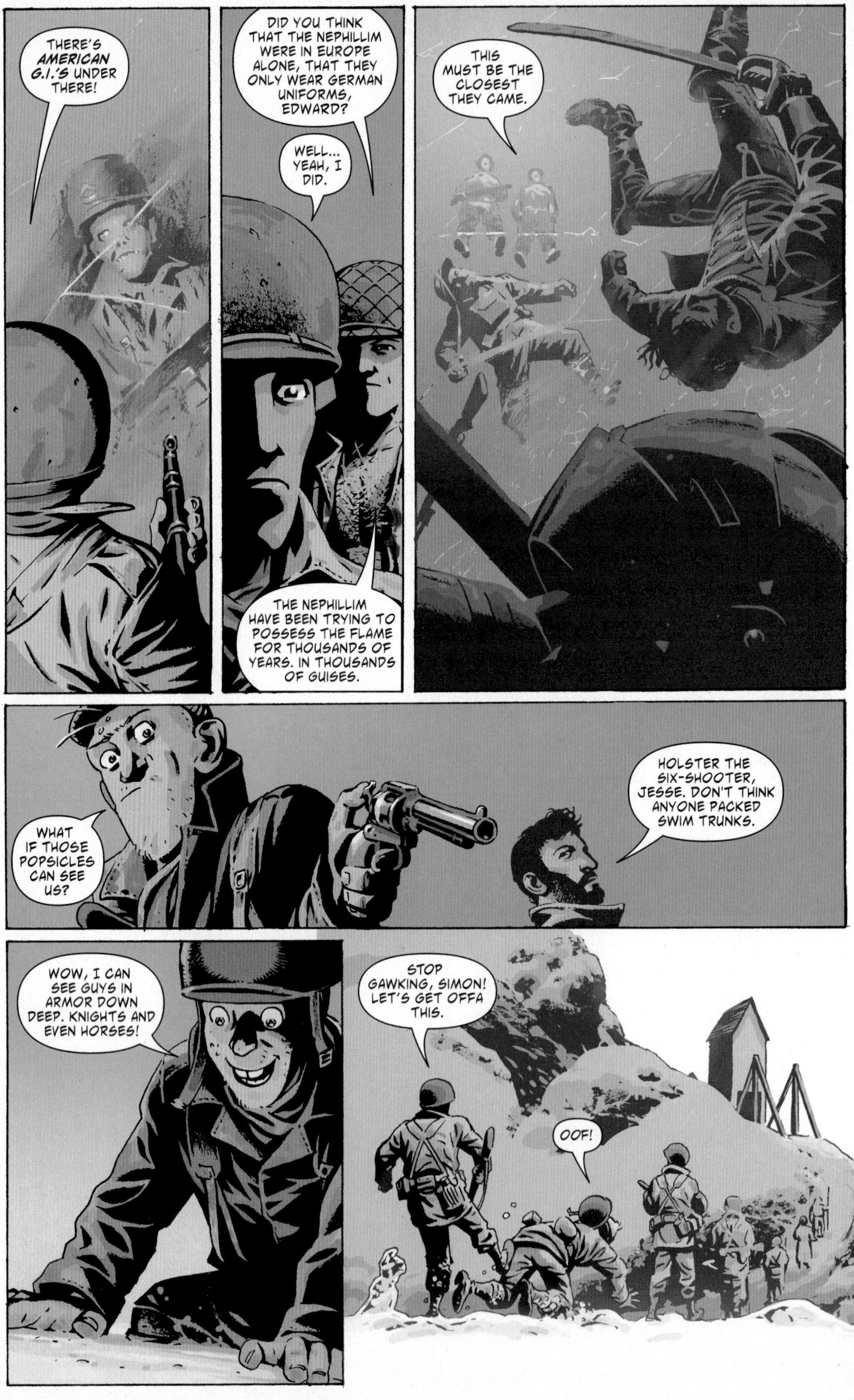
THERE'S AMERICAN G.I.'S UNDER THERE!
DID YOU THINK THAT THE NEPHILLIM WERE IN EUROPE ALONE, THAT THEY ONLY WEAR GERMAN UNIFORMS, EDWARD?
WELL... YEAH, I DID.
THE NEPHILLIM HAVE BEEN TRYING TO POSSESS THE FLAME FOR THOUSANDS OF YEARS. IN THOUSANDS OF GUISES.
THIS MUST BE THE CLOSEST THEY CAME.
WHAT IF THOSE POPSICLES CAN SEE US?
HOLSTER THE SIX-SHOOTER, JESSE. DON'T THINK ANYONE PACKED SWIM TRUNKS.
WOW, I CAN SEE GUYS IN ARMOR DOWN DEEP. KNIGHTS AND EVEN HORSES!
STOP GAWKING, SIMON! LET'S GET OFFA THIS.
OOF!

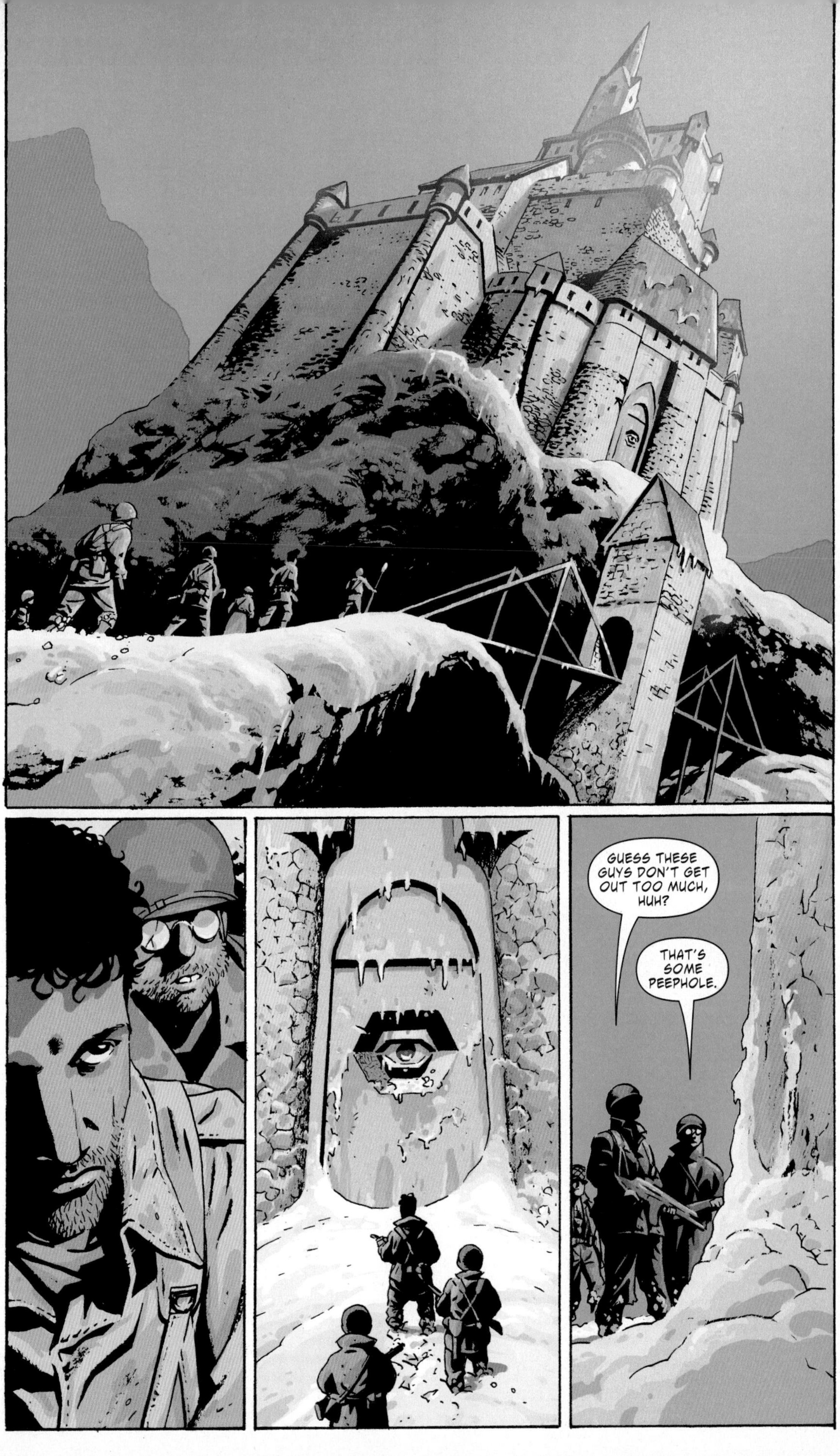
GUESS THESE GUYS DON'T GET OUT TOO MUCH, HUH?
THAT'S SOME PEEPHOLE.

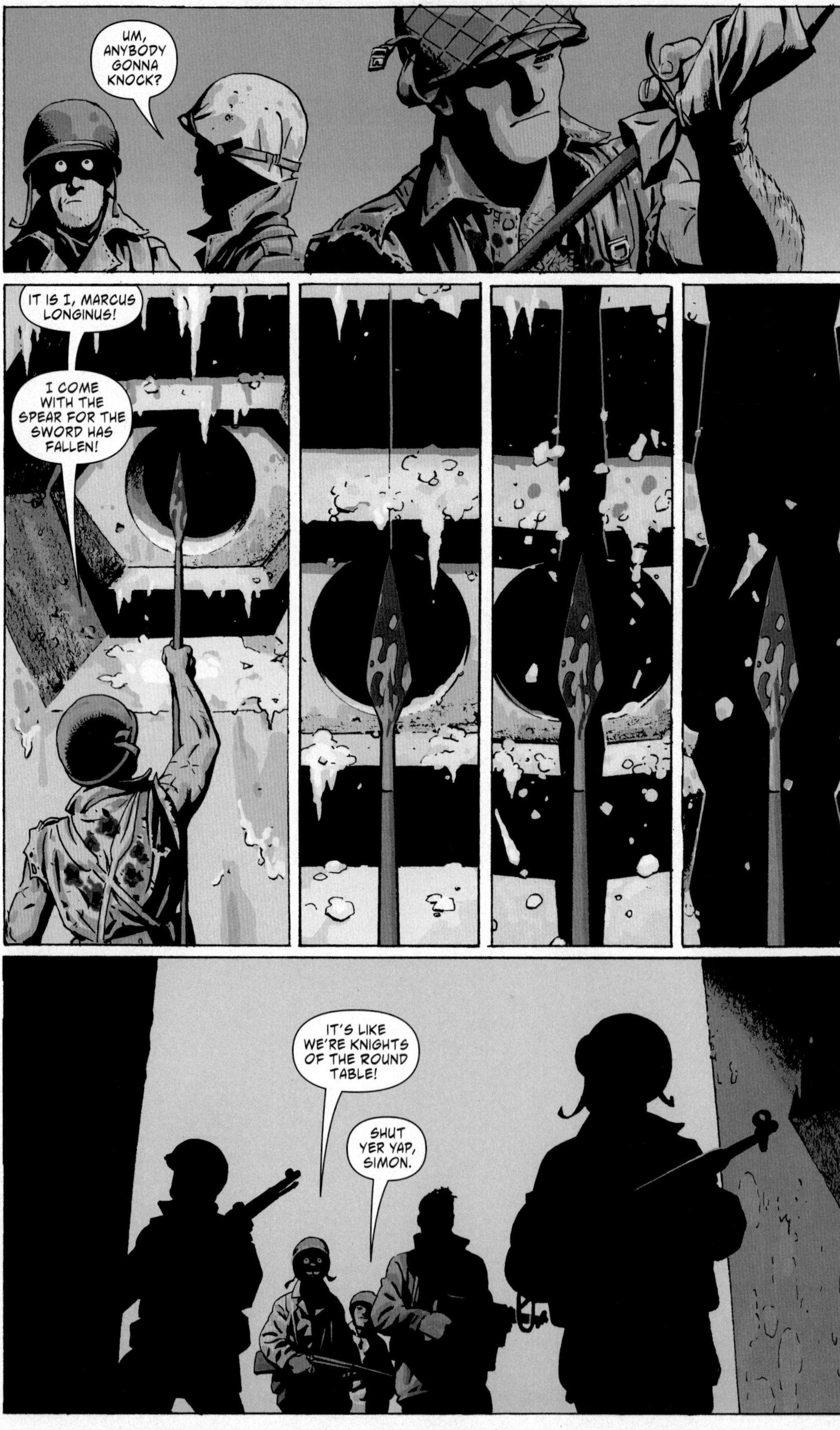
UM, ANYBODY GONNA KNOCK?
IT IS I, MARCUS LONGINUS!
I COME WITH THE SPEAR FOR THE SWORD HAS FALLEN!
IT'S LIKE WE'RE KNIGHTS OF THE ROUND TABLE!
SHUT YER YAP, SIMON.

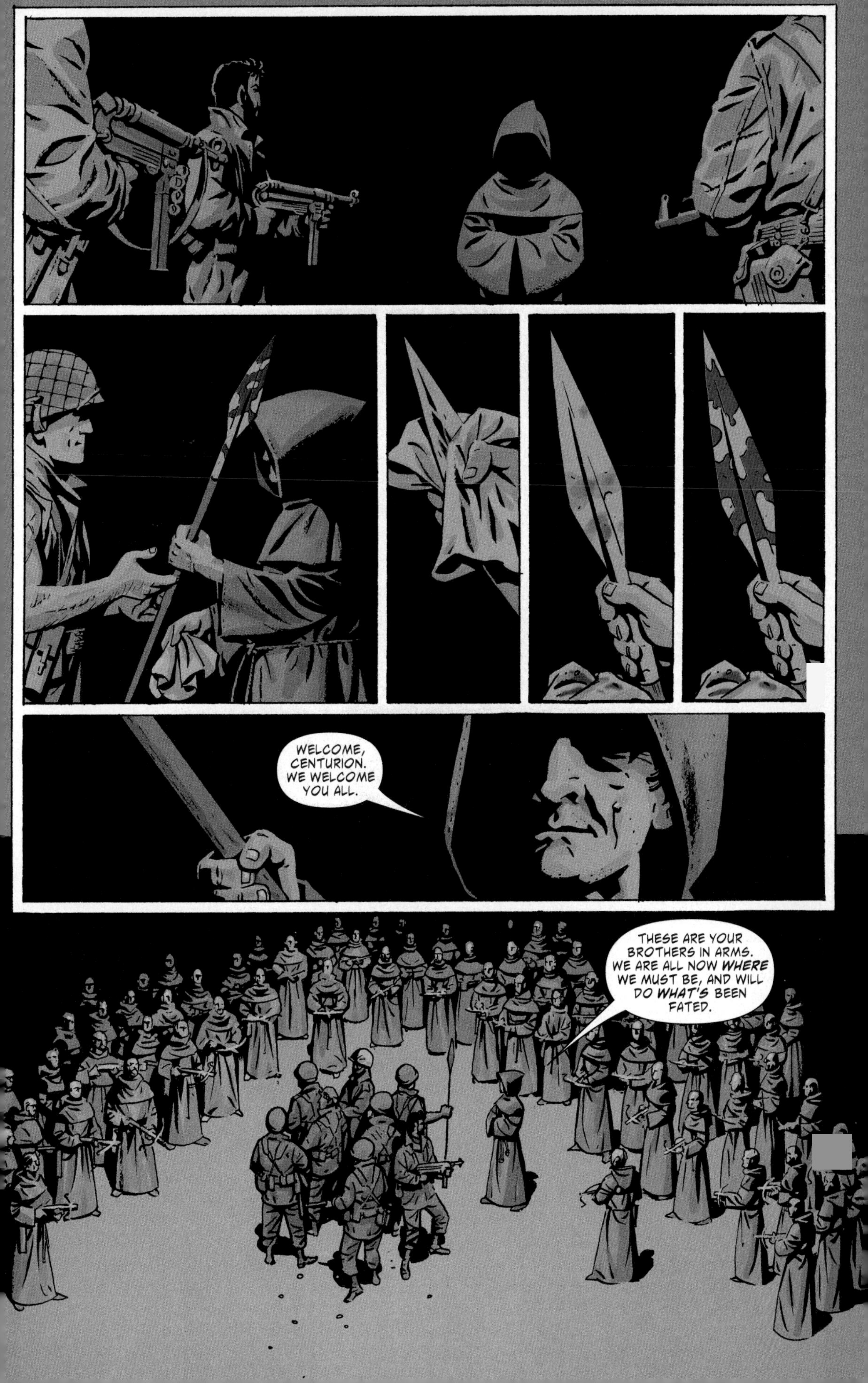
WELCOME, CENTURION. WE WELCOME YOU ALL.
THESE ARE YOUR BROTHERS IN ARMS. WE ARE ALL NOW WHERE WE MUST BE, AND WILL DO WHAT'S BEEN FATED.

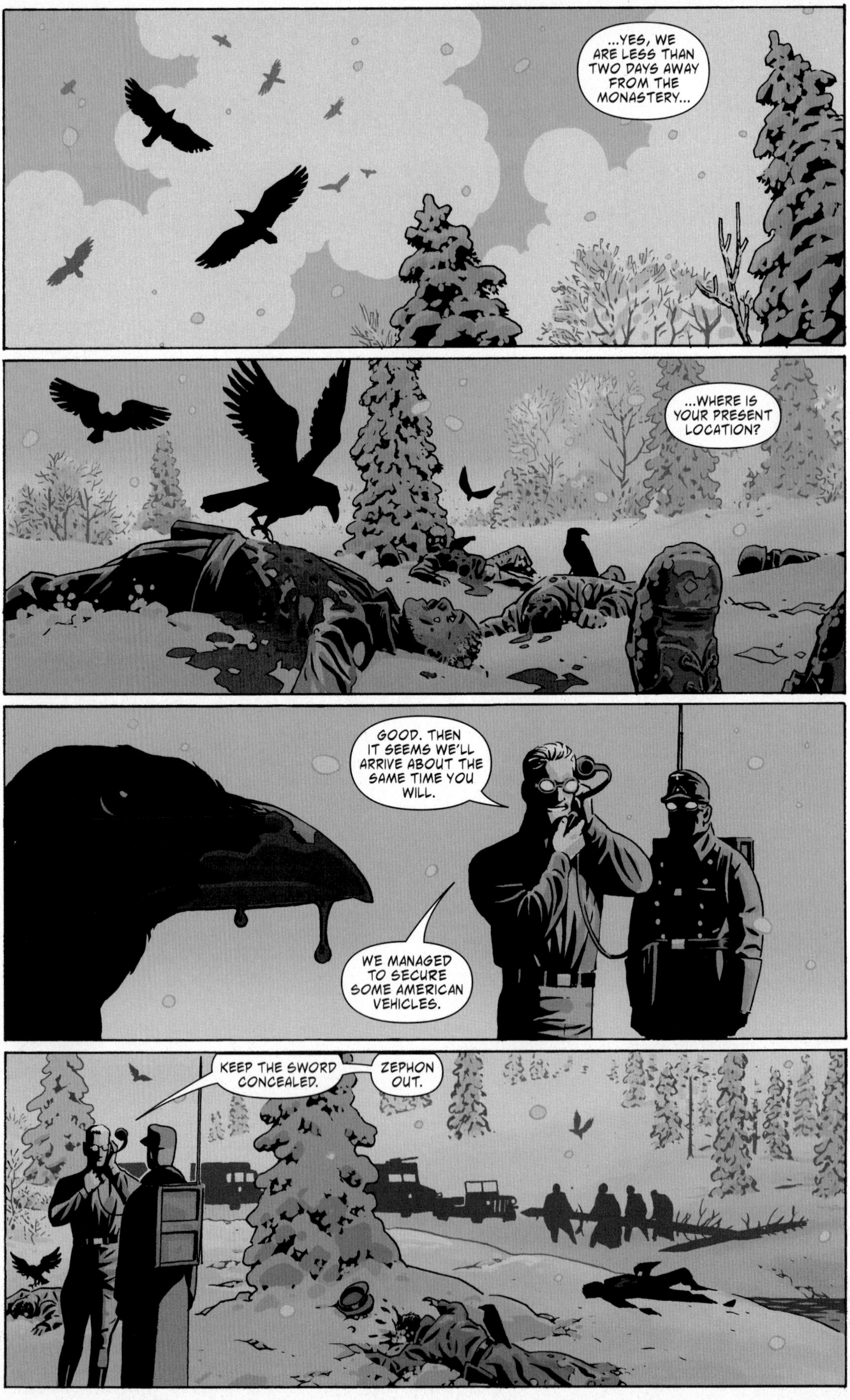

...YES, WE ARE LESS THAN TWO DAYS AWAY FROM THE MONASTERY...
...WHERE IS YOUR PRESENT LOCATION?
GOOD. THEN IT SEEMS WE'LL ARRIVE ABOUT THE SAME TIME YOU WILL.
WE MANAGED TO SECURE SOME AMERICAN VEHICLES.
KEEP THE SWORD CONCEALED.
ZEPHON OUT.

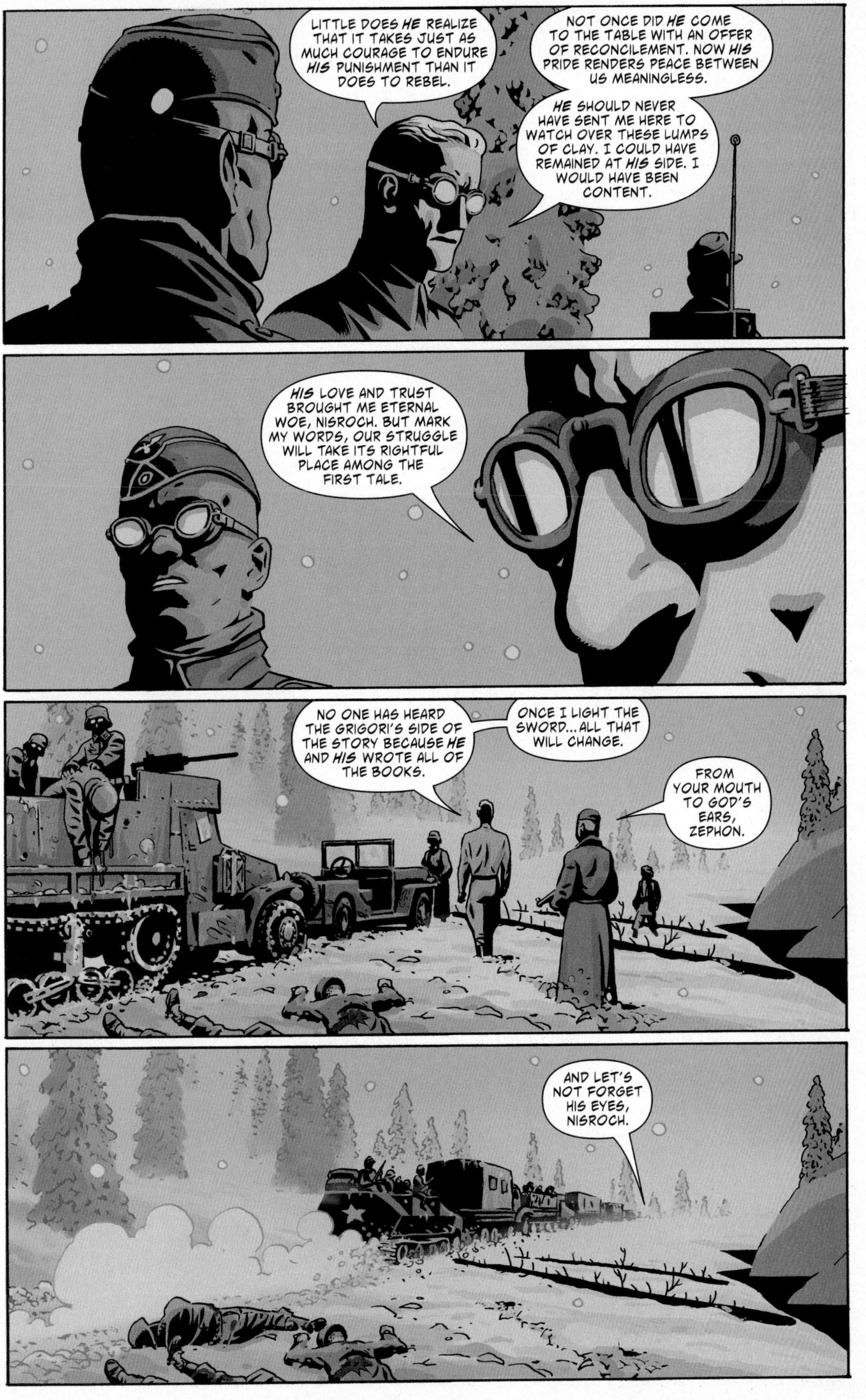
LITTLE DOES HE REALIZE THAT IT TAKES JUST AS MUCH COURAGE TO ENDURE HIS PUNISHMENT THAN IT DOES TO REBEL.
NOT ONCE DID HE COME TO THE TABLE WITH AN OFFER OF RECONCILEMENT. NOW HIS PRIDE RENDERS PEACE BETWEEN US MEANINGLESS.
HE SHOULD NEVER HAVE SENT ME HERE TO WATCH OVER THESE LUMPS OF CLAY. I COULD HAVE REMAINED AT HIS SIDE. I WOULD HAVE BEEN CONTENT.
HIS LOVE AND TRUST BROUGHT ME ETERNAL WOE, NISROCH. BUT MARK MY WORDS, OUR STRUGGLE WILL TAKE ITS RIGHTFUL PLACE AMONG THE FIRST TALE.
NO ONE HAS HEARD THE GRIGORI'S SIDE OF THE STORY BECAUSE HE AND HIS WROTE ALL OF THE BOOKS.
ONCE I LIGHT THE SWORD... ALL THAT WILL CHANGE.
FROM YOUR MOUTH TO GOD'S EARS, ZEPHON.
AND LET'S NOT FORGET HIS EYES, NISROCH.

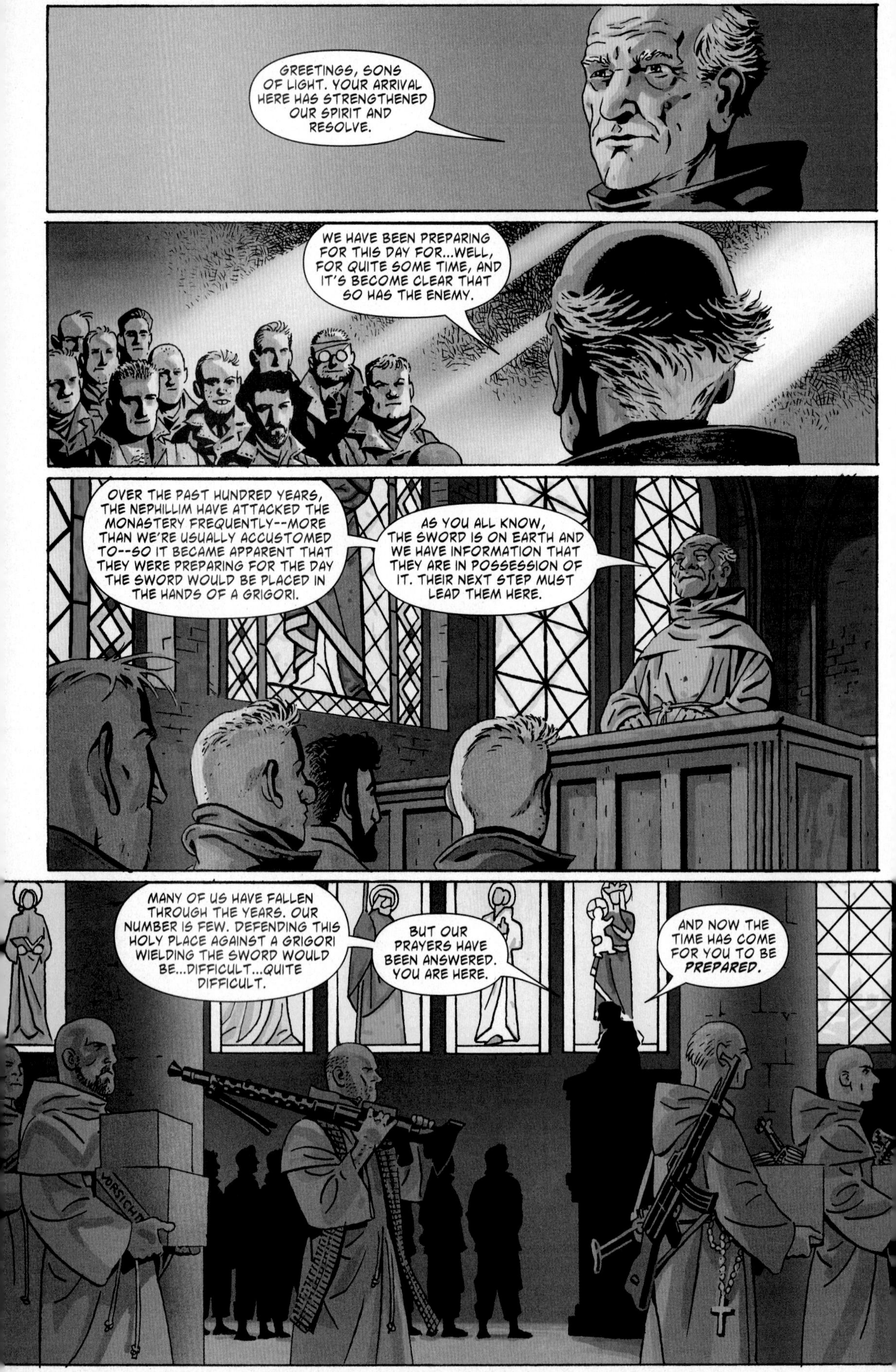
GREETINGS, SONS OF LIGHT. YOUR ARRIVAL HERE HAS STRENGTHENED OUR SPIRIT AND RESOLVE.
WE HAVE BEEN PREPARING FOR THIS DAY FOR...WELL, FOR QUITE SOME TIME, AND IT'S BECOME CLEAR THAT SO HAS THE ENEMY.
OVER THE PAST HUNDRED YEARS, THE NEPHILLIM HAVE ATTACKED THE MONASTERY FREQUENTLY--MORE THAN WE'RE USUALLY ACCUSTOMED TO--SO IT BECAME APPARENT THAT THEY WERE PREPARING FOR THE DAY THE SWORD WOULD BE PLACED IN THE HANDS OF A GRIGORI.
AS YOU ALL KNOW, THE SWORD IS ON EARTH AND WE HAVE INFORMATION THAT THEY ARE IN POSSESSION OF IT. THEIR NEXT STEP MUST LEAD THEM HERE.
MANY OF US HAVE FALLEN THROUGH THE YEARS. OUR NUMBER IS FEW. DEFENDING THIS HOLY PLACE AGAINST A GRIGORI WIELDING THE SWORD WOULD BE...DIFFICULT...QUITE DIFFICULT.
BUT OUR PRAYERS HAVE BEEN ANSWERED. YOU ARE HERE.
AND NOW THE TIME HAS COME FOR YOU TO BE *PREPARED*.

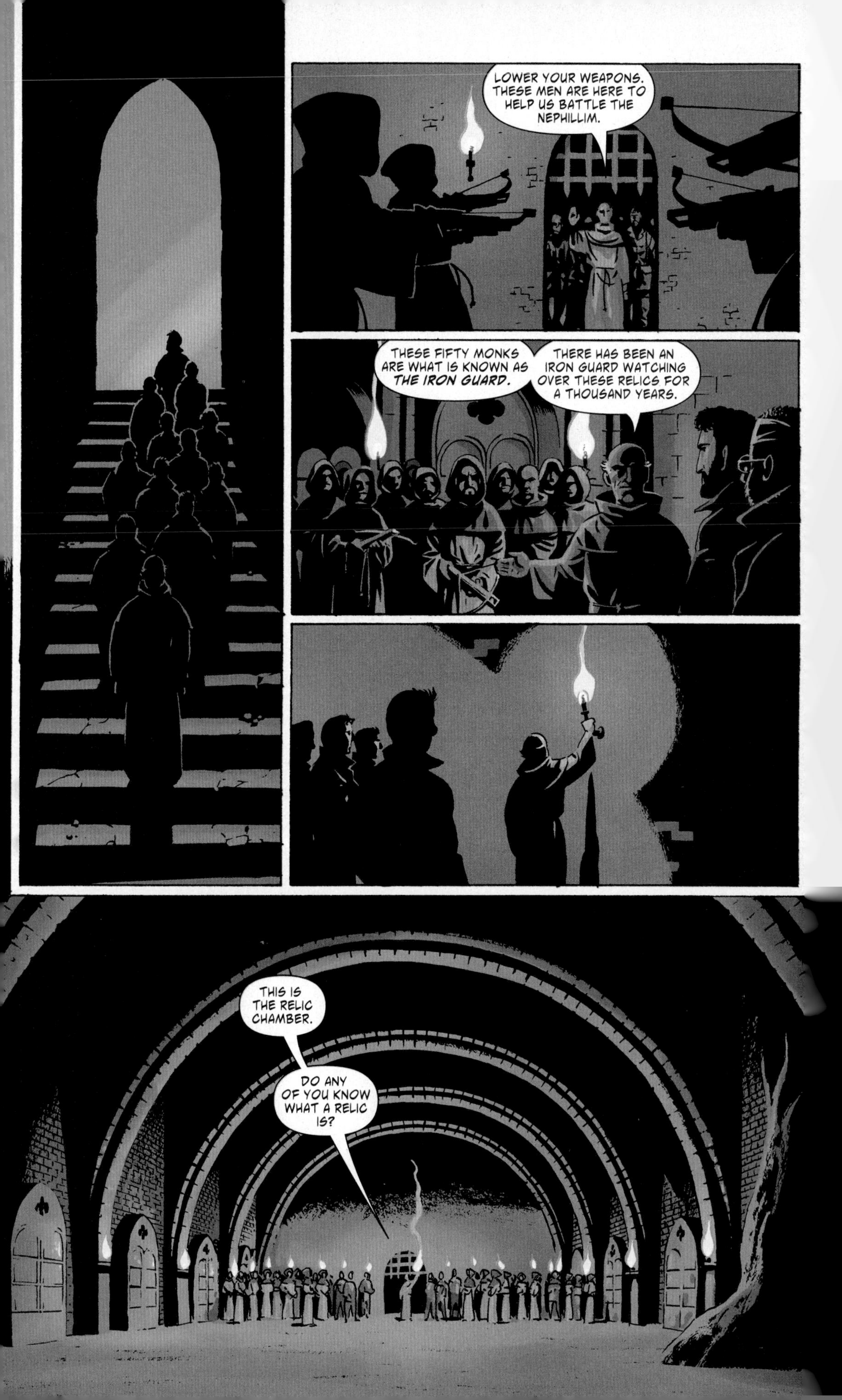

LOWER YOUR WEAPONS. THESE MEN ARE HERE TO HELP US BATTLE THE NEPHILLIM.
THESE FIFTY MONKS ARE WHAT IS KNOWN AS ***THE IRON GUARD.***
THERE HAS BEEN AN IRON GUARD WATCHING OVER THESE RELICS FOR A THOUSAND YEARS.
THIS IS THE RELIC CHAMBER.
DO ANY OF YOU KNOW WHAT A RELIC IS?

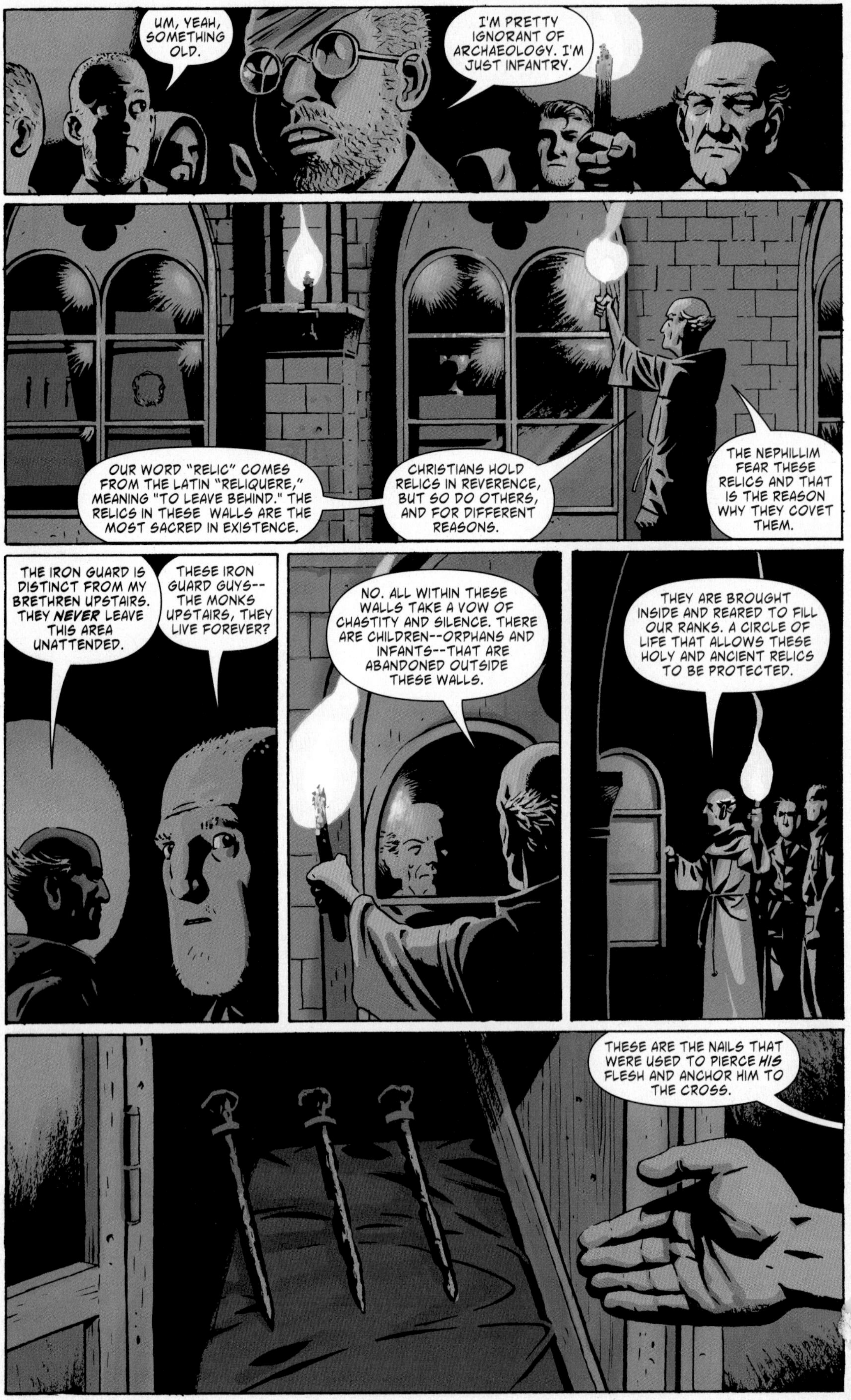
UM, YEAH, SOMETHING OLD.
I'M PRETTY IGNORANT OF ARCHAEOLOGY. I'M JUST INFANTRY.
OUR WORD "RELIC" COMES FROM THE LATIN "RELIQUERE," MEANING "TO LEAVE BEHIND." THE RELICS IN THESE WALLS ARE THE MOST SACRED IN EXISTENCE.
CHRISTIANS HOLD RELICS IN REVERENCE, BUT SO DO OTHERS, AND FOR DIFFERENT REASONS.
THE NEPHILLIM FEAR THESE RELICS AND THAT IS THE REASON WHY THEY COVET THEM.
THE IRON GUARD IS DISTINCT FROM MY BRETHREN UPSTAIRS. THEY *NEVER* LEAVE THIS AREA UNATTENDED.
THESE IRON GUARD GUYS-- THE MONKS UPSTAIRS, THEY LIVE FOREVER?
NO. ALL WITHIN THESE WALLS TAKE A VOW OF CHASTITY AND SILENCE. THERE ARE CHILDREN--ORPHANS AND INFANTS--THAT ARE ABANDONED OUTSIDE THESE WALLS.
THEY ARE BROUGHT INSIDE AND REARED TO FILL OUR RANKS. A CIRCLE OF LIFE THAT ALLOWS THESE HOLY AND ANCIENT RELICS TO BE PROTECTED.
THESE ARE THE NAILS THAT WERE USED TO PIERCE *HIS* FLESH AND ANCHOR HIM TO THE CROSS.

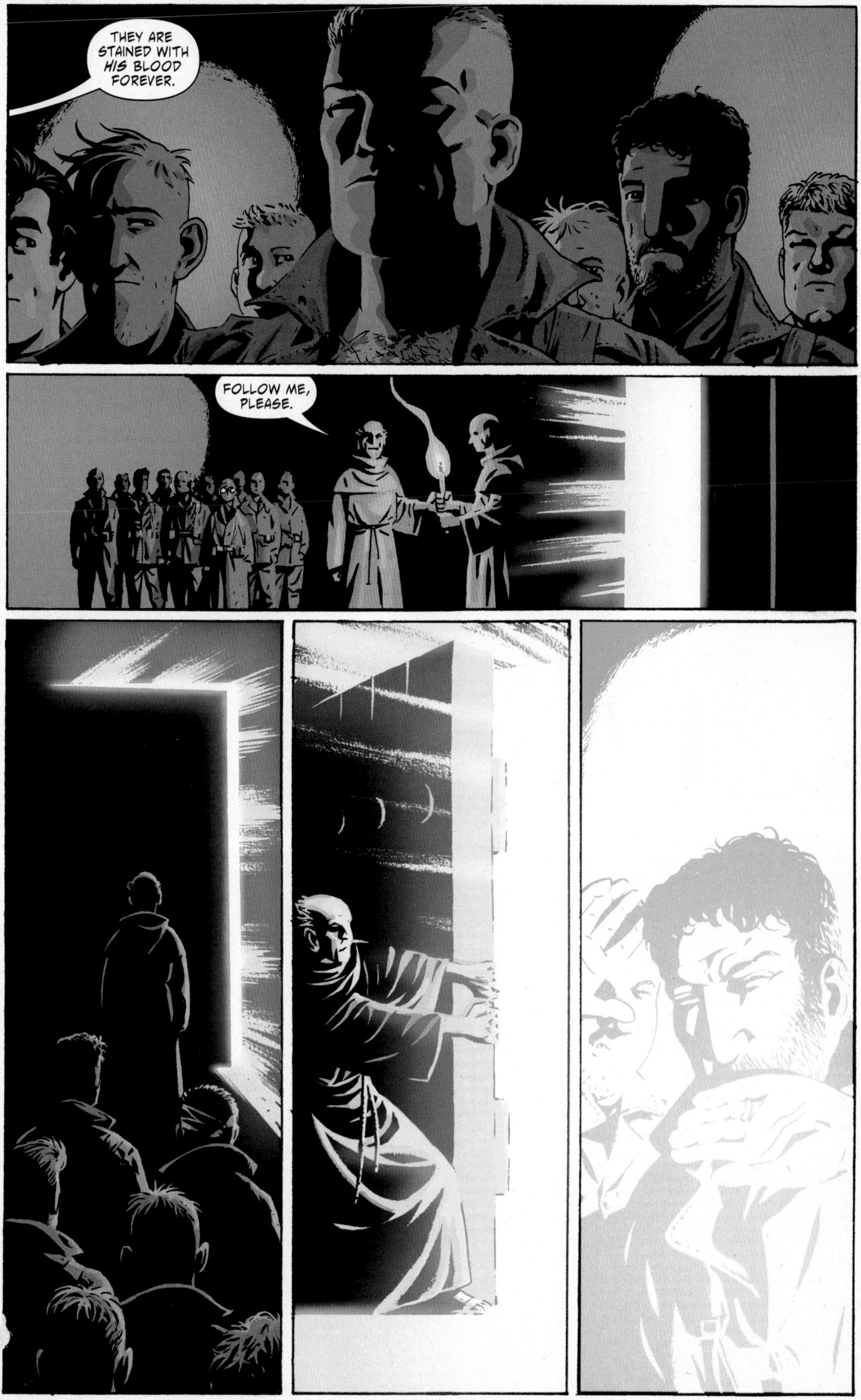
THEY ARE STAINED WITH HIS BLOOD FOREVER.
FOLLOW ME, PLEASE.

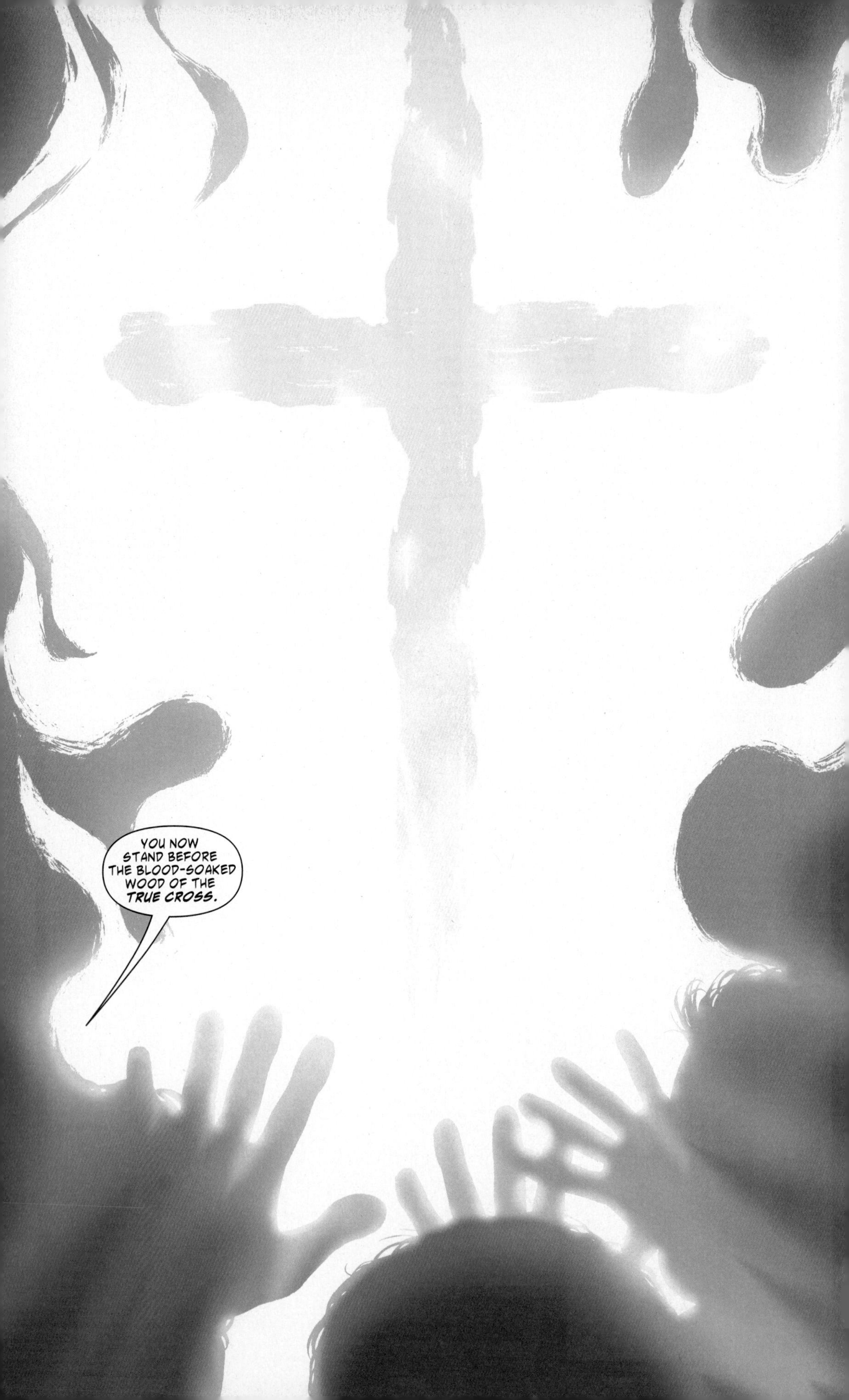
YOU NOW STAND BEFORE THE BLOOD-SOAKED WOOD OF THE TRUE CROSS.

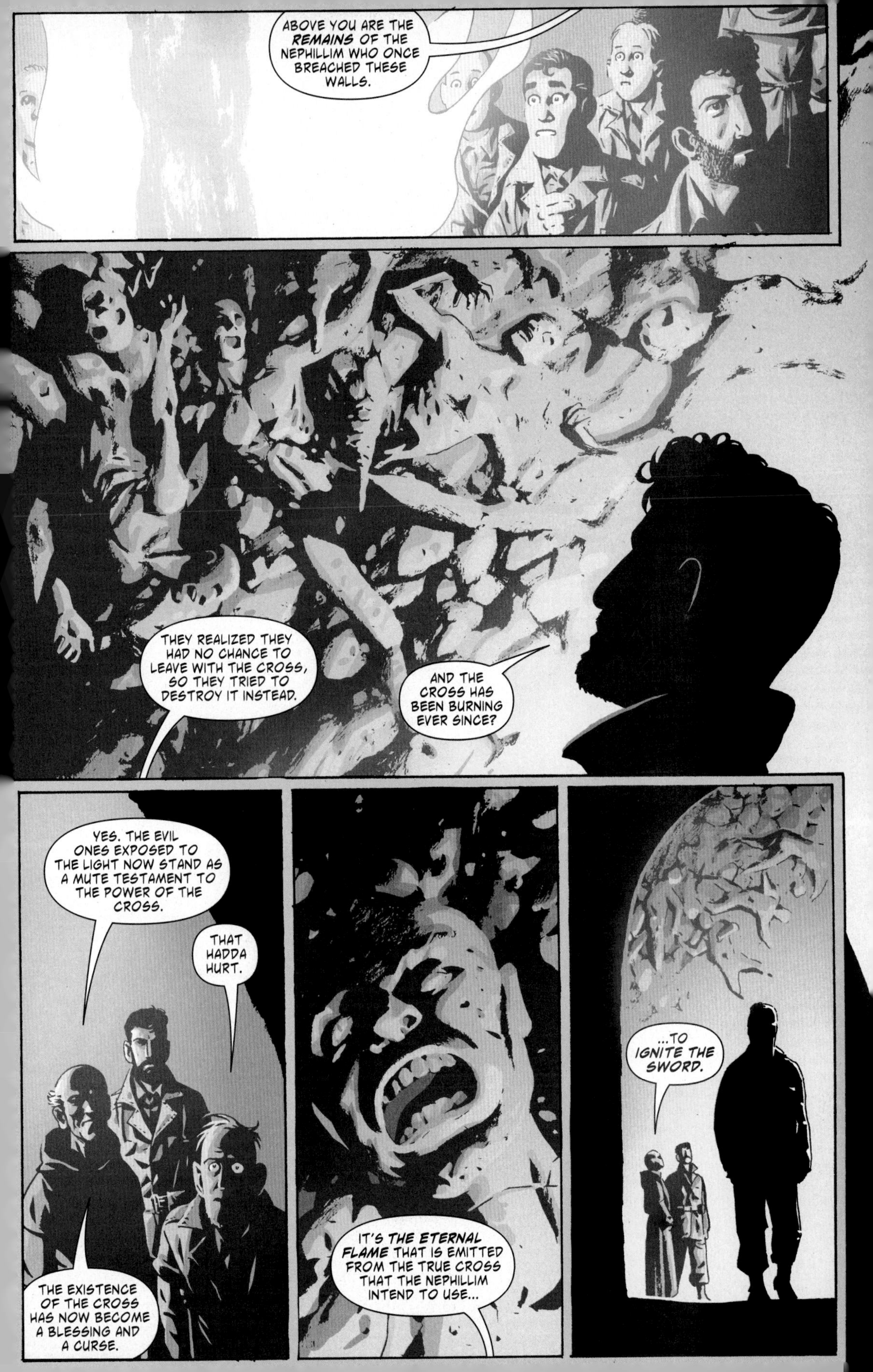
ABOVE YOU ARE THE *REMAINS* OF THE NEPHILLIM WHO ONCE BREACHED THESE WALLS.
THEY REALIZED THEY HAD NO CHANCE TO LEAVE WITH THE CROSS, SO THEY TRIED TO DESTROY IT INSTEAD.
AND THE CROSS HAS BEEN BURNING EVER SINCE?
YES. THE EVIL ONES EXPOSED TO THE LIGHT NOW STAND AS A MUTE TESTAMENT TO THE POWER OF THE CROSS.
THAT HADDA HURT.
THE EXISTENCE OF THE CROSS HAS NOW BECOME A BLESSING AND A CURSE.
IT'S *THE ETERNAL FLAME* THAT IS EMITTED FROM THE TRUE CROSS THAT THE NEPHILLIM INTEND TO USE...
...TO *IGNITE THE SWORD.*

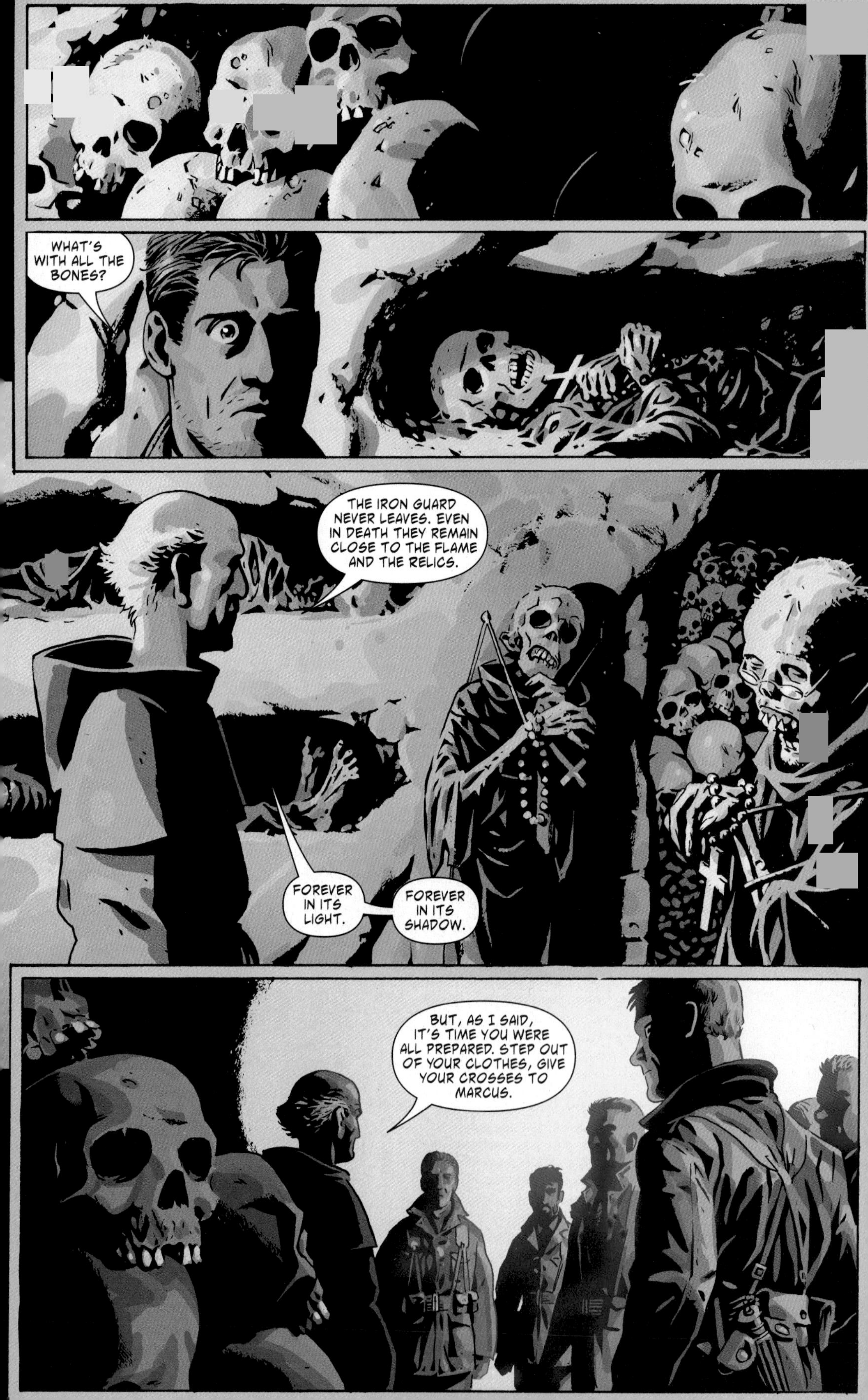
WHAT'S WITH ALL THE BONES?
THE IRON GUARD NEVER LEAVES. EVEN IN DEATH THEY REMAIN CLOSE TO THE FLAME AND THE RELICS.
FOREVER IN ITS LIGHT.
FOREVER IN ITS SHADOW.
BUT, AS I SAID, IT'S TIME YOU WERE ALL PREPARED. STEP OUT OF YOUR CLOTHES, GIVE YOUR CROSSES TO MARCUS.

YOU HAVE LISTENED TO MY WORDS. NOW PROCEED, SONS OF LIGHT.

IS IT GONNA HURT? I'M NOT A BIG FAN OF BURNING.

I'M ALL FOR RETHINKIN' OUR STRATEGY... MAYBE GET ANOTHER ANGEL'S OPINION...

C'MON, WE'VE ALL GOTTA GO TOGETHER.

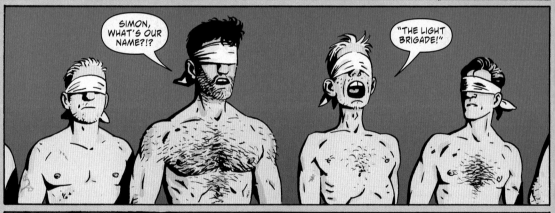

SIMON, WHAT'S OUR NAME?!?

"THE LIGHT BRIGADE!"

YOU'RE DAMN RIGHT.

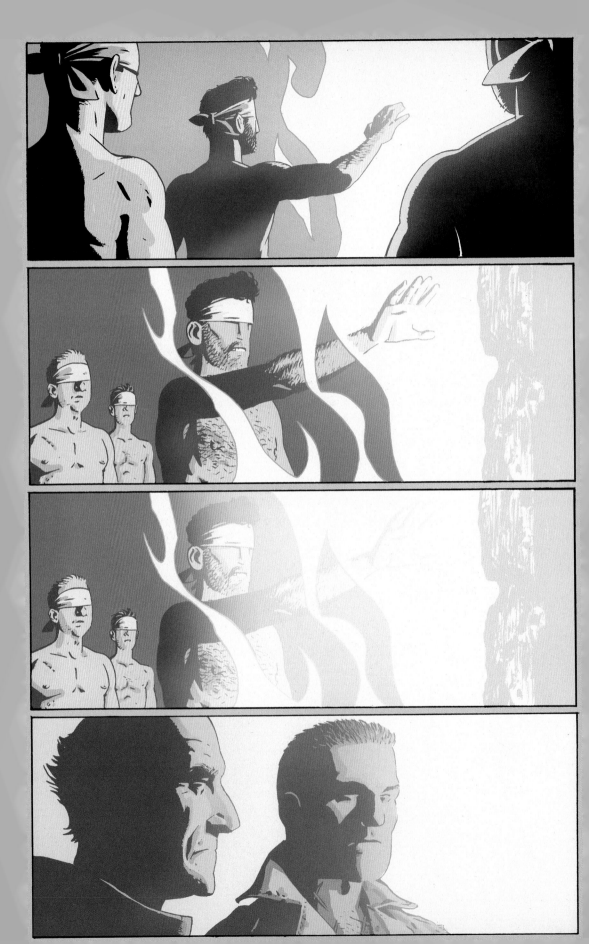

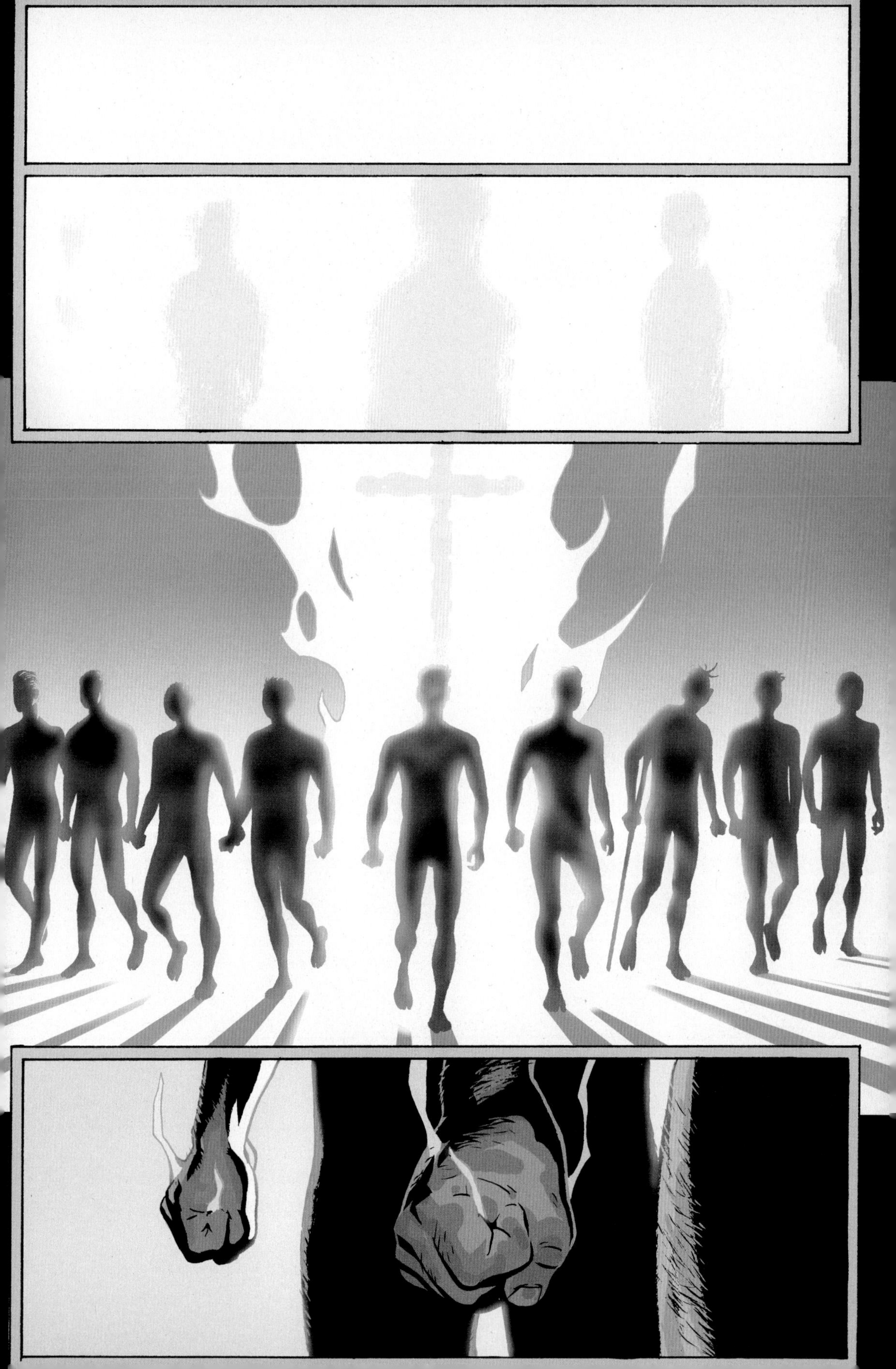

OPEN YOUR HANDS.

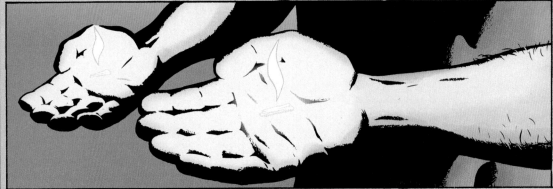

IS IT ENOUGH?

MORE THAN ENOUGH. YOU HAVE BEEN ALLOWED *THIS* GIFT BECAUSE OF YOUR MEETING WITH THE ARCHANGEL.

THIS IS WHY YOU ARE HERE.

THE GIFT THAT KEEPS ON GIVING, HUH?

NOW, THE FINAL STEP.

AM I DREAMING? AM I ACTUALLY GONNA TAKE A BATH AFTER SIX MONTHS?

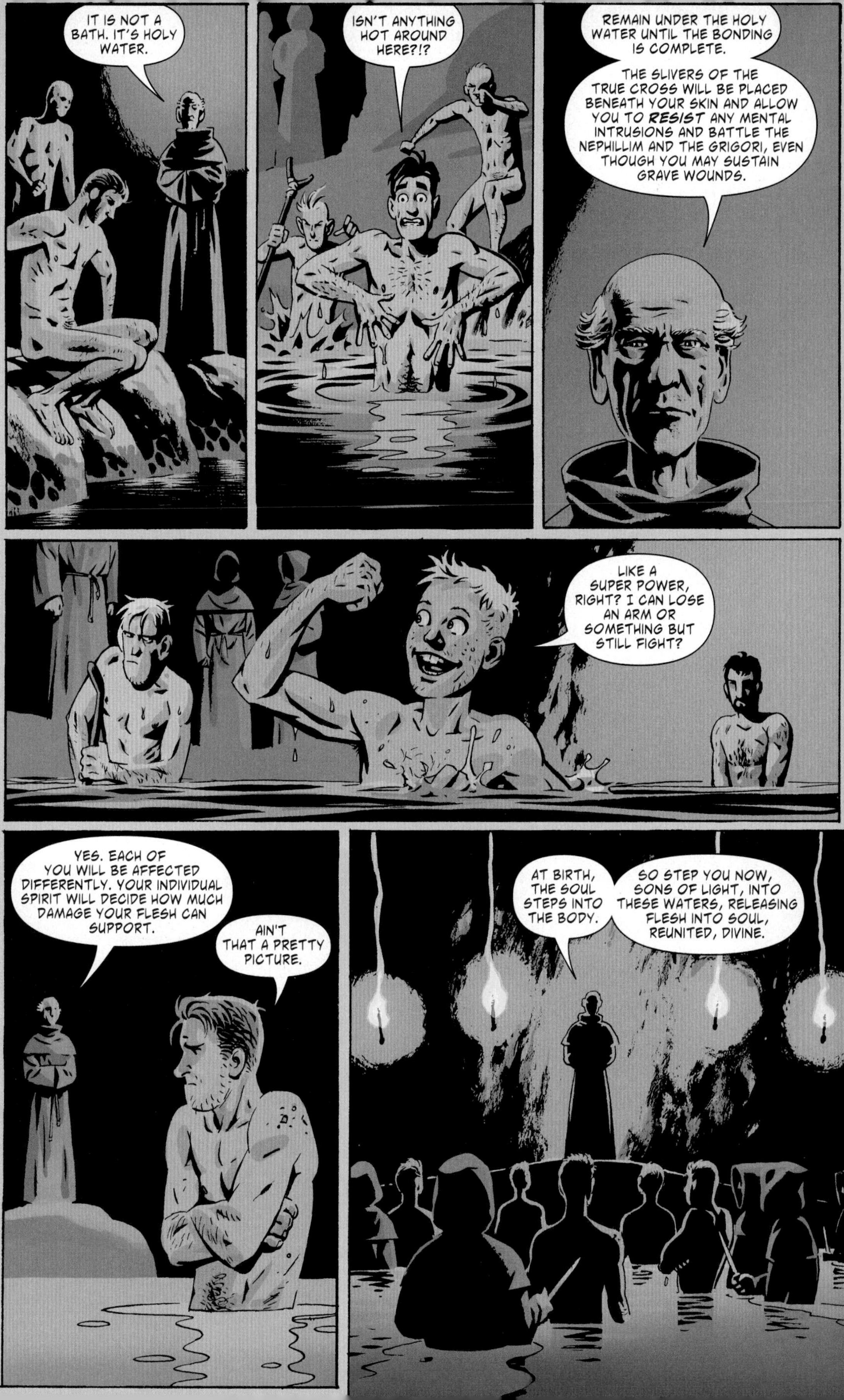
IT IS NOT A BATH. IT'S HOLY WATER.
ISN'T ANYTHING HOT AROUND HERE?!?
REMAIN UNDER THE HOLY WATER UNTIL THE BONDING IS COMPLETE.
THE SLIVERS OF THE TRUE CROSS WILL BE PLACED BENEATH YOUR SKIN AND ALLOW YOU TO RESIST ANY MENTAL INTRUSIONS AND BATTLE THE NEPHILLIM AND THE GRIGORI, EVEN THOUGH YOU MAY SUSTAIN GRAVE WOUNDS.
LIKE A SUPER POWER, RIGHT? I CAN LOSE AN ARM OR SOMETHING BUT STILL FIGHT?
YES. EACH OF YOU WILL BE AFFECTED DIFFERENTLY. YOUR INDIVIDUAL SPIRIT WILL DECIDE HOW MUCH DAMAGE YOUR FLESH CAN SUPPORT.
AIN'T THAT A PRETTY PICTURE.
AT BIRTH, THE SOUL STEPS INTO THE BODY.
SO STEP YOU NOW, SONS OF LIGHT, INTO THESE WATERS, RELEASING FLESH INTO SOUL, REUNITED, DIVINE.

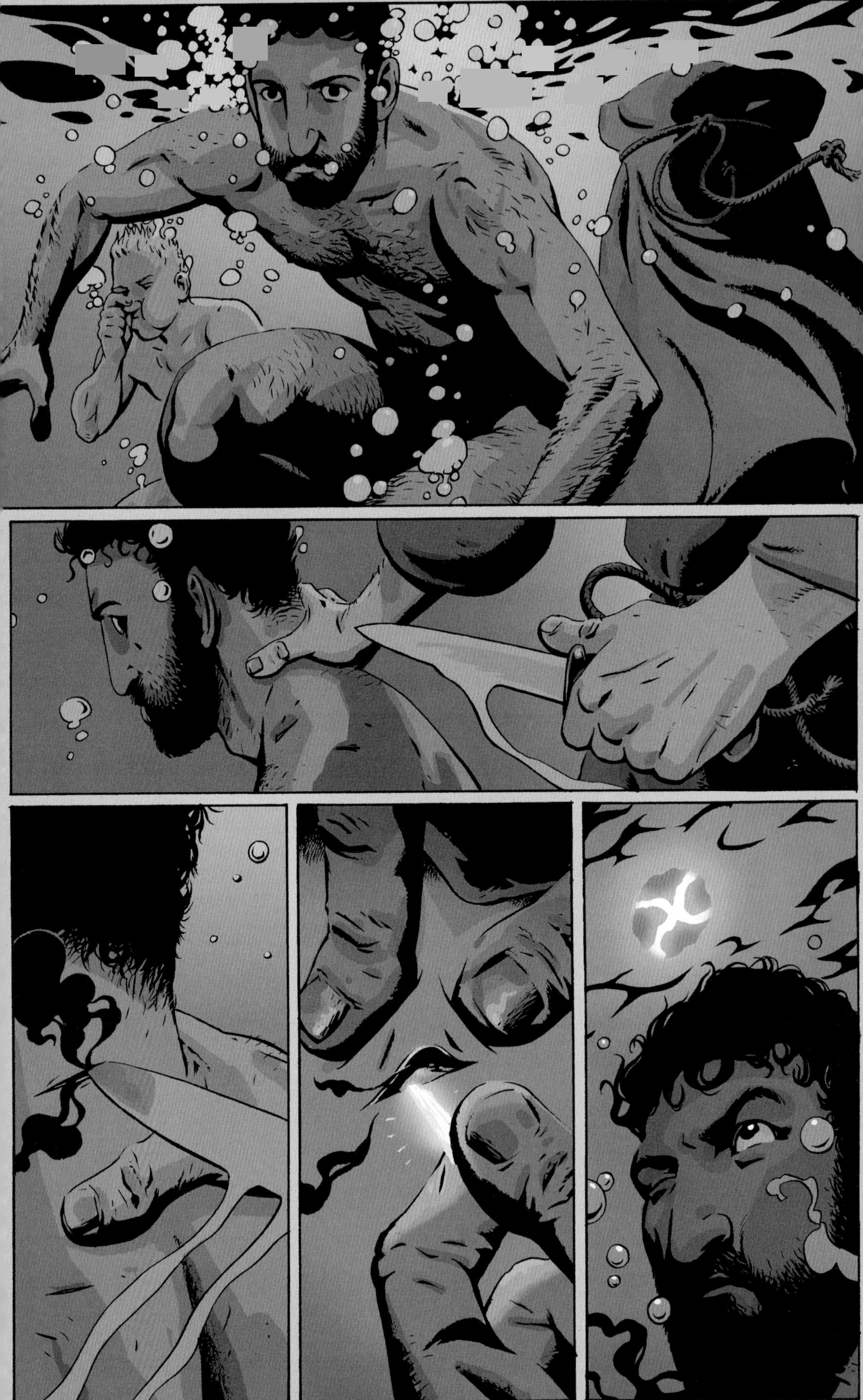

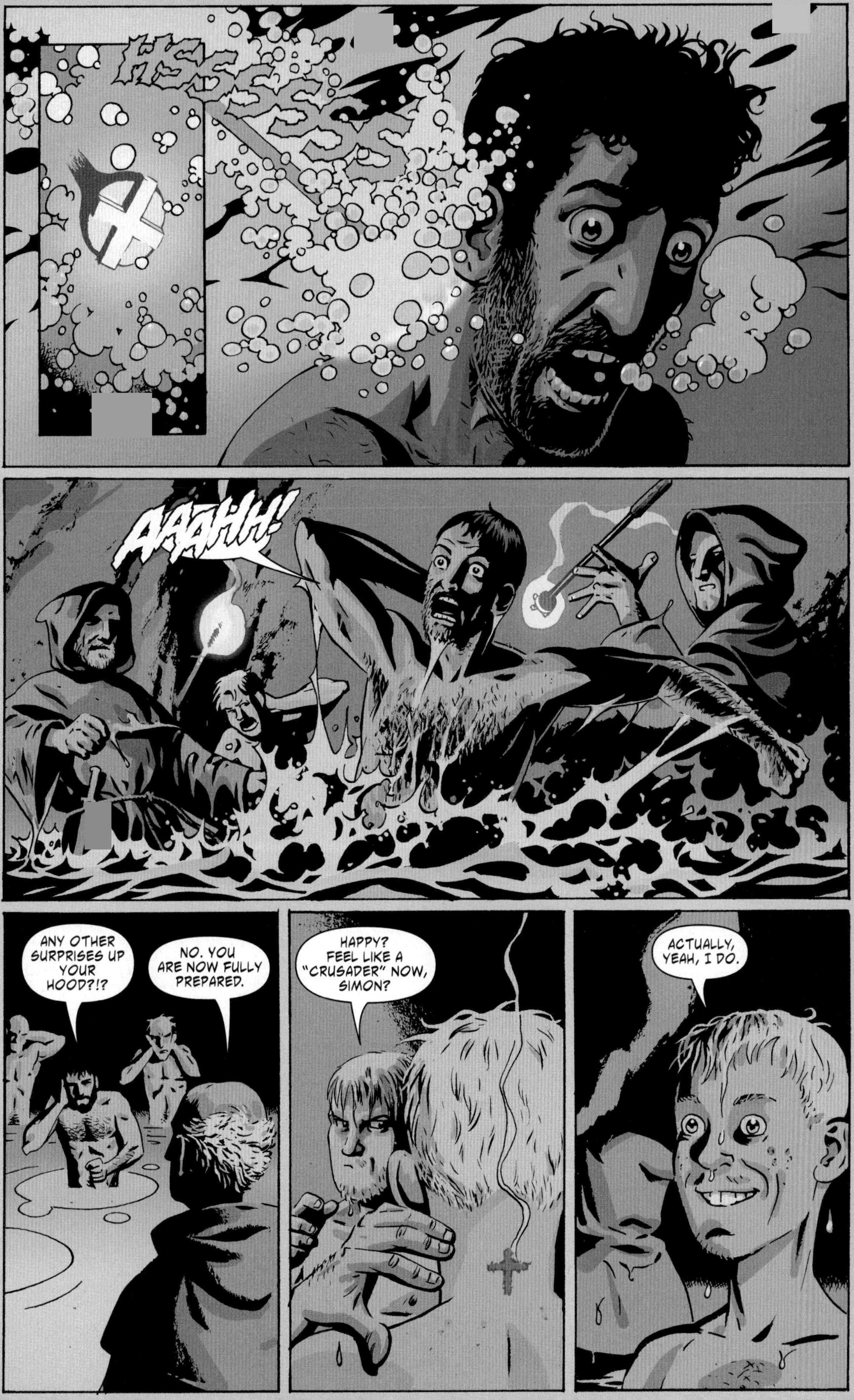
HSSSSS
AAAHH!
ANY OTHER SURPRISES UP YOUR HOOD?!?
NO. YOU ARE NOW FULLY PREPARED.
HAPPY? FEEL LIKE A "CRUSADER" NOW, SIMON?
ACTUALLY, YEAH, I DO.

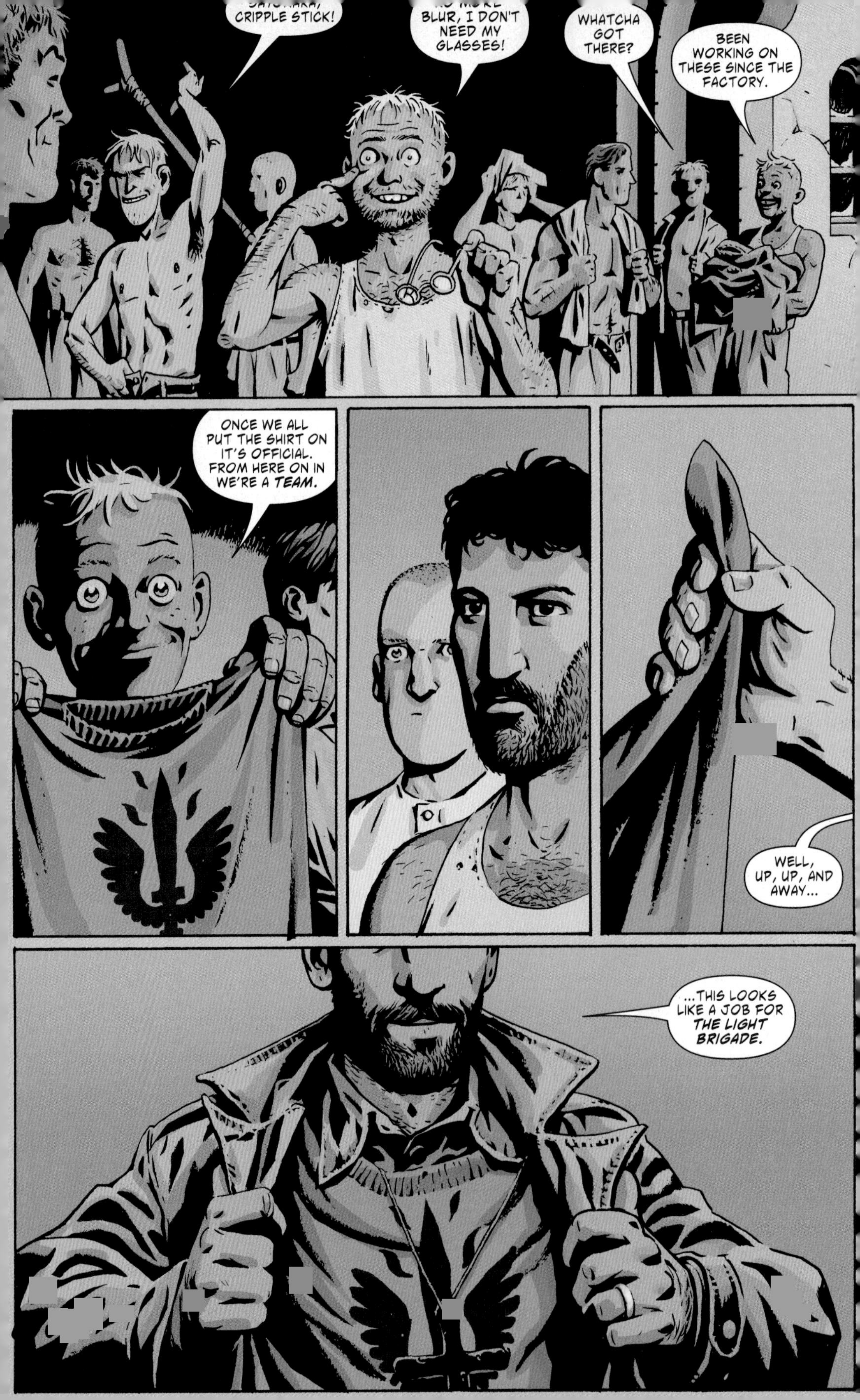
CRIPPLE STICK!
BLUR, I DON'T NEED MY GLASSES!
WHATCHA GOT THERE?
BEEN WORKING ON THESE SINCE THE FACTORY.
ONCE WE ALL PUT THE SHIRT ON IT'S OFFICIAL. FROM HERE ON IN WE'RE A *TEAM.*
WELL, UP, UP, AND AWAY...
...THIS LOOKS LIKE A JOB FOR *THE LIGHT BRIGADE.*

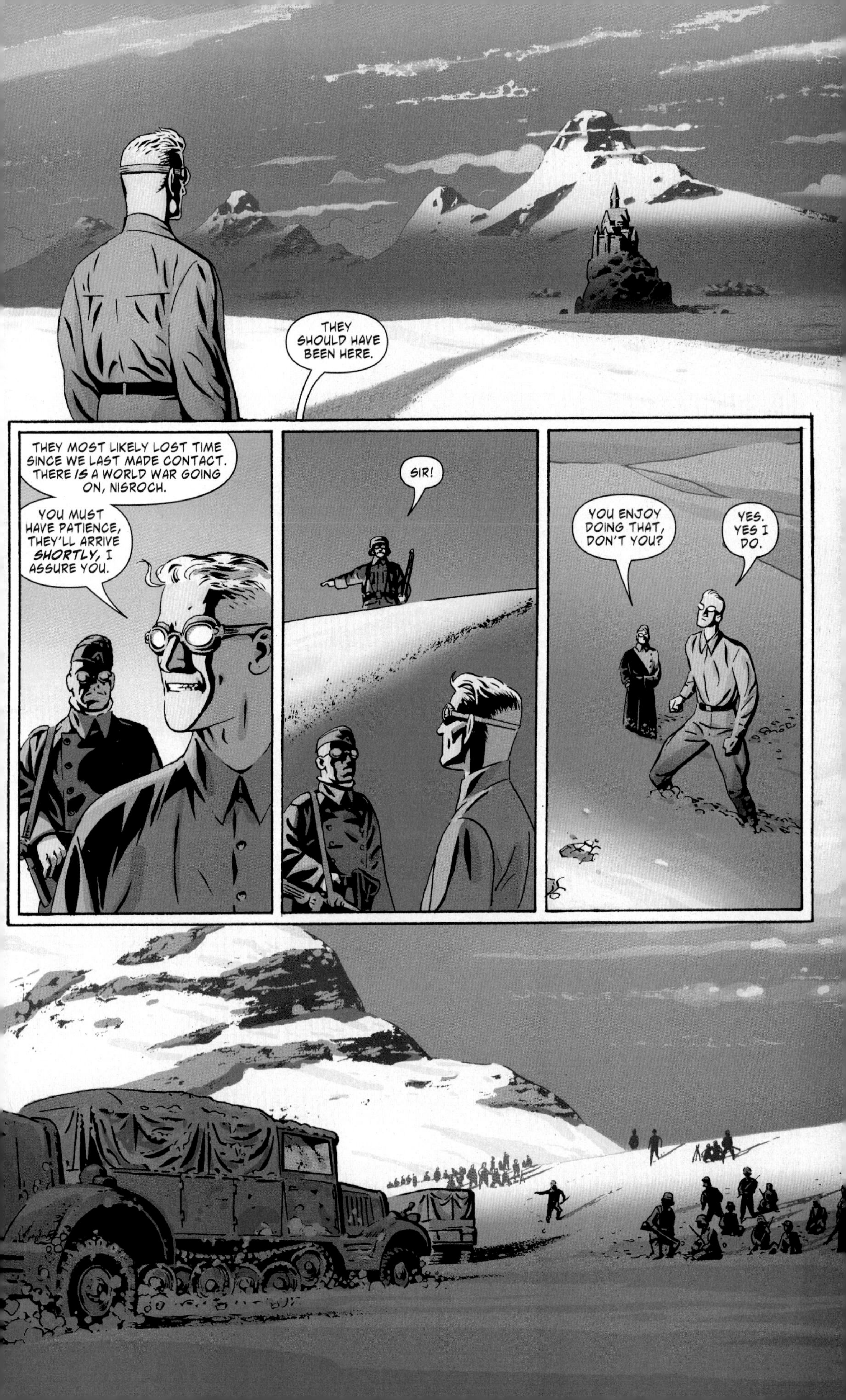
THEY SHOULD HAVE BEEN HERE.
THEY MOST LIKELY LOST TIME SINCE WE LAST MADE CONTACT. THERE *IS* A WORLD WAR GOING ON, NISROCH.
YOU MUST HAVE PATIENCE, THEY'LL ARRIVE *SHORTLY*, I ASSURE YOU.
SIR!
YOU ENJOY DOING THAT, DON'T YOU?
YES. YES I DO.

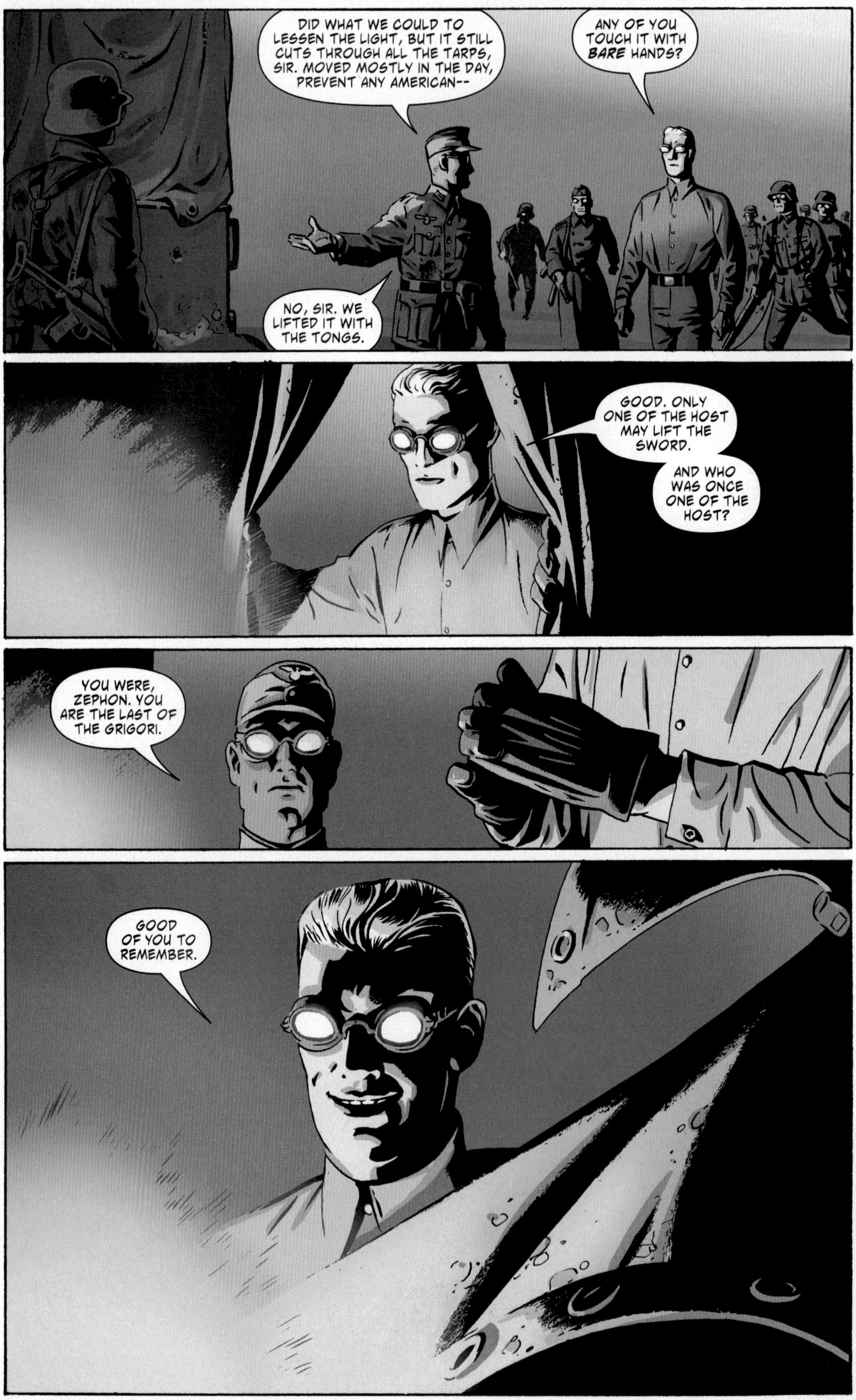
DID WHAT WE COULD TO LESSEN THE LIGHT, BUT IT STILL CUTS THROUGH ALL THE TARPS, SIR. MOVED MOSTLY IN THE DAY, PREVENT ANY AMERICAN--
ANY OF YOU TOUCH IT WITH BARE HANDS?
NO, SIR. WE LIFTED IT WITH THE TONGS.
GOOD. ONLY ONE OF THE HOST MAY LIFT THE SWORD.
AND WHO WAS ONCE ONE OF THE HOST?
YOU WERE, ZEPHON. YOU ARE THE LAST OF THE GRIGORI.
GOOD OF YOU TO REMEMBER.

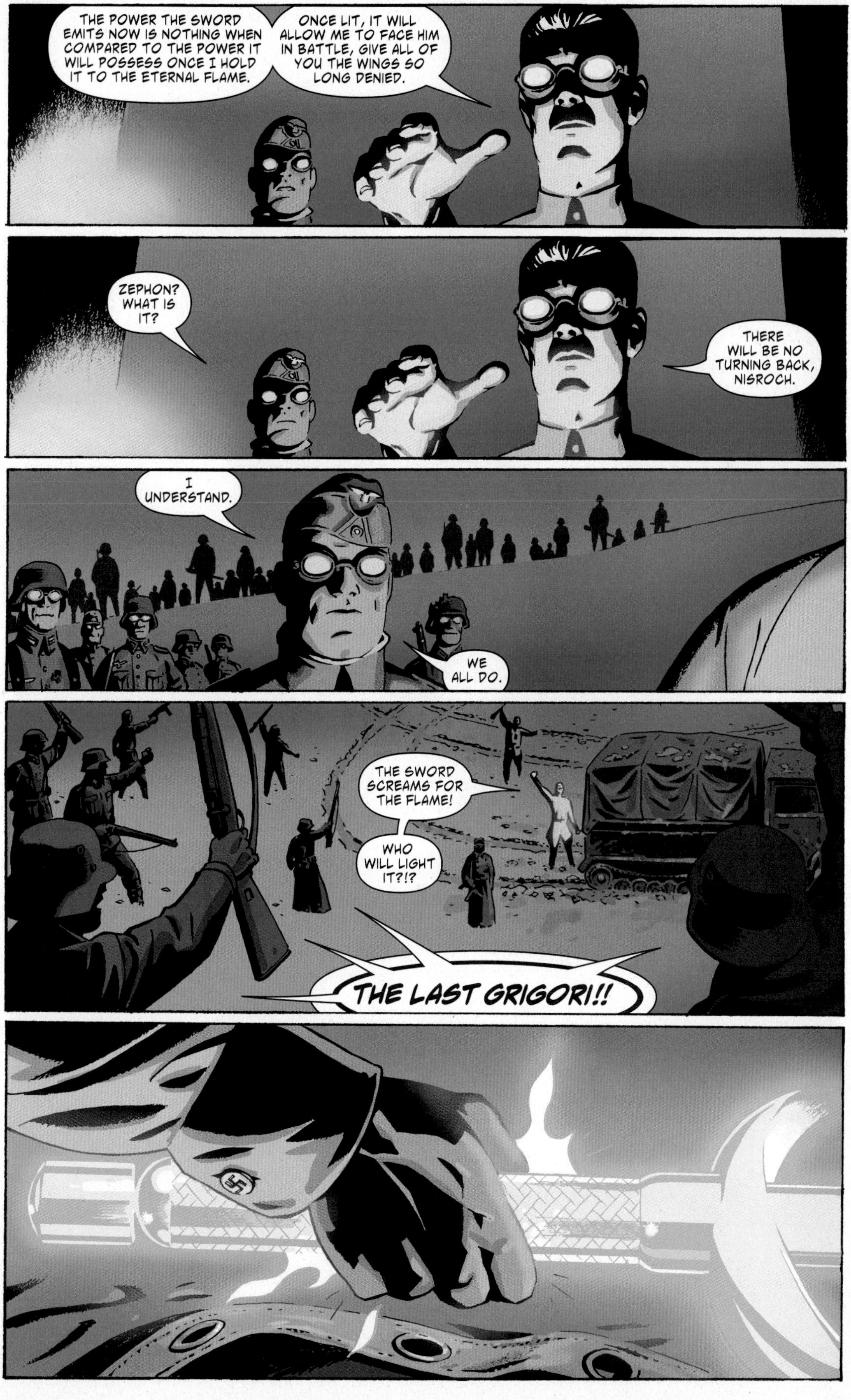
THE POWER THE SWORD EMITS NOW IS NOTHING WHEN COMPARED TO THE POWER IT WILL POSSESS ONCE I HOLD IT TO THE ETERNAL FLAME.
ONCE LIT, IT WILL ALLOW ME TO FACE HIM IN BATTLE, GIVE ALL OF YOU THE WINGS SO LONG DENIED.
ZEPHON? WHAT IS IT?
THERE WILL BE NO TURNING BACK, NISROCH.
I UNDERSTAND.
WE ALL DO.
THE SWORD SCREAMS FOR THE FLAME!
WHO WILL LIGHT IT?!?
THE LAST GRIGORI!!

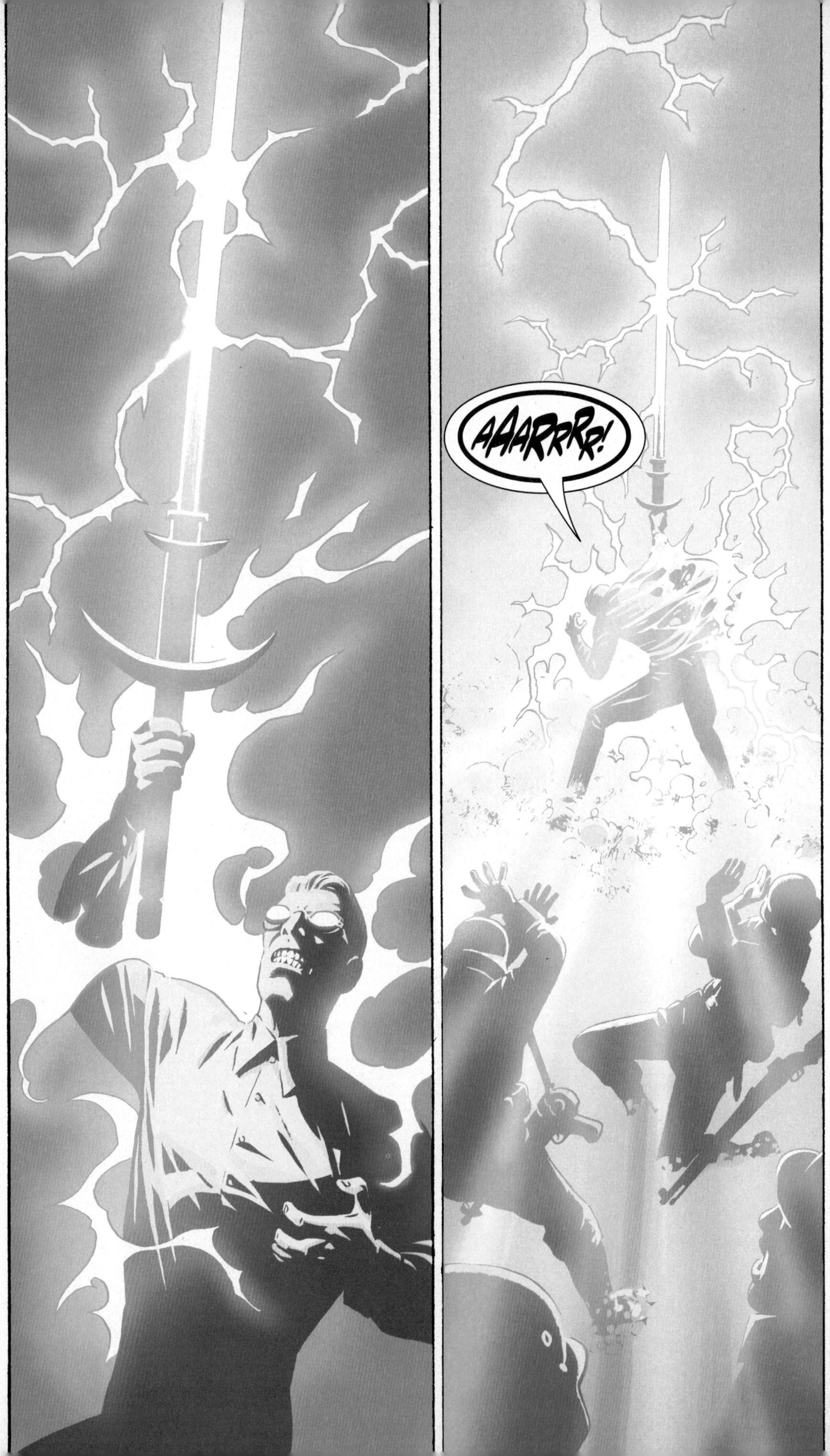
AAARRRR!

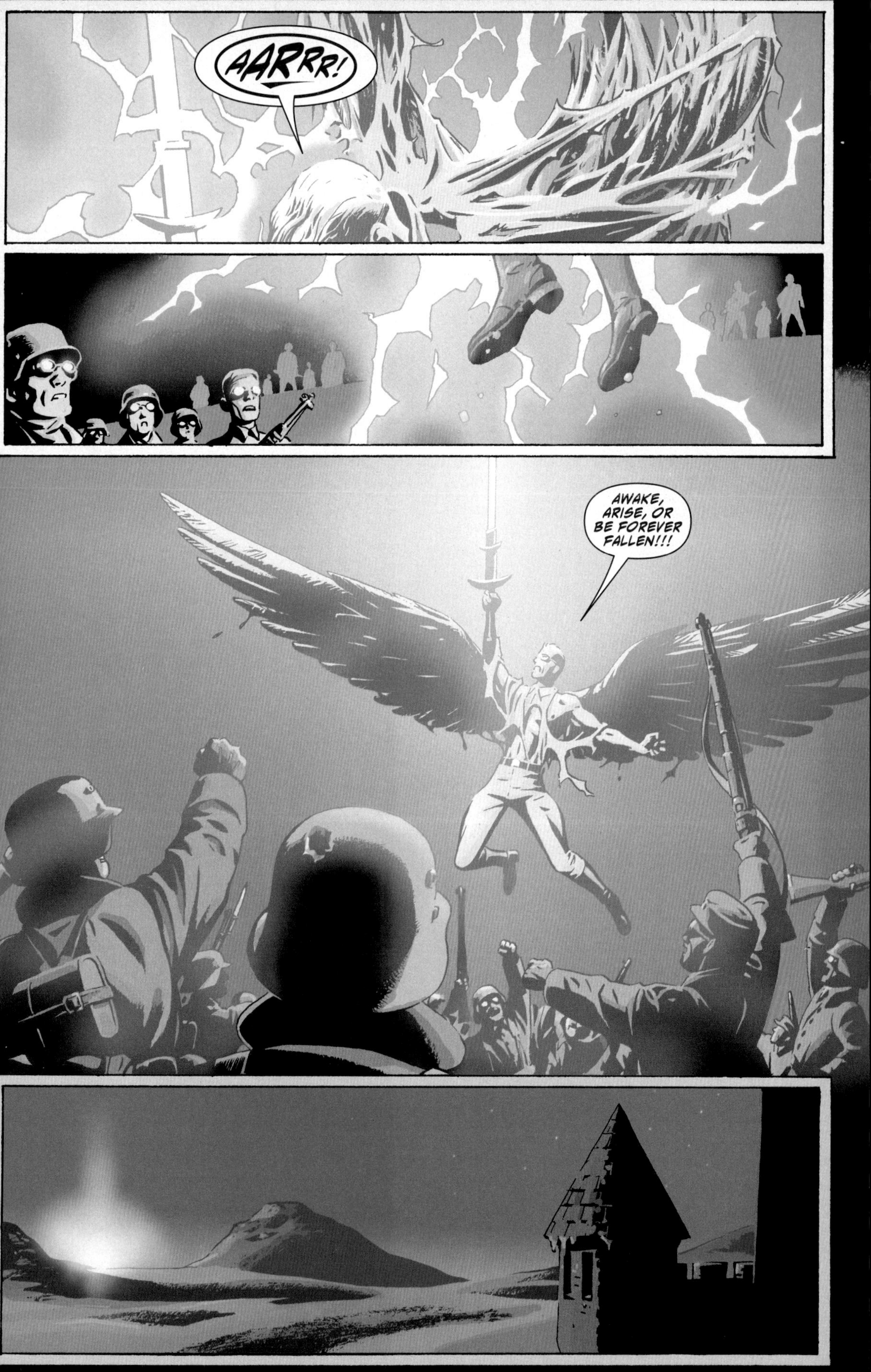
AARRR!
AWAKE, ARISE, OR BE FOREVER FALLEN!!!

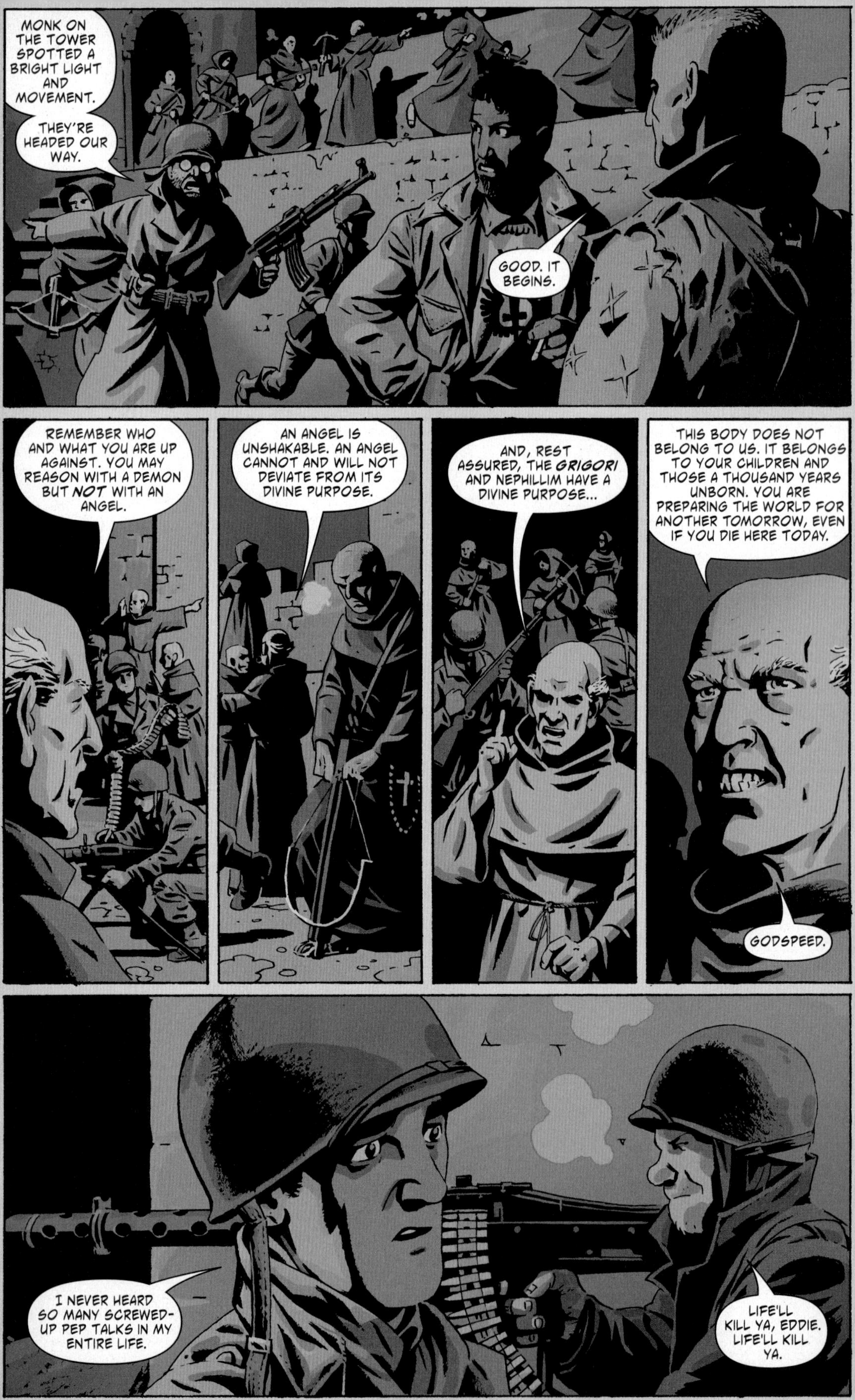
MONK ON THE TOWER SPOTTED A BRIGHT LIGHT AND MOVEMENT.
THEY'RE HEADED OUR WAY.
GOOD. IT BEGINS.
REMEMBER WHO AND WHAT YOU ARE UP AGAINST. YOU MAY REASON WITH A DEMON BUT NOT WITH AN ANGEL.
AN ANGEL IS UNSHAKABLE. AN ANGEL CANNOT AND WILL NOT DEVIATE FROM ITS DIVINE PURPOSE.
AND, REST ASSURED, THE GRIGORI AND NEPHILLIM HAVE A DIVINE PURPOSE...
THIS BODY DOES NOT BELONG TO US. IT BELONGS TO YOUR CHILDREN AND THOSE A THOUSAND YEARS UNBORN. YOU ARE PREPARING THE WORLD FOR ANOTHER TOMORROW, EVEN IF YOU DIE HERE TODAY.
GODSPEED.
I NEVER HEARD SO MANY SCREWED-UP PEP TALKS IN MY ENTIRE LIFE.
LIFE'LL KILL YA, EDDIE. LIFE'LL KILL YA.

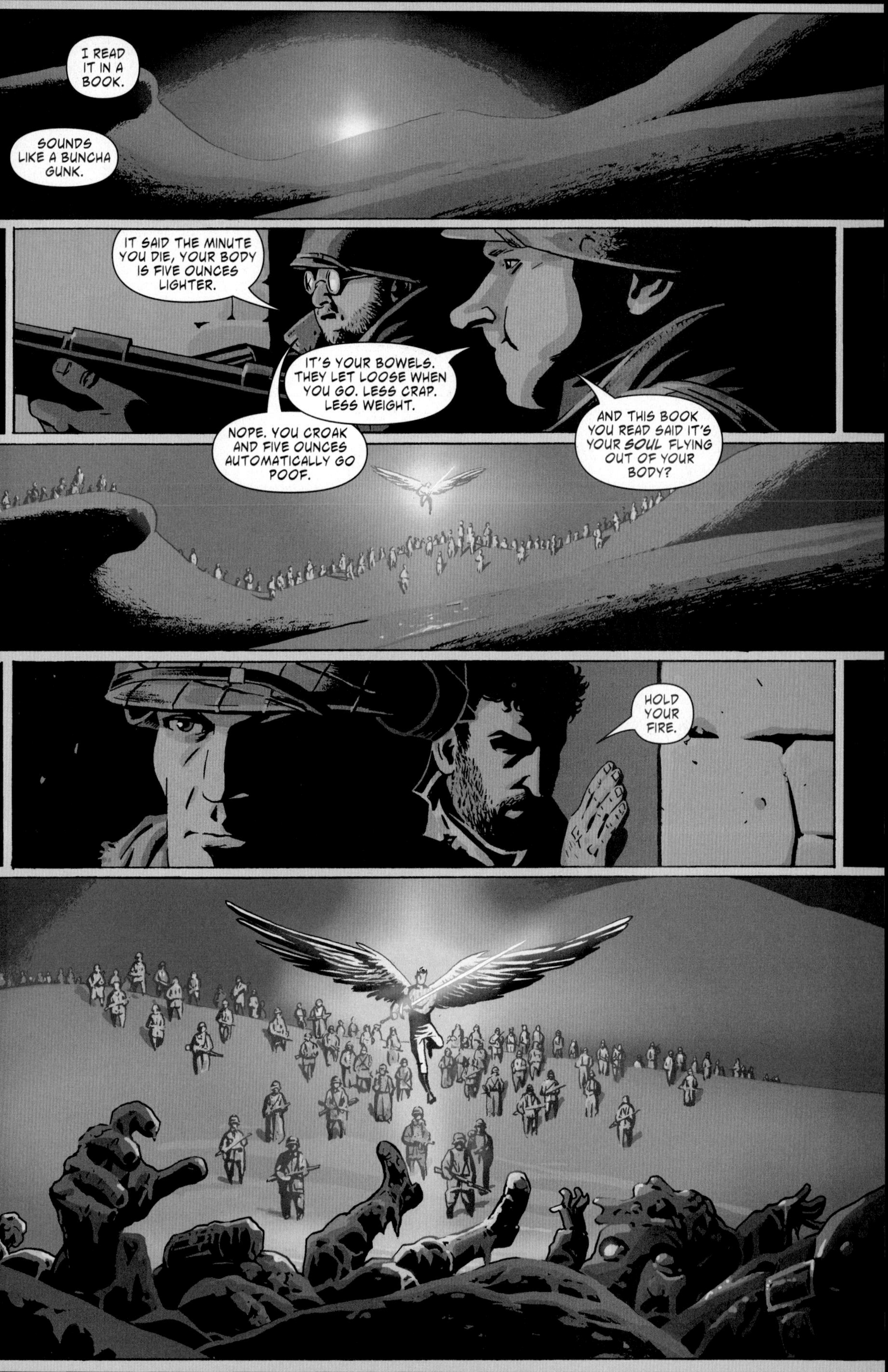

I READ IT IN A BOOK.
SOUNDS LIKE A BUNCHA GUNK.
IT SAID THE MINUTE YOU DIE, YOUR BODY IS FIVE OUNCES LIGHTER.
IT'S YOUR BOWELS. THEY LET LOOSE WHEN YOU GO. LESS CRAP. LESS WEIGHT.
NOPE. YOU CROAK AND FIVE OUNCES AUTOMATICALLY GO POOF.
AND THIS BOOK YOU READ SAID IT'S YOUR SOUL FLYING OUT OF YOUR BODY?
HOLD YOUR FIRE.

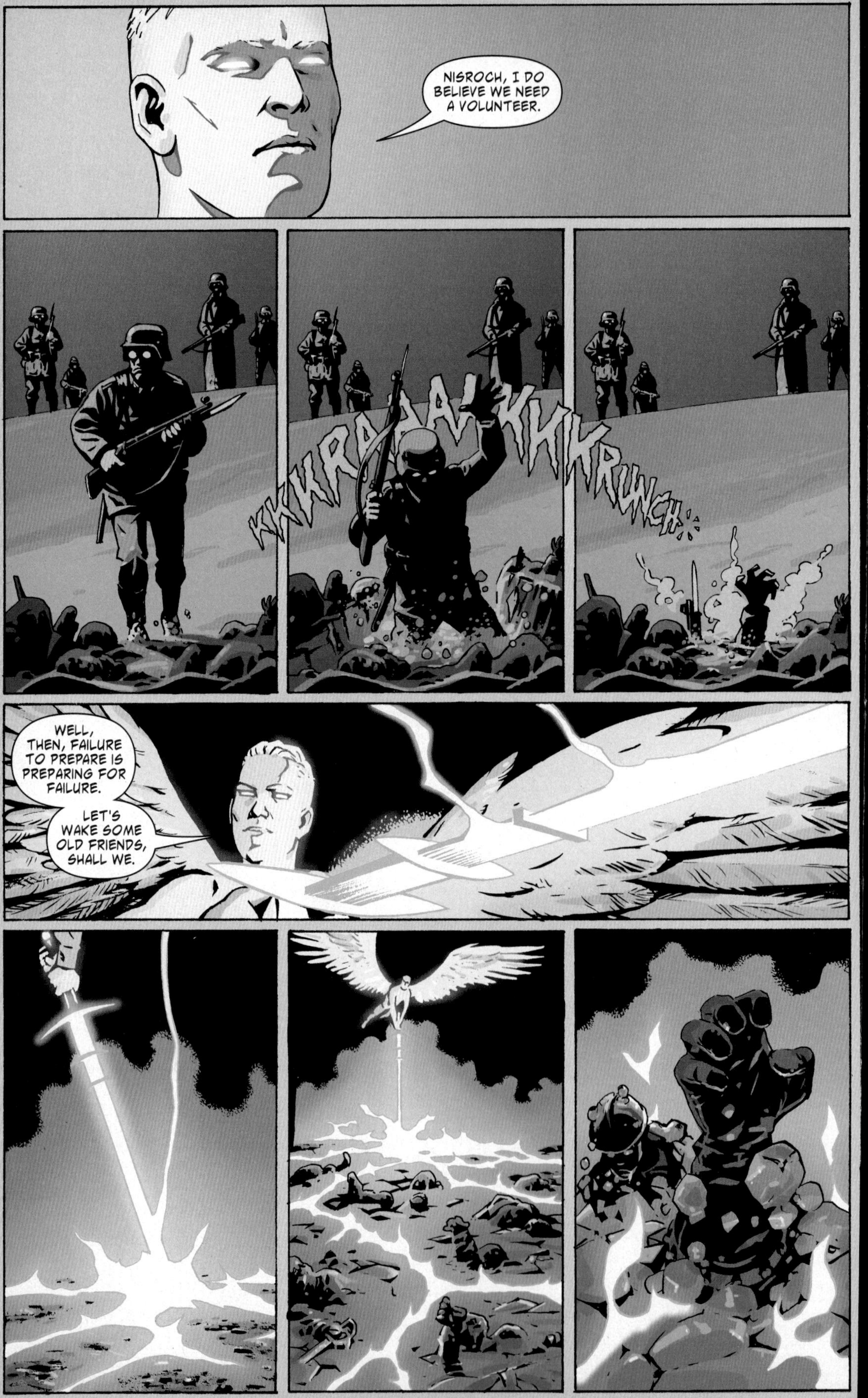
NISROCH, I DO BELIEVE WE NEED A VOLUNTEER.
KKKRRAAKKKKKRUNCH
WELL, THEN, FAILURE TO PREPARE IS PREPARING FOR FAILURE.
LET'S WAKE SOME OLD FRIENDS, SHALL WE.

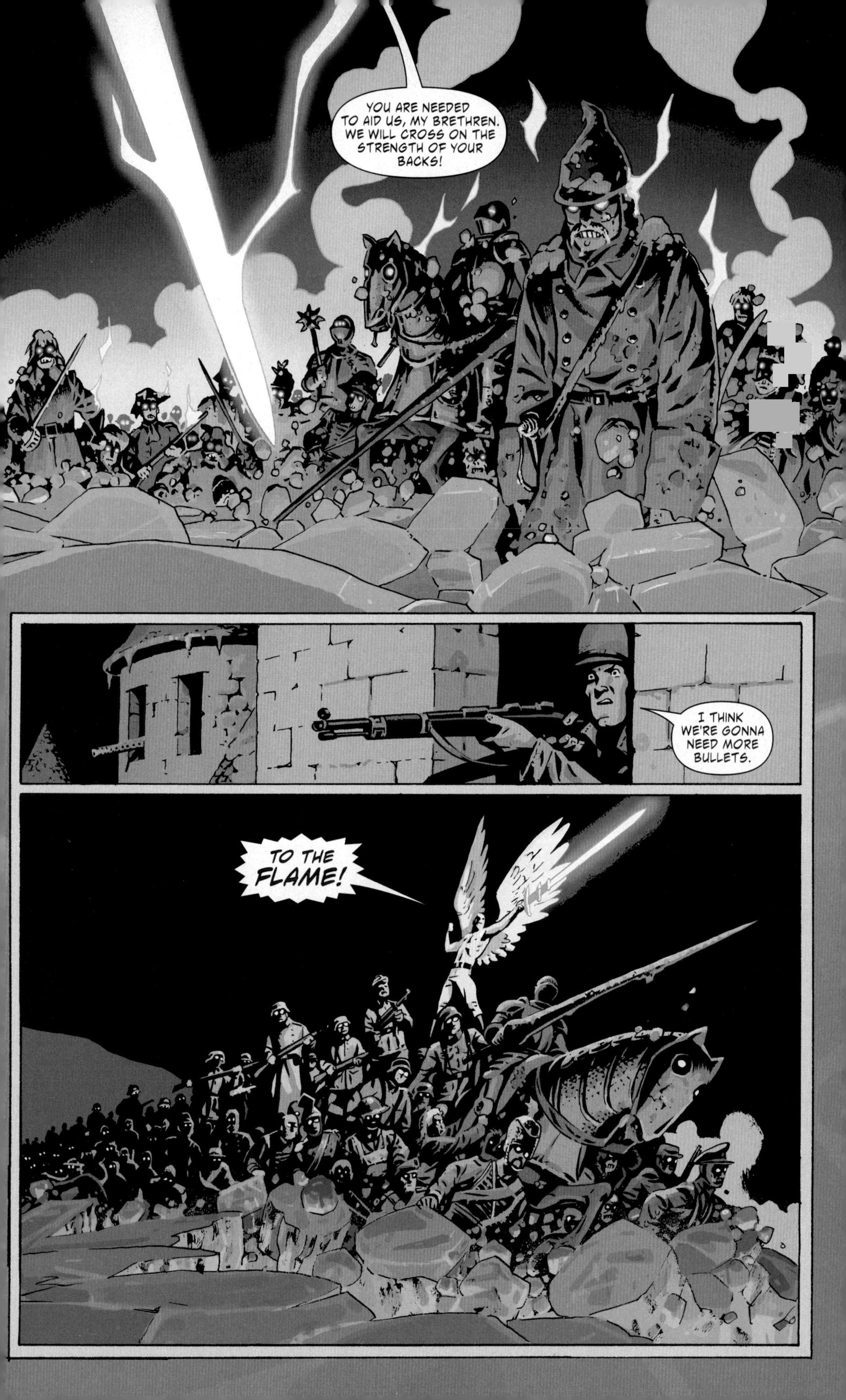
YOU ARE NEEDED TO AID US, MY BRETHREN. WE WILL CROSS ON THE STRENGTH OF YOUR BACKS!
I THINK WE'RE GONNA NEED MORE BULLETS.
TO THE FLAME!

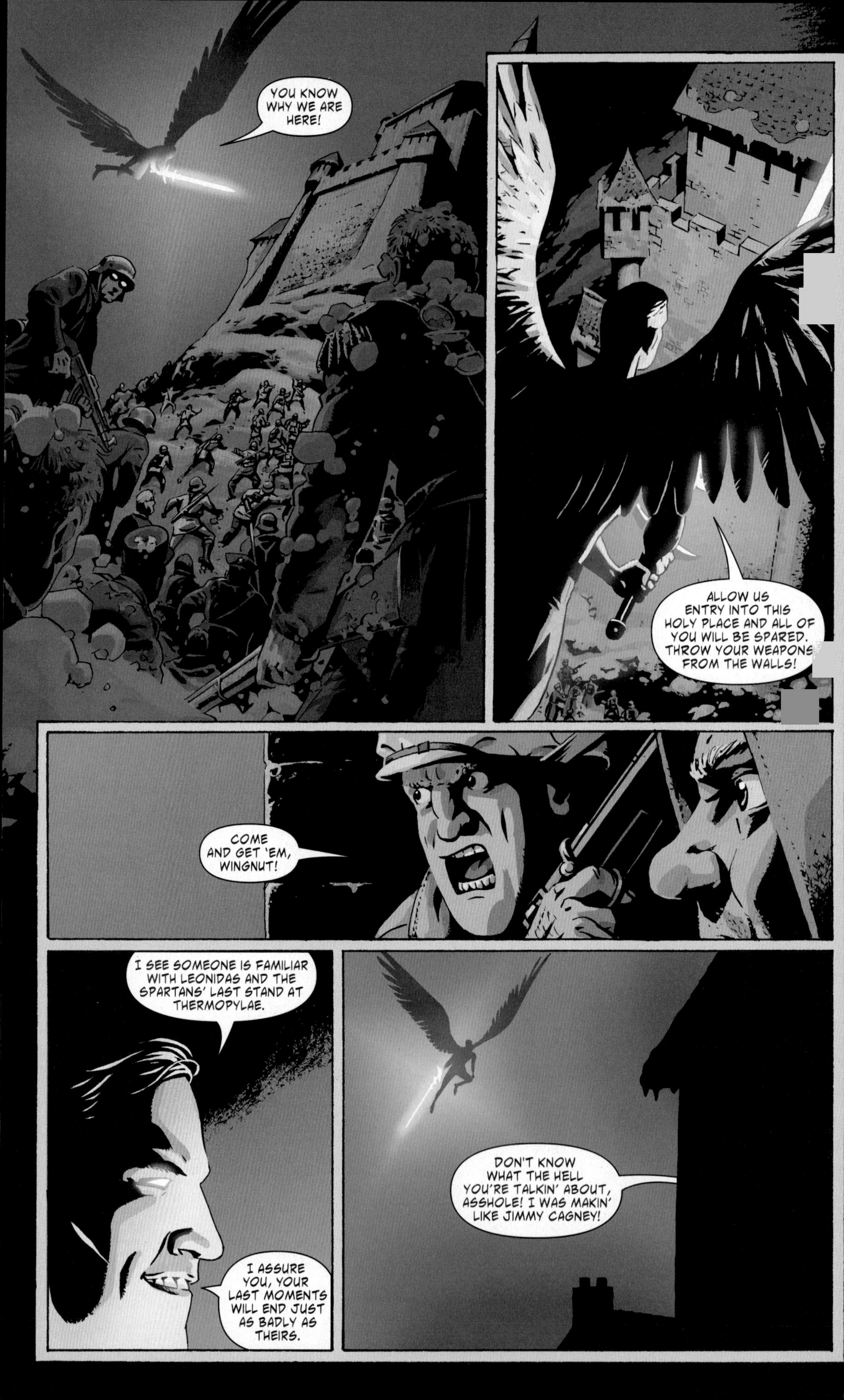
YOU KNOW WHY WE ARE HERE!
ALLOW US ENTRY INTO THIS HOLY PLACE AND ALL OF YOU WILL BE SPARED. THROW YOUR WEAPONS FROM THE WALLS!
COME AND GET 'EM, WINGNUT!
I SEE SOMEONE IS FAMILIAR WITH LEONIDAS AND THE SPARTANS' LAST STAND AT THERMOPYLAE.
I ASSURE YOU, YOUR LAST MOMENTS WILL END JUST AS BADLY AS THEIRS.
DON'T KNOW WHAT THE HELL YOU'RE TALKIN' ABOUT, ASSHOLE! I WAS MAKIN' LIKE JIMMY CAGNEY!

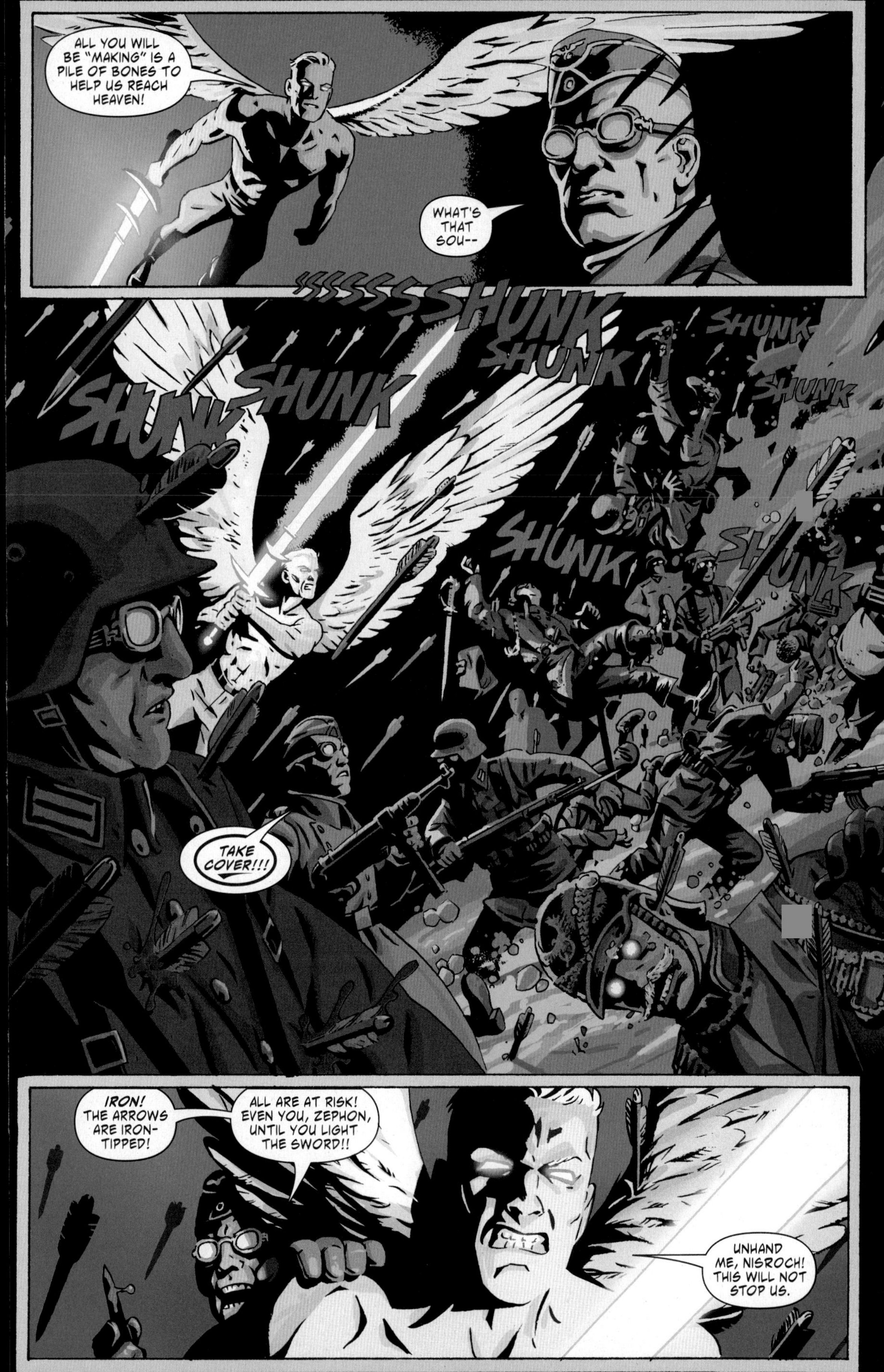
ALL YOU WILL BE "MAKING" IS A PILE OF BONES TO HELP US REACH HEAVEN!
WHAT'S THAT SOU--
SSSSSSSSHUNK
SHUNK
SHUNK
SHUNK
SHUNK
SHUNK
SHUNK
SHUNK
TAKE COVER!!!
IRON! THE ARROWS ARE IRON-TIPPED!
ALL ARE AT RISK! EVEN YOU, ZEPHON, UNTIL YOU LIGHT THE SWORD!!
UNHAND ME, NISROCH! THIS WILL NOT STOP US.

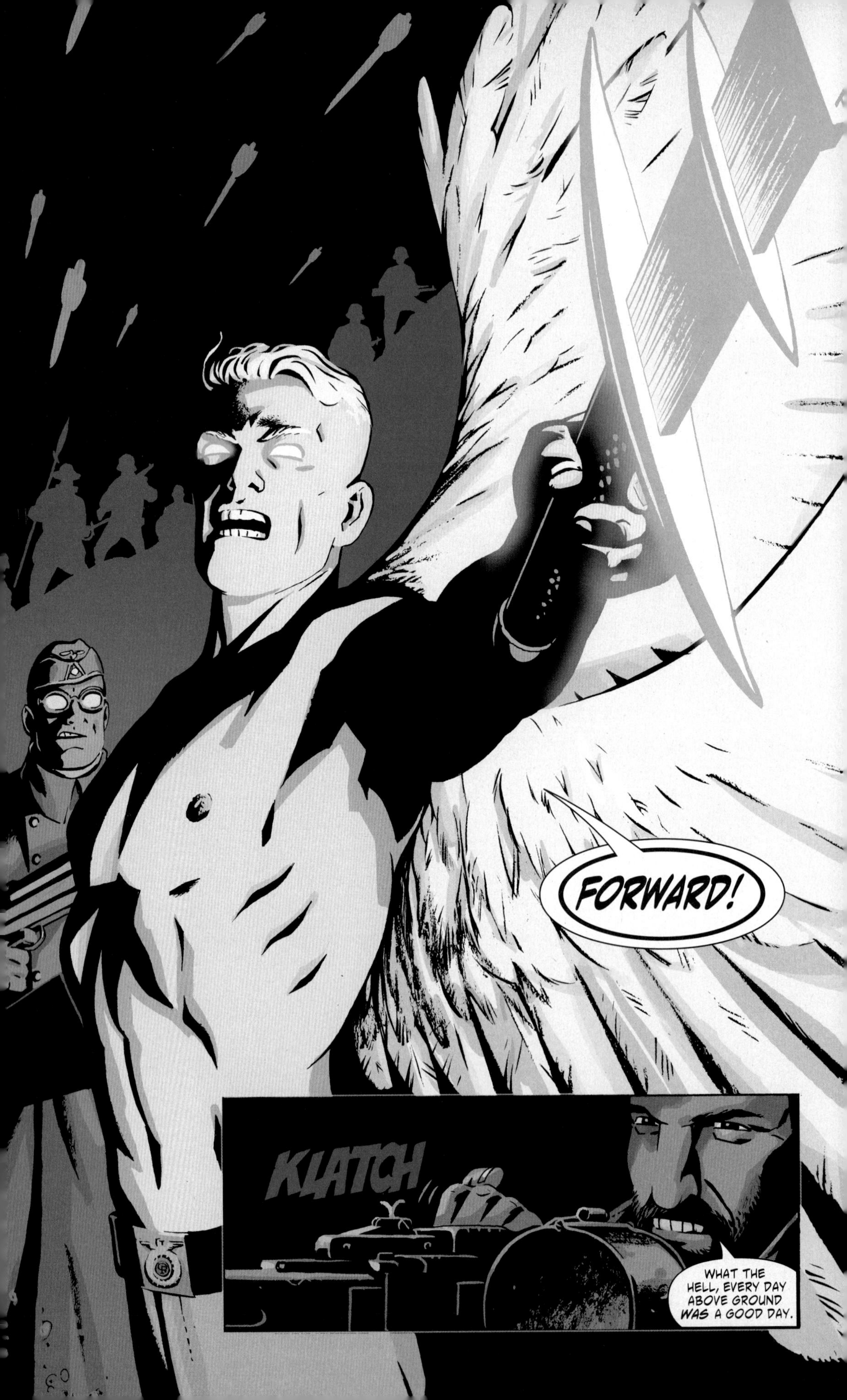
FORWARD!
KLATCH
WHAT THE HELL, EVERY DAY ABOVE GROUND WAS A GOOD DAY.

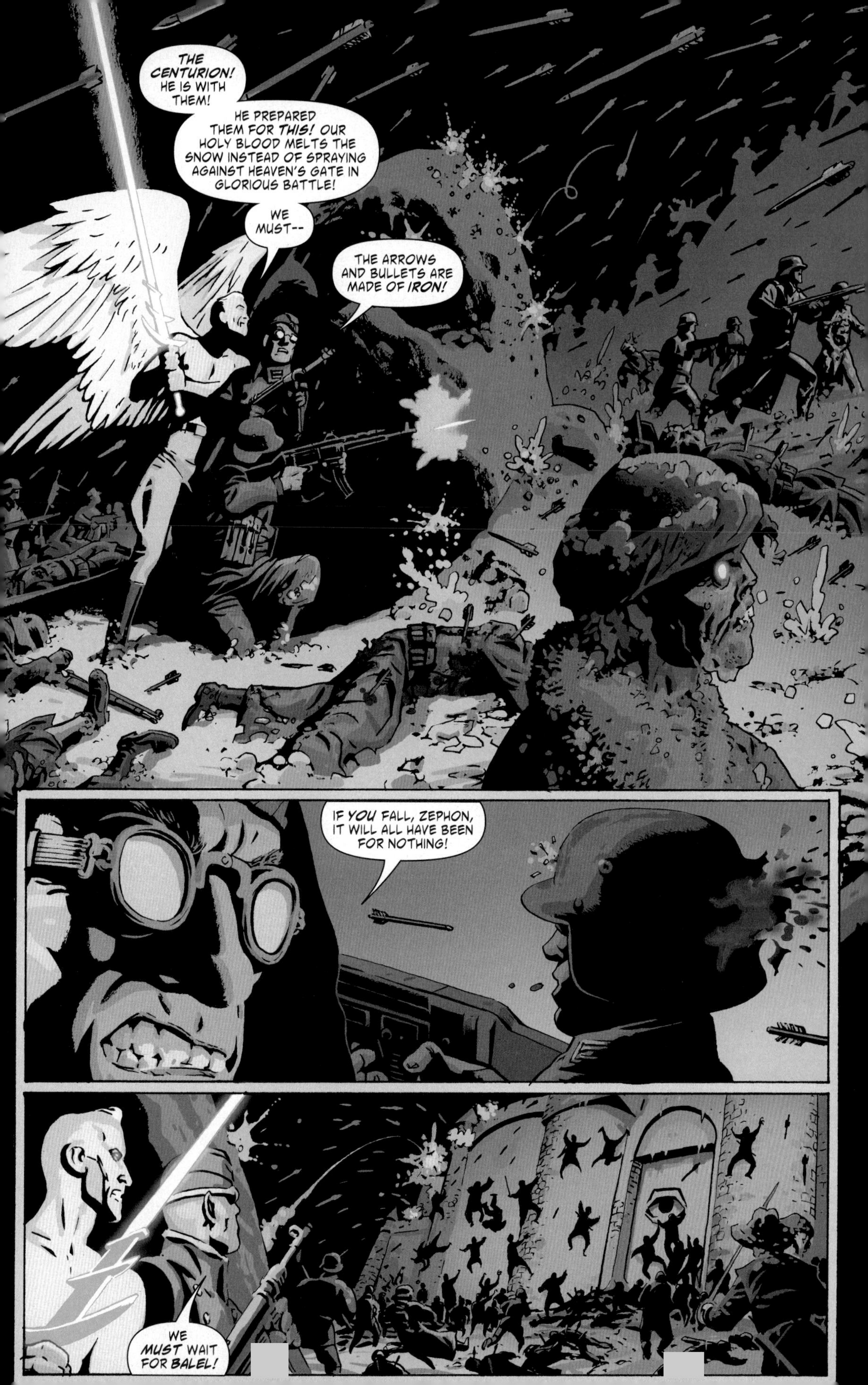
THE CENTURION! HE IS WITH THEM!
HE PREPARED THEM FOR THIS! OUR HOLY BLOOD MELTS THE SNOW INSTEAD OF SPRAYING AGAINST HEAVEN'S GATE IN GLORIOUS BATTLE!
WE MUST--
THE ARROWS AND BULLETS ARE MADE OF IRON!
IF YOU FALL, ZEPHON, IT WILL ALL HAVE BEEN FOR NOTHING!
WE MUST WAIT FOR BALEL!

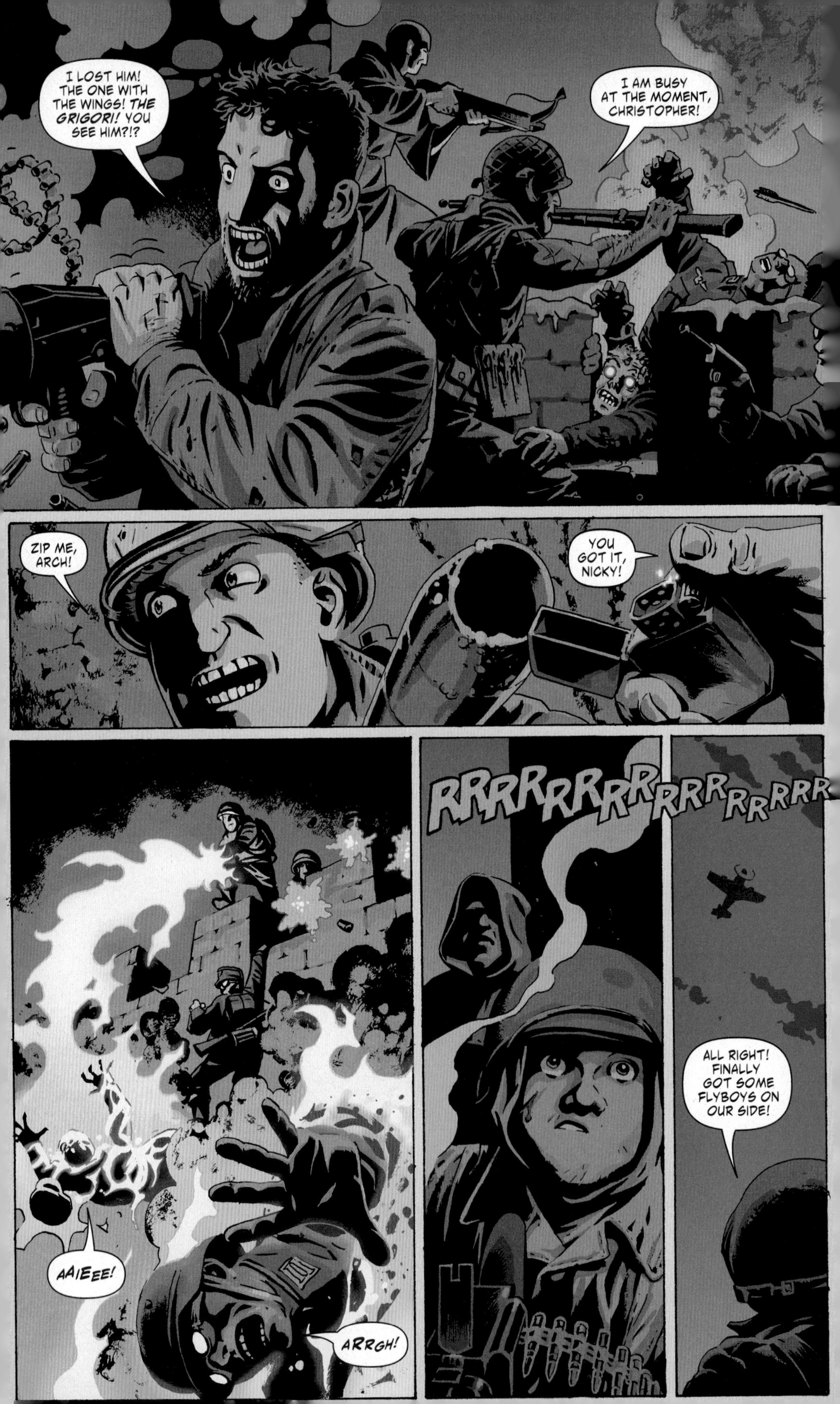
I LOST HIM! THE ONE WITH THE WINGS! THE GRIGORI! YOU SEE HIM?!?
I AM BUSY AT THE MOMENT, CHRISTOPHER!
ZIP ME, ARCH!
YOU GOT IT, NICKY!
AAIEEE!
ARRGH!
RRRRRRRRRRRRRRRRR
ALL RIGHT! FINALLY GOT SOME FLYBOYS ON OUR SIDE!

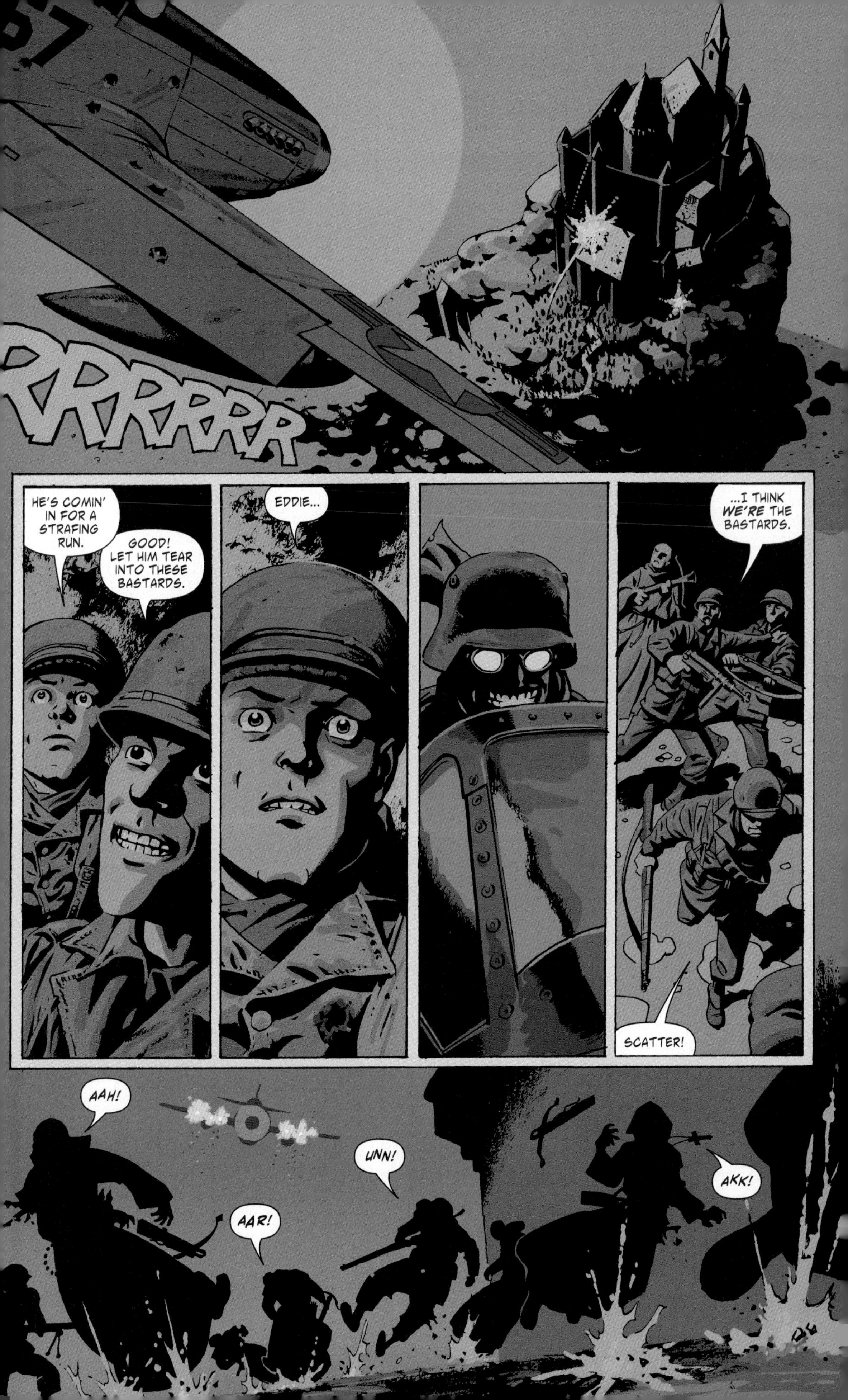
RRRRRRR
HE'S COMIN' IN FOR A STRAFING RUN.
GOOD! LET HIM TEAR INTO THESE BASTARDS.
EDDIE...
...I THINK WE'RE THE BASTARDS.
SCATTER!
AAH!
UNN!
AKK!
AAR!

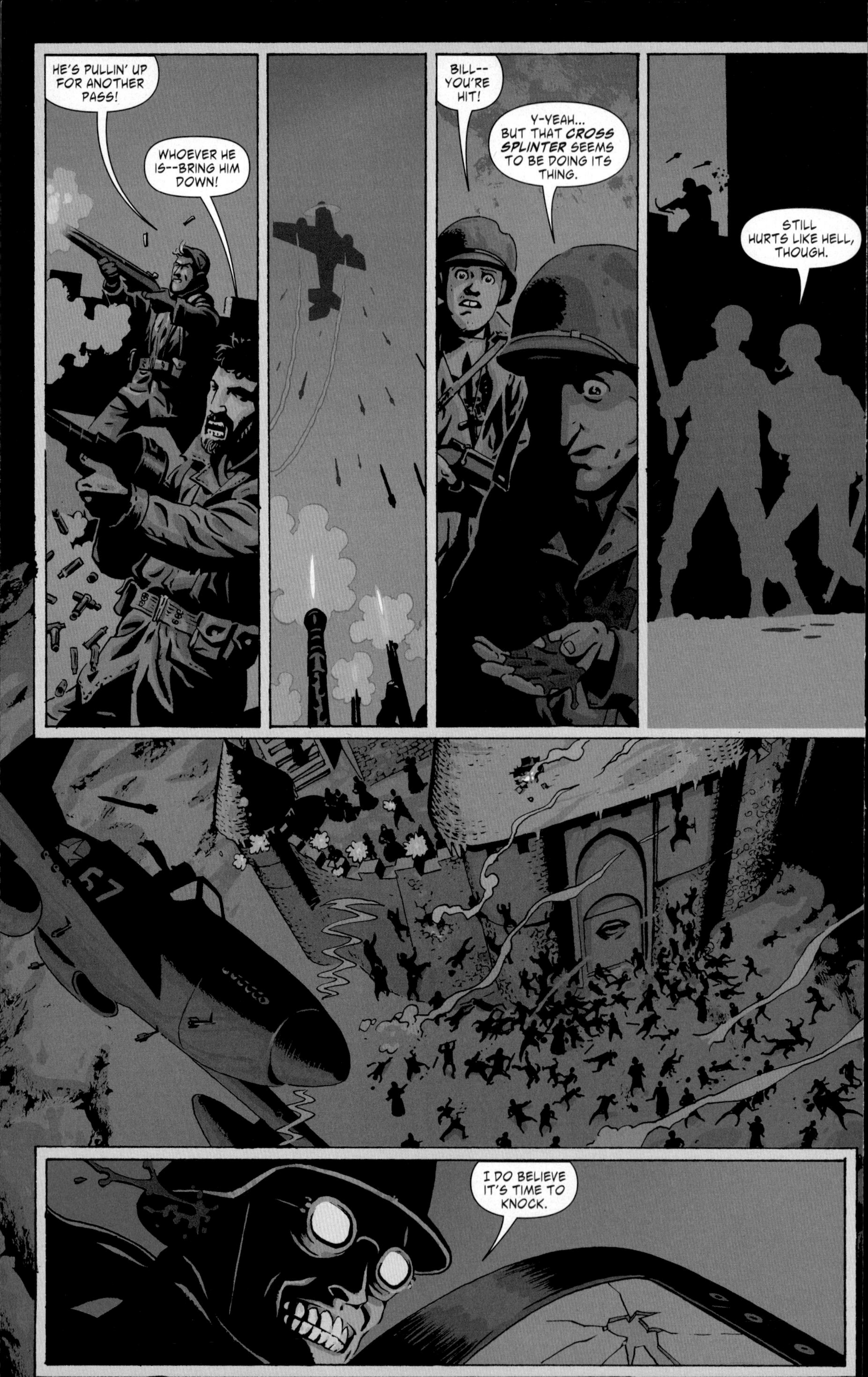
HE'S PULLIN' UP FOR ANOTHER PASS!
WHOEVER HE IS--BRING HIM DOWN!
BILL--YOU'RE HIT!
Y-YEAH... BUT THAT CROSS SPLINTER SEEMS TO BE DOING ITS THING.
STILL HURTS LIKE HELL, THOUGH.
I DO BELIEVE IT'S TIME TO KNOCK.

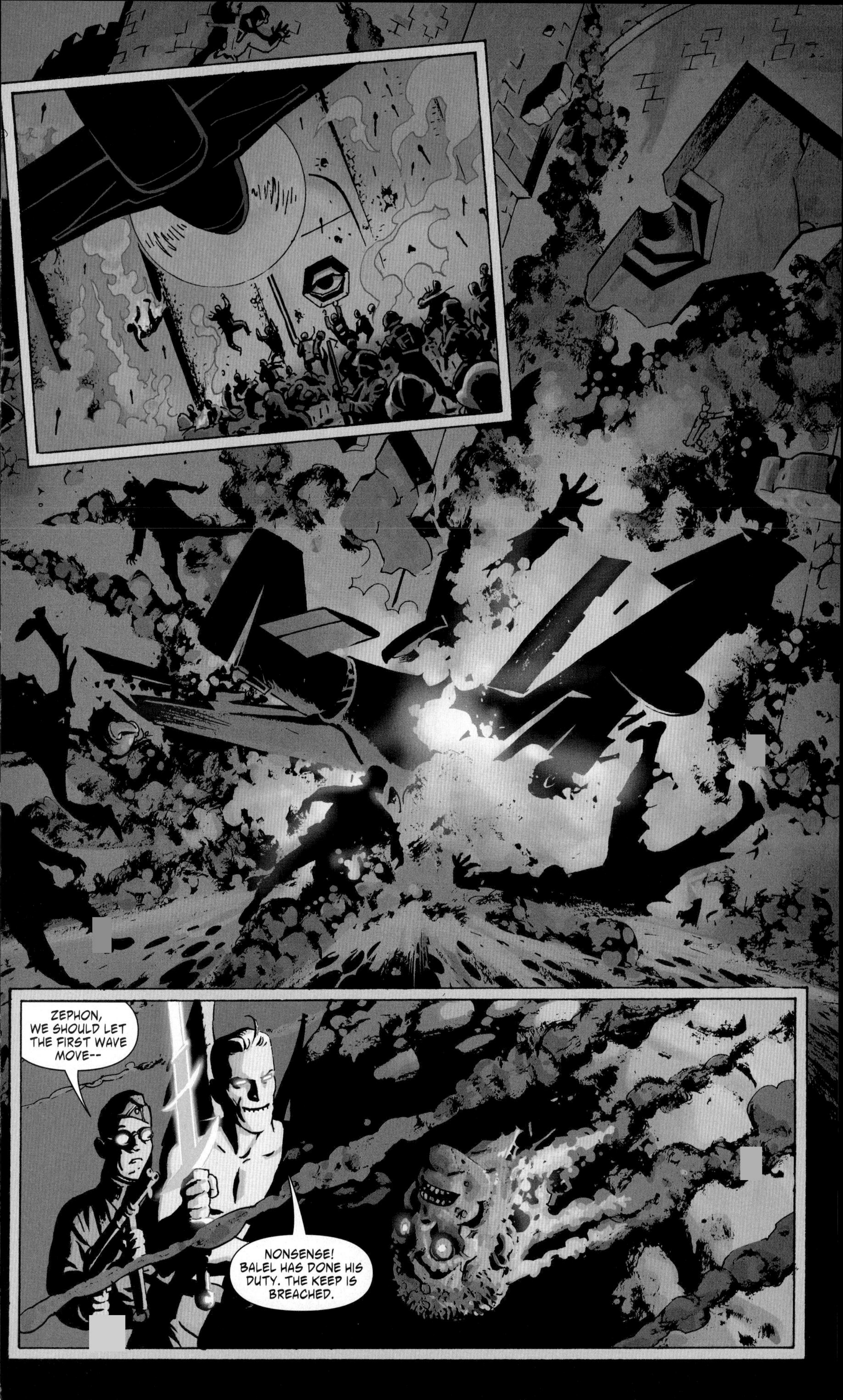
ZEPHON, WE SHOULD LET THE FIRST WAVE MOVE--
NONSENSE! BALEL HAS DONE HIS DUTY. THE KEEP IS BREACHED.

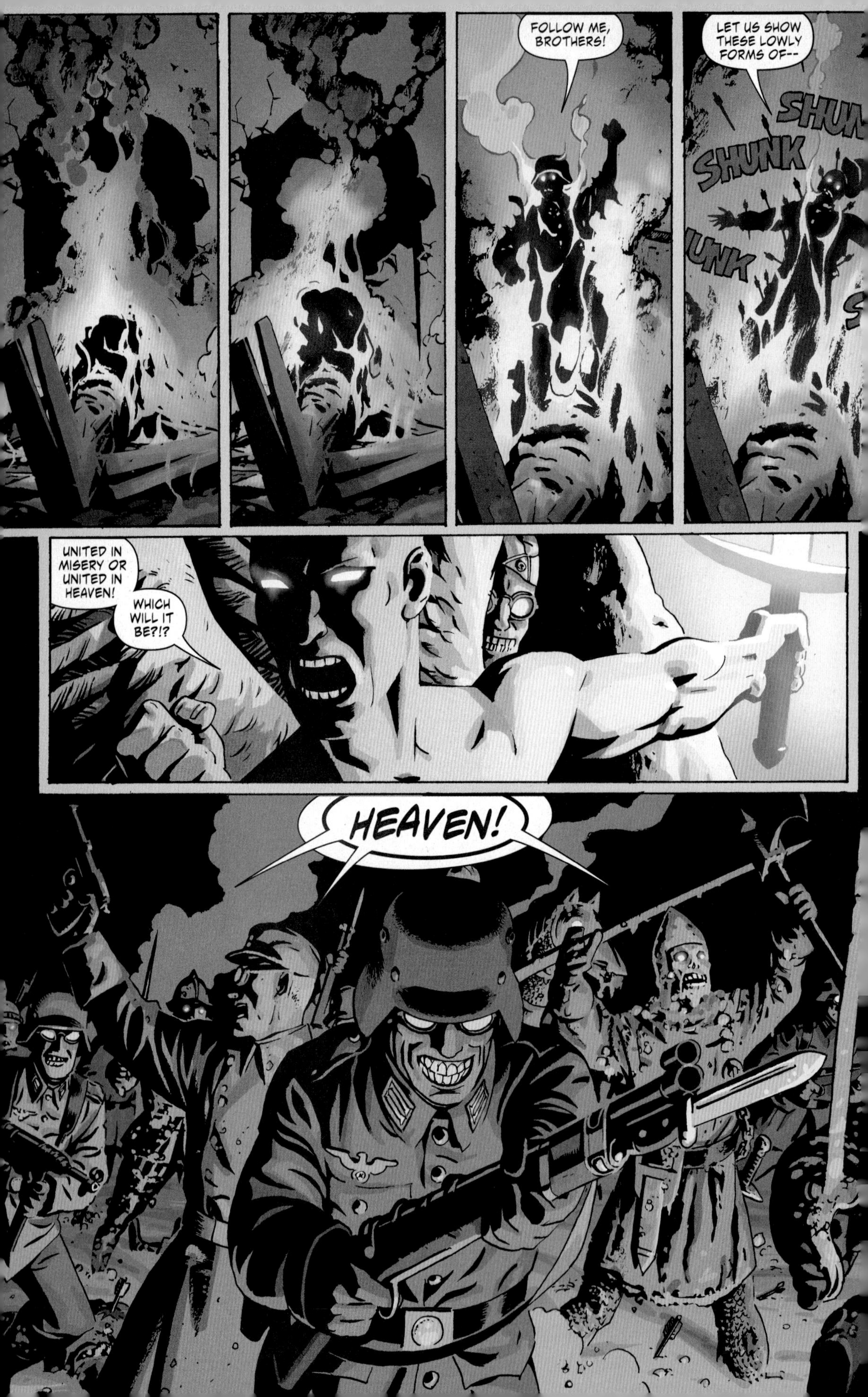
FOLLOW ME, BROTHERS!
LET US SHOW THESE LOWLY FORMS OF--
SHUNK
SHUNK
UNK
UNITED IN MISERY OR UNITED IN HEAVEN!
WHICH WILL IT BE?!?
HEAVEN!

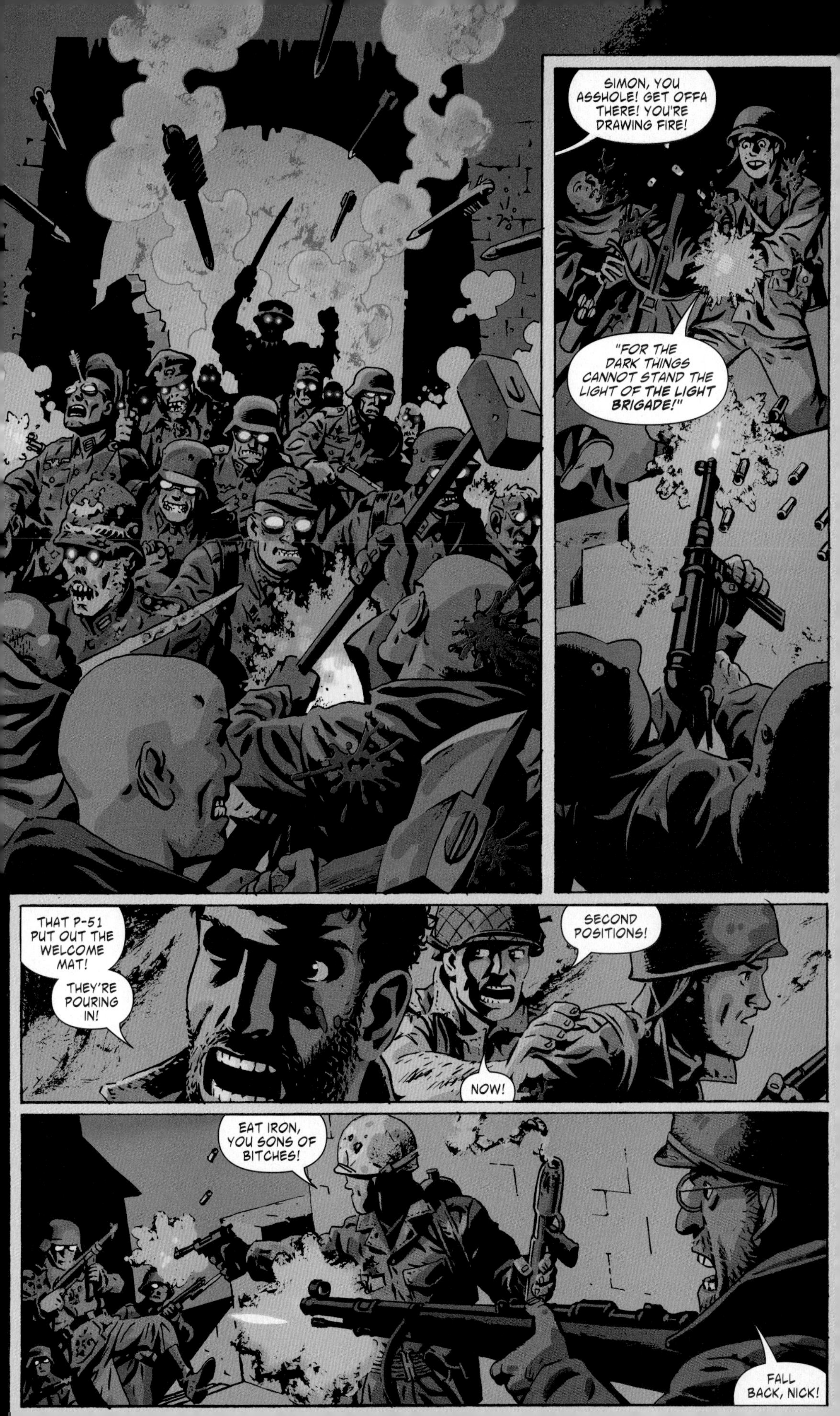
SIMON, YOU ASSHOLE! GET OFFA THERE! YOU'RE DRAWING FIRE!
"FOR THE DARK THINGS CANNOT STAND THE LIGHT OF THE LIGHT BRIGADE!"
THAT P-51 PUT OUT THE WELCOME MAT!
THEY'RE POURING IN!
SECOND POSITIONS!
NOW!
EAT IRON, YOU SONS OF BITCHES!
FALL BACK, NICK!

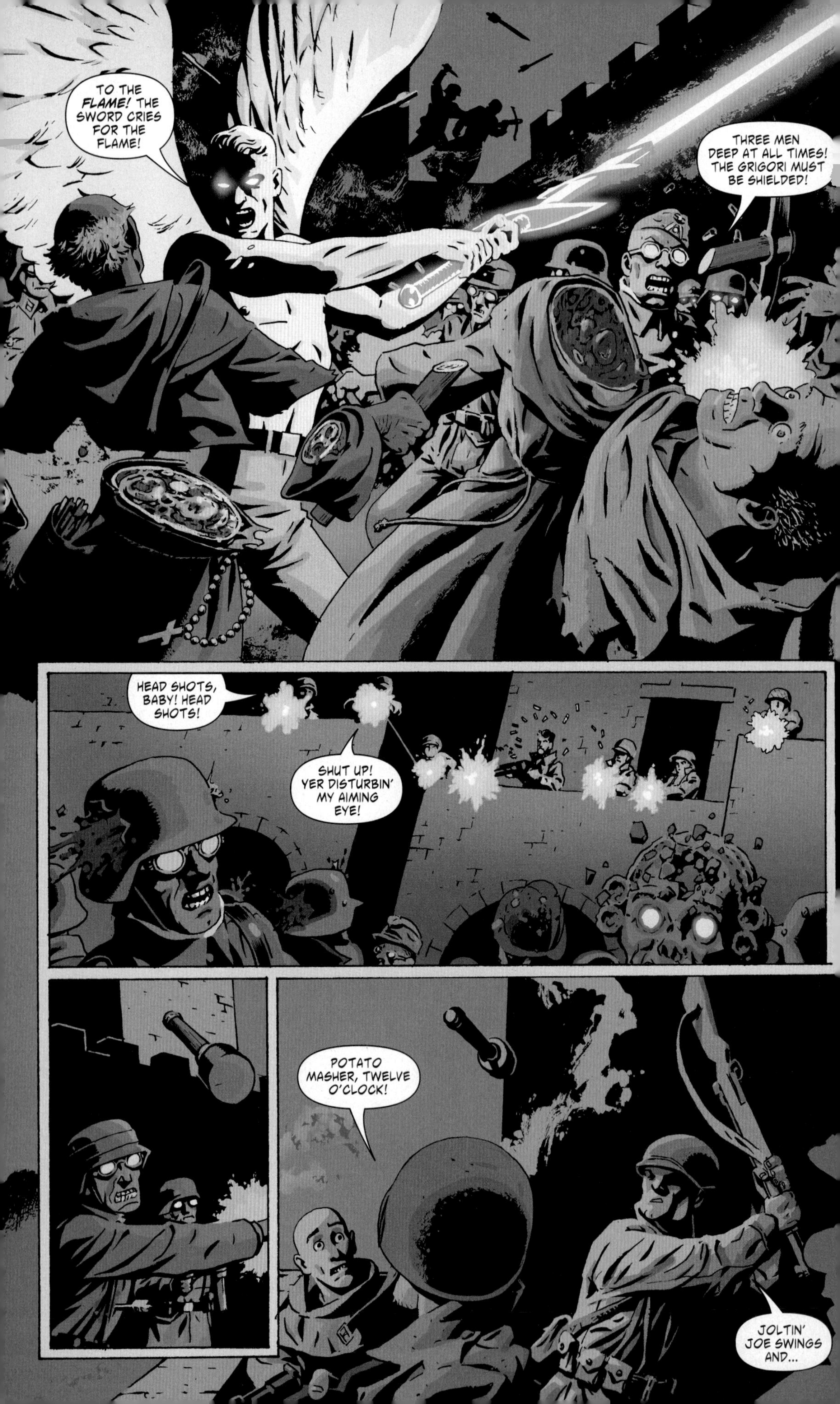
TO THE FLAME! THE SWORD CRIES FOR THE FLAME!
THREE MEN DEEP AT ALL TIMES! THE GRIGORI MUST BE SHIELDED!
HEAD SHOTS, BABY! HEAD SHOTS!
SHUT UP! YER DISTURBIN' MY AIMING EYE!
POTATO MASHER, TWELVE O'CLOCK!
JOLTIN' JOE SWINGS AND...

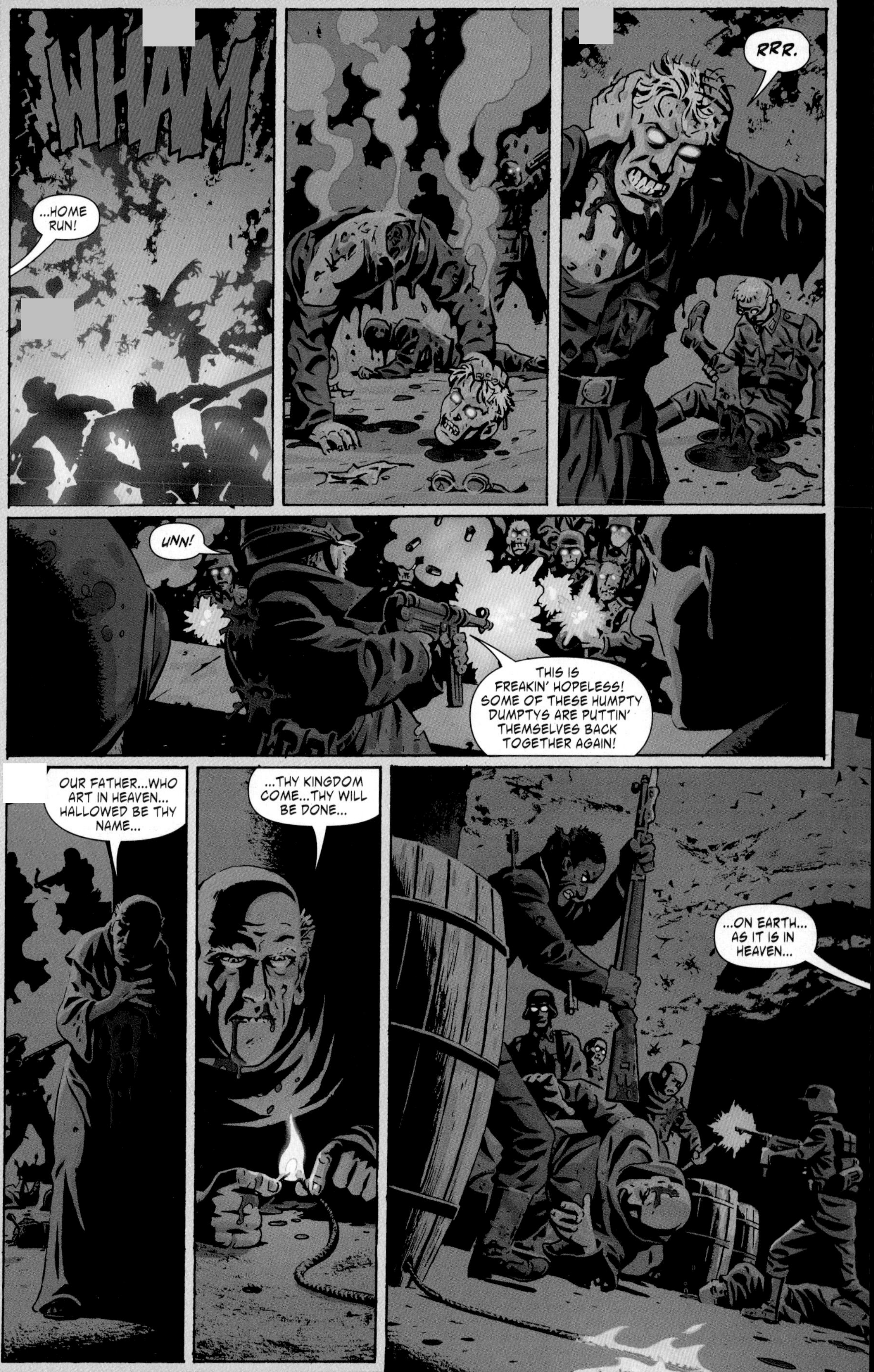
WHAM
...HOME RUN!
RRR.
UNN!
THIS IS FREAKIN' HOPELESS! SOME OF THESE HUMPTY DUMPTYS ARE PUTTIN' THEMSELVES BACK TOGETHER AGAIN!
OUR FATHER...WHO ART IN HEAVEN... HALLOWED BE THY NAME...
...THY KINGDOM COME...THY WILL BE DONE...
...ON EARTH... AS IT IS IN HEAVEN...

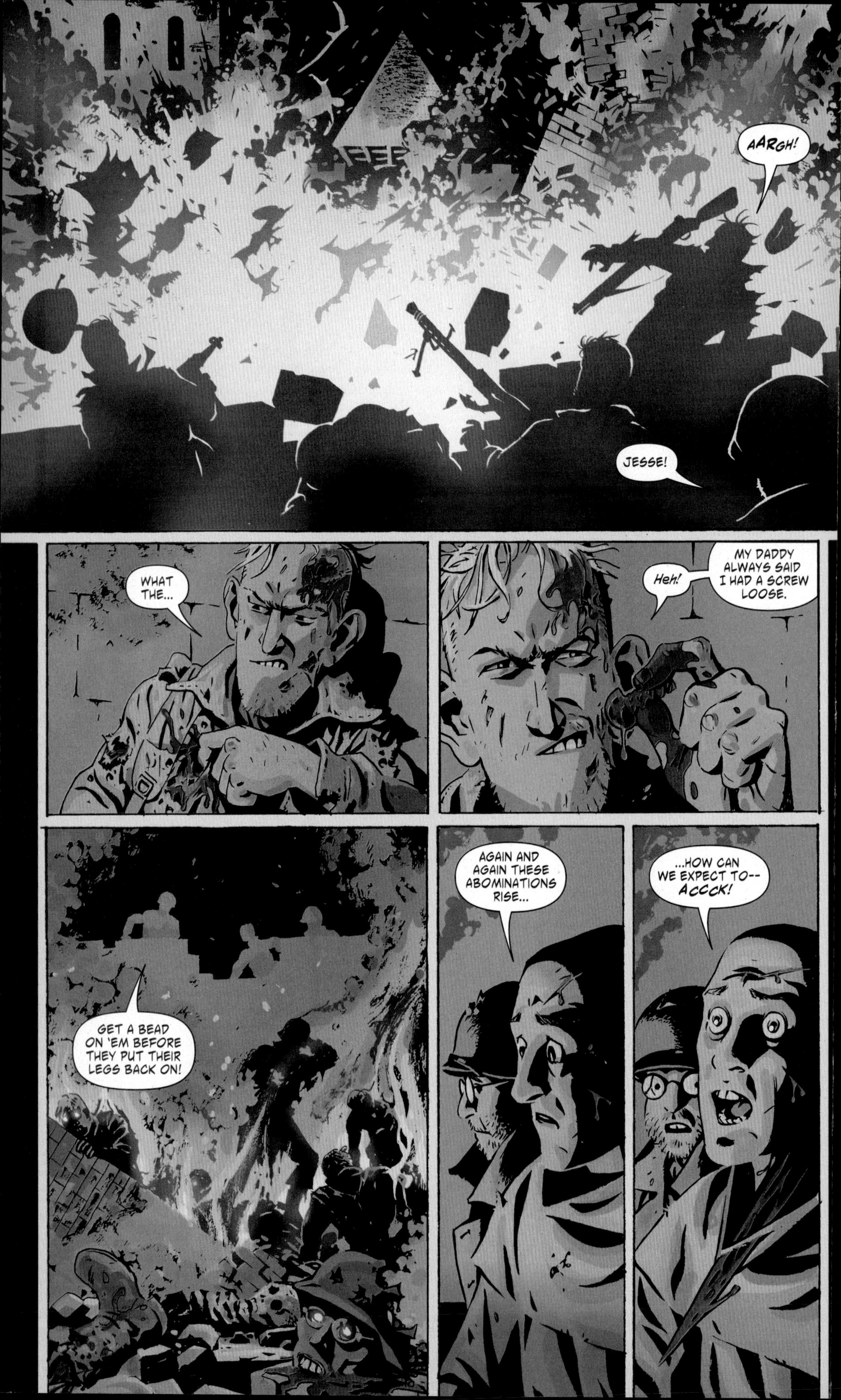
AARGH!
JESSE!
WHAT THE...
Heh!
MY DADDY ALWAYS SAID I HAD A SCREW LOOSE.
GET A BEAD ON 'EM BEFORE THEY PUT THEIR LEGS BACK ON!
AGAIN AND AGAIN THESE ABOMINATIONS RISE...
...HOW CAN WE EXPECT TO-- ACCCK!

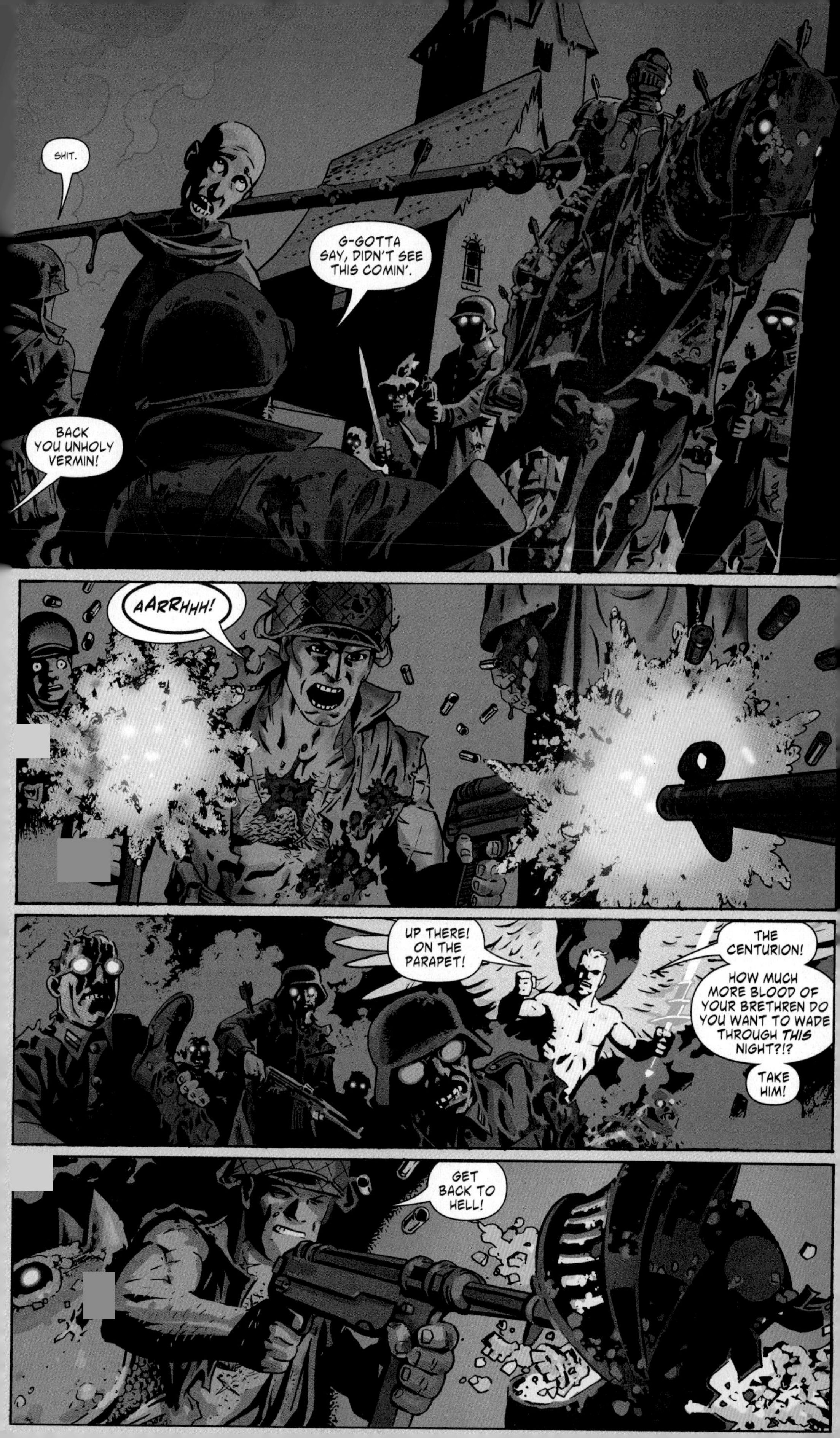
SHIT.
G-GOTTA SAY, DIDN'T SEE THIS COMIN'.
BACK YOU UNHOLY VERMIN!
AARRHHH!
UP THERE! ON THE PARAPET!
THE CENTURION!
HOW MUCH MORE BLOOD OF YOUR BRETHREN DO YOU WANT TO WADE THROUGH THIS NIGHT?!?
TAKE HIM!
GET BACK TO HELL!

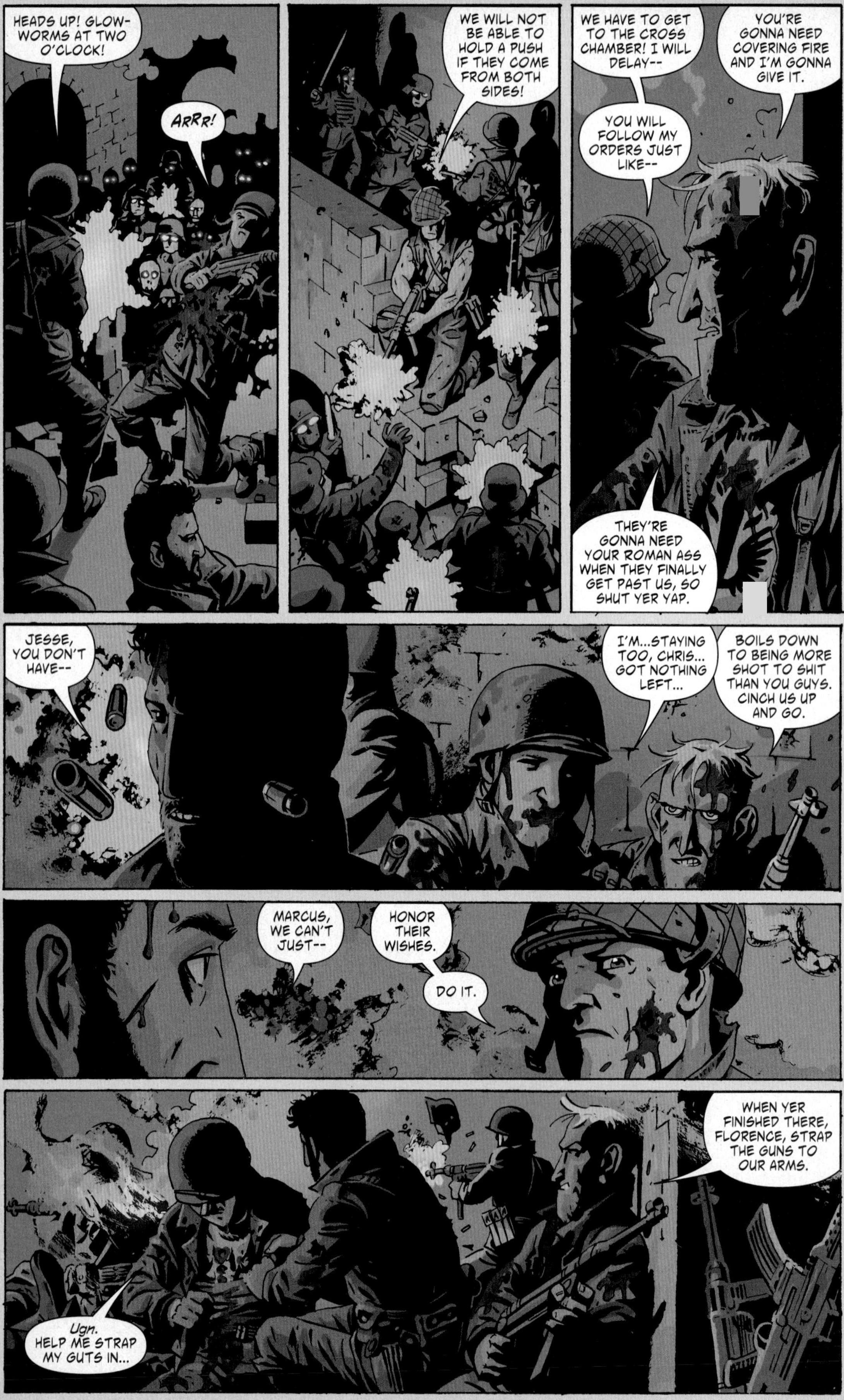
HEADS UP! GLOW-WORMS AT TWO O'CLOCK!
ARRR!
WE WILL NOT BE ABLE TO HOLD A PUSH IF THEY COME FROM BOTH SIDES!
WE HAVE TO GET TO THE CROSS CHAMBER! I WILL DELAY--
YOU WILL FOLLOW MY ORDERS JUST LIKE--
YOU'RE GONNA NEED COVERING FIRE AND I'M GONNA GIVE IT.
THEY'RE GONNA NEED YOUR ROMAN ASS WHEN THEY FINALLY GET PAST US, SO SHUT YER YAP.
JESSE, YOU DON'T HAVE--
I'M...STAYING TOO, CHRIS... GOT NOTHING LEFT...
BOILS DOWN TO BEING MORE SHOT TO SHIT THAN YOU GUYS. CINCH US UP AND GO.
MARCUS, WE CAN'T JUST--
HONOR THEIR WISHES.
DO IT.
WHEN YER FINISHED THERE, FLORENCE, STRAP THE GUNS TO OUR ARMS.
Ugn. HELP ME STRAP MY GUTS IN...

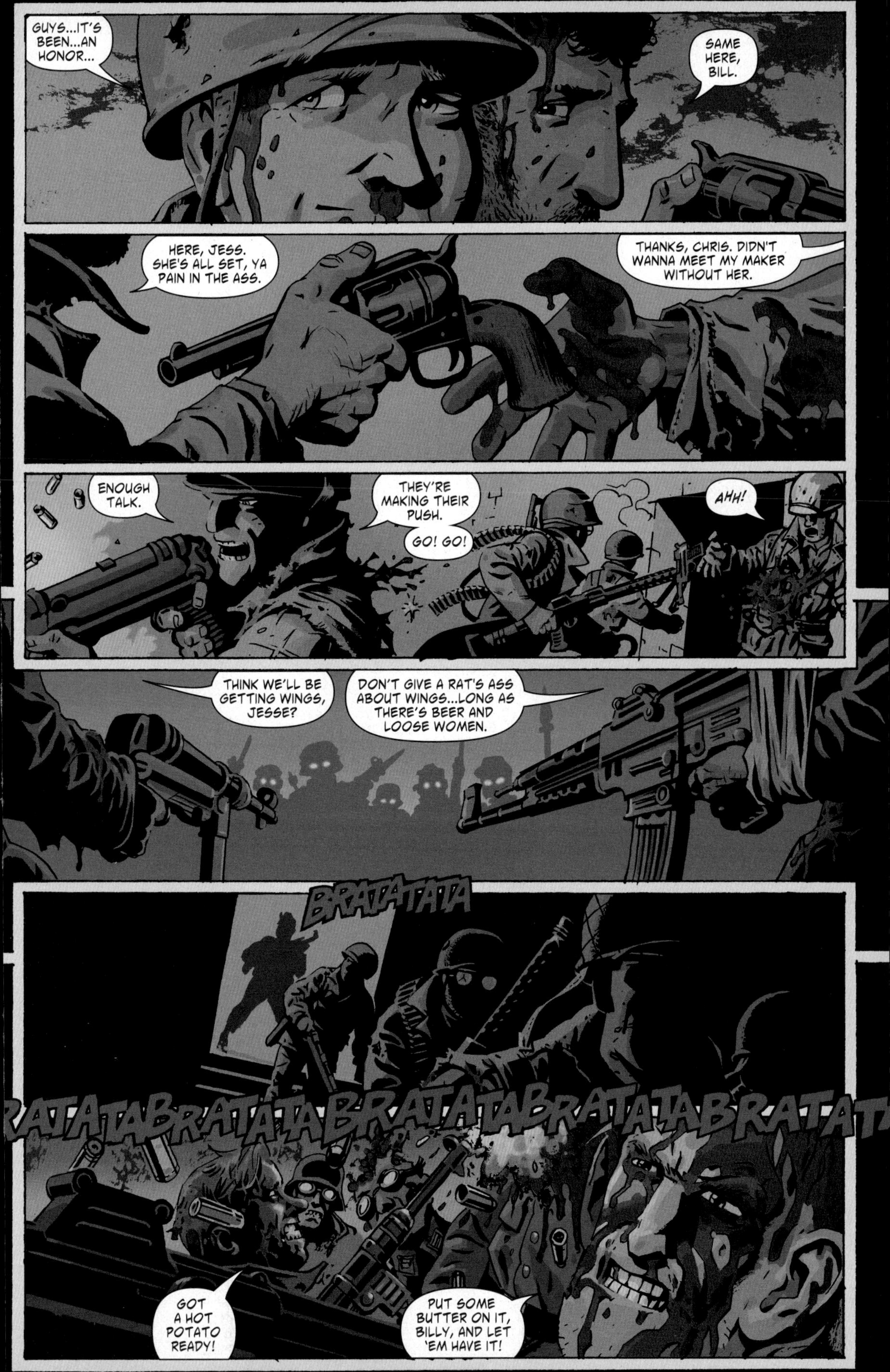
GUYS...IT'S BEEN...AN HONOR...
SAME HERE, BILL.
HERE, JESS. SHE'S ALL SET, YA PAIN IN THE ASS.
THANKS, CHRIS. DIDN'T WANNA MEET MY MAKER WITHOUT HER.
ENOUGH TALK.
THEY'RE MAKING THEIR PUSH.
GO! GO!
AHH!
THINK WE'LL BE GETTING WINGS, JESSE?
DON'T GIVE A RAT'S ASS ABOUT WINGS...LONG AS THERE'S BEER AND LOOSE WOMEN.
BRATATATA
RATATABRATATABRATATABRATATABRATAT
GOT A HOT POTATO READY!
PUT SOME BUTTER ON IT, BILLY, AND LET 'EM HAVE IT!

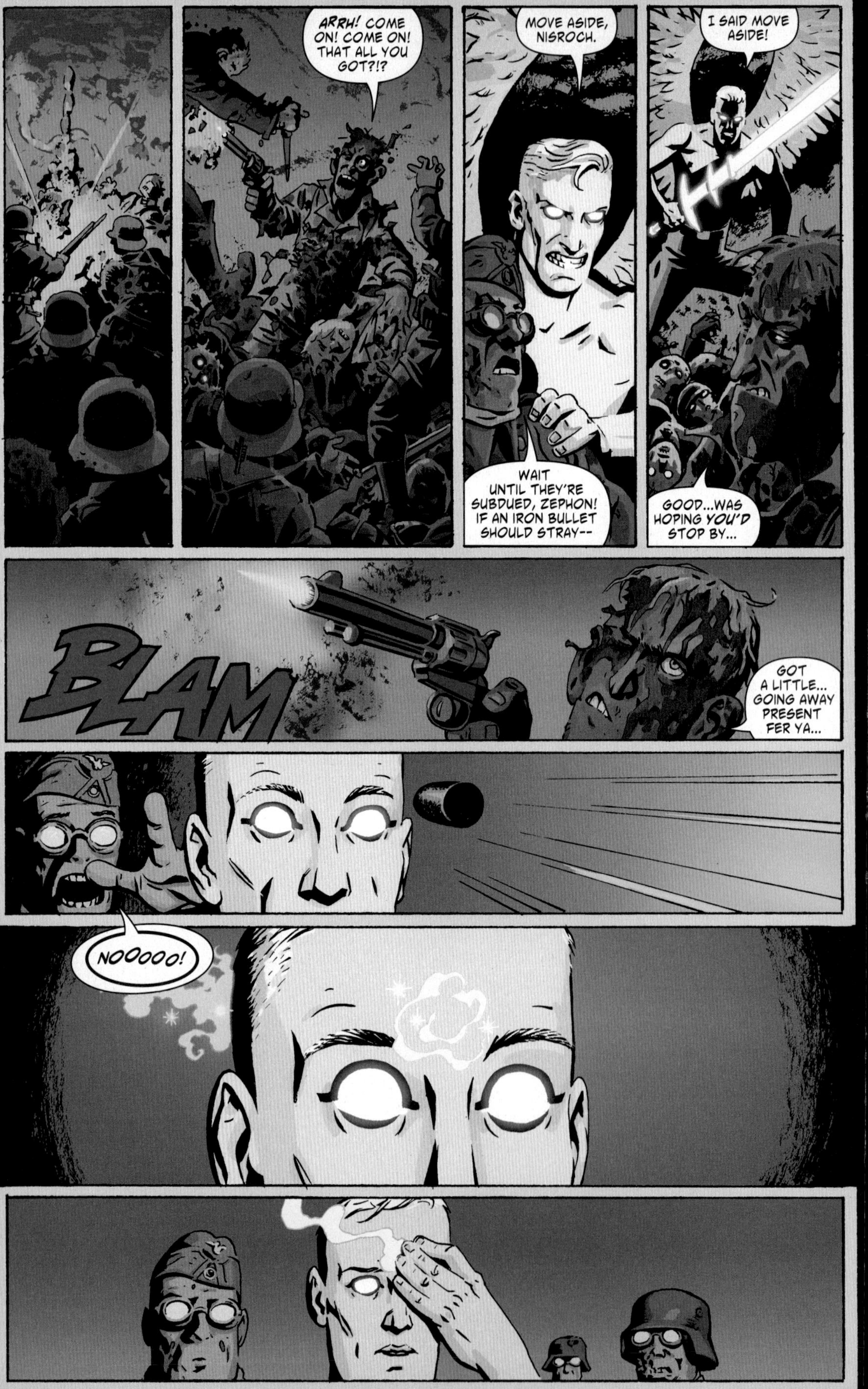
ARRH! COME ON! COME ON! THAT ALL YOU GOT?!?
MOVE ASIDE, NISROCH.
WAIT UNTIL THEY'RE SUBDUED, ZEPHON! IF AN IRON BULLET SHOULD STRAY--
I SAID MOVE ASIDE!
GOOD...WAS HOPING YOU'D STOP BY...
BLAM
GOT A LITTLE... GOING AWAY PRESENT FER YA...
NOOOOO!

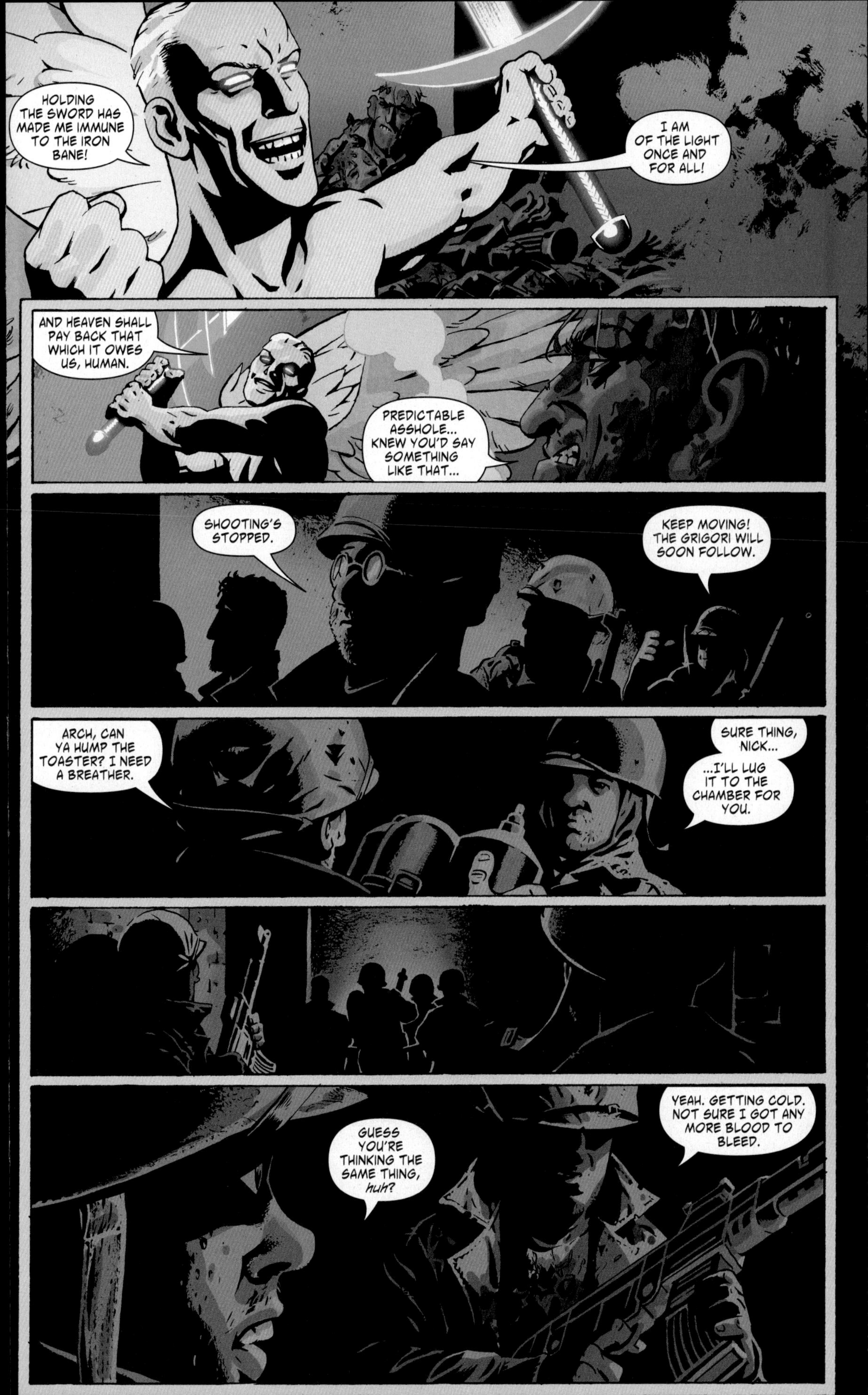
HOLDING THE SWORD HAS MADE ME IMMUNE TO THE IRON BANE!
I AM OF THE LIGHT ONCE AND FOR ALL!
AND HEAVEN SHALL PAY BACK THAT WHICH IT OWES US, HUMAN.
PREDICTABLE ASSHOLE... KNEW YOU'D SAY SOMETHING LIKE THAT...
SHOOTING'S STOPPED.
KEEP MOVING! THE GRIGORI WILL SOON FOLLOW.
ARCH, CAN YA HUMP THE TOASTER? I NEED A BREATHER.
SURE THING, NICK...
...I'LL LUG IT TO THE CHAMBER FOR YOU.
GUESS YOU'RE THINKING THE SAME THING, *huh*?
YEAH. GETTING COLD. NOT SURE I GOT ANY MORE BLOOD TO BLEED.

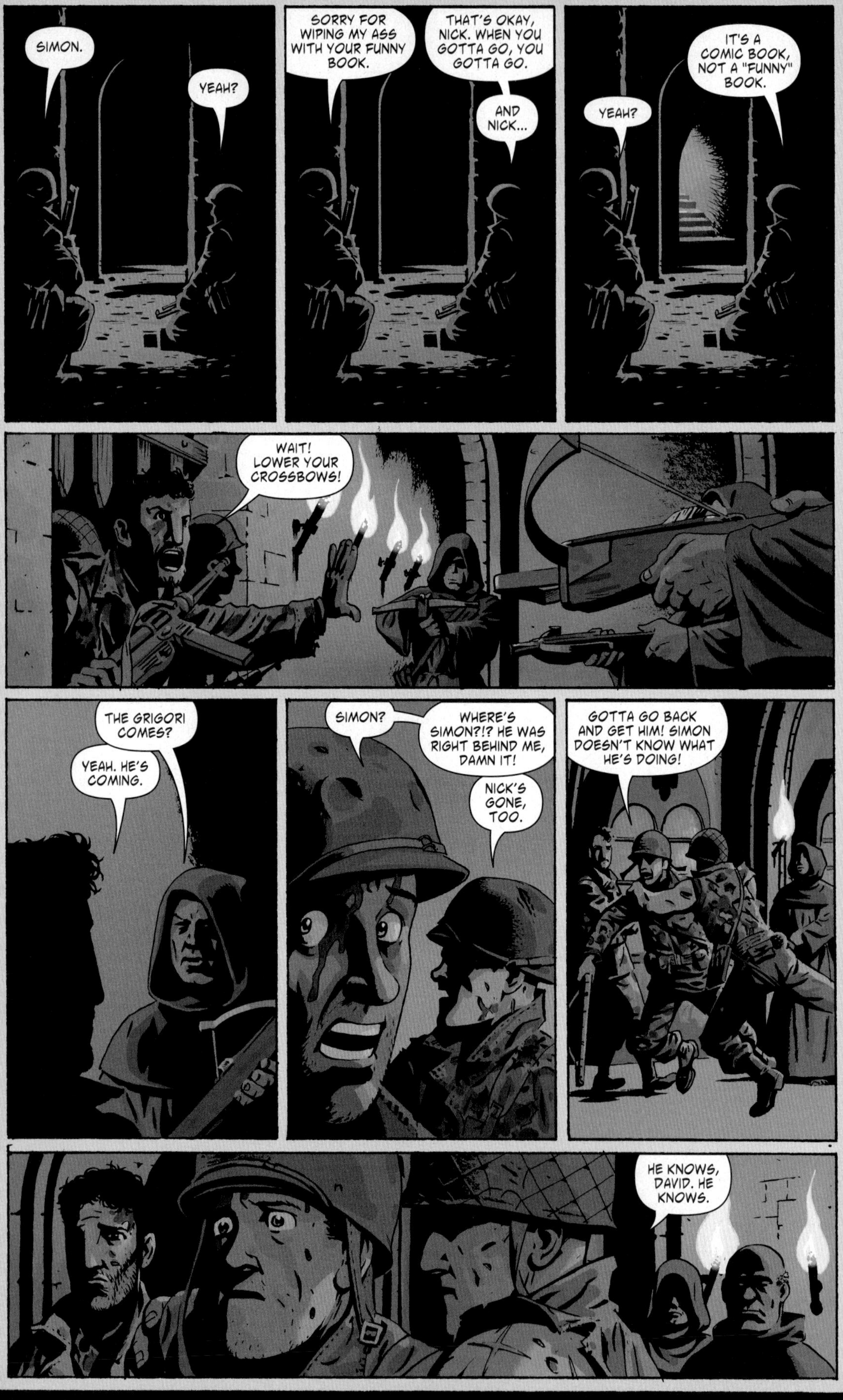
SIMON.
YEAH?
SORRY FOR WIPING MY ASS WITH YOUR FUNNY BOOK.
THAT'S OKAY, NICK. WHEN YOU GOTTA GO, YOU GOTTA GO.
AND NICK...
YEAH?
IT'S A COMIC BOOK, NOT A "FUNNY" BOOK.
WAIT! LOWER YOUR CROSSBOWS!
THE GRIGORI COMES?
YEAH. HE'S COMING.
SIMON?
WHERE'S SIMON?!? HE WAS RIGHT BEHIND ME, DAMN IT!
NICK'S GONE, TOO.
GOTTA GO BACK AND GET HIM! SIMON DOESN'T KNOW WHAT HE'S DOING!
HE KNOWS, DAVID. HE KNOWS.

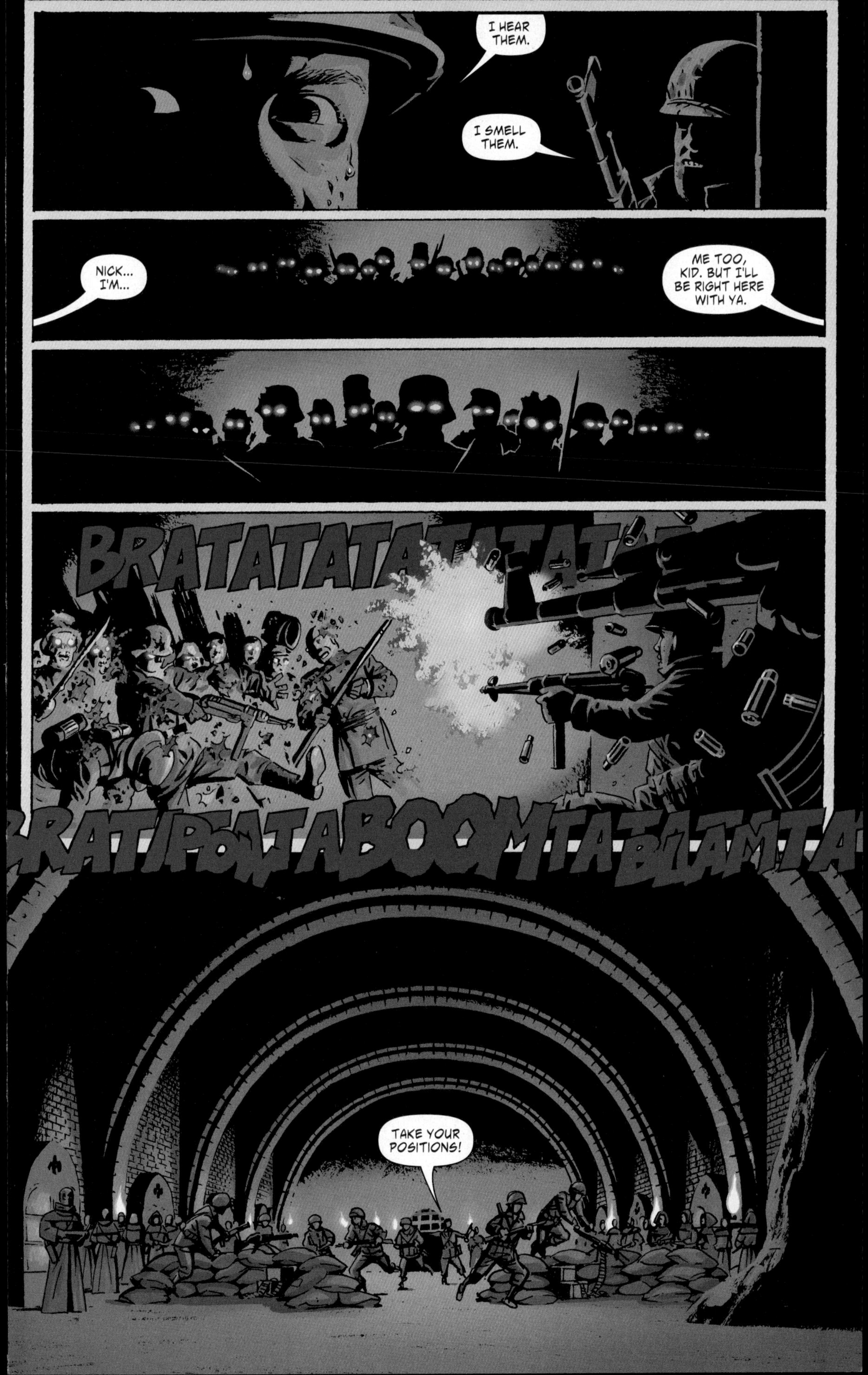
I HEAR THEM.
I SMELL THEM.
NICK... I'M...
ME TOO, KID. BUT I'LL BE RIGHT HERE WITH YA.
BRATATATATATAT
BRATIPOWTABOOMTATABLAMTAT
TAKE YOUR POSITIONS!

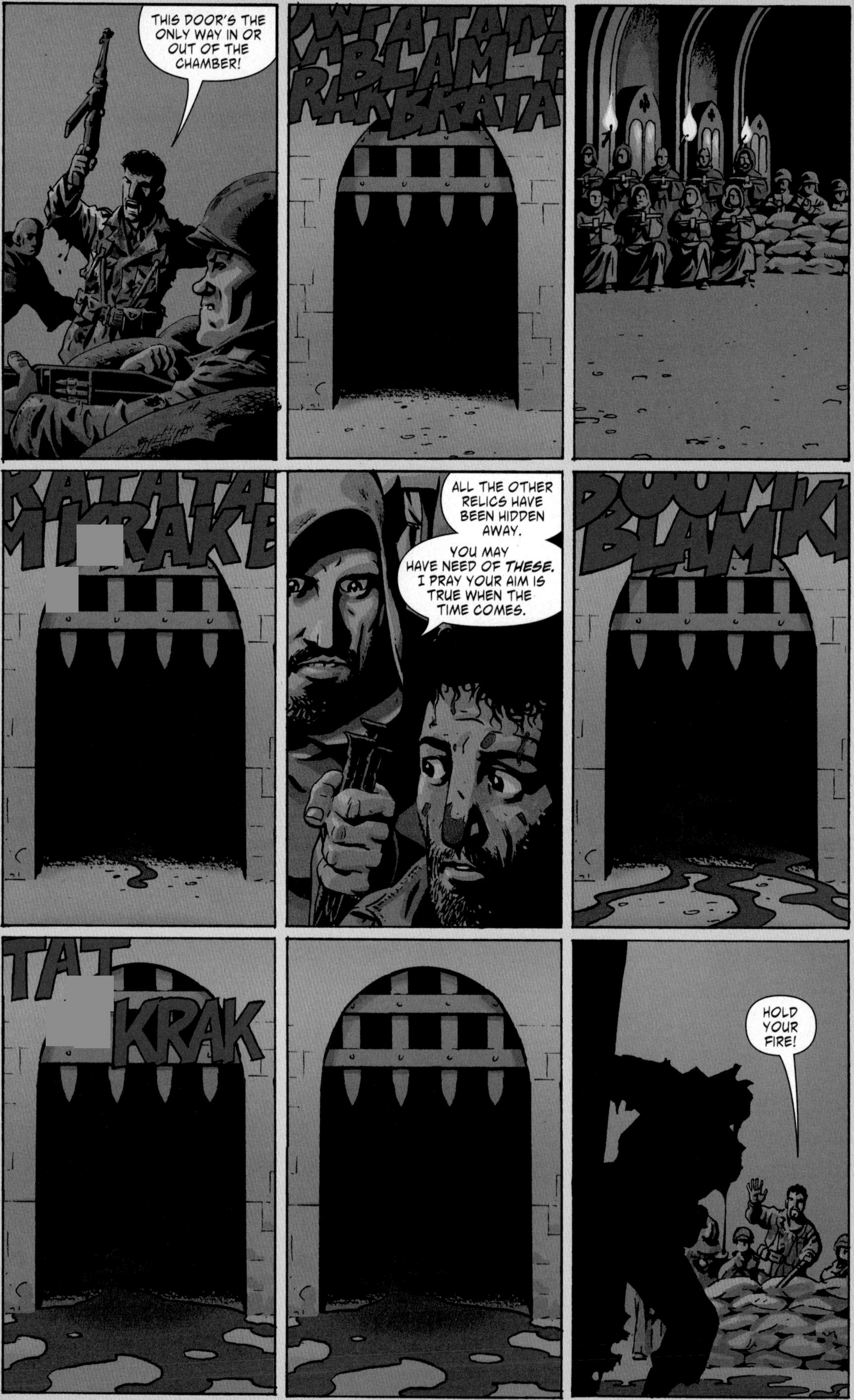
THIS DOOR'S THE ONLY WAY IN OR OUT OF THE CHAMBER!
BLAM
KRAK
ALL THE OTHER RELICS HAVE BEEN HIDDEN AWAY.
YOU MAY HAVE NEED OF *THESE*. I PRAY YOUR AIM IS TRUE WHEN THE TIME COMES.
BLAM
TAT
KRAK
HOLD YOUR FIRE!

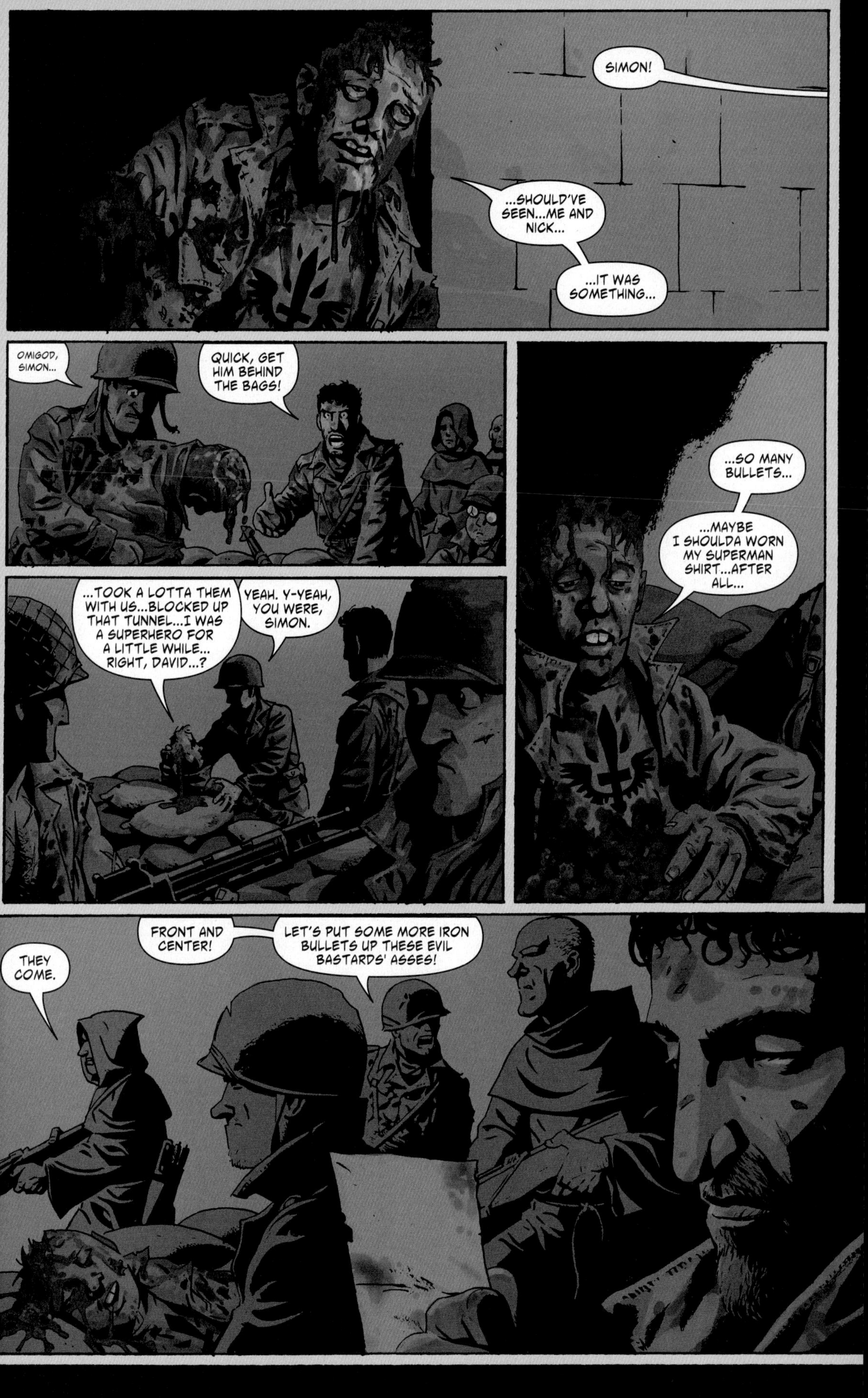
SIMON!
...SHOULD'VE SEEN...ME AND NICK...
...IT WAS SOMETHING...
OMIGOD, SIMON...
QUICK, GET HIM BEHIND THE BAGS!
...SO MANY BULLETS...
...MAYBE I SHOULDA WORN MY SUPERMAN SHIRT...AFTER ALL...
...TOOK A LOTTA THEM WITH US...BLOCKED UP THAT TUNNEL...I WAS A SUPERHERO FOR A LITTLE WHILE... RIGHT, DAVID...?
YEAH. Y-YEAH, YOU WERE, SIMON.
THEY COME.
FRONT AND CENTER!
LET'S PUT SOME MORE IRON BULLETS UP THESE EVIL BASTARDS' ASSES!

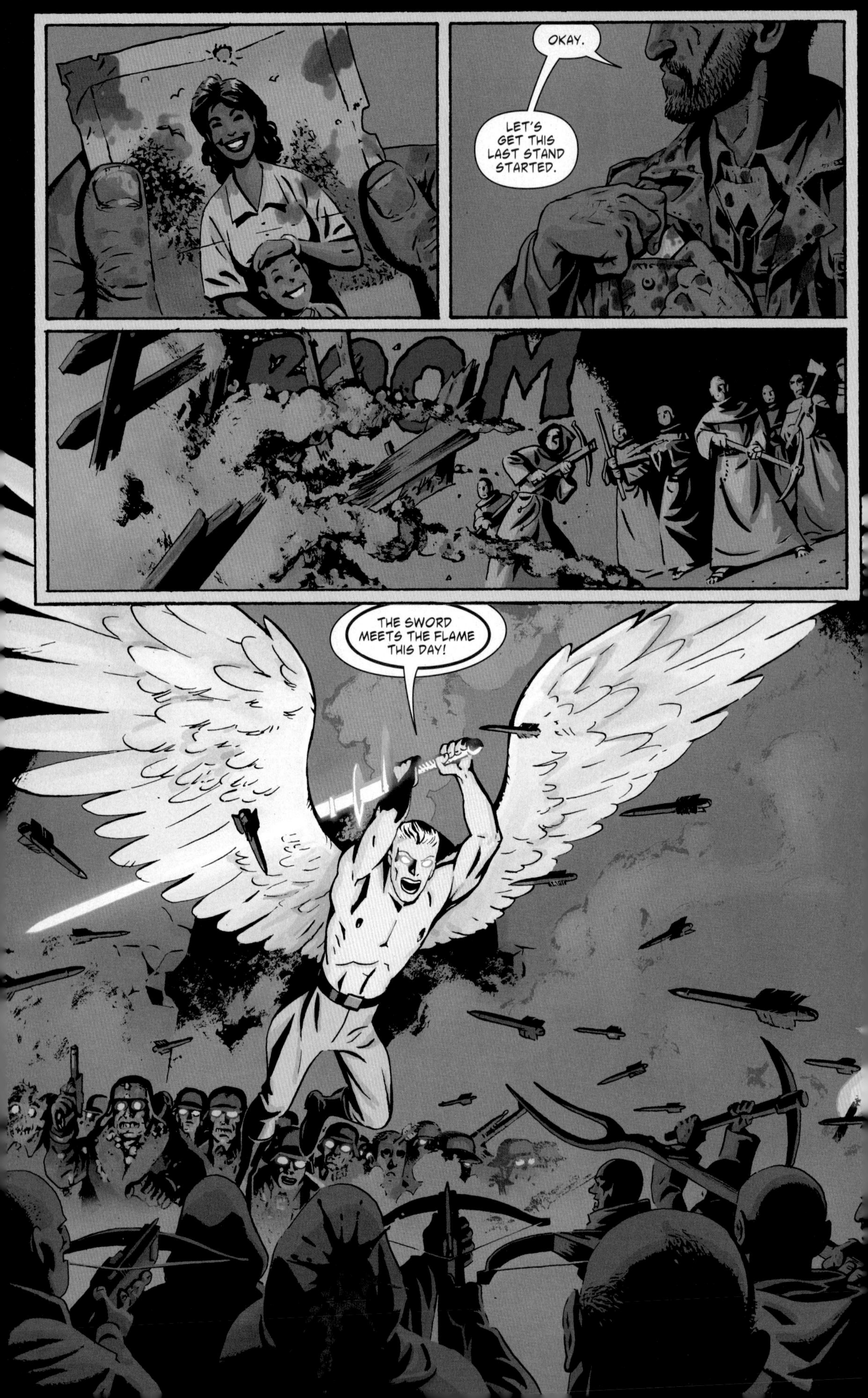
OKAY.
LET'S GET THIS LAST STAND STARTED.
BOOM
THE SWORD MEETS THE FLAME THIS DAY!

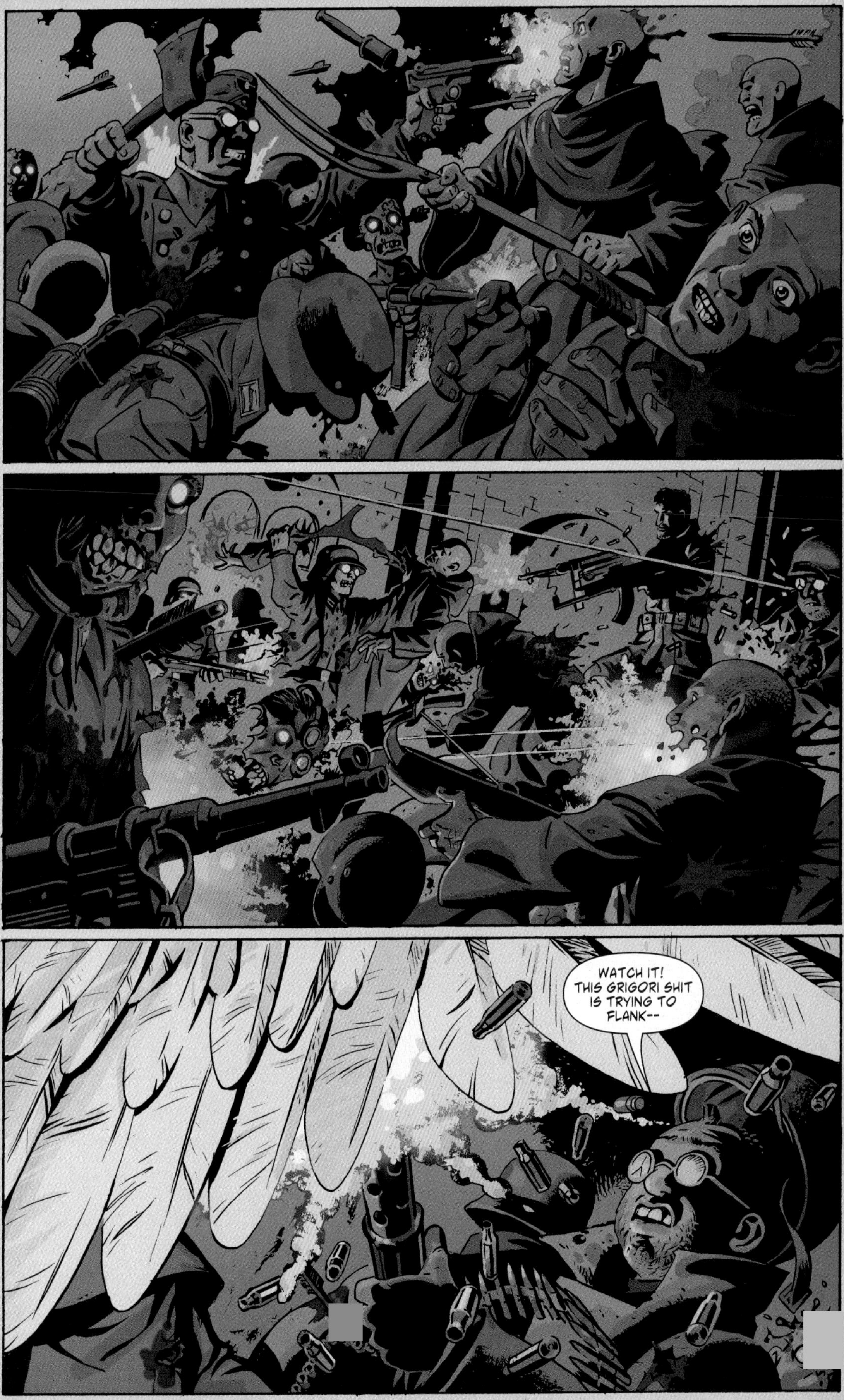
WATCH IT! THIS GRIGORI SHIT IS TRYING TO FLANK--

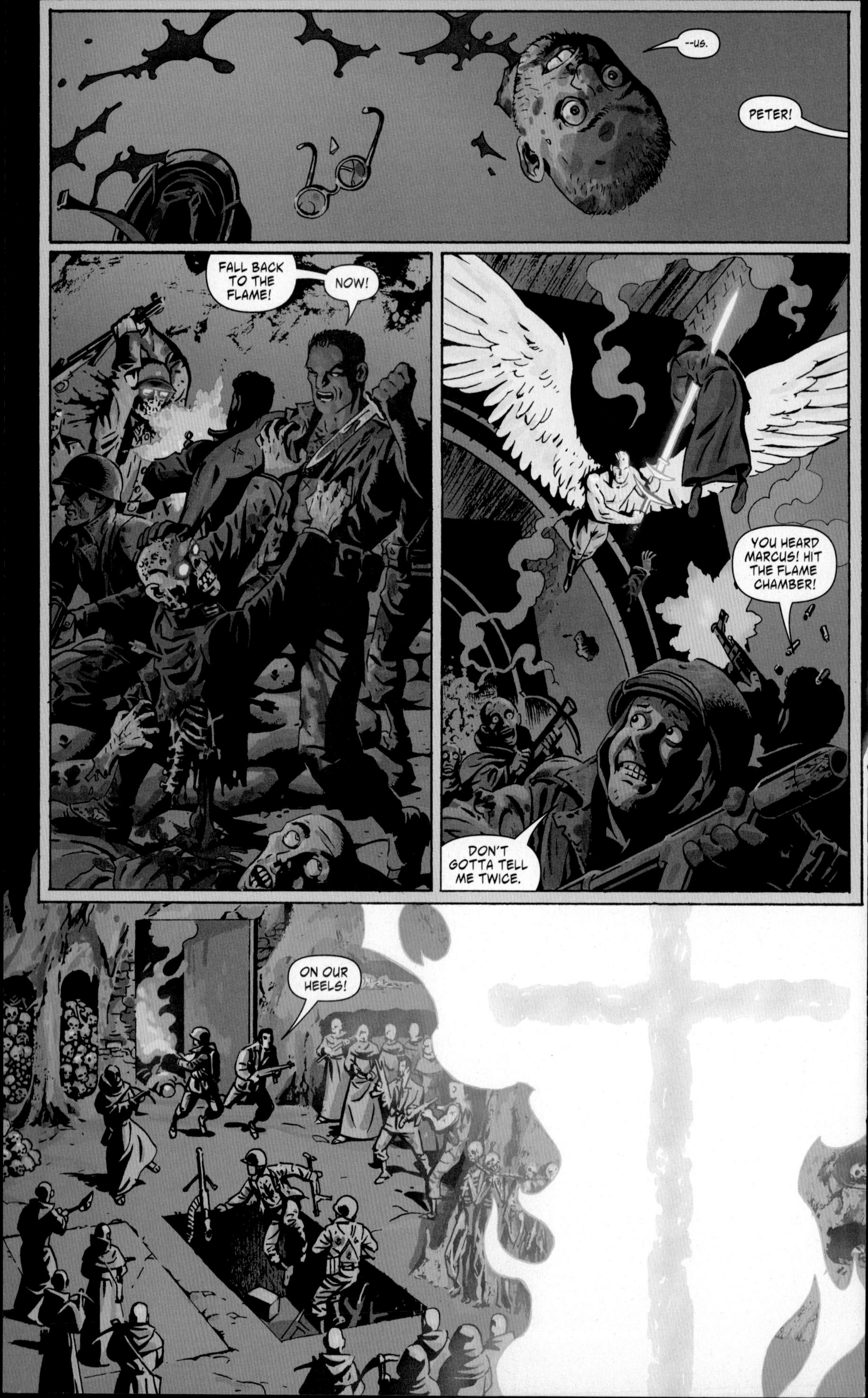
--US.
PETER!
FALL BACK TO THE FLAME!
NOW!
YOU HEARD MARCUS! HIT THE FLAME CHAMBER!
DON'T GOTTA TELL ME TWICE.
ON OUR HEELS!

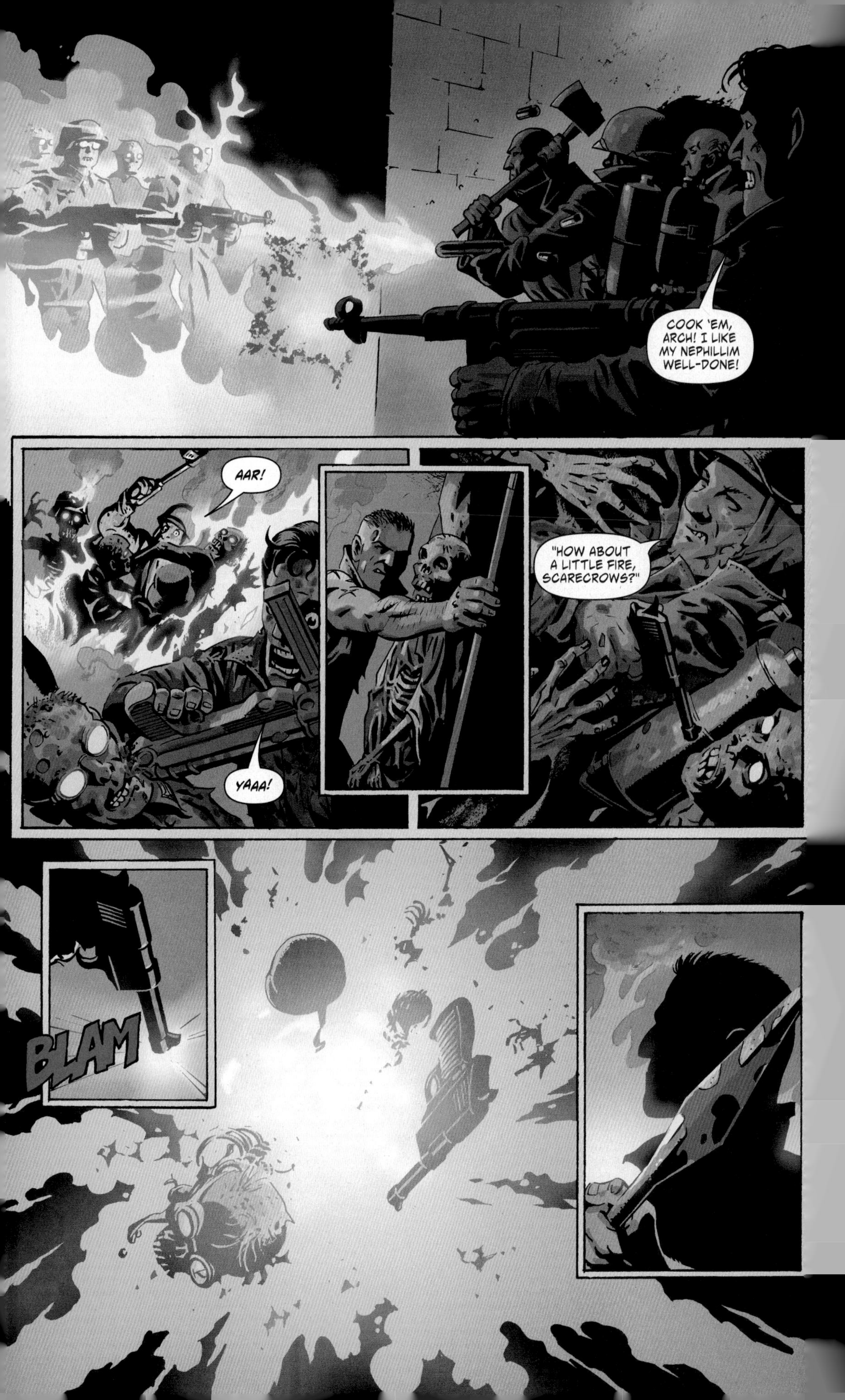
COOK 'EM, ARCH! I LIKE MY NEPHILLIM WELL-DONE!
AAR!
YAAA!
"HOW ABOUT A LITTLE FIRE, SCARECROWS?"
BLAM

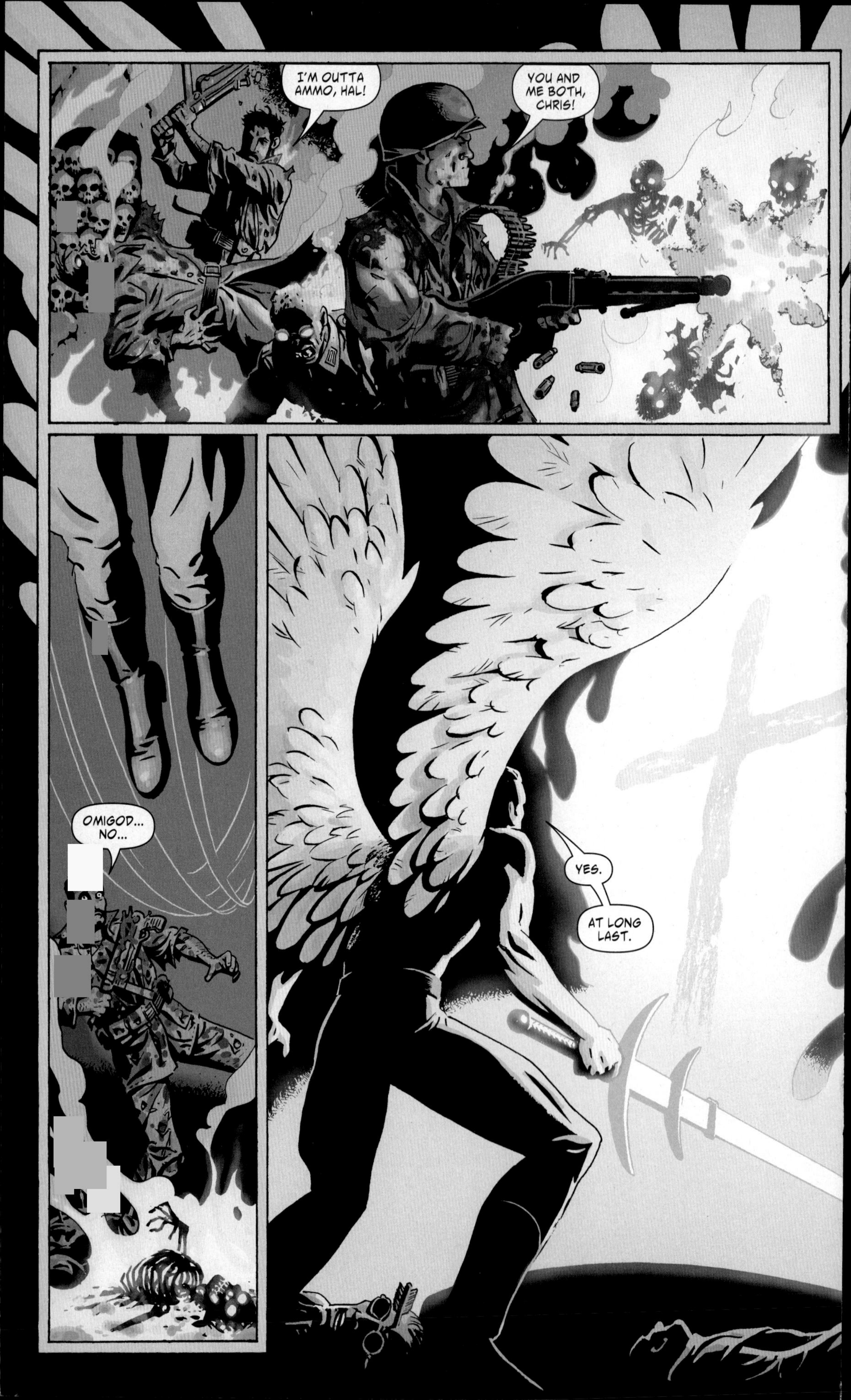
I'M OUTTA AMMO, HAL!
YOU AND ME BOTH, CHRIS!
OMIGOD... NO...
YES.
AT LONG LAST.

GRIGORI!

TURN AND FACE ME!

CENTURION.

I'M GLAD YOU'RE NOT DEAD.

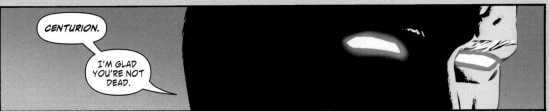

I WAS HOPING I WOULD GET TO KILL YOU.

LET US FINISH THIS AT LAST.

YES. LET'S.

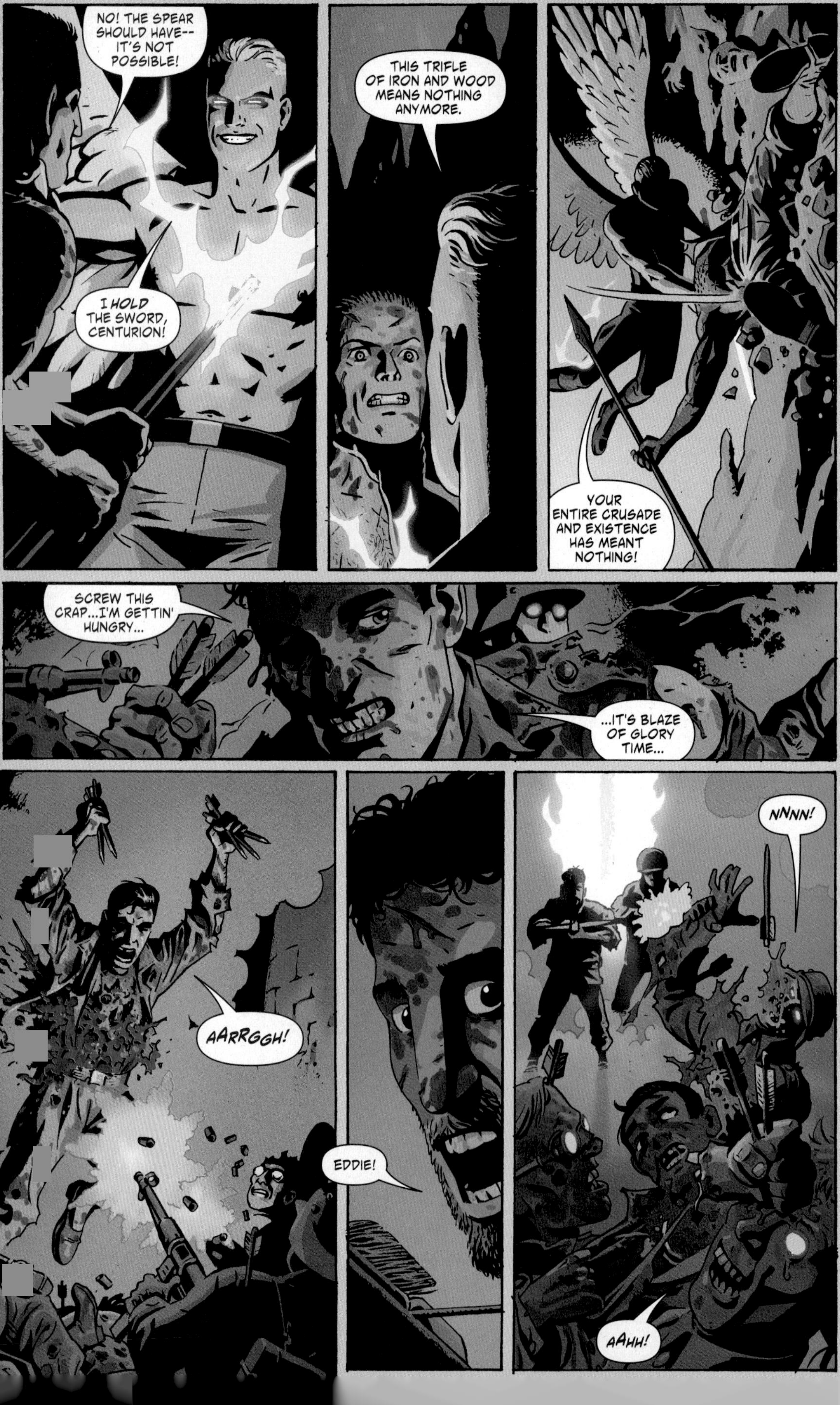
NO! THE SPEAR SHOULD HAVE-- IT'S NOT POSSIBLE!
I HOLD THE SWORD, CENTURION!
THIS TRIFLE OF IRON AND WOOD MEANS NOTHING ANYMORE.
YOUR ENTIRE CRUSADE AND EXISTENCE HAS MEANT NOTHING!
SCREW THIS CRAP...I'M GETTIN' HUNGRY...
...IT'S BLAZE OF GLORY TIME...
AARRGGH!
EDDIE!
NNNN!
AAHH!

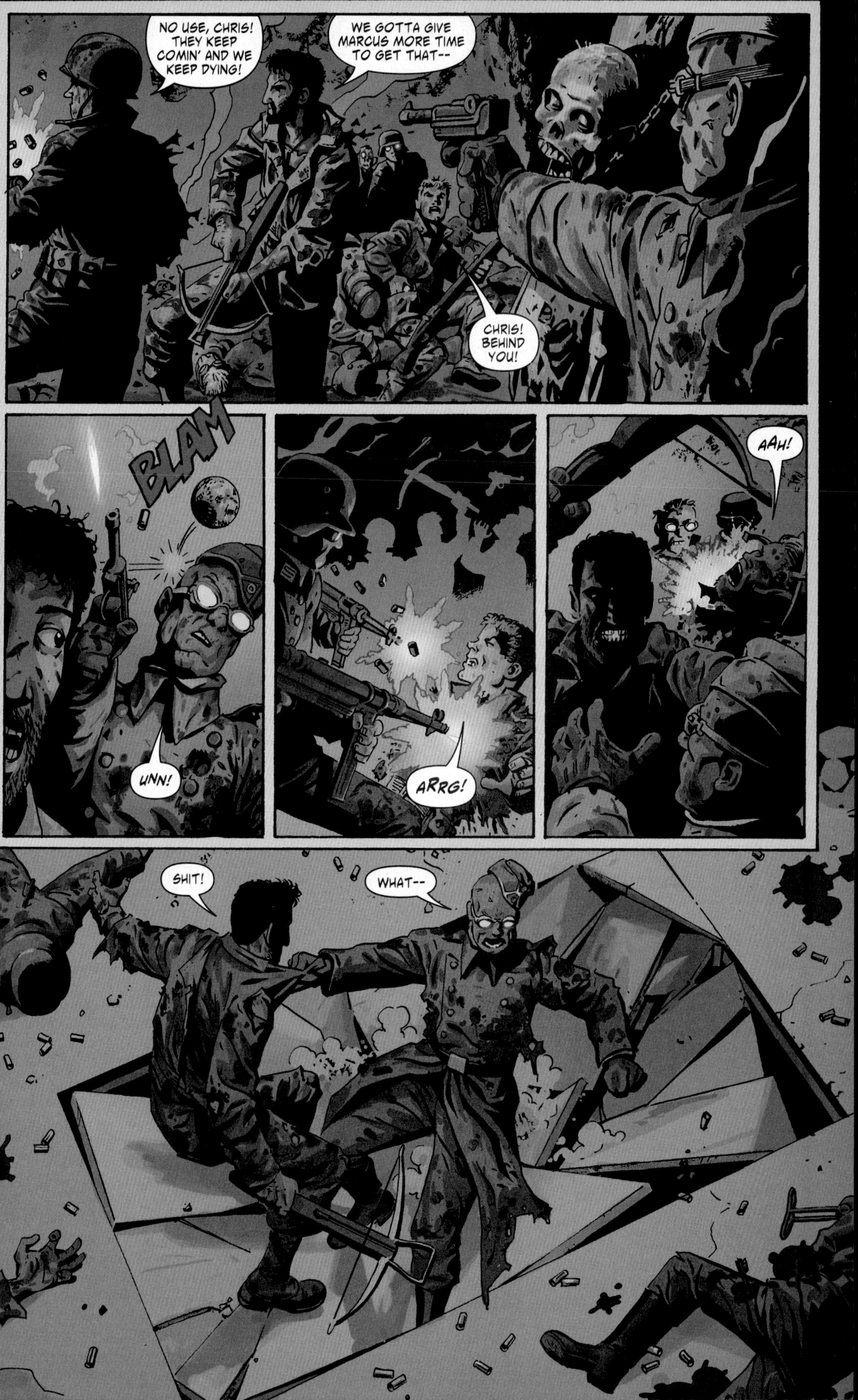
NO USE, CHRIS! THEY KEEP COMIN' AND WE KEEP DYING!
WE GOTTA GIVE MARCUS MORE TIME TO GET THAT--
CHRIS! BEHIND YOU!
BLAM
UNN!
ARRG!
AAH!
SHIT!
WHAT--

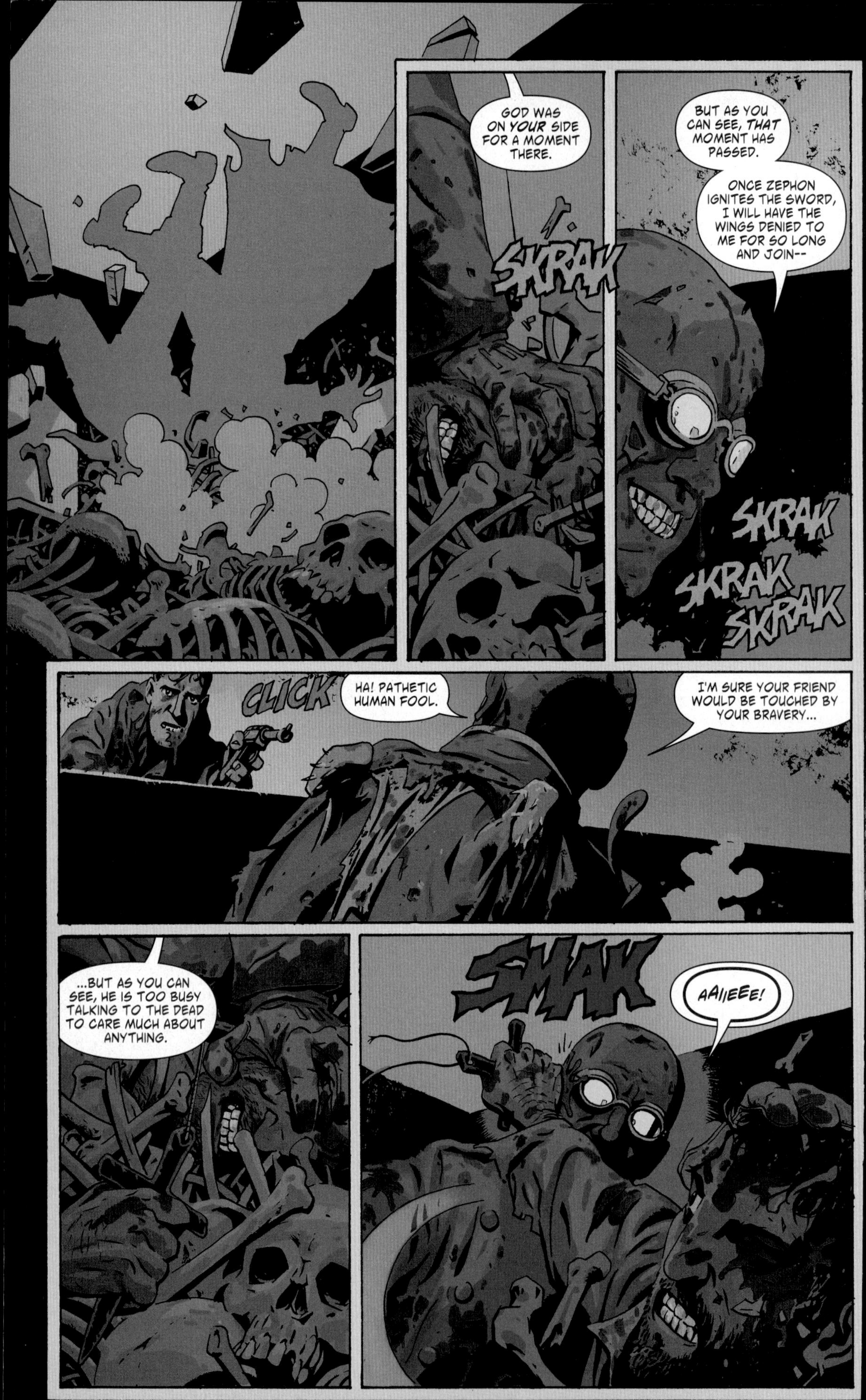
GOD WAS ON YOUR SIDE FOR A MOMENT THERE.
SKRAK
BUT AS YOU CAN SEE, THAT MOMENT HAS PASSED.
ONCE ZEPHON IGNITES THE SWORD, I WILL HAVE THE WINGS DENIED TO ME FOR SO LONG AND JOIN--
SKRAK
SKRAK
SKRAK
CLICK
HA! PATHETIC HUMAN FOOL.
I'M SURE YOUR FRIEND WOULD BE TOUCHED BY YOUR BRAVERY...
...BUT AS YOU CAN SEE, HE IS TOO BUSY TALKING TO THE DEAD TO CARE MUCH ABOUT ANYTHING.
SMAK
AAIIEEE!

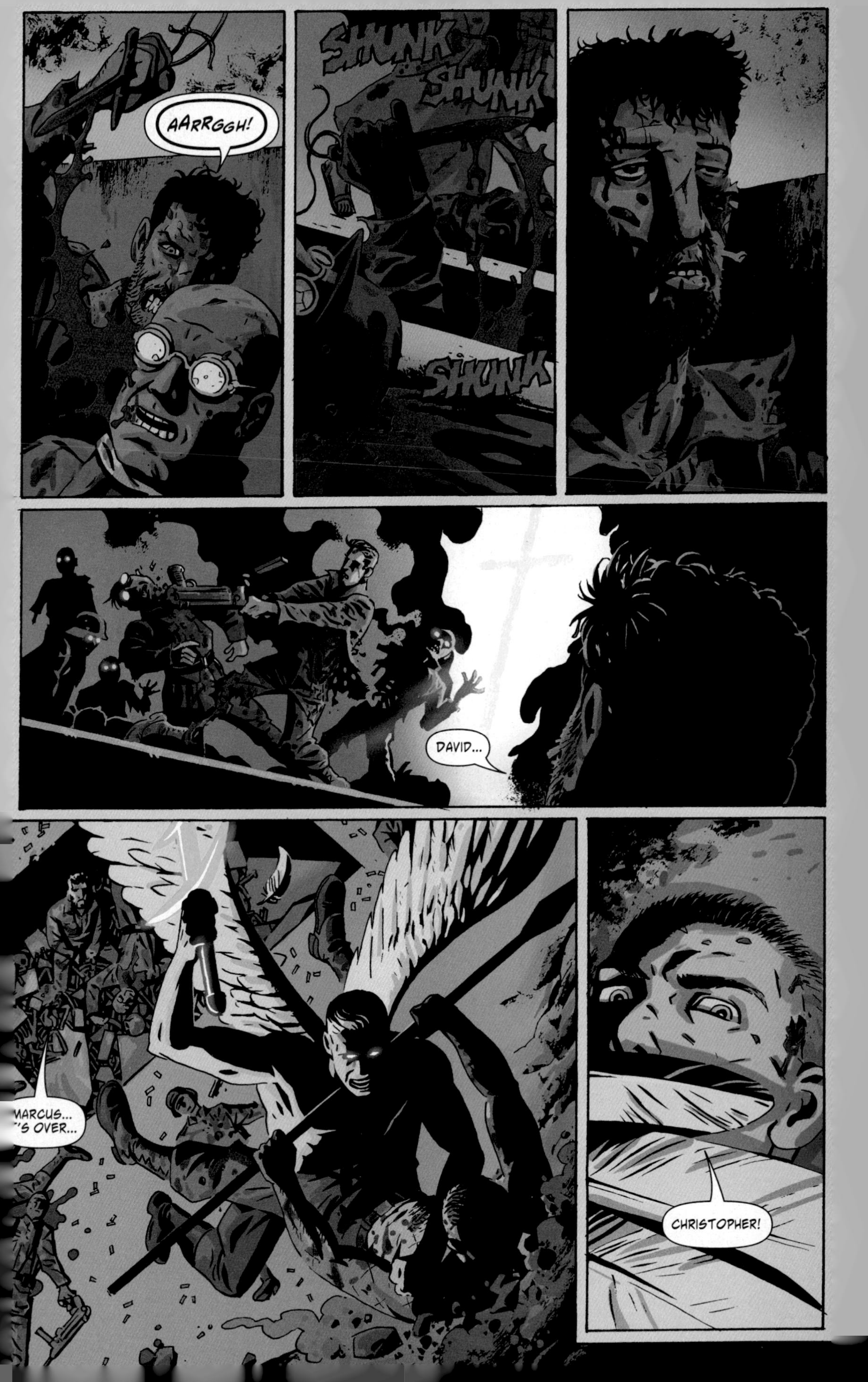
AARRGGH!
SHUNK
SHUNK
SHUNK
DAVID...
MARCUS...
'S OVER...
CHRISTOPHER!

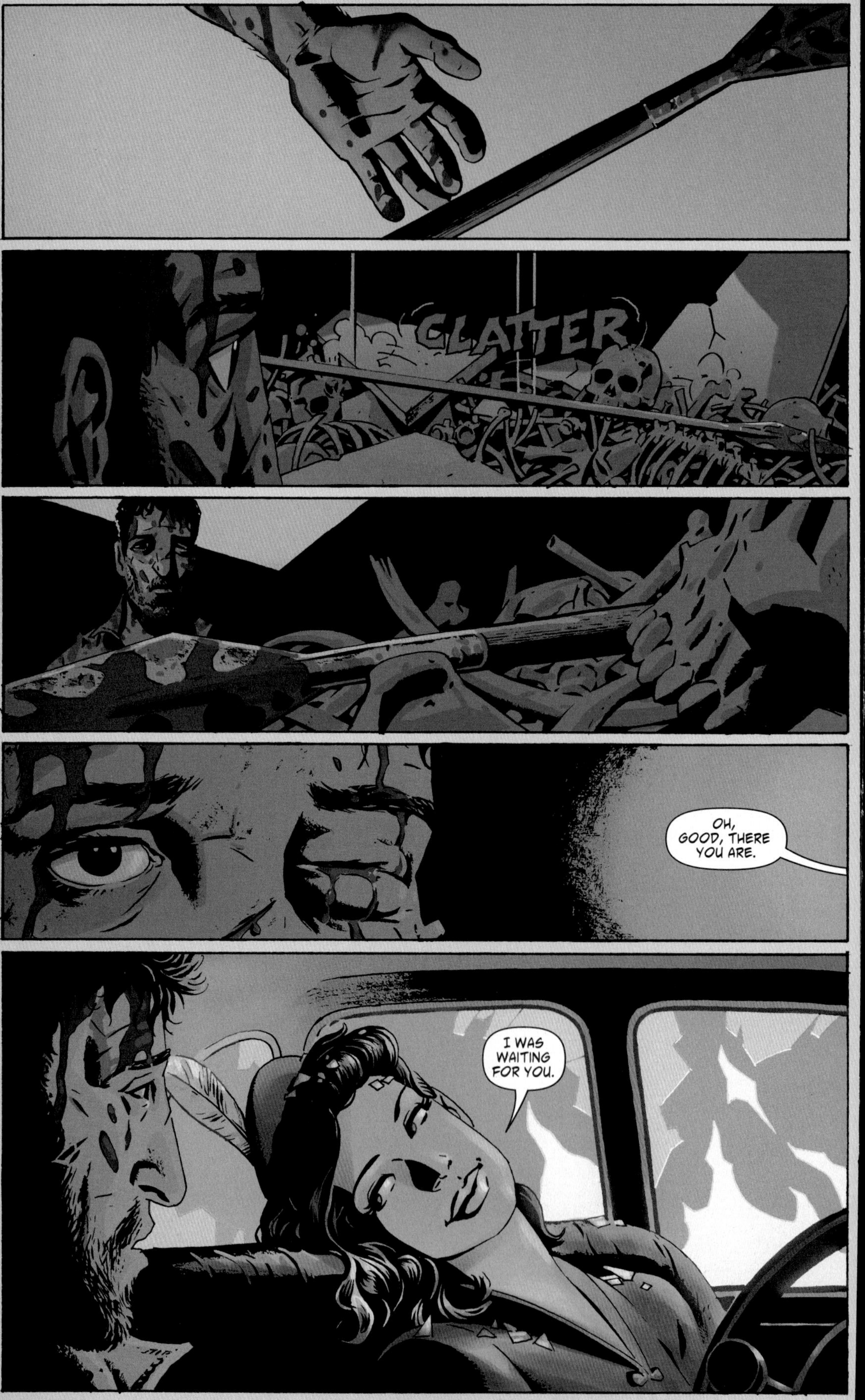
CLATTER
OH, GOOD, THERE YOU ARE.
I WAS WAITING FOR YOU.

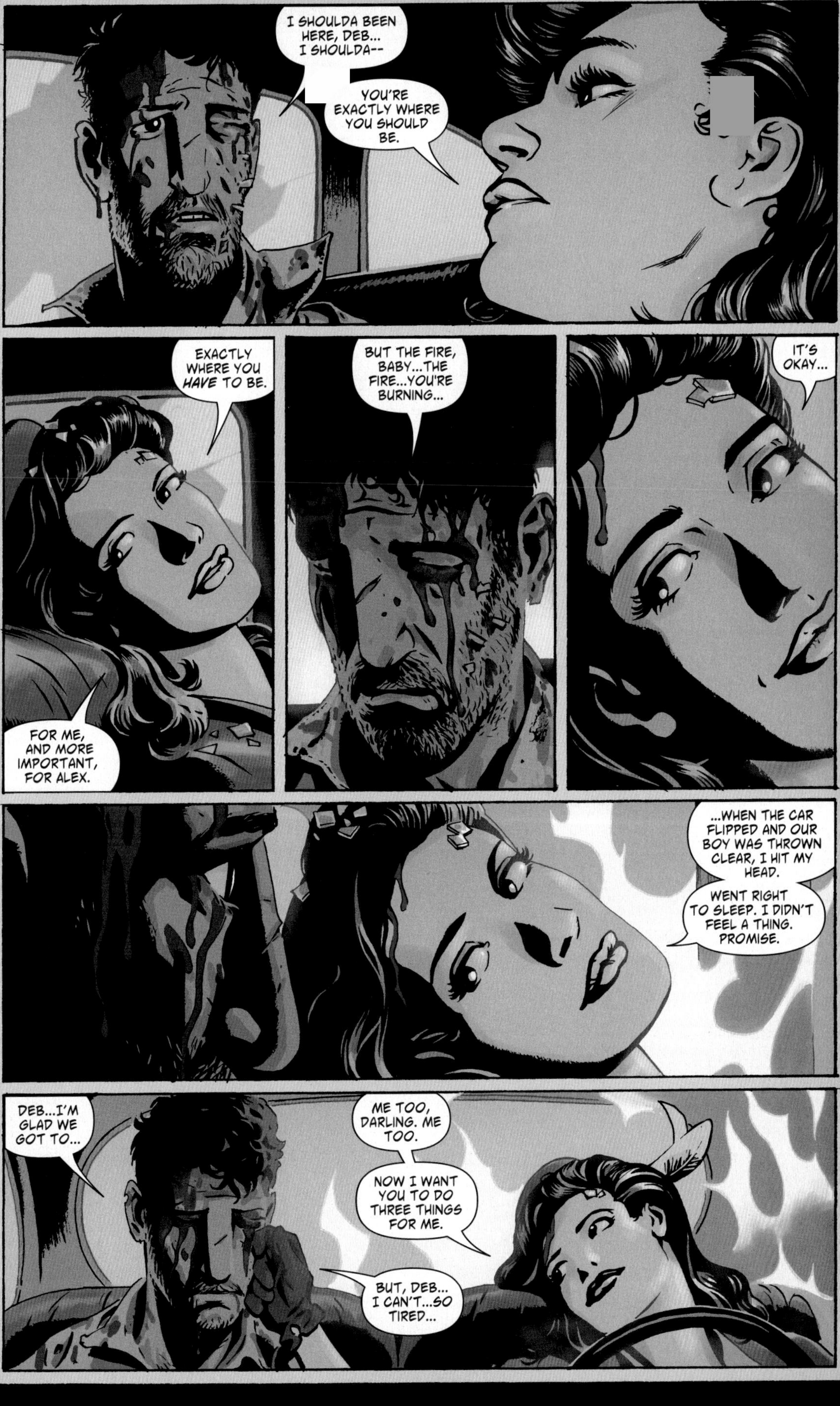
I SHOULDA BEEN HERE, DEB... I SHOULDA--
YOU'RE EXACTLY WHERE YOU SHOULD BE.
EXACTLY WHERE YOU *HAVE* TO BE.
FOR ME, AND MORE IMPORTANT, FOR ALEX.
BUT THE FIRE, BABY...THE FIRE...YOU'RE BURNING...
IT'S OKAY...
...WHEN THE CAR FLIPPED AND OUR BOY WAS THROWN CLEAR, I HIT MY HEAD.
WENT RIGHT TO SLEEP. I DIDN'T FEEL A THING. PROMISE.
DEB...I'M GLAD WE GOT TO...
ME TOO, DARLING. ME TOO.
NOW I WANT YOU TO DO THREE THINGS FOR ME.
BUT, DEB... I CAN'T...SO TIRED...

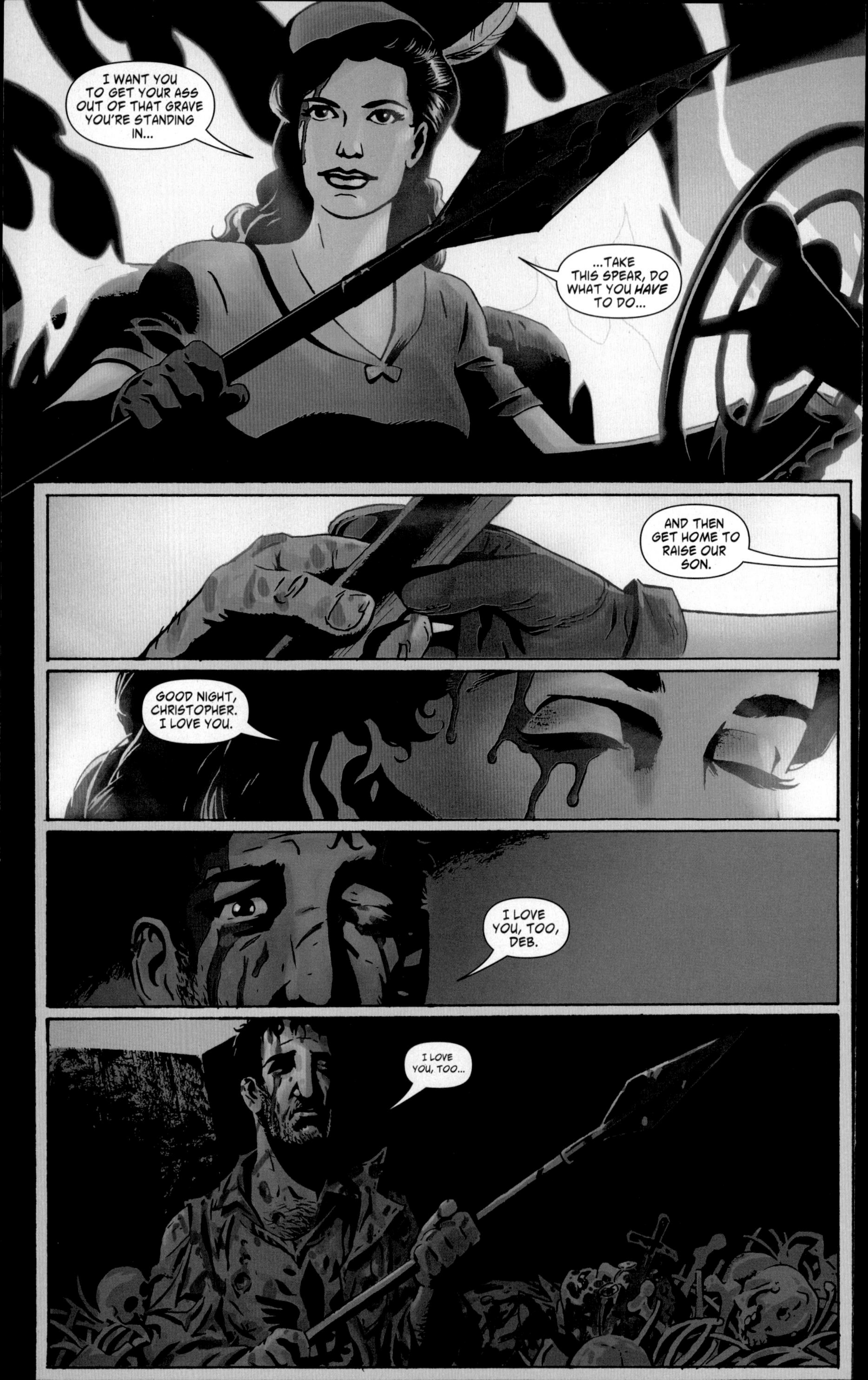
I WANT YOU TO GET YOUR ASS OUT OF THAT GRAVE YOU'RE STANDING IN...
...TAKE THIS SPEAR, DO WHAT YOU *HAVE* TO DO...
AND THEN GET HOME TO RAISE OUR SON.
GOOD NIGHT, CHRISTOPHER. I LOVE YOU.
I LOVE YOU, TOO, DEB.
I LOVE YOU, TOO...

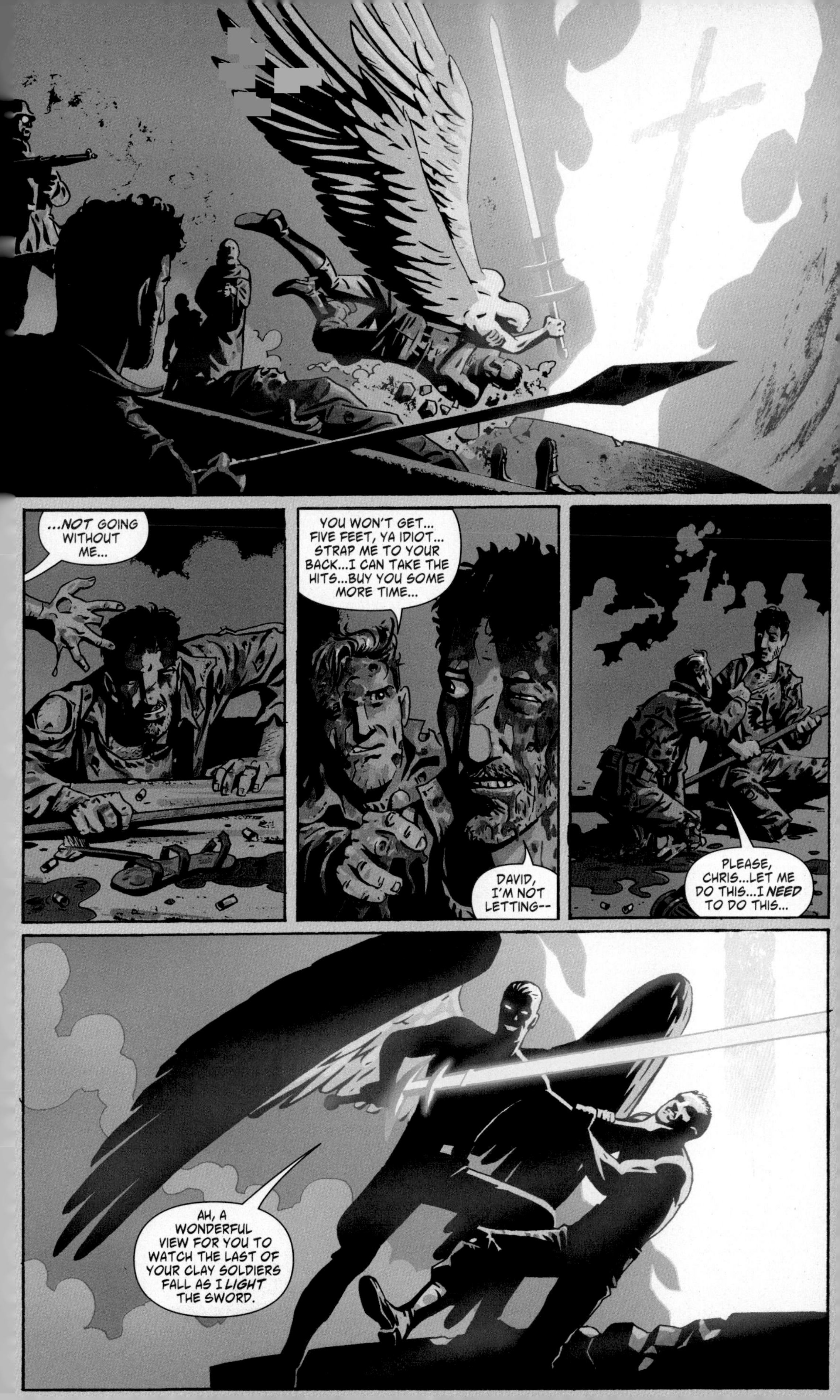
...NOT GOING WITHOUT ME...
YOU WON'T GET... FIVE FEET, YA IDIOT... STRAP ME TO YOUR BACK...I CAN TAKE THE HITS...BUY YOU SOME MORE TIME...
DAVID, I'M NOT LETTING--
PLEASE, CHRIS...LET ME DO THIS...I NEED TO DO THIS...
AH, A WONDERFUL VIEW FOR YOU TO WATCH THE LAST OF YOUR CLAY SOLDIERS FALL AS I LIGHT THE SWORD.

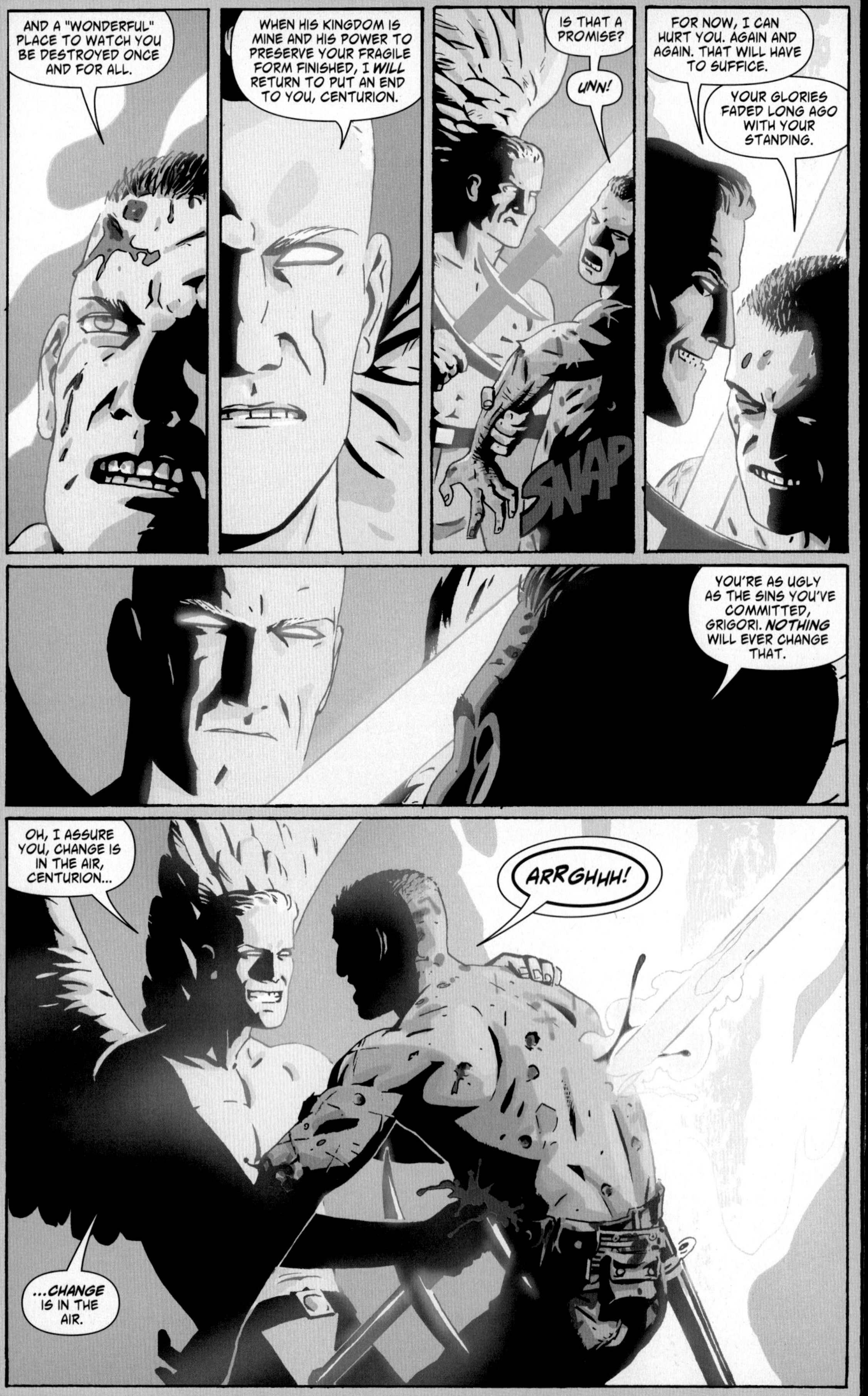
AND A "WONDERFUL" PLACE TO WATCH YOU BE DESTROYED ONCE AND FOR ALL.
WHEN HIS KINGDOM IS MINE AND HIS POWER TO PRESERVE YOUR FRAGILE FORM FINISHED, I *WILL* RETURN TO PUT AN END TO YOU, CENTURION.
IS THAT A PROMISE?
UNN!
SNAP
FOR NOW, I CAN HURT YOU. AGAIN AND AGAIN. THAT WILL HAVE TO SUFFICE.
YOUR GLORIES FADED LONG AGO WITH YOUR STANDING.
YOU'RE AS UGLY AS THE SINS YOU'VE COMMITTED, GRIGORI. *NOTHING* WILL EVER CHANGE THAT.
OH, I ASSURE YOU, CHANGE IS IN THE AIR, CENTURION...
ARRGHHH!
...*CHANGE* IS IN THE AIR.

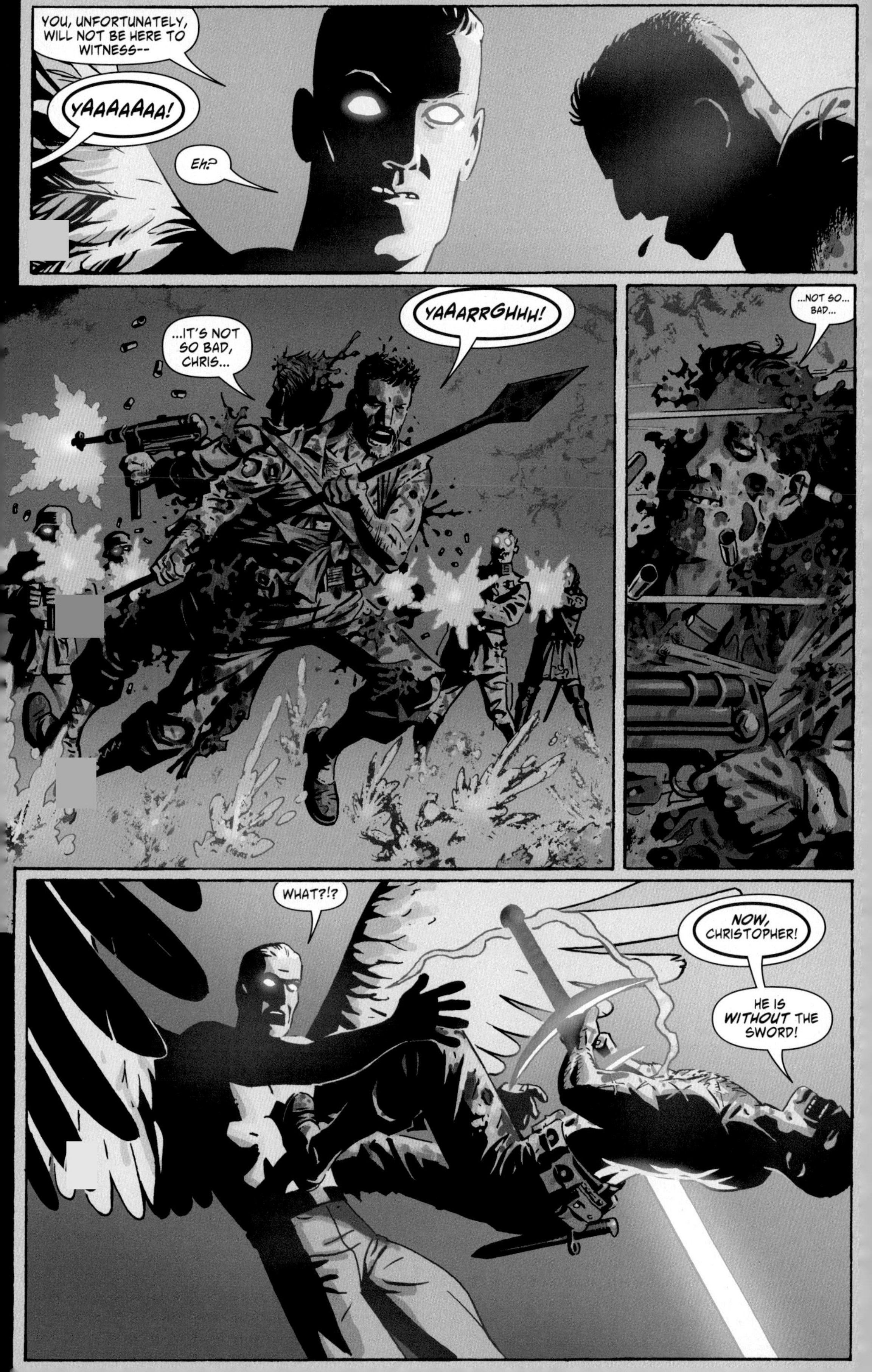
YOU, UNFORTUNATELY, WILL NOT BE HERE TO WITNESS--
YAAAAAAA!
Eh?
...IT'S NOT SO BAD, CHRIS...
YAAARRGHHH!
...NOT SO... BAD...
WHAT?!?
NOW, CHRISTOPHER!
HE IS WITHOUT THE SWORD!

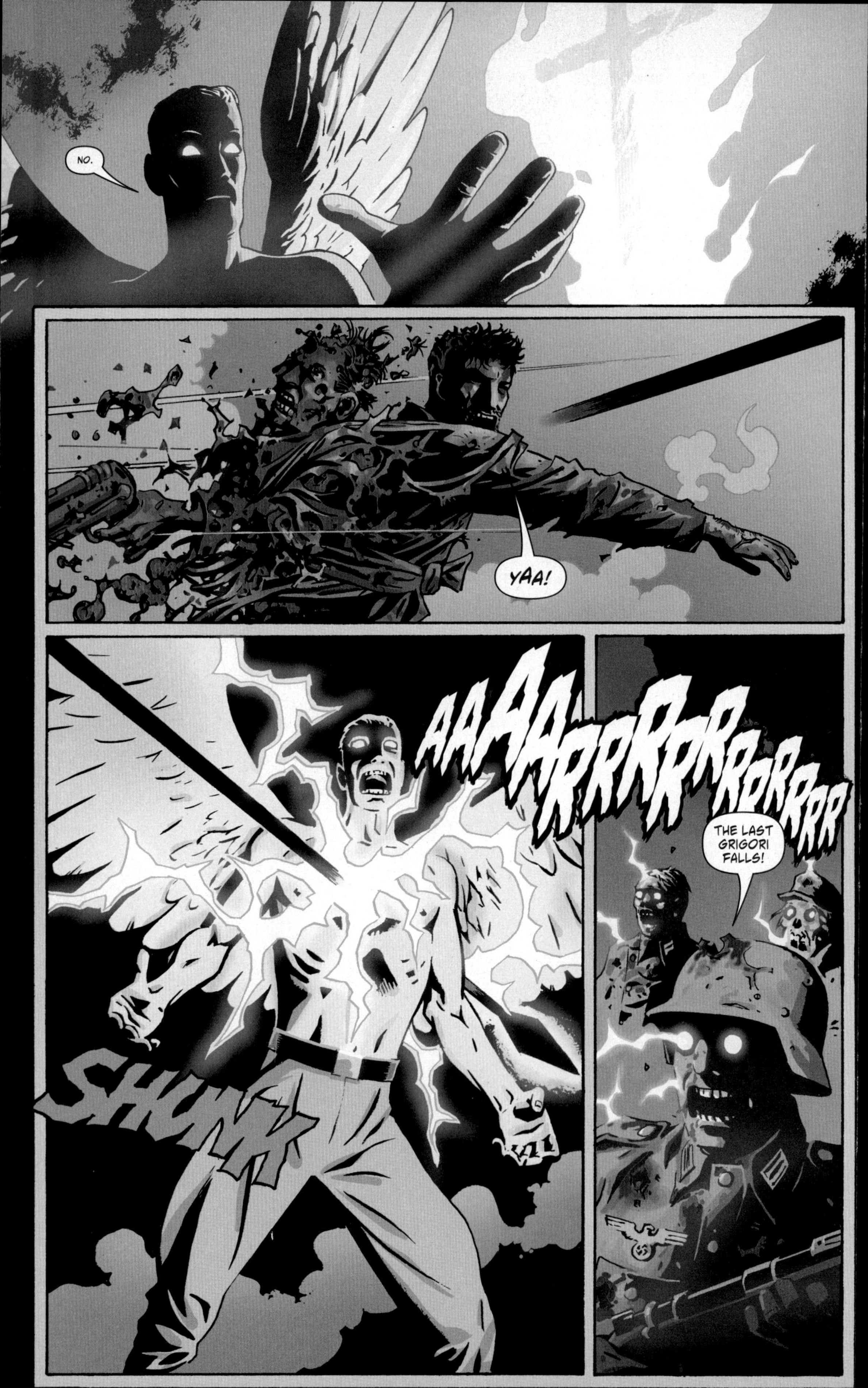
NO.
YAA!
AAAARRRRRRRRRRR
THE LAST GRIGORI FALLS!
SHUNK

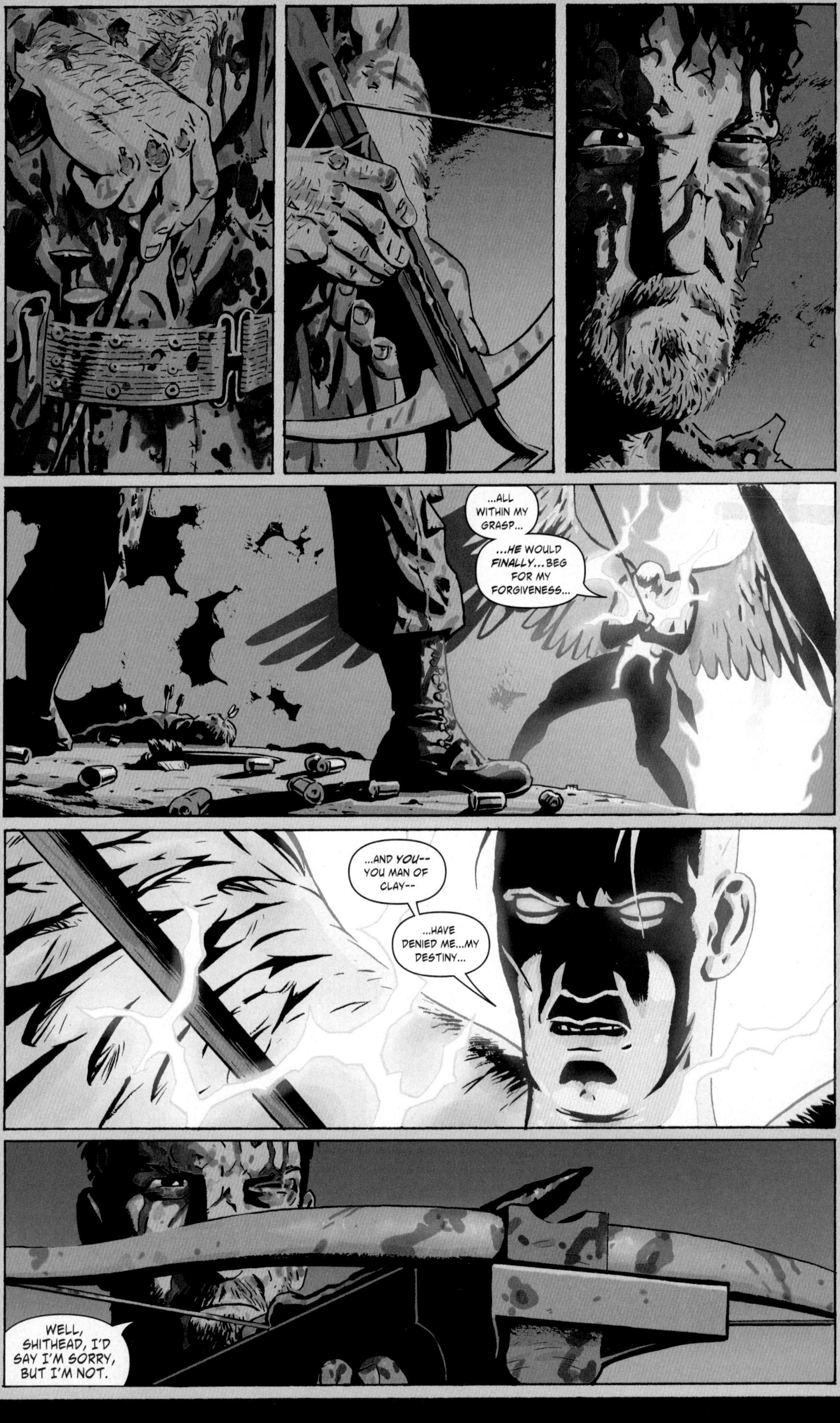
...ALL WITHIN MY GRASP...
...HE WOULD FINALLY...BEG FOR MY FORGIVENESS...
...AND YOU-- YOU MAN OF CLAY--
...HAVE DENIED ME...MY DESTINY...
WELL, SHITHEAD, I'D SAY I'M SORRY, BUT I'M NOT.

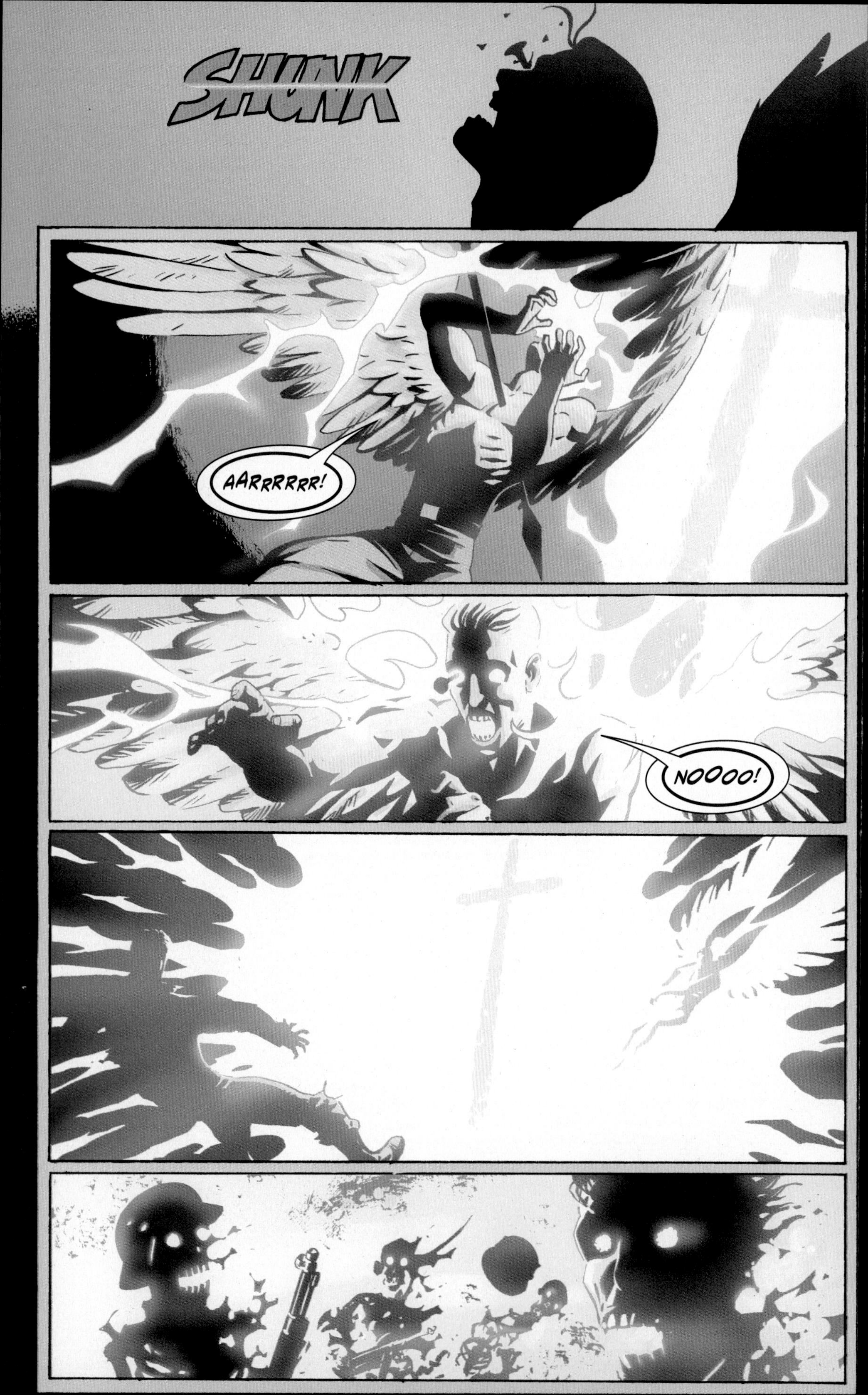
SHUNK
AARRRRRR!
NOOOO!

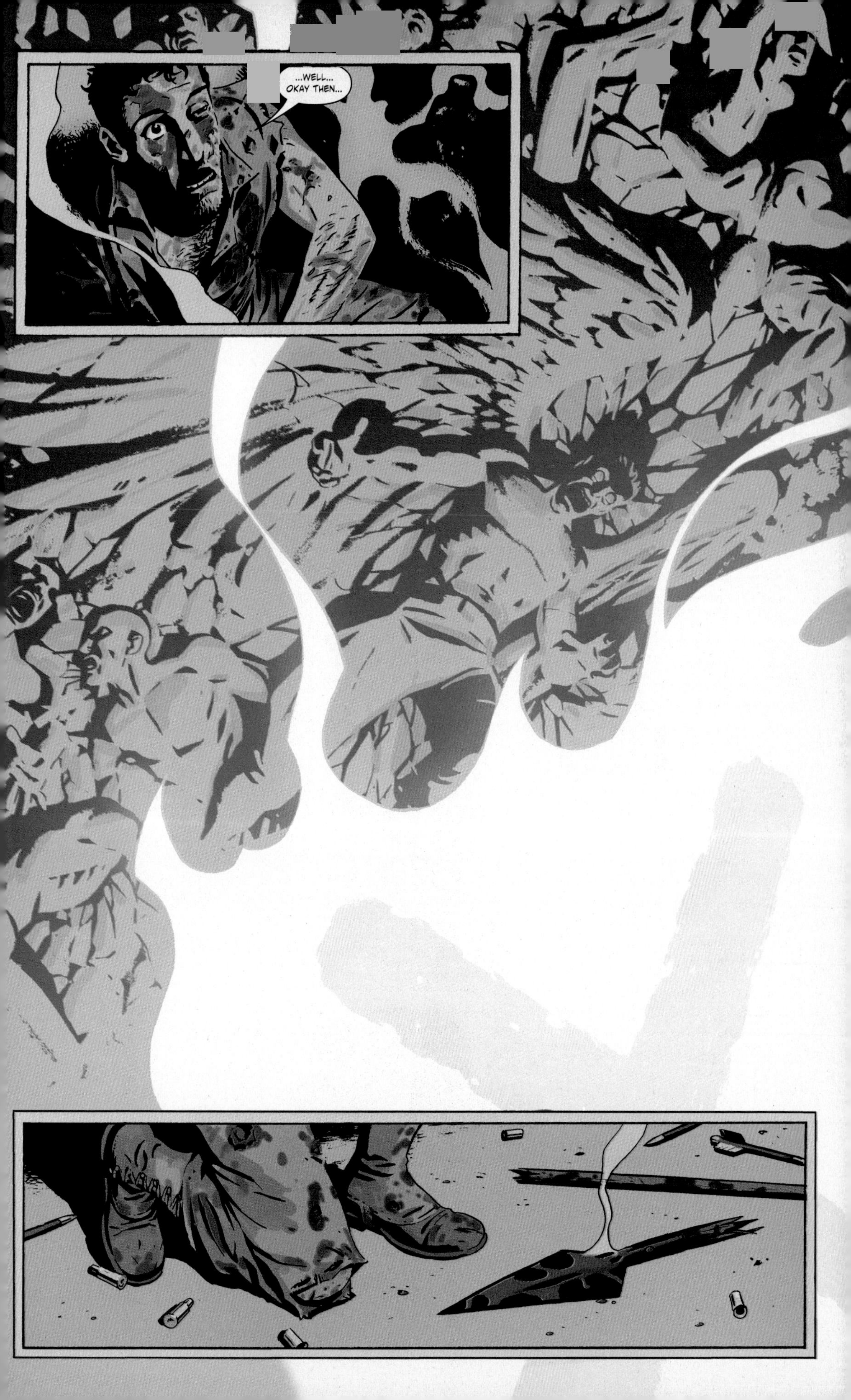
...WELL... OKAY THEN...

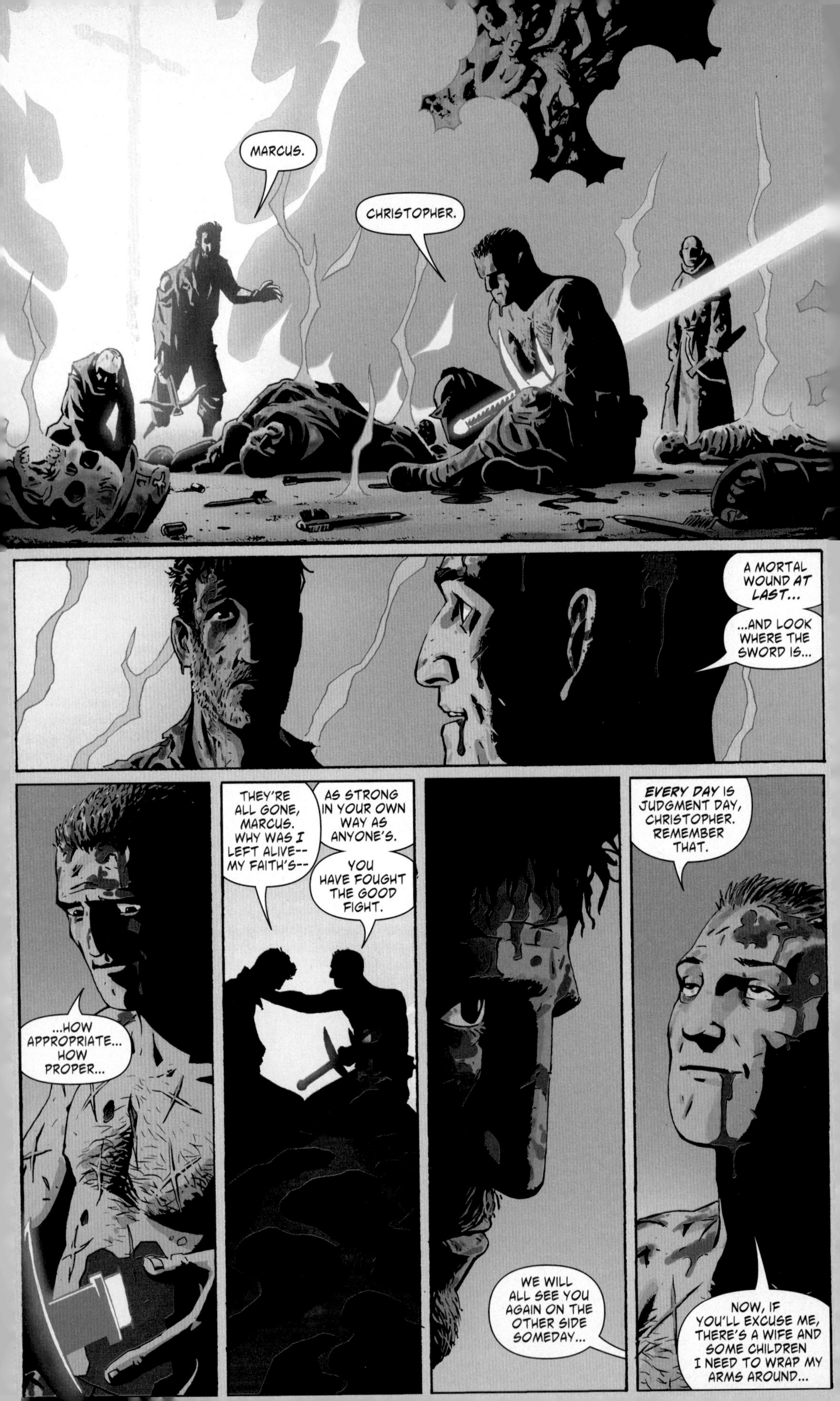
MARCUS.
CHRISTOPHER.
A MORTAL WOUND AT LAST...
...AND LOOK WHERE THE SWORD IS...
...HOW APPROPRIATE... HOW PROPER...
THEY'RE ALL GONE, MARCUS. WHY WAS I LEFT ALIVE-- MY FAITH'S--
AS STRONG IN YOUR OWN WAY AS ANYONE'S.
YOU HAVE FOUGHT THE GOOD FIGHT.
WE WILL ALL SEE YOU AGAIN ON THE OTHER SIDE SOMEDAY...
EVERY DAY IS JUDGMENT DAY, CHRISTOPHER. REMEMBER THAT.
NOW, IF YOU'LL EXCUSE ME, THERE'S A WIFE AND SOME CHILDREN I NEED TO WRAP MY ARMS AROUND...

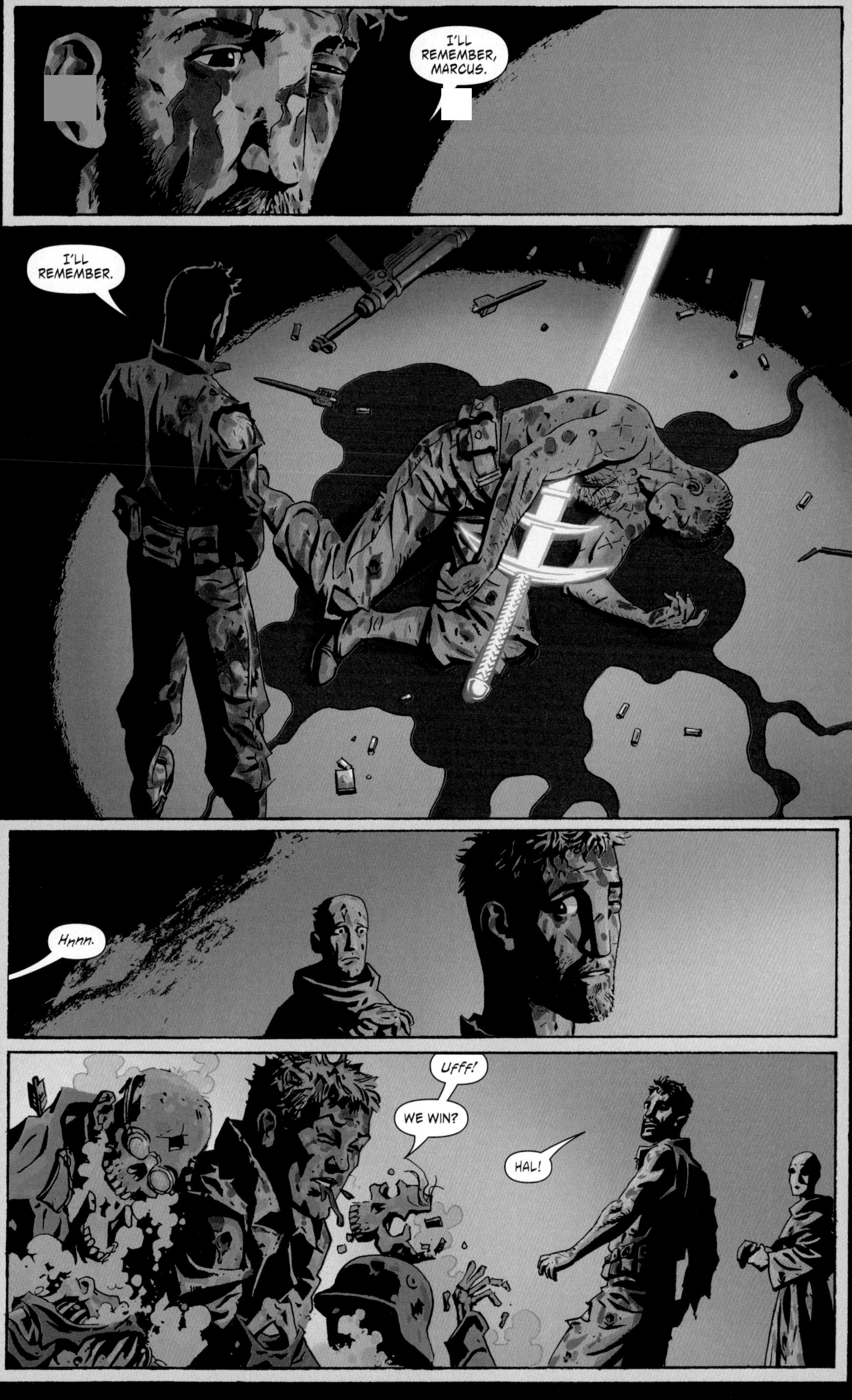
I'LL REMEMBER, MARCUS.
I'LL REMEMBER.
Hnnn.
Ufff!
WE WIN?
HAL!

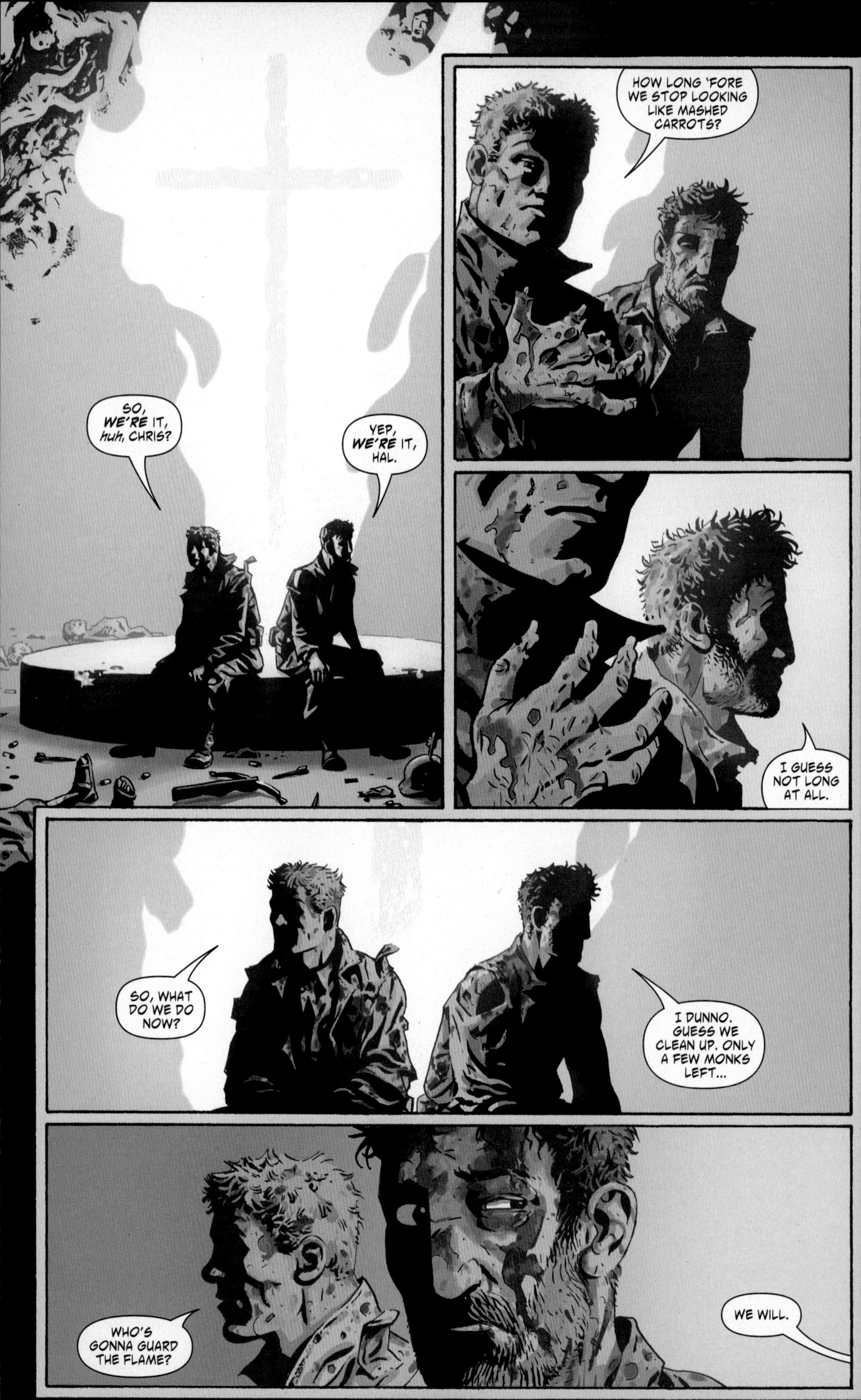
HOW LONG 'FORE WE STOP LOOKING LIKE MASHED CARROTS?
SO, WE'RE IT, huh, CHRIS?
YEP, WE'RE IT, HAL.
I GUESS NOT LONG AT ALL.
SO, WHAT DO WE DO NOW?
I DUNNO. GUESS WE CLEAN UP. ONLY A FEW MONKS LEFT...
WHO'S GONNA GUARD THE FLAME?
WE WILL.

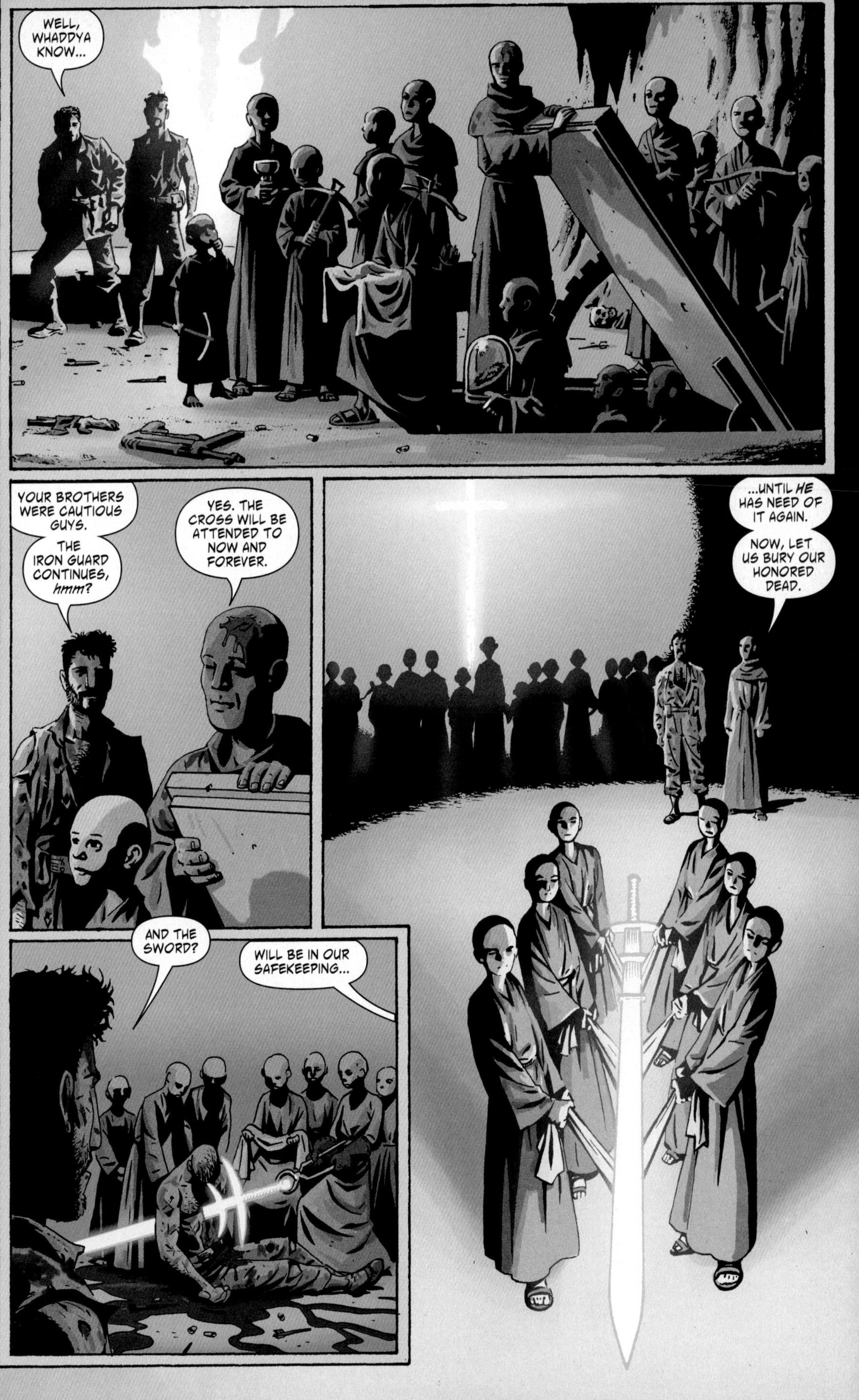
WELL, WHADDYA KNOW...
YOUR BROTHERS WERE CAUTIOUS GUYS.
THE IRON GUARD CONTINUES, *hmm*?
YES. THE CROSS WILL BE ATTENDED TO NOW AND FOREVER.
AND THE SWORD?
WILL BE IN OUR SAFEKEEPING...
...UNTIL *HE* HAS NEED OF IT AGAIN.
NOW, LET US BURY OUR HONORED DEAD.

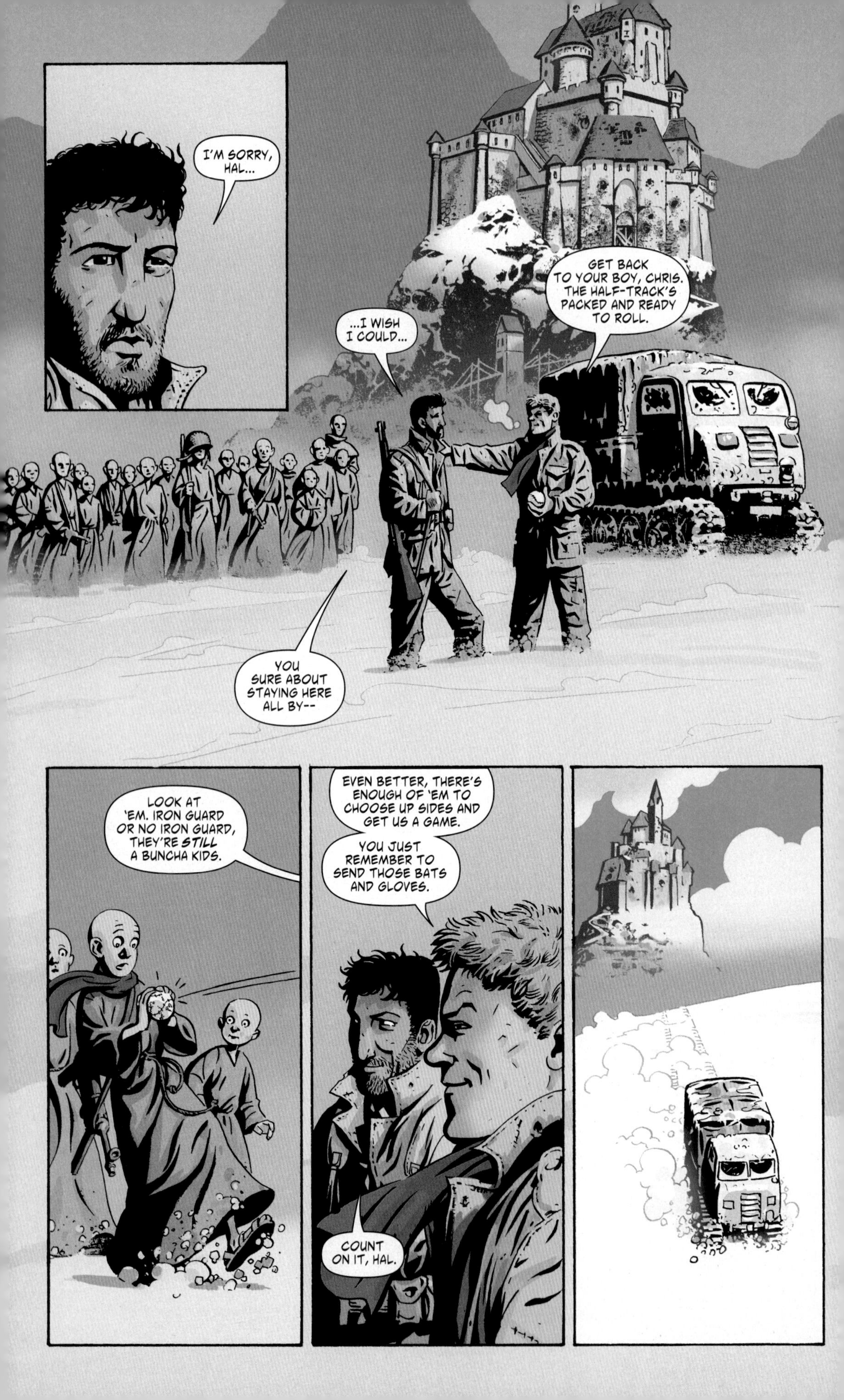
I'M SORRY, HAL...
...I WISH I COULD...
GET BACK TO YOUR BOY, CHRIS. THE HALF-TRACK'S PACKED AND READY TO ROLL.
YOU SURE ABOUT STAYING HERE ALL BY--
LOOK AT 'EM. IRON GUARD OR NO IRON GUARD, THEY'RE *STILL* A BUNCHA KIDS.
EVEN BETTER, THERE'S ENOUGH OF 'EM TO CHOOSE UP SIDES AND GET US A GAME.
YOU JUST REMEMBER TO SEND THOSE BATS AND GLOVES.
COUNT ON IT, HAL.

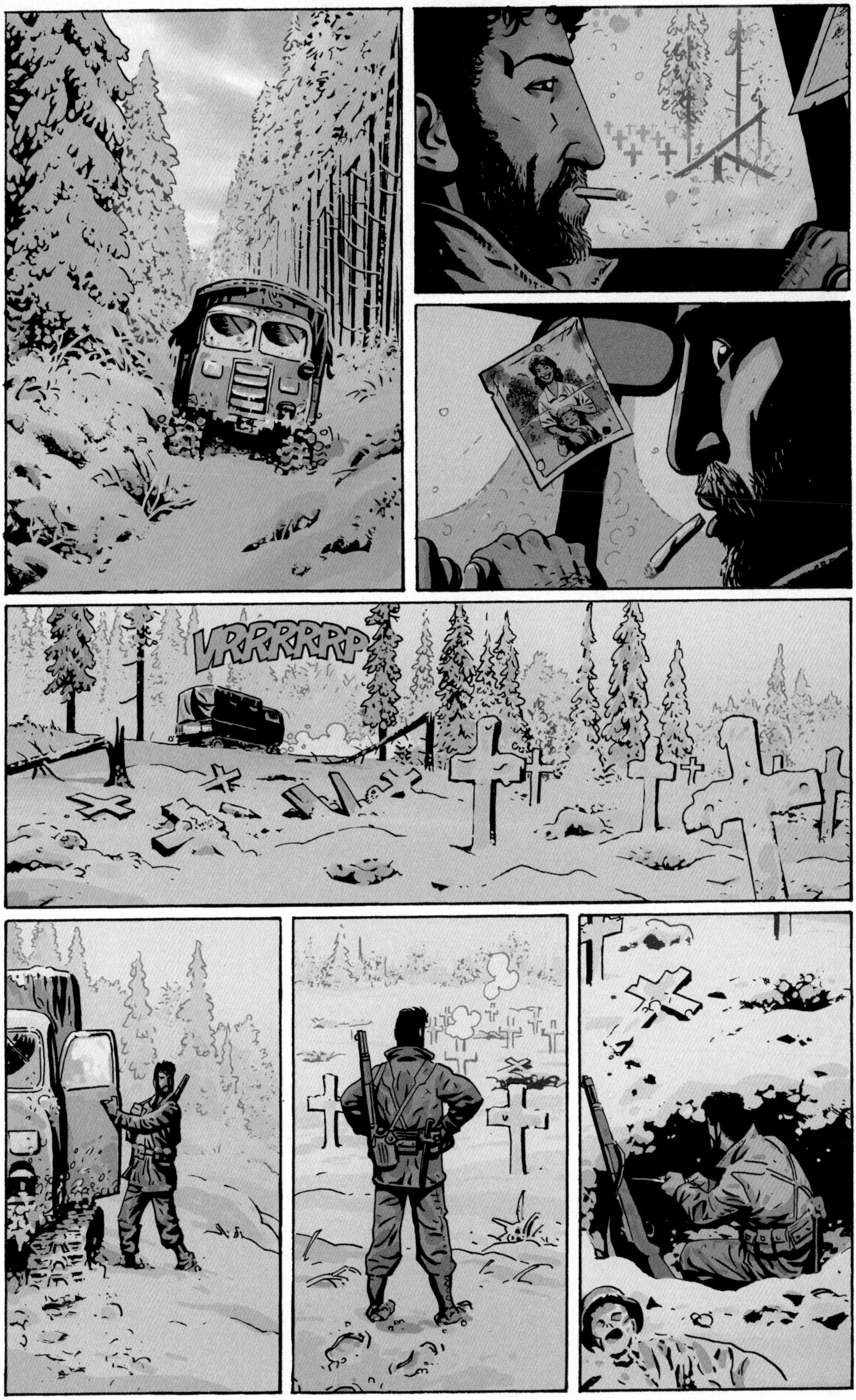
VRRRRRRP

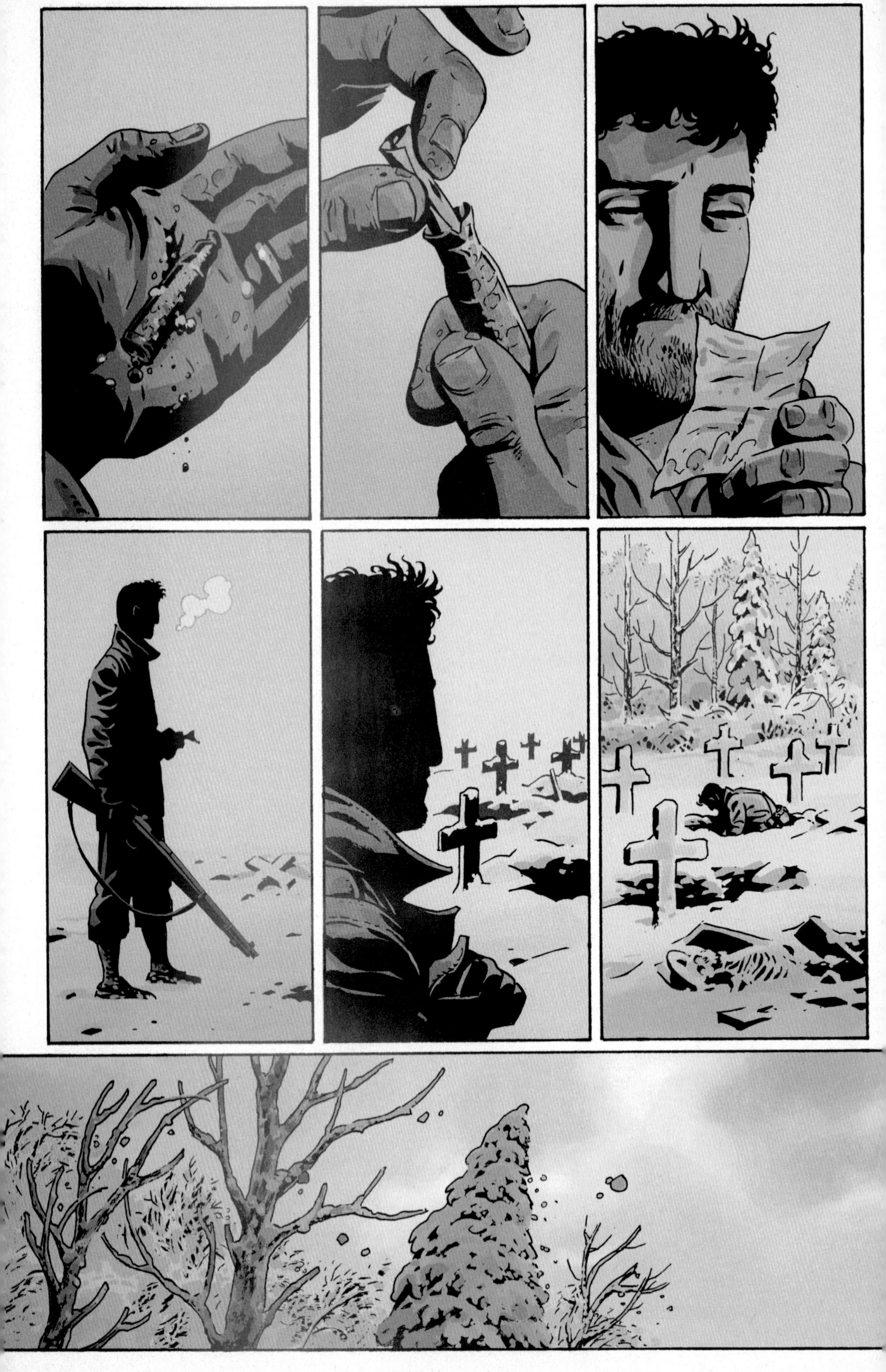

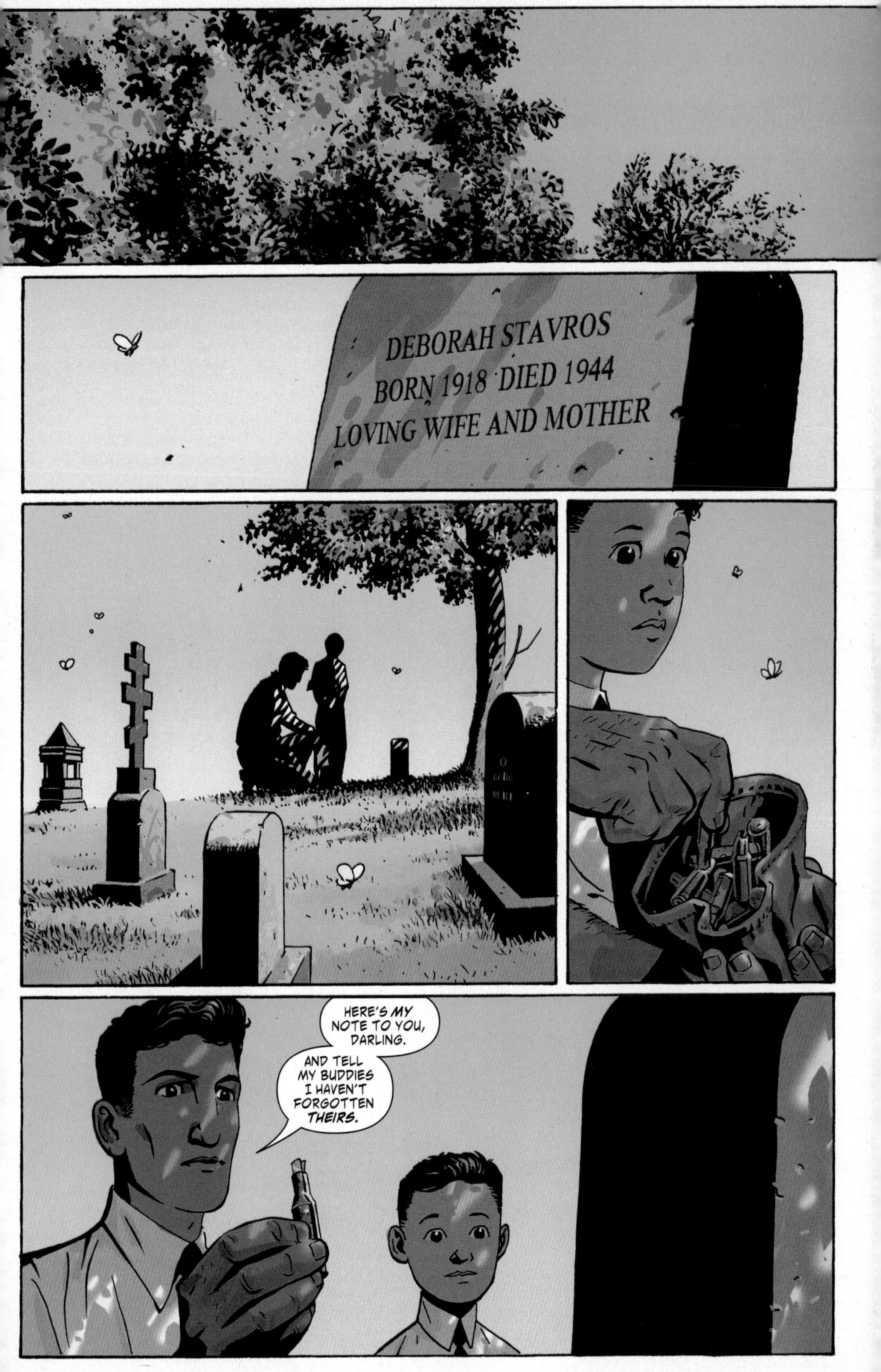
DEBORAH STAVROS
BORN 1918 DIED 1944
LOVING WIFE AND MOTHER
HERE'S MY NOTE TO YOU, DARLING.
AND TELL MY BUDDIES I HAVEN'T FORGOTTEN THEIRS.

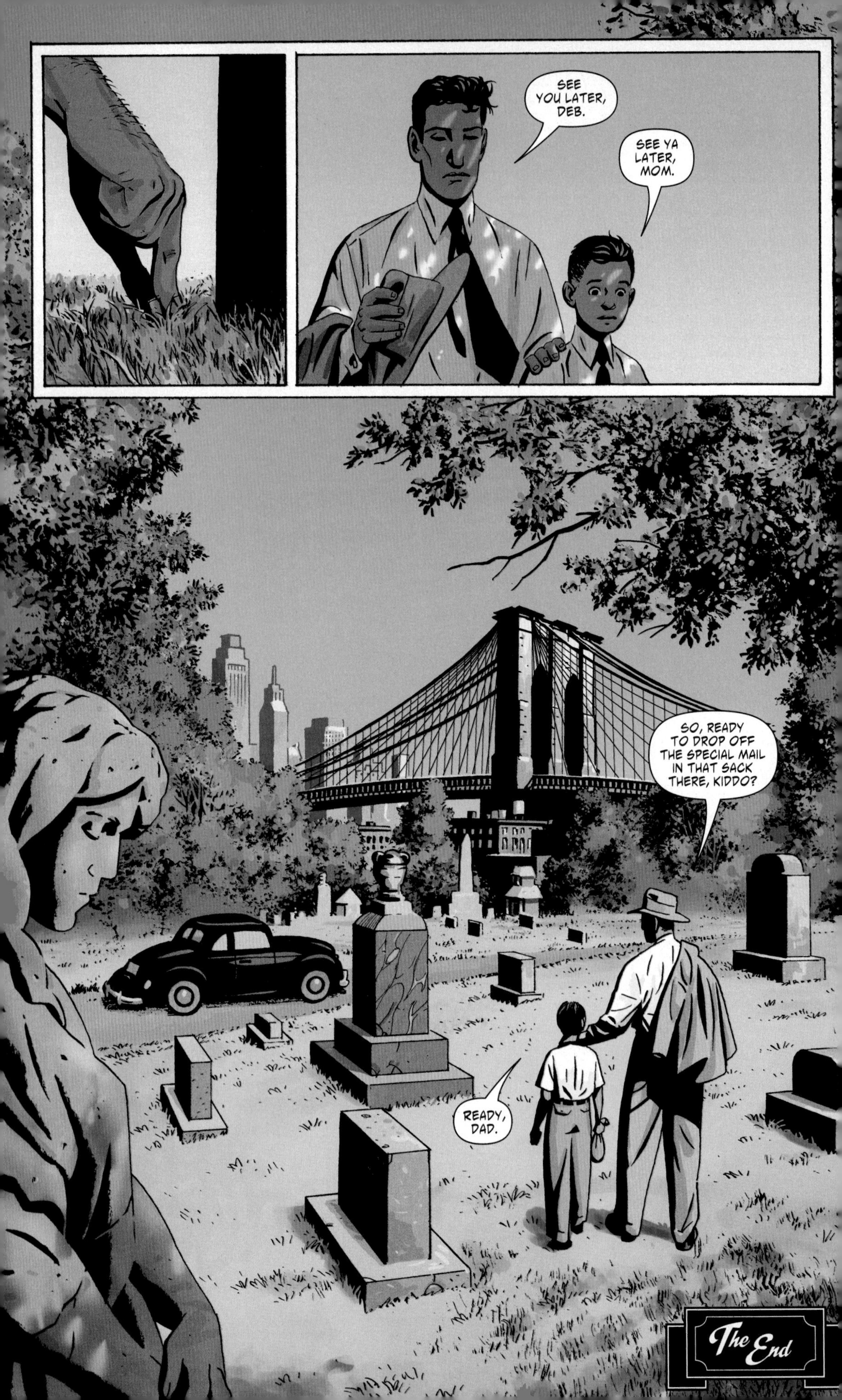
SEE YOU LATER, DEB.
SEE YA LATER, MOM.
SO, READY TO DROP OFF THE SPECIAL MAIL IN THAT SACK THERE, KIDDO?
READY, DAD.
The End

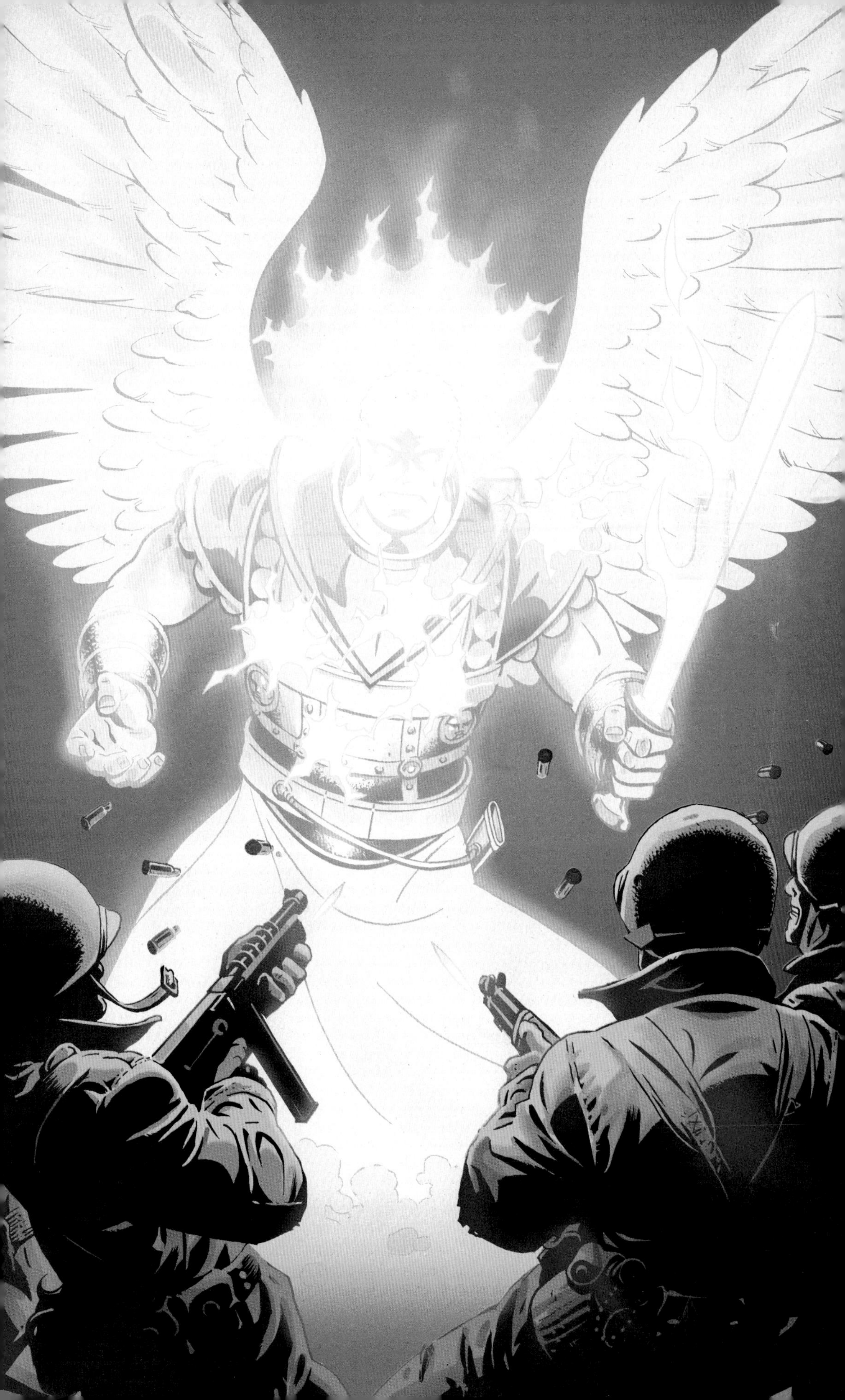

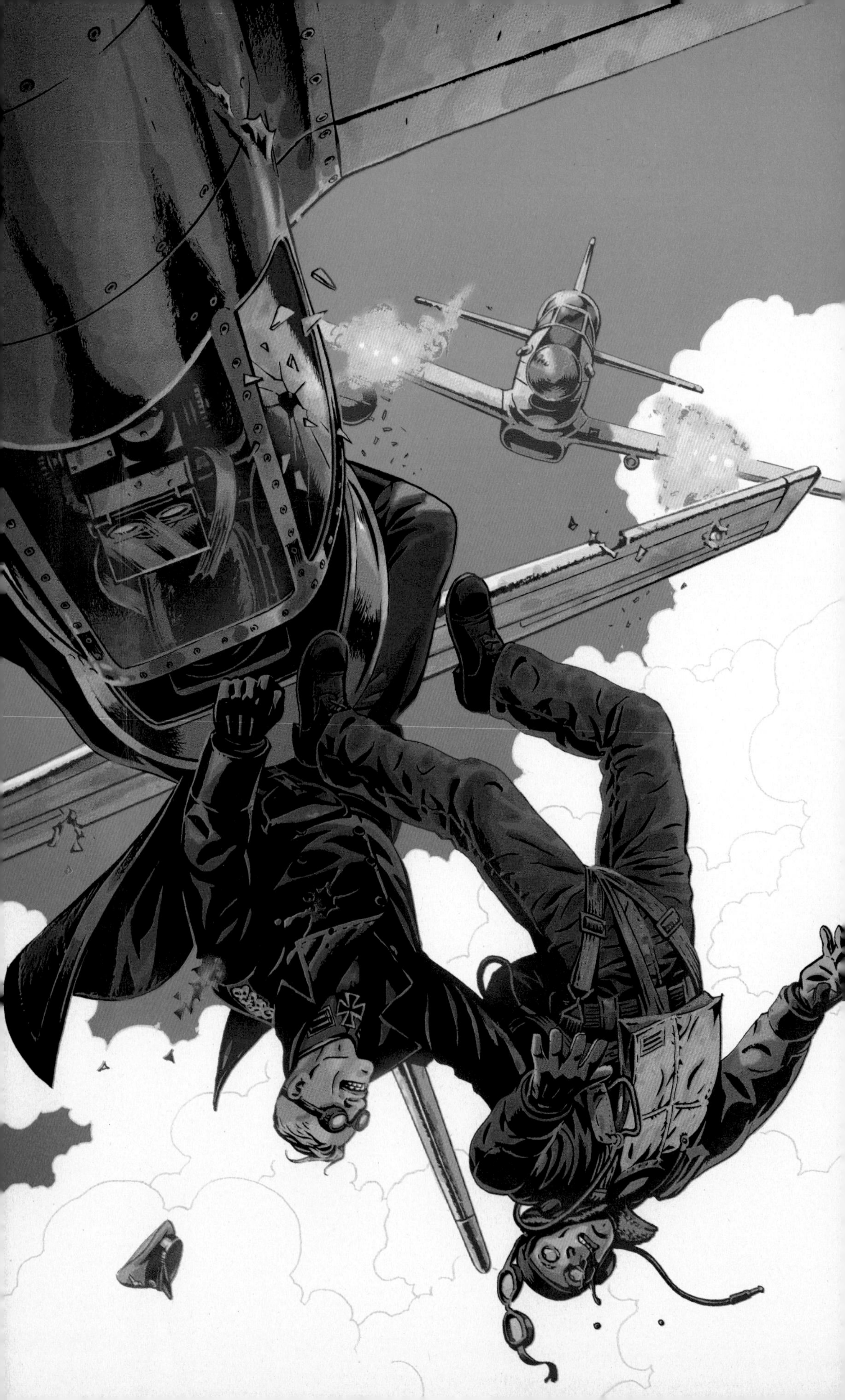

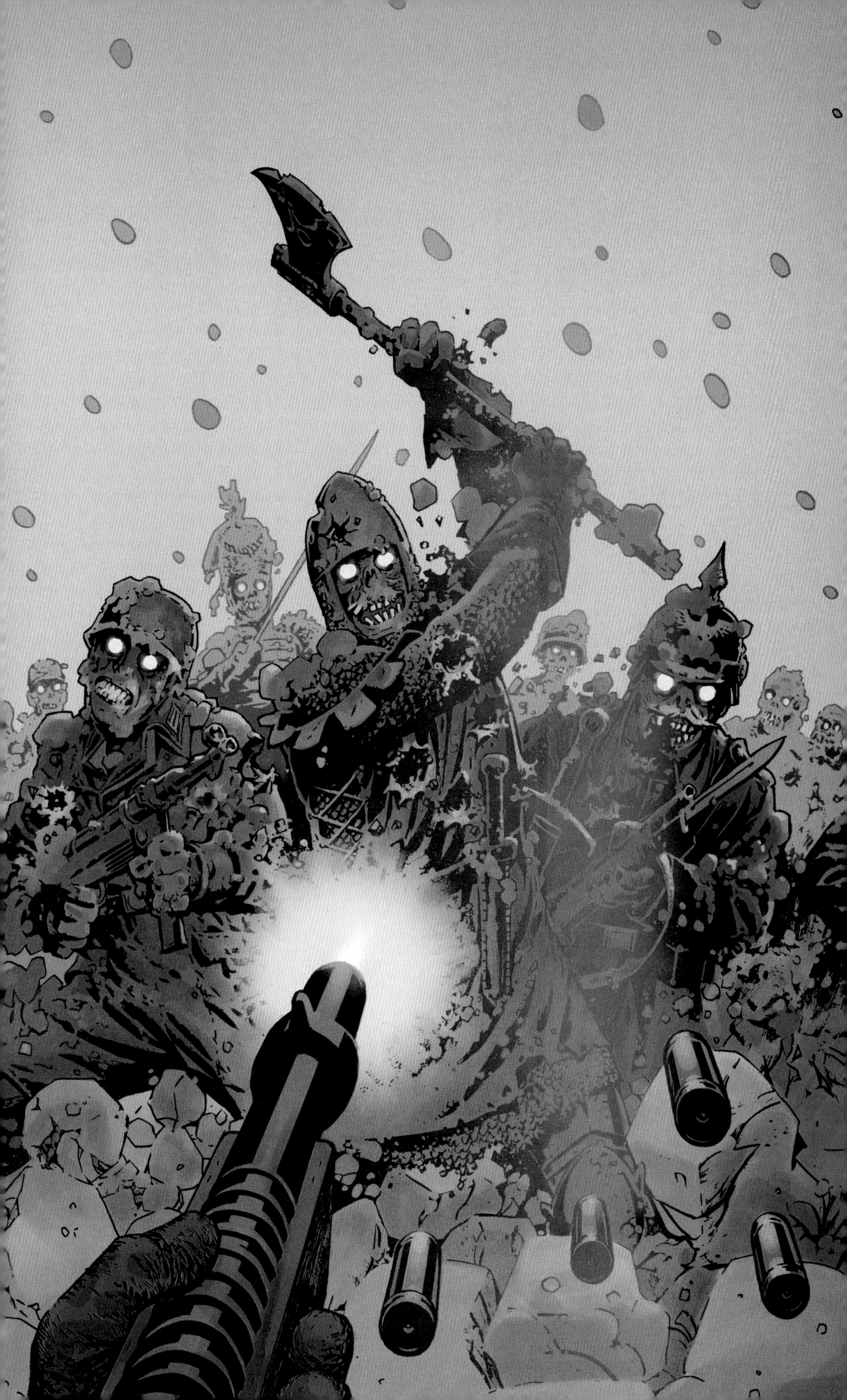

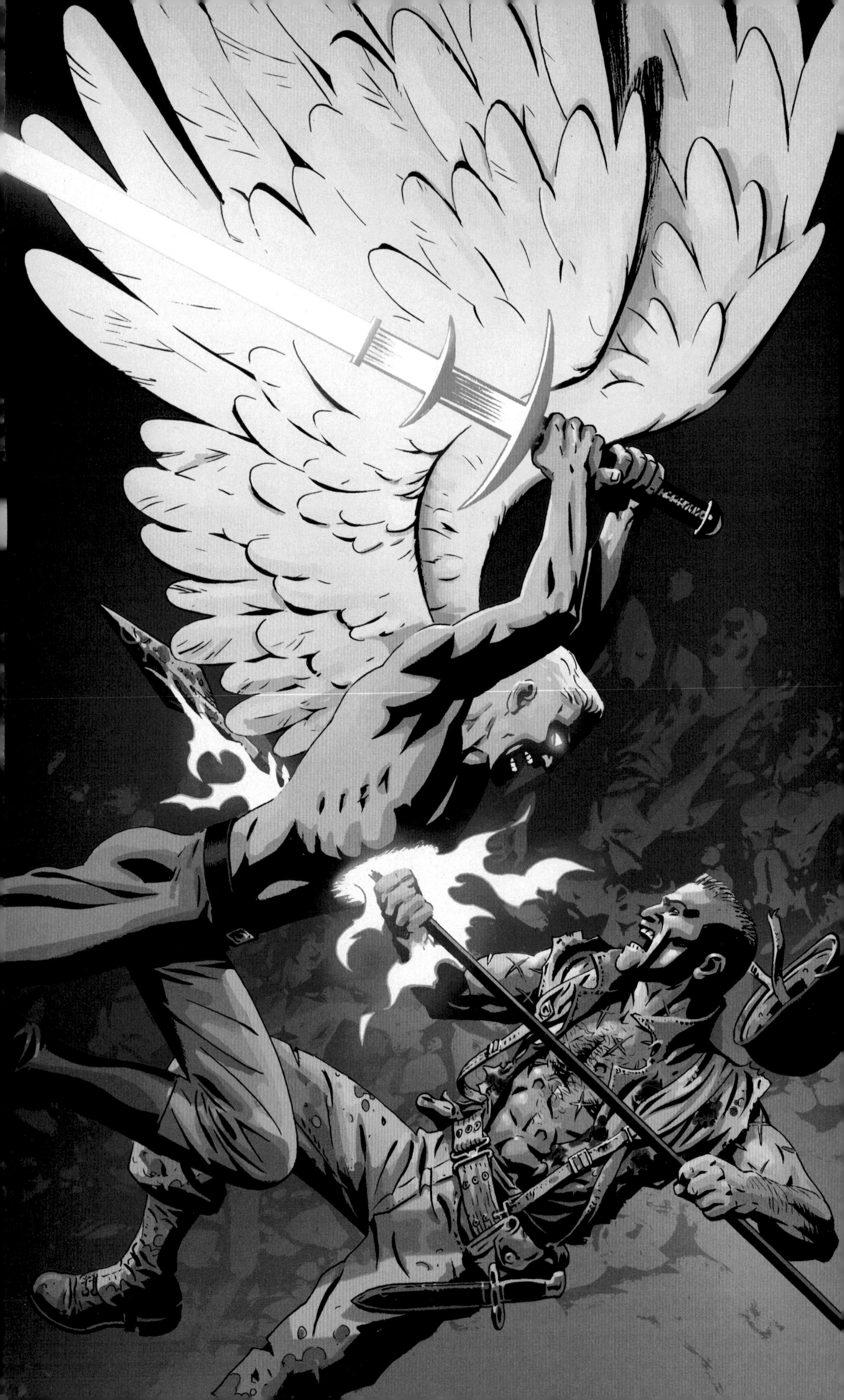